Hobson and Imperialism

Hobson and Imperialism

*Radicalism, New Liberalism,
and Finance 1887–1938*

P. J. CAIN

OXFORD
UNIVERSITY PRESS

OXFORD

UNIVERSITY PRESS

Great Clarendon Street, Oxford OX2 6DP

Oxford University Press is a department of the University of Oxford.
It furthers the University's objective of excellence in research, scholarship,
and education by publishing worldwide in

Oxford New York

Auckland Bangkok Buenos Aires Cape Town Chennai
Dar es Salaam Delhi Hong Kong Istanbul Karachi Kolkata
Kuala Lumpur Madrid Melbourne Mexico City Mumbai Nairobi
São Paulo Shanghai Singapore Taipei Tokyo Toronto
and an associated company in Berlin

Oxford is a registered trade mark of Oxford University Press
in the UK and in certain other countries

Published in the United States
by Oxford University Press Inc., New York

© Peter Cain 2002

The moral rights of the author have been asserted
Database right Oxford University Press (maker)

First published 2002

British Library Cataloguing in Publication Data
Data available

Library of Congress Cataloging in Publication Data
Data available

ISBN 0–19–820390–X

1 3 5 7 9 10 8 6 4 2

Typeset in Sabon
by Florence Production Ltd, Stoodleigh, Devon
Printed in Great Britain
on acid-free paper by
Biddles Ltd, Guildford and King's Lynn

Preface

MY FIRST SERIOUS encounter with Hobson's *Imperialism: A Study* took place while sitting on a bench waiting for a bus in Birmingham in September 1972. I have been reading him ever since so this book is very obviously overdue. Work on Hobson has frequently been put aside for tasks that, at the time at any rate, seemed more important or more necessary. About ten years ago I decided to seize the day and, with Tony Morris's encouragement and some kind reviews of my proposals, I signed a contract to produce the book by 1995. It was then delayed by the feeling that I was not up to the task, that my intellectual stance was becoming increasingly old-fashioned and my interpretation redundant. However, a bulging filing cabinet has been a constant reminder of work unfinished. More recently, my sixtieth birthday has brought home to me that time is not so much passing as accelerating and that I may soon not have the luxury of choosing whether I will or nay. A late flowering of egoism has also played its part: I have now convinced myself that the world would be a better place if my notes were translated into a finished book. Finally, the approach of the hundredth anniversary of the first edition of *Imperialism* not only gave me a passable excuse to publish but also shamed me into finally settling my account with a writer to whom I have been heavily indebted for many years. Even so, the manuscript would not have been complete by now had it not been for the generosity of the Arts and Humanities Research Board whose support in 2001 gave me the chance to get the key chapters of the present volume written.

This is my first single-authored book and, since it could prove my last, I think it important to take the opportunity to thank my parents for their unflagging support for my youthful academic aspirations. I also remember with gratitude my teachers of economics and history in the sixth form at Thornleigh College, Bolton, who first kindled my interest in the movement of ideas. A book so long in the making and one that has changed its shape in the author's head on a number of occasions is the product of many influences. My first head of department at Birmingham, Harry Court, helped enormously by boosting my fragile self-confidence and by encouraging my belief that the history of ideas was a suitable area of study for an economic historian. The fact that Terence Hutchison, one of the finest historians of economic thought, lived across the corridor in the Ashley Building was a stimulus to action and gave me an exacting standard to measure my own efforts against. When I first wrote about Hobson, Peter Clarke gently exposed some of the weaknesses in my approach, forced me to rethink my position, and afterwards offered welcome support on a number of occasions. In the 1980s and early 1990s, teaching the history of economic thought alongside Roger Backhouse proved one of the most difficult and exciting episodes in my academic life and enriched my understanding of Hobson's intellectual context and antecedents. Roger also took on the tedious task of reading the whole manuscript and his penetrating comments have led to a number of improvements. Michael Freeden kindly read drafts of Chapters 2 and 3 and sharpened up my understanding of New Liberalism in its early days. Tony Taylor also read these chapters and gave me the benefit of his wide knowledge of British social and political history. Chapter 8 proved the most difficult to write and Roger Lloyd-Jones and Ian Phimister read some of my earlier efforts and helped me to get my thoughts in order. A special mention should be made of Tony Hopkins, who also commented on Chapter 8 and has been a constant source of encouragement in all my intellectual adventures for thirty years.

The book is a rather different one from the one I could have produced in 1995 because my working environment has changed dramatically. In Birmingham I was mainly exposed to the views of economic historians, economists, and other social scientists. At Sheffield Hallam, where I have always been treated with great generosity, the stimulation has come from a different mix of historical interests and from living next door to an English department. Their influence can be traced in parts of Chapters 3, 4, 5, and 7. Needless to say, neither they nor anyone else mentioned here shares the blame for the mistakes and misinterpretations which no doubt litter the following pages.

I dedicate the book to my wife Christine, with love and gratitude. It is not easy living with academics, especially one who is in constant communication with someone who died sixty years ago.

P. J. C.

Totley
29 November 2001

Contents

Contents

CHAPTER ONE

Introduction

In my first essay on Hobson, published over twenty years ago, I excused my venture into print by claiming that he was 'both well-known and neglected'.[1] What I believed was a rather clever way of saying that, although Hobson was remembered both as a critic of imperialism and for his work on unemployment and its causes, he had received relatively little academic attention, was already questionable when uttered. It took no account of the fact that Hobson's textbook *The Evolution of Modern Capitalism*, first written in the 1890s, had been reprinted again as late as 1965 or that a number of his major works had been recently reissued.[2] It was also rather misleading given recent work on Hobson's theory of underconsumption and his welfare economics;[3] Bernard Porter's brilliant extended analysis of Hobson's imperial thought in the critical years 1898–1902;[4] Emy's account of the evolution of ideas in the Liberal party after Gladstone in which Hobson figured prominently;[5] Freeden's pioneering essays on Hobson and the philosophy

[1] P. J. Cain, 'J. A. Hobson, Cobdenism and the Radical Theory of Economic Imperialism, 1898–1914', *Economic History Review*, 2nd ser. 31 (1978), 565.
[2] Including *The War in South Africa* (1900) and *The Economics of Distribution* (1900), both reprinted in New York in 1972. Other notable reprints include *Richard Cobden: The International Man* (1918; repr. 1968); *The Crisis of Liberalism* (1909; repr. Brighton, 1974); and *Confessions of an Economic Heretic* (1938; repr. Brighton, 1976).
[3] D. J. Coppock, 'A Reconsideration of Hobson's Theory of Unemployment', *Manchester School*, 21 (1953); E. E. Nemmers, *Hobson and Underconsumption* (Amsterdam, 1956). See also H. B. Davis, 'Hobson and Human Welfare', *Science and Society*, 21 (1957).
[4] B. Porter, *Critics of Empire: British Radical Attitudes to Colonialism in Africa, 1895–1914* (Cambridge, 1968), esp. chs. 6 and 7. H. Mitchell's sensitive study of aspects of Part II of *Imperialism: A Study* should also be mentioned. See 'Hobson Revisited', *Journal of the History of Ideas*, 26 (1965). There is also a perceptive analysis of Hobson in R. Koebner and H. D. Schmidt, *Imperialism: The History and Significance of a Political Word, 1840–1960* (Cambridge, 1964).
[5] H. V. Emy, *Liberals, Radicals and Social Politics, 1892–1914* (Cambridge, 1973).

of New Liberalism;[6] and the production of two weighty theses whose greatest merit was to provide the comprehensive bibliography of Hobson's writings necessary to a true scholarly appraisal.[7] My judgement was then rendered totally redundant even as it was printed by the publication of Freeden's and Clarke's major contributions to the understanding of New Liberalism[8] and Collini's volume on Hobson's intellectual confrère L. T. Hobhouse.[9] These last three books have provided the foundations of most subsequent work on New Liberalism in general and on Hobson and the political and ideological context in which he lived and worked in particular.

Porter's great achievement was not only to illuminate Hobson's own work but to see it as part of a complex and evolving critique of overseas expansion at the turn of the twentieth century. Similarly, Freeden and Clarke rescued Hobson from his lonely position of economic heretic and showed him to be a key figure in a wide-ranging movement engaged in redefining liberalism both in philosophical and in practical terms. So what was this New Liberalism to which Hobson devoted most of his best years? New Liberalism claimed that it pursued the same goal as the older liberalism but it had a different perspective on how it might be best achieved. On the economic front, for example, most liberals believed that the existing market economy dispensed a rough and ready justice, though there were always radicals who believed that no satisfactory social system was possible while land remained in the possession of a small elite. New Liberals agreed with the radicals on the land question. However, they claimed that inherited privilege and monopolies, in business and the professions as well as on the land, also created 'unearned income' and denied the mass of the population the means to achieve their full potential, both physical and mental. Moreover, in their view, the coming of political democracy

---

[6] M. Freeden, 'J. A. Hobson as a New Liberal Theorist', *Journal of the History of Ideas*, 34 (1973); id., 'Biological and Evolutionary Roots of the New Liberalism in England', *Political Theory*, 4 (1976).

[7] A. J. Lee, 'The Social and Economic Thought of J. A. Hobson' (unpub. Ph.D. thesis, University of London, 1970); J. Townshend, 'J. A. Hobson and the Crisis of Liberalism' (unpub. Ph.D. thesis, University of Southampton, 1973).

[8] M. Freeden, *The New Liberalism: An Ideology of Social Reform* (Oxford, 1978); P. F. Clarke, *Liberals and Social Democrats* (Cambridge, 1978).

[9] S. Collini, *Liberalism and Sociology: L. T. Hobhouse and Political Argument in England, 1880–1915* (Cambridge, 1979).

under the Reform Acts of 1867 and 1884 made it legitimate for the state, as the representative of the whole community, to tax that unearned income. New Liberals were not socialist revolutionaries but worked to produce a reformed capitalism in which the classes would live in harmony. The redistribution of what Hobson was later to call 'the surplus' to the majority, through welfare provision and better education, was intended to ensure equality of opportunity rather than the dead-level equality proposed by socialists. Hobson became the foremost economist of the movement as well as contributing to its philosophical and sociological underpinnings. His underconsumption theory was only one part of a complex theoretic structure aimed at justifying the redistribution of income New Liberals espoused, a structure that was only completed with the full development of his concept of surplus just before the First World War. As we shall see, Hobson's theory of economic imperialism was one outcome of his New Liberal economic ideas and was also in a direct line of succession from earlier radical thought on the matter.

Since the late 1970s the flow of publications has been steady and covered most aspects of Hobson's career as a radical economic and social thinker. There are now, for example, two more full-length studies of Hobson as an economic theorist;[10] Freeden has extended his study of liberalism to cover the First World War and the interwar period and given an in-depth account of Hobson's later political thought;[11] Hobson's ideas on international government, which became a major preoccupation after 1914, have also received attention in a major monograph;[12] Townshend has provided a convenient short account of much of the recent research on Hobson;[13] and there are now two collections of essays covering most aspects

[10] J. Allett, *New Liberalism: The Political Economy of J. A. Hobson* (Toronto, 1981); M. P. Schneider, *J. A. Hobson* (1996). See also W. H. Richmond, 'John A. Hobson: Economic Heretic', *American Journal of Economics and Sociology*, 37 (1978).
[11] M. Freeden, *Liberalism Divided: A Study of British Political Thought, 1914–1939* (Oxford, 1986). In this context one should also note J. Meadowcroft, *Conceptualising the State: Innovation and Dispute in British Political Thought, 1880–1914* (Oxford, 1995), and A. Vincent and R. Plant, *Philosophy, Politics and Citizenship: The Life and Thought of British Idealists* (1984), both of which have substantial material on Hobson.
[12] D. Long, *Towards a New Liberal Internationalism: The International Theory of J. A. Hobson* (Cambridge, 1996).
[13] J. Townshend, *J. A. Hobson* (Manchester, 1990).

of his intellectual career.[14] Many more of his key writings have also been reprinted in recent years.[15]

Since Porter, however, the harvest of research on Hobson's imperial thought has not been quite so rich. There are a number of good, brief accounts and analyses of the main lines of argument of *Imperialism: A Study*.[16] There have also been some enlivening attempts in recent times to reinterpret *Imperialism* in the context of the evolution of imperial thought in general[17] and of the British anti-imperial tradition in particular.[18] The links between Hobson's thought on the economics of imperialism and that of classical economic thinkers such as Smith and James Mill have been investigated[19] and some recent historians of British imperialism have made imaginative use of Hobson's theories, as Chapter 8 of the present book indicates. However, leaving aside my own work,[20] not much

---

[14] M. Freeden (ed.), *Reappraising J. A. Hobson: Humanism and Welfare* (1990); J. Pheby (ed.), *J. A. Hobson after Fifty Years: Freethinker of the Social Sciences* (Basingstoke, 1994).

[15] Including *Imperialism: A Study* (1902; repr. 1988.) and *The Social Problem* (1901 repr. Bristol, 1996). There is also an excellent selection of Hobson's work in *J. A. Hobson: A Reader*, ed. M. Freeden (1988). See also *J. A. Hobson: A Collection of his Writings* (Bristol, 1992), a six-volume set which includes *J. A. Hobson: Writings on Welfare and Distribution*, ed. R. E. Backhouse, and *J. A. Hobson: Writings on Imperialism and Internationalism*, ed. P. J. Cain. The 1919 edition of *Democracy after the War* has also been printed as part of an eight-volume set, P. J. Cain (ed.), *The Empire and its Critics, 1899–1939* (Bristol, 1998).

[16] In my opinion, the most stimulating of these are: Allett, *New Liberalism*, ch. 5; A. Brewer, *Marxist Theories of Imperialism* (2nd edn. 1990), ch. 4; L. Magnusson, 'Hobson and Imperialism: An Appraisal', in Pheby (ed.), *J. A. Hobson after Fifty Years*; and G. Nowell, 'Hobson's *Imperialism*: A Defence', in R. M. Chilcote (ed.), *The Political Economy of Imperialism: Critical Appraisals* (Boston, 1999); J. C. Wood, 'J. A. Hobson and British Imperialism', *American Journal of Economics and Sociology*, 42 (1983).

[17] See, in particular, N. Etherington, 'The Capitalist Theory of Capitalist Imperialism', *History of Political Economy*, 15 (1983); id., *Theories of Imperialism War, Conquest and Capital* (1984), chs. 2, 3, and 4. For commentary on Etherington's views see P. J. Cain, 'Hobson, Wilshire and the Capitalist Theory of Capitalist Imperialism', *History of Political Economy*, 17 (1985). See also B. Semmel, *The Liberal Ideal and the Demons of Empire* (Baltimore, 1993), esp. ch. 6; S. Edgell and J. Townshend, 'John Hobson, Thorstein Veblen and the Phenomenon of Imperialism: Finance Capitalism, Patriotism and War', *American Journal of Economics and Sociology*, 51 (1992).

[18] M. Taylor, 'Imperium et Libertas? Rethinking the Radical Critique of Imperialism during the Nineteenth Century', *Journal of Imperial and Commonwealth History*, 19 (1991).

[19] P. J. Cain, 'International Trade and Economic Development in the Thought of J. A. Hobson before 1914', *History of Political Economy*, 11 (1979).

[20] Cain, 'J. A. Hobson, Cobdenism and the Radical Theory of Economic Imperialism'; id., 'Variations on a Famous Theme: Hobson, International Trade and

interest has been shown in Hobson's other writings on imperialism and the difference between them and *Imperialism*.[21] So, the main aim of the present book is to offer a detailed discussion of the evolution of Hobson's thoughts on economic imperialism from his earliest comments on the subject in his father's newspaper in the late 1880s to the publication of the third edition of *Imperialism* two years before his death in 1940.

In 1978 I argued that *Imperialism* was only a 'snapshot' of Hobson's views on imperialism and that his thoughts were in continuous evolution.[22] Clarke and Wood responded by emphasizing the continuities in Hobson's thinking.[23] *Imperialism* was undoubtedly Hobson's most comprehensive treatise on the subject as well as his most impassioned and readable contribution. It was also the book he chose to republish, without serious amendment, just before his death and it is now assumed, by most readers, to be the alpha and omega of his thinking. Whether *Imperialism* is the book most representative of his views during his lifetime is, however, a different matter. Both Clarke and Wood ignore Hobson's writings on imperialism in the early 1890s, which were pro-imperialist in sentiment and which need to be recovered. It is also the case that, until his death in 1940, Hobson continued to produce new ideas on empire. Many of these fresh insights were undoubtedly elaborations upon themes in *Imperialism*. But I also believe that in some of his works, most notably in *An Economic Interpretation of Investment* (1911), he took an approach to imperial expansion and its outcomes that contradicted some of the key arguments in *Imperialism* on which his fame as a theorist rests. Moreover, looking at Hobson's writings from the late 1890s onwards, it seems to me that the ideas presented in *An Economic Interpretation* were, perhaps, more representative of his thinking—

Imperialism', in Freeden (ed.), *Reappraising J. A. Hobson*. My view of Hobson's development before 1914 was revised in 'Free Trade, Social Reform and Imperialism: J. A. Hobson and the Dilemmas of Liberalism, 1890–1914', in A. Marrison (ed.), *Free Trade and its Reception 1815–1960: Freedom and Trade*, (Manchester, 1998).

[21] The exceptions are J. C. Wood, *British Economists and the Empire* (1983), ch. 10, and id., 'J. A. Hobson and British Imperialism'.

[22] Cain, 'J. A. Hobson, Cobdenism and the Radical Theory of Economic Imperialism', 565.

[23] P.F. Clarke, 'Hobson, Free Trade and Imperialism', *Economic History Review*, 2nd ser. 34 (1981) and my reply, 'Hobson's Developing Theory of Imperialism', in the same issue; Wood, *British Economists and the Empire*, 249, 261 n. 98.

and of the radical tradition that he was part of—than those found in *Imperialism*. The bulk of the book, Chapters 2–7, is, therefore, taken up with a largely chronological account of Hobson's thought on imperialism and imperial expansion in order to illustrate its diversity and changefulness.

Chapters 2 and 3 concentrate upon Hobson's early intellectual journey, something relatively neglected in the literature. Chapter 2 demonstrates that his radicalism was not inherited but something he had to learn after he came to London in the mid-1880s and began writing 'A London Letter' for his father's newspaper in Derby. The new faith was acquired only slowly. Writing his now-famous book, *The Physiology of Industry*, with A. F. Mummery in 1889 was only the beginning of the process. It was not completed until the mid-1890s, mediated by his experiences of London poverty and by the influence of Ruskin as well as the Fabians and the Rainbow Circle, the intellectual hothouse of the New Liberal thinking that Hobson finally espoused. The publication of the *Evolution of Modern Capitalism* (1894), a book discussed in some detail in this chapter, marked the point when New Liberalism became his established mode of thought. In Chapter 2 I also investigate the links between Hobson's New Liberal stance and traditional radical thinking from Paine onwards, with special reference to the way that he developed the concept of unearned income as handed down from John Stuart Mill. His famous doctrines of underconsumption and oversaving were directly linked to his concern with the 'unearned increment', a concern that reached its climax in the Edwardian period with his most elaborate statement of the concept of surplus in the *Industrial System* (1909). Some of Hobson's most enduring insights were expressed in the language of social biology, and the importance of that receives some attention here with an eye to the fact that such language was later a critical element in forming the argument of Part II of *Imperialism*.

Chapter 3 tries to show that his conversion into a radical critic of imperialism and of imperial expansion was even more prolonged than his transformation into a New Liberal. Initially, Hobson's Liberal Unionist background made support for 'free trade imperialism' appealing. In the early 1890s, he even showed some sympathy with protection and imperial federation. Indeed, he was still writing about the latter in a positive spirit in 1896. A growing hostility to Rhodes's behaviour in South Africa, the influence of the Rainbow

Circle, and contributions to the *Progressive Review* under William Clarke's editorship began to push him in a radical direction. However, it was not until 1898 that he successfully merged his radical stance on domestic issues with his growing hostility to imperial expansion. In 'Free Trade and Foreign Policy' he brought his theory of underconsumption and oversaving together with his new aversion to imperialism when he claimed that oversaving led to foreign investment and that the need to find more outlets for the latter was the key to understanding modern imperial expansion. It is noticeable that his chief concern in 1898 was the scramble for China rather than the storm brewing in South Africa. As in Chapter 2, one of my purposes is to show how Hobson's critique of imperialism was an important moment in a long-standing but evolving radical discourse. His innovations were, in a very real sense, an attempt to bring up to date Spencer's analysis of militarism as a causal factor in imperialism by incorporating the role of finance more firmly into the sources of unearned income upon which militancy was supposedly based.

Chapters 4 and 5 deal with Hobson's writings in 1899–1902, a period that covers the Boer War and the publication of *Imperialism: A Study*.[24] Chapter 4 charts the development of his ideas before and during his visit to South Africa in 1899 and shows how books such as *The War in South Africa* (1900) and *The Psychology of Jingoism* arose out of that visit. It also tries to illustrate the tension between Hobson's interest in financiers as a body of men capable of using politics for their own sinister ends and his growing awareness of the evolution of a new kind of capitalism based on the growth of big business. The chapter ends with a sustained analysis and critique of Part I of *Imperialism: A Study*[25] and of the sections of Part II that are directly linked to the economic analysis presented by Hobson in Part I. Partly because of the speed with which it was put together

---

[24] Some of the material in these chapters can also be found in P. J. Cain, 'British Radicalism, the South African Crisis and the Origins of the Theory of Financial Imperialism', in D. Omissi and A. S. Thompson (eds.), *The Impact of the South African War* (2002).

[25] *Imperialism: A Study* was first published in 1902. Some significant changes were made for the second edition of 1905 and these differences are noted in Chapter 6. The third edition of 1938 was virtually a reprint of the 1905 edition with a new introduction and with the statistical material updated. The 1988 edition, with an introduction by Jules Townshend, reprints the third edition entire. Unless otherwise stated, the 1988 edition is the one used here.

and partly because Hobson wanted to extend his analysis to cover all industrially developed countries, the analysis suffered from a number of internal contradictions and inconsistencies. The greatest point of tension in his account was that between his sense of the financier as conspirator—inherited from the radical tradition and seemingly confirmed by his South African experiences—and a more analytical approach to financial capitalism as part of the changing structure of advanced industrial societies. As for the latter, Part II contained a number of scattered insights into the growth of big business and into the formation of coalitions of propertied interests which, it is argued, have a Gramscian flavour and were intrinsically of much greater interest than his oft-repeated insistence on the financier as demon king.

In Chapter 5 the focus of attention shifts to Part II of *Imperialism*, the part least often read in modern times. Part II was twice as long as Part I, it contained some of Hobson's finest writing and in it were discussed a range of issues which Hobson undoubtedly believed were of equal importance to the more nakedly economic arguments at the beginning of the book. In Part II, Hobson first investigated the political, social, and ideological forces making for expansion in Britain and then went on to discuss the impact of imperialism upon Africa, India, and China and upon the settlement colonies, the emerging Dominions. He also tried to forecast what the outcomes would be in the twentieth century if present imperialist policies were pursued indefinitely. The discussion made it plain that he believed that the fate of the world depended more on what might happen in China than upon any other set of events. Besides offering a more detailed account than hitherto of Hobson's most famous text, the main aim of the discussion is to highlight the extent which the book was an attempt to update and refine the radical anti-imperialist discourse that Hobson had adopted in the 1890s. In Part I this was achieved by linking together oversaving, foreign investment, and the malign influence of financiers. In Part II, it is argued, Hobson dramatized the struggle as one between 'industry'—the source of liberty, democracy, and prosperity for all—and 'parasitism'. The latter word became something of a commonplace among liberal and socialist critics and clearly developed from the concern with evolutionary biology and the medical discoveries that were such a feature of the age. As used by Hobson it might be crudely defined as 'militancy + finance'. Put more subtly, Part II of *Imperialism* represents

Hobson's attempt to find a language in which to describe the changing balance of economic power in Britain in his time, as the 'Few' or the 'classes' of historical radicalism changed their economic shape and political and social colouring. Hobson aimed to transform and modernize the inherited radical discourse while retaining strong links with it, thus making it plausible for him to claim that he was in the true line of succession from Spencer and from Cobden.

The chapter ends with a short survey of the reception of *Imperialism*. It shows that *Imperialism* was not received with acclaim even amongst those opposed to British policy in South Africa. Many critics of the Boer War found Hobson's root-and-branch hostility to the conflict too extreme and many felt that his attitude to Britain's role in the world was far too negative. His social and economic radicalism and his hostility to white empire unity also distanced him from many liberals who were suspicious of further expansion. Even within the New Liberal fraternity there was stern opposition from critics like Herbert Samuel who believed that domestic radicalism and the extension of Britain's mission abroad were perfectly compatible.

The extended treatment given to *Imperialism* implicitly contradicts my earlier view on its importance in the history of Hobson's thought. In truth, *Imperialism* is Hobson's most extended and powerful piece of writing on the subject. Nonetheless, his opinions did change frequently after 1902 and Chapters 6 and 7 chart the major shifts in them. Chapter 6 argues that, in the Edwardian period, Hobson's thinking on imperial matters was, at worst, schizoid and, at best, puzzling. One strand of his writings was in a direct line of succession from *Imperialism*. The book was republished in 1905 and contained alterations to Part I that in some ways hardened the stance he had adopted in 1902. He also printed numerous articles in which he warned of the dangers of parasitism and its consequences. This was accompanied (rather than followed) by a stream of writings contradicting some key arguments in *Imperialism*. From 1903, Hobson spent much of his time attacking Chamberlain's campaign to introduce protection and imperial preference because, in true radical fashion, he saw protection as a device for extending privilege and unearned income. But his advocacy of free trade led him into dangerous intellectual territory. In *Imperialism* Hobson had presented international trade as the chief carrier of a diseased capitalism and of imperialism. He had claimed that the problem of imperialism could be resolved by a redistribution of income and wealth that would drastically reduce foreign investment and marginalize foreign trade. As Chapter 2 shows, the argument had a considerable radical pedigree though it was hardly consistent with the thinking of Cobden, whom Hobson claimed to follow. Yet, in support of free trade, Hobson committed himself after 1903 to the Cobdenite position that an extended foreign trade was good for internationalism and thus for democracy and prosperity. The outcome was *An Economic Interpretation of Investment* (1911), where Hobson presented imperialism not as a reversion to militancy and barbarism so much as a necessary stage in an economic globalization that would eventually lead every area of the world, whether advanced or 'backward', towards liberty and prosperity. Chapter 6 explores these contradictions and also tries to account for them in terms of the tensions within Hobson's radical stance and within radicalism in general.

Hobson lived until 1940 and thus encountered the First World War and the beginning of the next, as well as the great depression of the 1930s. His views on imperialism were influenced by these seismic events in complex ways laid out in Chapter 7. Not surprisingly, during the First World War his views gradually shifted back towards those he had put forward in *Imperialism*, as is evident in *The New Protectionism* (1916) and especially in *Democracy after the War* (1917). After the war and through to the mid-1930s his views moved in the opposite direction, back to those expressed in *An Economic Interpretation of Investment* though without ever quite matching the heady optimism of that work. As the great depression lingered and another world conflict became more likely, Hobson decided that early thoughts were best and reissued *Imperialism* in a third edition in 1938. Between 1914 and 1940, however, Hobson's work on imperialism was not simply a steady recycling of old ideas adapted to changing times. He carried on thinking, providing a number of new insights into the phenomenon of imperialism and, especially during 1916–17, he investigated a number of specific episodes in Britain's imperial past with an attention to detail not equalled since his early work on South Africa. In rethinking his stance on imperialism after 1914 he also became a pioneer in the field of what was later to be called 'development economics'. In the 1920s and 1930s he also seriously considered for the first time the idea that, as an inspiration for imperial domination and expansion, the desire for power might be more important than the pursuit of wealth.

Hobson republished *Imperialism* again in 1938 partly because he felt that its message was pertinent again, partly because the book was attracting widespread attention. *Imperialism* had only a few supporters in the Edwardian period, and at times before 1914 Hobson himself repudiated a number of its core statements, as Chapter 6 tries to show. After the war, and to some extent because of it, Hobson's views as expressed in *Imperialism* slowly became more acceptable in academic circles and on the left of politics. The story of the resurrection of *Imperialism* as a classic text is a complex one. What can be said here is that the book's emergence as a classic had its costs. These included the suppression of Hobson's other writings on imperial themes, a suppression which Hobson endorsed in his autobiography, *Confessions of an Economic Heretic*, also published in 1938 and subsequently one of his most frequently read texts. Chapter 7 ends with a brief summary of Hobson's views on imperialism over the period 1887–1938.

The last chapter changes the perspective to ask whether Hobson's *Imperialism* is more than just a classic illuminating its time. Is it a book that is still useful to present-day historians attempting to understand the motivation behind imperial expansion in the late nineteenth and early twentieth centuries? In pursuit of an answer[26] Chapter 8 looks at the book in the context of our modern knowledge of the size, distribution, and ownership of foreign investment and its place in the British economy. In *Imperialism*, Hobson contended that the costs of empire were paid by the nation as a whole but that only a very small elite got the benefits: Chapter 8 tests this argument against recent scholarly attempts to understand whether the empire was worth having. Besides addressing the vexed question of whether or not Hobson meant his theory to apply to the tropical African partition of the 1880s and 1890s, there are also three brief cases studies. The first is concerned with the background to the occupation of Egypt in 1882, the second with the origins of the Boer War of 1899–1902, and the third investigates the British

[26] This builds upon an earlier attempt. P. J. Cain, 'Hobson Lives? Finance and British Imperialism, 1870–1914' in S. Groenweld and D. Wintle (eds.), *State and Trade: Government and the Economy in Britain and the Netherlands since the Middle Ages* (Zutphen, 1992).

role in the scramble for China between 1895 and 1914. Hobson saw all these episodes as examples of financial imperialism and his convictions are tested against the work of modern specialists. Hobson emerges with some credit from this bruising encounter with modernity. Nonetheless, the chief finding of the chapter is that there may be more mileage in future in developing his thoughts on the rise of big business and cartels in *Imperialism* and in *The Evolution of Modern Capitalism* than in pursuing the more traditional lines of Hobsonian thinking.

I make no claim to have read every word that Hobson wrote on imperialism and empire. In pursuit of my theme, I have largely concentrated my efforts on close reading of what I take to be the key books and articles and Hobson's vast store of journalism and other ephemeral writings[27] has been consulted only when it seemed imperative to do so. Hobson is intended to be the centre of attention throughout. I have introduced the writings of his contemporaries, and filled in the political and social context in which he worked, only when it seemed important to an understanding of the twists and turns of Hobson's mental development or necessary to bring his ideas into sharper focus by comparing and contrasting them with those of his contemporaries. In other words, this is a book about Hobson *in* his time rather than about Hobson *and* his times. It is in no sense a definitive work on its subject. Rather, it offers an interpretation of Hobson's intellectual journey and its significance that, with luck, will stimulate other scholars to reread him and to challenge my own account.

What follows is mainly an exercise in the history of economic thought though one that, I hope, interprets this marvellous field of knowledge in a more imaginative way than was evident in my early encounters with Hobson. Reacting to one of the latter, Peter Clarke accused me, with some justice, of treating Hobson too much as an academic thinker concerned with ironing out faults in the logic of his arguments. Instead, he thought, I should have been looking out for a politically committed writer reacting to his changing environment and using whatever intellectual weapons came to hand at the time.[28] While I continue to support a rather different inter-

---

[27] Lee and Townshend list over 700 items in their bibliographies of Hobson's writings, many of which are from newspapers and other fleeting sources.
[28] Clarke, 'Hobson, Free Trade and Imperialism', 308.

pretation of Hobson's intellectual trajectory from Clarke's, I hope that my work now shows more Skinnerian traces than it did then.[29] Nonetheless, I believe that texts can have meanings beyond those intended by the author and I have been encouraged in this thinking by some of my recent colleagues, from whom I have learned a great deal about language and its intricacies. Nonetheless, I make no pretence to any degree of knowledge or understanding allowing me to practice as a master of discourse analysis. My rather hesitant probing into Hobson's use of language especially in Chapter 5 owes rather more to memories of the works of T. S. Eliot, F. R. Leavis, and Raymond Williams than it does to the diverse outpourings of Michel Foucault and his successors.

Unlike many of his famous contemporaries, Hobson is little known as a person. Few private papers have survived and his autobiography must be one of the most self-effacing ever produced. Even his comments on those who influenced him have a singularly bloodless character.[30] Though frequently mentioned in the memoirs and diaries of the time, Hobson always appears as a shadowy figure, a set of ideas and opinions rather than a living, breathing being: intellectual biography is all the historian can aspire to in his case. Hobson can appear intellectually as well as personally remote. His philosophy, based as it was on notions of a rational pursuit of a common good, looks out of place in our age when the incommensurability of human desires is largely taken for granted. His anti-Semitism and his authoritarian eugenics cast doubt on the authenticity of his liberalism and are an embarrassment now. Hobson also had marked intellectual limitations. Over the years I have been frequently puzzled by his inconsistencies—as Chapter 6 bears witness—and have long despaired of his lack of academic rigour which, as a young scholar, I too often tried to excuse or deny. I can now accept with a certain equanimity the knowledge that Hobson not only contradicts himself at different points in his life but that he was quite capable of holding two opposed sets of ideas at the same time. Yet his intellectual stature is still considerable and his economic ideas far from dead. The range of his know-

---

[29] Q. Skinner, 'Meaning and Understanding in the History of Ideas', *History and Theory*, 8 (1969), repr. in J. Tully (ed.), *Meaning and Context: Quentin Skinner and his Critics* (Princeton, 1988).

[30] See G. D. H. Cole's comments on Hobson's autobiography *Confessions of an Economic Heretic* in *Political Quarterly*, 9 (1938), 441.

ledge makes modern scholars seem ridiculously overspecialized. Politics and political science, sociology, economics, history, biology, and social psychology were all subjects on which his reading was wide and his thoughts often penetrating. He carried on thinking long past conventional retirement age and he often showed moral courage in first embracing, and then persisting in believing, ideas that many of his contemporaries thought wrongheaded and some thought wicked. When moved by great causes he could also write with eloquence as well as clarity as *Imperialism* testifies. Moreover, though no Keynes (who *can* compare with him?), he can certainly claim to be one of the chief intellectual inspirations behind the welfare state and the mixed economy that came into being in the 1940s and are still, albeit shakily, in place in 2002 despite the assaults of Thatcherism.[31] It is often said of biographers that too close an acquaintance with their subject can turn initial interest and liking into boredom and even hostility. Despite moments of disillusion, this has not been my experience in reading Hobson. He has been part of my life for so long that I have come to think of him as a distant member of the family, a rather quirky intellectual uncle from whom I have learned much. What follows is written in a necessarily critical spirit: but is also an extended tribute to the intellectual legacy of a man who, for the last thirty years, has been one of my guides to a better understanding of Victorian and Edwardian thought and society, and an inspiration for my own work on British imperialism.

[31] I thus dissociate myself from the rather condescending verdict on Hobson delivered by F. Inglis, *Radical Earnestness: English Social Theory, 1880–1980* (1982), 59–60, 62.

CHAPTER TWO

Becoming a New Liberal, 1887–1898

HOBSON'S LIBERAL INHERITANCE

John Atkinson Hobson (1858–1940) was not born into the cause of radical anti-imperialism. He described himself as springing from 'the middle stratum of the middle-class of a middle sized industrial town in the Midlands'.[1] Perhaps this was too modest an assessment, since his father, William Hobson, was the joint proprietor of a weekly paper, the *Derbyshire Advertiser and Journal*, and was twice mayor of Derby, in 1883 and 1885.[2] William's paper gave its support to the Liberal party; and that party was a loose coalition of forces ranging from the remnants of the Whig aristocracy on one side to a motley collection of 'single issue' radical groups keen to bend the party to their cause on the other. Its core support came from provincial business and the better-off artisan and what held it together was hostility to the great landed aristocrats and to the interventionist state the aristocracy had once created to extend and consolidate their privileges and which had been popularly known as 'Old Corruption'. Under Gladstone's masterly leadership, the party presided over a classic compromise in which, in return for the loss of many of their privileges such as agricultural protection and the creation of a low-tax, minimalist state, the aristocracy was left to enjoy its rents in peace and also to run the much-reduced government machine. It is only in recent times that historians have made plain how much popular support there was for this brand of liberalism and the extent to which, despite the pressures of class

---

[1] J. A. Hobson, *Confessions of an Economic Heretic*, ed. M. Freeden (1974), 15. The *Confessions* was first published in 1938.

[2] Alan Lee, 'John Atkinson Hobson, 1858–1940', in J. M. Bellamy and J. Saville (eds.), *Dictionary of Labour Biography*, i (1972), 176.

hostility, middle- and working-class forces in the provinces and in the 'Celtic fringe' banded together to preserve it.[3] Nonetheless, as we shall see, class conflict was growing in the 1880s and was beginning to threaten the coherence of the party. Indeed, it can be argued that one compelling reason why Gladstone was converted to the cause of Irish Home Rule in 1886 was that he saw it as a unifying issue to counteract the growing clamour within the movement for state action on class lines which would unsettle the 'producers' alliance' on which the party relied. Whatever were Gladstone's motives, they did not appeal to William Hobson. He followed the declining Whig-aristocratic end of the Liberal coalition who objected to Home Rule and he supported the Liberal Unionists who stood for the status quo and for imperial unity.

Hobson was undoubtedly raised in an atmosphere where free market capitalism and the Gladstonian state were largely taken for granted as guarantors of individual freedom. However, one of the weaknesses in Hobson's own account of his early life is his insistence that, in his youth, he was completely surrounded by economic and political complacency and that he was an entirely self-taught economic heretic. In truth, there was a great deal of heresy about in Hobson's younger days and he was exposed to some of it himself when, at the age of 16, he took a University Extension course in economics led by William Moore Ede. Ede was following Arnold Toynbee as well as John Stuart Mill in arguing that the Industrial Revolution had brought little benefit to the bulk of the population; and he supported trades unionism and the cause of income redistribution.[4] In his autobiography, Hobson remembered attending the classes but omitted to mention their radical stance and made no reference to Mill's schemes for worker co-operation to raise living standards in his remarkable discussion of distribution in the

---

[3] John Vincent, *The Formation of the Liberal Party, 1857–1868* (1966), remains a classic account of the diverse elements within the party. On its popular foundations see E. F. Biagini, *Liberty, Retrenchment and Reform: Popular Liberalism in the Age of Gladstone, 1860–1880* (Cambridge, 1992); and J. Lawrence, 'Popular Radicalism and the Socialist Revival in Britain', *Journal of British Studies*, 31 (1992). On its leadership, see the magnificent biography by H. C. G. Matthew, *Gladstone, 1809–1898* (Oxford, 1996), esp. 59–86, 103–48, 330–50. For a brief description of the Gladstonian 'nightwatchman' state see P. J. Cain, 'British Free Trade, 1850–1914: Economics and Policy', *ReFRESH* 29 (1999), 1–2.

[4] Alon Kadish, 'Rewriting the *Confessions*: Hobson and the Extension Movement', in Freeden (ed.), *Reappraising J. A. Hobson*, 137–40.

Principles of Political Economy. He claimed instead that it was his own reading of the *Principles* which sowed the seeds of doubt about 'Mill's dogma' that wages were paid out of savings (the so-called wages fund) and that, therefore, the welfare of the working class was dependent on the thrift of the rich.[5] Howsoever implanted, such ideas had little effect upon him for many years.

Already bereft of religious beliefs, he went up to Oxford in the late 1870s to read classics, did poorly in examinations, and, his intellectual self-assurance undermined, went off to teach at a school in Exeter. What induced him to move to London in the mid-1880s is not known: but it is evident from the 'London Letter' he then began to write for his father's newspaper that his views were still close to home. He supported Liberal Unionism, claiming that its leaders 'represent the force of solid intelligence and respectability which has given firmness to our constitution and order to [Britain's] progress'. In 1887 he was also writing of 'the inbred idleness of the Irish peasant' and 'the obstinate indolence which lies at the root of Irish grievances'; and his comment that the current methods of relieving poverty made the problem worse by increasing the life expectancy of the poor also suggests a certain superficiality in analysis.[6] Nonetheless, his exposure to metropolitan life and ideas slowly began to jog him out of his apparent complacency, though his first essays into print were on religious rather than social and economic themes.

Liberalism, Idealism, and Social Reform

Hobson arrived in the capital in interesting times. The 1880s in Britain were characterized by falling prices and pressure on profits in both agriculture and in manufacturing. Provincial business-men routinely complained of a tendency to 'overproduction' and their views were endorsed by the famous Royal Commission on

[5] *Confessions*, 25. Hobson makes no acknowledgement here of the fact that Mill had given up the wage fund idea towards the end of his life. It is, however, not clear from Kadish's account whether Hobson would have learned this from Ede.

[6] *Derbyshire Advertiser and North Staffordshire Journal*, 7 Oct. 1887 and 4 Nov. 1887. He had an equally dim view of the Irish in America saying that 'the only thing they are good for is political agitation' and claiming that the average American supported Home Rule 'because they think that more of the Irish would then stay at home'. Ibid. 4 Nov. 1887.

Depression in Trade and Industry, which reported in 1886, and by a host of amateur economists.[7] Unemployment was certainly higher on average than in the mid-Victorian period and at the depths of severe slumps, such as those of 1879 and 1886, rose to socially alarming heights.[8] Part of the problem was increasing foreign competition under free trade. Arable agriculture was severely affected by imports of grain flowing in from the new global economy created by railways and cheap steam shipping, and displaced labour poured off the land into urban Britain. Manufacturing imports, especially in iron and steel, also grew rapidly fuelling demands for a return to protection. Protectionists, known at the time as 'Fair Traders', objected to Britain's policy of unilateral free trade and argued that it led to reduced investment and growth in Britain and induced foreign investment and emigration thus contributing to the strength of Britain's rivals in Europe and the United States.[9] Despite much calamitous talk, however, it is evident that the economy continued to grow[10] and that, despite a sharp rise in foreign investment in the 1880s, domestic investment was not significantly curtailed. Much of the dynamism of the economy came from the service sector especially transport, distribution, commerce, and finance. The growth of services was fastest in the south-east of England, especially in London, where the City expanded with great rapidity. The latter was the chief conduit for the growth of that 'invisible' income—from insurance, shipping, short-term credits, and returns on foreign investment—which compensated for the sluggish growth of manufactured exports.[11]

London's economy was dynamic and innovative. Besides the City's income, much of it dependent on London's position as the

---

[7] Alon Kadish, 'The Non-canonical Context of the *Physiology of Industry*', in Pheby (ed.), *J. A. Hobson after Fifty Years*.

[8] 'Unemployment' became a serious matter of concern in the 1880s. J. Harris, *Unemployment and Politics: A Study in English Social Policy, 1880–1914* (Oxford, 1972), 4. See also R. W. Garside, *The Measurement of Unemployment: Methods and Sources in Great Britain, 1850–1970* (1980).

[9] *Minority Report of the Royal Commission on Depression in Trade and Industry*, Cd. 4893 (1886). Hobson took part in debates on fair trade in Oxford in the late 1870s. *Confessions*, 25.

[10] S. B. Saul, *The Great Depression, 1873–1896: Myth or Reality?* (1969).

[11] C. H. Lee, 'Regional Growth and Structural Change in Victorian Britain', *Economic History* Review, 2nd ser. 34 (1981); R. C. Michie, *The City of London* (1991); P. J. Cain and A. G. Hopkins, *British Imperialism, 1688–2000* (2001), chs. 3 and 5.

biggest port in the country, it also enjoyed enormous revenues from hosting central government services and from the activities of 'High Society'. It was the centre of the service economy and also the home of many new industries attracted by the high level of demand in the capital.[12] Nonetheless it also contained vast reservoirs of poverty and unemployment and parts of east London were suffering from particularly acute problems of economic and social transition in the 1880s. Already a major magnet for migrants from other parts of Britain, London was also attracting refugees from Europe at the same time that it was losing out as a centre of shipbuilding and other heavy industries under pressure from the provinces. Unemployment in the poorer areas reached heights that sparked riots in the latter part of the decade, forcing the government of the day to initiate emergency public works programmes. It was the crisis in London that persuaded Charles Booth to begin his famous study of poverty levels in east London. Booth's conclusion that about 30 per cent of London's population had incomes insufficient to ensure minimum subsistence levels shocked the nation's elite. His suggested remedies, including old age pensions, also posed a severe challenge to laissez-faire individualism. Booth's findings and policy proposals were beginning to reverberate around the capital as Hobson settled in.[13]

Booth's survey—the serious beginnings of applied sociology in Britain—attracted Hobson's attention early,[14] but it was only one part of an intellectual and political ferment to which he was now exposed.[15] The Social Democratic Federation was formed in the 1880s under H. M. Hyndman's leadership and Marxism also famously captured William Morris for the cause. Despite its Marxist ideology, the SDF still had strong affinities with liberal and radical thinking especially in its hostility to the remnants of the aristocratic state.[16] But its stress on the inevitability of class conflict and the

---

[12] L. D. Schwartz, *London in the Age of Industrialisation: Entrepreneurs, Labour Force and Living Conditions, 1750–1850* (Cambridge, 1992); T. C. Barker, 'London: A Unique Megalopolis?', in T. C. Barker and A. Sutcliffe (eds.), *Megalopolis. The Giant City in History* (1993).

[13] G. Stedman Jones, *Outcast London: A Study in the Relationship between Classes in Victorian Society* (Oxford, 1971).

[14] *Confessions*, 28.

[15] Some indication of the bewildering variety of movements and opinions can be found in S. Pierson, *Marxism and the Origins of British Socialism: The Struggle for a New Consciousness* (Ithaca, NY, 1973).

[16] Lawrence, 'Popular Radicalism and the Socialist Revival in Britain', 175–9.

need for revolution did not have a wide appeal amongst British intellectual elites. Most had no fundamental hostility to capitalism, believed in equality of opportunity rather than equality itself, and yearned for some solution to the social problems of the age that would reconcile all sections of society.[17] This quest for moral community was an almost instinctive, and sometimes overpowering, urge amongst Britain's liberal intellectual elites:[18] even so fierce an individualist as Herbert Spencer believed that evolution was slowly bringing into being individuals whose main concern would be the common good rather than their own.[19] Moreover, there was general agreement amongst liberal thinkers that what was most needed to bring about a harmonious community was the constant improvement of 'character' with its 'constantly self-reviewing disposition to form virtuous habits of conduct and its focus on the welfare of others as the object of moral action'.[20] Mill, for example, despite agreeing with Spencer that society was simply an aggregate of the individuals composing it, earnestly believed that all right-thinking persons could and should strive for altruism in their relations with others and that all merely 'self-regarding' acts were necessarily selfish.[21] T. H. Green and his followers emphasized this in subsequently shifting away from the individualism of Spencer and Mill, offering instead an Idealist approach to society as an organic entity, one which was more than the sum of its parts. In such a society, the individual had his or her true meaning as a member of a community and found creative purpose in furthering the good of the whole.[22] Green's thought had an enormous influence on generations of Oxford students from the 1870s onwards,[23] and the assumptions behind it were carried into the British Idealist

---

[17] Hobson thought the SDF and Morris were 'too inflammatory'. *Confessions*, 29.

[18] S. den Otter, *British Idealism and Social Explanation: A Study in Late Victorian Thought* (Oxford, 1996), 83.

[19] M. W. Taylor, *Men versus the State: Herbert Spencer and Late Victorian Individualism* (Oxford, 1992), 94.

[20] S. Collini, *Public Moralists: Political Thought and Intellectual Life in Britain, 1850–1950* (Oxford, 1991), 133.

[21] Ibid., 62–7; id., 'Liberalism and the Legacy of Mill', *Historical Journal*, 20 (1977).

[22] On Green see M. Richter, *The Politics of Conscience: T. H. Green and his Age* (1964).

[23] Hobson felt that the influence of Jowett, Green, and Pattison had done something, even in his undergraduate days, to liberate him from the 'materialistic and narrowly utilitarian' ideas of the age. *Confessions*, 26.

movement by the likes of Bernard Bosanquet, D. G. Richie, and J. H. Muirhead.[24]

Since it encouraged people to co-operate with each other to produce commodities rather than fight—or, in Spencer's words, it furthered the movement from a 'militant' society to an 'industrial' one—most liberal and radical thinkers were clear that the Industrial Revolution had been a progressive force. Indeed, for liberals, the word 'industry' and 'industrial' still evoked the idea of energy and progress rather than the simple process of producing commodities.[25] As Samuel Smiles averred, 'the spirit of self-help, as exhibited in the energetic action of individuals, has in all times been a marked feature in the English character'; and that energetic individualism based on 'industry, sobriety and upright honesty of purpose in life' was chiefly encountered 'in our homes, in the streets, behind counters, in workshops, at the loom and the plough, in counting houses and manufactories, and in the busy haunts of men'.[26] Yet Mill and Green were concerned, as was Smiles himself, that the character-forming benefits of industrialism would be lost if wealth became the primary concern of individuals because such materialism would inevitably lead, via luxury, to corruption and the degradation of character.[27] Also, like the later Mill, Green did not believe in any Smithian 'invisible hand' reconciling all claims in the market. Writing when the agricultural depression was in full swing and when the horrors of urbanism were again coming to elite attention, Green thought of the market as divisive, as exacerbating poverty and threatening social collapse. Cultivating character in order to encourage the social virtues was, he believed, vital to prevent class warfare and to preserve liberalism as a force.[28]

---

[24] Den Otter, *British Idealism, passim.* The notion of character here described also played a crucial role in the thinking of the greatest British economist of the time, Alfred Marshall. See S. Collini, D. Winch, and J. Burrow, *That Noble Science of Politics: A Study in Nineteenth Century Intellectual History* (Cambridge, 1983), ch. 10.

[25] My stress here is different from that in R. Williams, *Keywords: A Vocabulary of Culture and Society* (1976), 137.

[26] S. Smiles, *Self Help*, ed. A. Briggs (1958), 38–9. The first edition was in 1859.

[27] R. Bellamy, *Liberalism and Modern Society: An Historical Argument* (1992), ch. 1.

[28] T. H. Green, *Prolegomena to Ethics* (4th edn. 1899), paras. 245, 257, 282–3; den Otter, *British Idealism*, 158.

Mill's and Green's arguments raised large issues about income redistribution and the role of the state in economic welfare which challenged not only Gladstonian orthodoxies but divided their intellectual heirs who disagreed about how much state intervention or 'collectivism' was required to achieve moral community. Mill had become convinced by the 1840s that the time had come to change the emphasis in society from producing wealth in favour of the more character-building tasks of redistributing income towards the poor—who had received little benefit from industrialization so far—and concentrating on moral and mental improvement.[29] Society, he hoped, was now ready to turn away from materialism to the virtuous life where all worked for common ends rather than for themselves alone.[30] Mill himself initially favoured self-help schemes, including population restraint and co-operative forms of production, to raise standards of living for the poor to levels where 'improvement' was possible.[31] As we shall see, in his later years he proposed more active intervention by the state. Spencer, of course, always objected to the use of the state as encouraging the return of that militarism and authoritarianism which the growth of free competitive industry had so effectively combated.[32] Bosanquet, who was a leading light in the Charity Organization Society the largest philanthropic body in England, also believed that too much public intervention would undermine the individual's desire to strive for a better life. Richie, on the other hand, felt that the state, as the representative of the moral community, had a much bigger role to play and that economic inequalities within society would have to be redressed somewhat if the majority were to progress as moral beings.[33] But nearly all members of the liberal elite whether emerging New Liberals such as L. T. Hobhouse, Fabian Socialists like Sidney Webb,[34] or the Christian Socialists led by Stuart

---

[29] J. S. Mill. *Principles of Political Economy* (1st edn. 1848), in id., *Collected Works*, iii (Toronto, 1965), 752–7.

[30] B. Semmel, *John Stuart Mill and the Pursuit of Virtue* (New Haven, 1984).

[31] G. Claeys, 'Justice, Independence, Industrial Democracy: The Development of John Stuart Mill's Views on Socialism', *Journal of Politics*, 49 (1987); O. Kurer, 'J. S. Mill and Utopian Socialism', *Economic Record*, 68 (1992).

[32] Herbert Spencer, *Man versus the State* (1884).

[33] Den Otter, *British Idealism*, esp. 100–1, 112.

[34] Collini, *Liberalism and Sociology*. For Webb, see W. Woolf, *From Radicalism to Socialism: Men and Ideas in the Formation of Fabian Socialist Doctrines, 1881–1889* (New Haven, 1975), 275–84.

Headlam, Scott Holland, and Sidney Ball,[35] shared the belief that everyone was capable, with the right education and training, of understanding what was the common good and of working towards it. All agreed similarly that the training of individual moral character was a key element in furthering progress and that the pursuit of mere wealth was a danger to that process.[36] Hobson, who joined the London Ethical Society where Bosanquet and Muirhead were prominent figures, was profoundly influenced by these assumptions about wealth and about moral community which became crucial elements in his social theorizing in the 1890s and beyond.

Initially, more attention was paid by social reformers to the problems of landlordism than to those generated by industry. After 1870, economic problems in towns had raised the issue of the morality of rent there even more sharply than in the countryside. Ricardian principles dictated that the rent accruing to landowners was the result of monopoly and was an 'unearned increment'.[37] Towards the end of his life, Mill moved from simply arguing this in an abstract fashion to active support for land reform, including land taxation, and for municipal ownership and disposal of land. He also wished to use the proceeds of land tax and sales to fund social programmes, especially in public education. He won the support of Frederic Harrison's Comtean positivists and other intellectual groups within the liberal movement: but the land issue only became a matter of intense and widespread public concern in the early 1880s when Henry George published *Progress and Poverty*. George attributed all economic and social ills to land monopoly, proposing at first nationalization and later a 'single tax' on land that could fund infrastructural investments and public utilities, while leaving the rest of capitalist society to function freely.[38] The widespread popularity of George's campaign encouraged Joseph Chamberlain to adopt a mild version of it as part of his attempt to steer the Liberal party

---

[35] Den Otter, *British Idealism*, 117–19. See also Sidney Ball, 'The Socialist Ideal', *Economic Record*, 9 (1899), 430–1. Ball was a Fabian as well as a Christian Socialist and a keen supporter of the New Liberal cause. There are frequent references to Ball in M. Freeden, *The New Liberalism: An Ideology of Social Reform* (Oxford, 1978).

[36] J. Burrow, *Whigs and Liberals: Continuities and Change in English Political Thought* (Oxford, 1988), 77–94.

[37] A. Offer, 'Ricardo's Paradox and the Movement of Rent in England, c1870–1914', *Economic History Review*, 2nd ser. 33 (1980).

[38] On Mill and George see the excellent discussion in Woolf, *From Radicalism to Socialism*, esp. 45–65, 85–93.

in a leftwards direction.[39] Hobson claimed never to have been a Georgeite but he was aware of George's powerful influence in radicalizing many small capitalists in urban Britain;[40] and the land issue remained a powerful element in the Liberal party for many years as the popularity of Lloyd George's pre-1914 land campaign attests.[41]

Of more importance in this context was that Mill's ideas on rent were very influential with the emerging Fabian socialist group. Sidney Webb led the way within the movement, generalizing Mill's claims and arguing that rents accrued to any factor of production which had some kind of monopoly, whether it was capitalist business, a group of professional persons with privileged access to education, or even trade unions which could severely restrict the supply of labour. It was the state's role to tax away these rents because they were not made through effort and, therefore, belonged not to individuals but to society as a whole. Thus, they could be used to support a whole raft of social reforms that would make Britain a more efficient society in what Webb thought of as the coming Darwinian struggle for survival between nations.[42] Fabianism was in a direct line of descent from earlier radical thought. It rejected Marxist analysis, divided society into the industrious and the idle rich, and argued that existing political structures were designed to maintain unearned income.[43] Nonetheless, one of their number, William Clarke, had identified emerging big business rather than land as the chief repository of rent,[44] and it was obvious that the new theory of rent could easily become a weapon in a class war.

---

[39] J. Chamberlain et al., *The Radical Programme*, ed. D. Hamer (Brighton, 1971).This was first published in 1885.

[40] *Confessions*, 27–8; J. A. Hobson, 'The Influence of Henry George in England', *Fortnightly Review*, NS 62 (1897), 835–44.

[41] A. Offer, *Property and Politics: Landownership, Law, Ideology and Urban Development in England* (Cambridge, 1981), chs. 20–3; Emy, *Liberals, Radicals and Social Politics*, ch. 6.

[42] Woolf, *From Radicalism to Socialism*, 199–204, 213–14, 275–84; D. M. Ricci, 'Fabian Socialism: A Theory of Rent as Exploitation', *Journal of British Studies*, 11 (1969), 105–21; A. M. McBriar, *Fabian Socialism and English Politics, 1884–1918* (Cambridge, 1966), 29–47. Rent theory was also being developed independently by a number of economists at the time including more mainstream figures such as Marshall. See Frank A. Fetter, *Capital, Interest and Rent: Essays in the Theory of Distribution* (Kansas City, 1977).

[43] Lawrence, 'Popular Radicalism and the Socialist Revival in Britain', 179–85.

[44] William Clarke, 'The Industrial Basis of Socialism', in G. B. Shaw and H. Bland (eds.), *Fabian Essays in Socialism* (1899). The essay was reprinted in *William Clarke: A Collection of his Writings*, ed. (H. Burrows and J. A. Hobson 1908).

Indeed, the renewed stress on land reform on the radical wing of the Liberal party from the 1880s was partly due to the need to find some cause which could keep the 'producers alliance' together and prevent the emergence of class politics in urban Britain.[45]

'THE PHYSIOLOGY OF INDUSTRY'

Hobson learned much from Fabian analyses of the condition of Britain but he never became a member of the society. When *Fabian Essays* was first published in 1889, Hobson still adhered to the Liberal Unionism of his youth. Later, when his own radicalism began to blossom, he found that their solutions to the social and economic crisis left too little scope for individual initiative. In the meantime, his emerging quest for an overarching conception of society was interrupted by his involvement in what he was later to call 'a narrower economic heresy'[46] yet one which had a profound influence on his thinking in the long run. While still in Exeter he met the businessman, A. F. Mummery, who 'had a natural zest for a path of his own finding and a sublime disregard for intellectual authority'.[47] In common with many capitalists, Mummery interpreted the falling prices and profits and the heavy unemployment of the time in terms of 'overproduction'. By Hobson's own account, he eventually persuaded the latter that the usual academic assumption that unemployment of resources was not a chronic problem of existing capitalist society was incorrect.[48] The result of this encounter was a jointly written book, *The Physiology of Industry*, published in 1889.

The authors offered two main explanations for capitalist instability.[49] First, it was suggested that, because of uncertainty, people might wish to hold money rather than spend it. This hoarding

---

[45] D. Nicholls, 'The English Middle Class and the Ideological Significance of Radicalism, 1760–1886', *Journal of British Studies*, 24 (1985).

[46] *Confessions*, 29.

[47] Ibid. 30.

[48] John Stuart Mill had recognized the existence of short-run unemployment during business cycles and his successors took this for granted. J. S. Mill, *Essays on Some Unsettled Questions in Political Economy* (1844), in id., *Collected Works*, iv (Toronto, 1967), 262–79.

[49] The following relies heavily on R. E. Backhouse, 'Mummery and Hobson's *The Physiology of Industry*', in Pheby (ed.), *J. A. Hobson after Fifty Years*, 78–99 and on the same author's 'Hobson as a Macroeconomic Theorist', in Freeden (ed.), *Reappraising J. A. Hobson*, 127–34.

version of underconsumption opened the possibility of a Keynesian-style gap between intended savings and intended investment: but it was undeveloped in the book and lacked even the sophistication of Mill's earlier work on the subject which it failed to acknowledge.[50] The second argument, which had a strongly Malthusian, even a Marxist, flavour was that the drive to accumulate in a competitive society forced capitalists to oversave and to overinvest resulting in a chronic tendency to overproduction, and its natural corollary underconsumption, and in the crises continuously racking the commercial world. The book had explosive political and social implications. It challenged the Smithian and Ricardian assumption that growth (and the welfare of the workforce) was dependent on capital accumulation and, therefore, on savings or thrift, asserting instead that consumption was crucial to capital formation rather than at the expense of it. As a result, the authors asserted that a healthy economic society was one where consumption was encouraged, where the burden of taxation was shifted from consumer goods to savings, and where the working class took a larger share of the national cake.[51] In so doing, they were also reflecting the fact that, as incomes for all sections of the working population rose in the late nineteenth century, mass consumption began to become a matter of serious interest to economists and sociologists as Thorstein Veblen's famous masterpiece, *The Theory of the Leisure Class* first published in 1891, vividly indicates. Nonetheless, despite its anti-Smithian attitude to thrift, the book retained the macroeconomic framework of analysis preferred by the classical economists rather than the focus on individual choice that characterized the emergent neo-classical theory of Jevons and Alfred Marshall.

Hobson was later to claim that he had no idea of the long history of underconsumptionist economics until enlightened by J. M. Robertson's *The Fallacy of Saving* (1892) and that he was blissfully unaware that his attack on thrift might provoke scandal.[52] Given the current welter of publicity on such issues this is hard to believe:[53]

---

[50] Hobson's later arguments about underconsumption also lacked a firm monetary base. See Backhouse, 'Hobson as a Macroeconomic Theorist', 116–27.

[51] *The Physiology of Industry*, ed. R. E. Backhouse (Bristol, 1992), 203–5, 209–10.

[52] *Confessions*, 30–2.

[53] See Kadish, 'The Non-canonical Context', *passim*. Robertson also claimed to have anticipated Hobson and Mummery's arguments. J. M. Robertson, *The Fallacy of Saving* (1892), p.v.

but it is likely that Mummery was the chief driving force behind the book,[54] which maintained throughout a dispassionate analytical tone and was not inspired by any obvious social philosophy. Indeed, while Hobson may have become an intellectual heretic, there is no reason to believe that at that time he had become, in any true sense, a convinced radical. This is evident from an article he published in 1890 which attacked the idea, mildly supported in the *Physiology*,[55] that the Eight Hour Day movement could advantage the working man. This conclusion was challenged by liberal reformists such as Bradlaugh who thought that reducing working hours would reduce both profits and wages and encourage capital flight[56] so Hobson's recantation was not in itself evidence of conformism to orthodoxy. However, he wrote in a Tory-inspired journal, and statements such as 'The rigid application of industrial law forbids the possibility of a general rise in wages, or of any increase in the proportion of aggregate wealth which goes in wages, except in accordance with the slow operation of the motive to save' and his assertion that 'refuse to feed capital and you will starve production and lower wages' sound remarkably like the Smith–Ricardo doctrines attacked so effectively in the *Physiology* and do not differentiate Hobson's position from that of more cautious, mainstream economists such as Marshall.[57]

In the following year, Hobson published a theory of rent that was so similar to that of the Fabians as to arouse the suspicion that he had stolen it from them.[58] This article was an exercise in pure

---

[54] In one of its most brilliant sections, the *Physiology* contains an anticipation of the acceleration principle that did not appear in Hobson's later writings. Backhouse, 'Mummery and Hobson's *The Physiology of Industry*', 81–2.

[55] *The Physiology of Industry*, 213–14.

[56] C. Bradlaugh, *Labour and Law* (1891), 101–3; Robertson, *The Fallacy of Saving*, ch. 8.

[57] J. A. Hobson, 'The Cost of a Shorter Working Day', *National Review*, 15 (1890), esp. 196, 202. For Alfred Marshall's position see his *Principles of Economics* (variorum edn. Cambridge, 1961), i. 693–702. For the Tory principles on which the *National Review* was run see Walter E. Houghton (ed.), *The Wellesley Index of Victorian Periodicals*, ii (Toronto, 1972), 529–32.

[58] J. A. Hobson, 'The Law of the Three Rents', *Quarterly Journal of Economics*, 5 (1890–1), 263–88; repr. in *J. A. Hobson: Writings on Welfare and Distribution*, ed. Backhouse. Sidney Webb was annoyed that Hobson made no acknowledgement of his article 'The Rate of Interest and the Laws of Distribution', *Quarterly Journal of Economics*, 2 (1888). See A. M. McBriar, *An Edwardian Mixed Doubles: The Bosanquets versus the Webbs. A Study in British Social Policy, 1890–1929* (Oxford, 1987), 75 n. 67. In fairness to Hobson, it must be noted that he was developing a position already indicated in the *Physiology*. (Backhouse, 'Mummery and Hobson's *The Physiology of Industry*', 89–92.)

theory: it also helped to create the marginal productivity theory of income distribution, according to which factors of production each received the value of their contribution (at the margin) to production, that Hobson would later repudiate vigorously.[59] In 1891 he also published a book inspired by Booth's revelations about London poverty.[60] This was a painstaking, heavily empirical investigation in the manner of Booth himself and the Webbs. It was well reviewed,[61] went through several editions over the next thirty years, and established Hobson's reputation as a social critic. In *Problems of Poverty*, chronic unemployment amongst unskilled workers was taken for granted and poverty was identified as a social disease rather than the product of individual misfortune or weakness: but this simply followed Booth's lead and the book was hardly original in analysis. Reform proposals were cautiously introduced[62] and discussed in piecemeal fashion. There was no reference to underconsumption and oversaving or to the reformist possibilities opened up by his work with Mummery.[63] What is more, Hobson took over Booth's idea that the very poor, the 'residuum', was more or less unemployable, that the poverty, bad housing, and alcoholism of London made them both physically and morally degenerate and that they were incapable of moral self-development. The biologist, R. E. Lankester had argued in 1880 that degeneration of species was as likely as progressive evolution and that the worst features of life in Britain's sprawling urban areas were an example of it. He believed that the London poor had reverted to a simpler, parasitic life in order to survive their hostile environment. The statistician and eugenicist Francis Galton held similar beliefs and 'urban degeneration' became a middle-class commonplace along with the equally common notion that the towns were only kept alive by a constant influx of healthy migrants from rural Britain.[64] Hobson did not use

---

[59] The article was published alongside another by J. B. Clark, 'Distribution as Determined by a Law of Rent', *Quarterly Journal of Economics*, 5 (1891). Clark, an American economist, argued that marginal productivity theory provided an ethical justification for the existing distribution of income. For Hobson's repudiation of marginalism see Ch. 6.

[60] *Problems of Poverty* (1st edn. 1891).

[61] For the reviews, see Kadish, 'Rewriting the *Confessions*', 149–50.

[62] See, for example, the discussion of public works in relieving distress in *Problems of Poverty*, 118–24.

[63] See here the comments by Clarke, *Liberals and Social Democrats*, 49.

[64] Stedman Jones, *Outcast London*, chs. 6 and 16. See also D. Pick, *Faces of Degeneration: A European Disorder c1848–1918* (Cambridge, 1989), esp. 32, 173,

the term 'parasitic' to describe London but he accepted the degeneration thesis and, commenting on the flow of rural labour into towns and the higher death rates there he wrote, 'thus the City figures as a mighty vampire, continually sucking the strongest blood of the country to keep up the enormous supply of energy it has to give out in the excitement of a too fast and unwholesome life'.[65] The *Physiology* received a hostile review from the Oxford economic theorist, F. Y. Edgeworth. Its attack on thrift as rational for individuals but irrational for society also attracted the hostility of H. S. Foxwell, who was prominent in the University Extension movement, but Hobson exaggerated the consequences of his breach with orthodoxy.[66] The hostility did not prevent him from taking up a career as an Extension lecturer in economics in later years. Nor was a promising University career blighted. Leaving aside the fact that Hobson twice taught at the London School of Economics (in 1896–7 and 1914–16), he was temperamentally and intellectually best suited for Extension teaching.[67] In his autobiography, Hobson also failed to mention that he came close to repudiating the *Physiology* altogether when faced with Foxwell's opposition to his taking up an economics Extension course via the London Ethical Society in 1892. In a letter to Foxwell, he wrote that 'I hold with no fanatical pertinacity the views I put forward in [*The Physiology of Industry*]. I would gladly yield them up before the pressure of argument.'[68] Kadish regards this as 'less than heroic'[69] and it is

---

197–8, 214–17; W. Greenslade, *Degeneration, Culture and the Novel* (Cambridge, 1994), 38–46; and G. R. Searle, *Eugenics and Politics in Britain, 1900–1914* (Leiden, 1976), ch. 3.

[65] *Problems of Poverty*, 57. Hobson's language probably reflects the widespread vampire literature of the time which culminated in Bram Stoker's *Dracula* (1897).

[66] For Edgeworth's review see T. W. Hutchison, *A Review of Economic Doctrines, 1870–1929* (Oxford, 1953), 118–19. On Foxwell, see Kadish, 'Rewriting the *Confessions*', 145.

[67] Compare Hobson's own account in *Confessions*, 30–1, with Kadish, 'Rewriting the *Confessions*', 151–66. Hobson argued, early in his career, that the professionalization of economics within universities harmed the subject by removing economists from contact with the everyday world. J. A. Hobson, 'The Academic Spirit in Education', *Contemporary Review*, 63 (1893). For the intellectual context of this argument see T. W. Heyck, *The Transformation of Intellectual Life in Victorian England* (1982), esp. ch. 8. Clarke believes that Hobson was too slapdash in his methods to become a full-time academic (*Liberals and Social Democrats*, 48). Alfred Marshall thought Hobson had much ability but was a 'hasty' writer and 'he disappoints me when the only good work is slow work' (*Principles of Economics*, ii. 430).

[68] Hobson to Foxwell, 12 Jan. 1892, in Kadish, 'Rewriting the *Confessions*', 146.

[69] Ibid. 166.

possible that his writings of 1890–1 were a somewhat craven attempt to win back academic respectability. However, such a view implies that the Hobson who co-wrote the *Physiology* was, in all essentials, the same as the one who wrote the famous radical works of later years and this is not the case. It may be best to see the *Physiology* as an abstract piece of reasoning, something Hobson was drawn into by Mummery out of sheer intellectual curiosity without realizing the full implications of these heretical ideas for his own inherited beliefs. What he wrote in 1890–1 certainly reflected his original political and social views more closely than did *The Physiology of Industry*. It may have been difficult, even impossible, for Hobson to integrate these new and exciting ideas into his general frame of reference and to reconcile his theoretical heresy with the rest of his cultural and emotional baggage at this early stage in his development as a social critic.

HOBSON, RUSKIN, AND NEW LIBERALISM

Hobson's transformation into the New Liberal thinker with which we are familiar began in earnest in 1892 and was largely complete by 1896, at which point the social and economic philosophy which underpinned his most famous later works—such as *The Industrial System* (1909) and *Work and Wealth* (1914)—was largely in place. His speedy shift towards the left of the liberal spectrum was highlighted by his association with the famous Rainbow Circle, one of the intellectual cradles of New Liberalism. Hobson became a founding member in 1894 along with Ramsey MacDonald, the future Labour Prime Minister who was the Circle's first secretary, former Fabian essayist William Clarke, Murray MacDonald the Liberal MP for Bow and Bromley, and Sydney Olivier, a Fabian and future colonial governor.[70] It was consolidated by his association with the *Progressive Review* begun in 1896 and edited by Clarke and Ramsey MacDonald.[71] The *Review* lasted only two years but the Circle flourished throughout the Edwardian age attracting new members along the way such as Herbert Samuel and Hobson's old friend, J. M. Robertson, both of whom became prominent Liberal MPs before the war.

[70] M. Freeden (ed.), *Minutes of the Rainbow Circle, 1894–1924* (1989).
[71] Ibid. 7–9.

In 1892, he followed up his first article on rent with another distinguishing between 'generic' rents, payments necessary to bring scarce factors of production into play and thus attributable to individuals, and 'specific' rents due entirely to monopoly powers dependent on mere social contrivance. The latter, which Hobson was later to call 'surplus', was thus the property of society rather than individuals. In a paper read to the National Liberal Club in the same year, Hobson also emphasized the importance of the monopoly rents arising from capitalist business as well as land; and he argued that society could tax them away without disturbing enterprise and growth. Both papers show a striking shift back to the macroeconomic concerns informing *The Physiology of Industry*.[72] At this point, Hobson's position was similar to that of the Fabians and some of his later writings emphasize these similarities.[73] What distinguished him from them over the next few years was, first, the reiteration and refinement of his 1889 claims about underconsumption; secondly, his determination to place his economic analysis within an organic conception of society which, although it owed something to Spencer and to evolutionary Idealism,[74] was also profoundly affected by his reading of John Ruskin.

Hobson had already argued that, although the widespread adoption of machinery had raised living standards for many workers, it was usually introduced because it was labour saving and had thus created unemployment and put pressure on the wage levels of lower grades of labour.[75] In 1893 he went further, claiming that overproduction and unemployment were endemic features of highly mechanized capitalist societies and that 'the reluctance of those who hold the purchasing power to demand consumptive goods is the true

---

[72] J. A. Hobson, 'The Element of Monopoly in Prices', *Quarterly Journal of Economics*, 6 (1891–2); repr. in *Hobson: Writings on Distribution and Welfare*, ed. Backhouse; J. A. Hobson, 'Monopoly Rents of Capital', *National Liberal Club: Political Economy Circle Transactions*, 2 (1895), 38–52. The paper was read on 19 Oct. 1892.

[73] Especially his *Economics of Distribution* (1900),which was based on lectures given at the Webb-inspired London School of Economics in 1896–7.

[74] For the influence of Spencer and of the Idealist J. S. McKenzie's *An Introduction to Social Philosophy* (1890) on Hobson in this context, see M. Freeden, 'Hobson's Evolving Conceptions of Human Nature', in id. (ed.), *Reappraising J. A. Hobson*, 56–60. See also Hobson's obituary notice 'Herbert Spencer', *South Place Magazine*, 9 (1904); repr. in *J. A. Hobson: A Reader*, ed. Freeden (1988), 60–4.

[75] *Problems of Poverty*, 45.

cause of the disease which figures on the surface as overproduction'.
He went on to say, expanding on the analysis of 1889, that

> When production was slower, markets narrower, credit less developed,
> there was less danger of this big miscalculation, and the corrective forces
> of industry were more speedily effective. But modern machinery has enor-
> mously expanded the size of markets, the scale of competition, the
> complexity of demand, and no longer produces for a small local present
> demand but for a large world future demand.[76]

Hobson also incorporated this thinking into his next major book,
*The Evolution of Modern Capitalism: A Study in Machine Pro-
duction*, first published in 1894.[77] And in the second edition of
Problems of Poverty (1895) he was emboldened enough to argue
that the central remedy for poverty was the elimination of underconsumption.[78] He made his next big step forward in an article of
1895 when, for the first time, he linked together oversaving (and
therefore underconsumption) with maldistribution of income and
wealth rather than associating it with the competition of capitalists
as hitherto. In doing so, he brought his analyses of economic rent
and underconsumption together since the latter was now held to
result from the oversaving which naturally accompanied monopoly:
according to Hobson, income gained without effort was almost
automatically saved. Radical methods of redistribution of this
unearned income would remedy the problem.[79] These findings were
published in book form in 1896 and represent Hobson's most
consistently held position on the subject of underconsumption for
the rest of his life.[80]

---

[76] J. A. Hobson, 'The Influence of Machinery upon Employment', *Political Science
Quarterly*, 8 (1893), 108. As Backhouse notes, Hobson was here arguing that
unemployment was a problem of 'temporal disequilibrium'. 'Hobson as a Macroeconomic Theorist', 128–9.

[77] Hobson took over the task of writing this book from William Clarke, then a
Fabian. *Confessions*, 36.

[78] Compare pp. 147–8 of the first and second editions.

[79] J. A. Hobson, 'The Economic Cause of Unemployment', *Contemporary
Review*, 67 (1895), esp. 756–60.

[80] J. A. Hobson, *The Problem of the Unemployed* (1896). For an analysis of
Hobson's underconsumption in its classic form see Allett, *New Liberalism*. Hobson
of course, assumes, without proof, that demand for commodities is connected with
origin of income, as Backhouse notes in 'Hobson as a Macroeconomic Theorist',
131–3. The same point was made by Hobson's friend, J. M. Robertson, who had no
doubt that the rich could go on increasing their consumption whatever their level of
income. See his *The Eight Hour Day* (1899), 100. However, it has been noted that

Having linked together rent or surplus with oversaving and underconsumption, Hobson also strove to integrate his economic thinking into a much wider analysis of an evolutionary, organic, but still liberal, society. Some impetus to this was given by his reading of the work of Simon Patten, an American pioneer in the economics of consumption. Patten took the line that the continuous extension of customary production would eventually lead to resource depletion and diminishing returns to the factors of production but that, in a dynamic society, the increasing diversity of production mitigated this tendency. Hobson extrapolated from this to wonder whether 'in a progressive community, whose variety of new consumption took more and more the shape of intellectual artistic, and moral commodities which are free from the strict limits of matter' the tendency might not even be reversed.[81] A year later, he was pointing out that the purpose of machinery was to produce standardized goods but that, as the machine advanced, the economy became more and more prone to crisis and big business, and monopoly, in the form of trusts and price-fixing cartels, became increasingly necessary to ensure stability.[82] But if consumers shifted their tastes to more artistic, individualized goods over time there need be fewer machines, less monopoly, and less instability.[83] Clearly, Hobson was beginning to think of art as a key element in the enlightened economic society of the future and to see also that 'nothing but a change in morals'[84] influencing patterns of consumption could bring it to the fore. In coming to such conclusions he increasingly relied on the authority of John Ruskin to enforce them.

When Hobson first encountered Ruskin seriously is not clear. The latter rated a favourable mention in the *Physiology*[85] but this may

Hobson's stress on oversaving as the key to growth not only distinguishes his analysis from the investment-centred analyses of Keynes, Domar, and Harrod but even seems to fit present-day macroeconomic experience better than their approach. M. Schneider, 'Modelling Hobson's Underconsumption Theory', in Pheby (ed.), *J. A. Hobson after Fifty Years*, 120–1.

[81] See Hobson's review of Patten's *The Theory of Dynamic Economics* (1892) in *Economic Journal*, 2 (1892), 687–90. The significance of Patten in Hobson's development has been noted by Freeden (ed.), *Reappraising J. A. Hobson*, 7–8.

[82] On the formation of trusts see J. A. Hobson, *The Evolution of Modern Capitalism: A Study in Machine Production* (1st edn. 1894), 117–66. Cf. Clarke, 'The Industrial Basis of Socialism', 89–92.

[83] 'The Influence of Machinery Upon Employment', 123.

[84] Ibid. 110.

[85] *Physiology of Industry*, 6–7.

just reflect Mummery's reading and it had no discernible effect on the book's arguments. He may have been influenced in Ruskin's direction through Idealist connections, through his association with Robertson and his reading of Shaw's denunciation of 'illth', or simply by the fact that Ruskin was such an important force in the Extension movement where Hobson earned his bread.[86] Whatever its origin, his attitudes appear to have changed swiftly. In 1892 he was making rather disparaging references to Ruskin but the influence of the latter was clearly visible from 1893 onwards when he began to provide Hobson with more intellectual ammunition for the qualitative approach to economics signalled in his review of Patten.[87] Ruskin attacked conventional economic theory because it was interested only in the crude question of growth in material production without reference to the quality of what was produced or how it was consumed, or how material wealth contributed to the life of society in general. In practice, the mindless pursuit of profit and material wealth had delivered 'illth' instead of true wealth and subjected the masses to degrading machine-driven work for poverty wages in ugly and unhealthy towns rather than producing 'souls of good quality'.[88] Consequently, Ruskin was always keen to remind the wealthy that their consumption patterns determined to a large extent the lives of the poorer part of the population, that

[86] Freeden, 'Hobson's Changing Conceptions of Human Nature', 57; H. C. G. Matthew, 'Hobson, Ruskin and Cobden', in Freeden (ed.), *Reappraising J. A. Hobson*, 15; G. B. Shaw, 'The Economic Basis of Socialism', in Shaw and Bland (eds.) *Fabian Essays*, 22–3. Robertson's *Fallacy of Saving* shows Ruskinian influence and Robertson was also picked out by Hobson in later life as someone with whom he was particularly closely associated in the 1890s. See *Confessions*, 49–51. Indeed, many of the ideas that Hobson developed in the early 1890s can be seen in Robertson's writing. Neither Fabian nor New Liberal nor Idealist, Robertson is a neglected figure whose economic and sociological ideas deserve greater attention. For an introduction to his work, see G. A. Wells (ed.), *J. M. Robertson (1856–1933): Liberal, Rationalist and Scholar* (1987).

[87] Hobson speaks of being persuaded by a friend to write a critical study of Ruskin (which eventually appeared in 1898 and is quoted below) in 'the mid-nineties' but this ignores the evidence of earlier Ruskinian influence. *Confessions*, 38. See also Clarke, *Liberals and Social Democrats*, 48–9. For the dismissive reference to Ruskin see Hobson's 'London Letter' in *Derbyshire Advertiser*, 2 Sept. 1892.

[88] Ruskin's best-known work on these themes is *Unto This Last* (1862) but perhaps his plainest, most readable statements are in *The Crown of Wild Olive* (1865) and *Time and Tide* (1867). All appear in *The Works of John Ruskin,* ed. E. T. Cook and A. Wedderburn, xviii (1905). On Ruskin's social and economic thought see P. D. Antony, *John Ruskin's Labour: A Study of Ruskin's Social Theory* (Cambridge, 1983) and J. F. Spear, *Dreams of an English Eden: Ruskin and his Tradition in English Social Criticism* (1984).

production and consumption were organically connected and had a profound ethical import. So, according to Ruskin, it was the duty of elites to demand products of a quality that would create an invigorating and healthy working and living environment very different from the monstrous wens produced by machine civilization. He also expected the state, under the control of a revived landed elite, to take a lead by funding workshops which would pay fair wages and establish high standards in the manner of medieval guilds.

Hobson was deeply smitten by Ruskin's vision of the organic nature of economic society but he had to reread the latter's paternalist Tory radicalism in a way which made it compatible with his own emerging evolutionary liberalism. He began this in 1893 by grafting Ruskin's ideas on to the normal utilitarian calculus used by economists. He argued for a distinction between 'objective' costs and utilities rated in money, and 'subjective' costs and utilities that measured the welfare produced by this objective wealth. Any amount of objective wealth could yield very varying levels of subjective satisfaction depending upon how it was produced and consumed: wealth and welfare were not synonymous. Hobson was keen to emphasize that it was quite possible to increase subjective utilities and reduce subjective costs while also reducing objective wealth if 'crude quantitative consumption' (which depended on machines) was replaced by that inspired by art and personal creativity. Further than that, the simple association of production with cost and consumption with utility was too limiting since the two were organically connected. The more artistic production became the less it cost in both objective and subjective terms and the more utility the work itself brought with it. Similarly, bad forms of consumption brought high costs in terms of ill-health and other evils. He concluded that since conventional economics only concerned itself with objective wealth it would have to be 'subjectivized'. Only then would it be brought into a right relation with ethics and politics and become an effective part of that wider sociology he wished to construct and which the 'most enlightened and poetic of political economists' gave him the confidence to build.[89]

---

[89] J. A. Hobson, 'The Subjective and Objective View of Distribution', *Annals of the American Academy of Political and Social Science* 4 (1893–4), 42–67; and repr. in *Hobson: Writings on Distribution and Welfare*, ed. Backhouse. The same analysis is carried further in 'Human Cost and Utility', *Economic Review*, 6 (1896), 10–20, repr. ibid.

Most of his thinking on these lines between 1892 and 1894 was brought together in the final chapter (entitled 'Civilisation and Industrial Development') of *The Evolution of Modern Capitalism*, a book which Hobson later said, and with justice, contained the germ of all his subsequent writings.[90] In this chapter Hobson repeated his arguments about the ill-effects of machine civilization and the stark contrast it enforced between the mass of underpaid alienated labour on one side and the idle consuming few on the other. He also argued that this must be replaced by another, more qualitative, economy which would be less ravenous of the earth's resources and guarantee more fulfilling lives for all. Bringing about the new moral world would require 'an education in the art of consumption such as may assign proper limits to the sphere of machine production'[91] encouraged by the active economic intervention of the state. For the ugly, illth-ridden, excessively mechanical industrial society of modern capitalism, with its extremes of wealth and poverty, arose from a maldistribution of wealth which was itself the product of private monopolies and economic rents and suffered from maladies such as chronic underconsumption.

Hobson recognized that many basic products, ideal for standardization, would continue to be in heavy demand and that machine production was the most efficient way of meeting that demand. Since these industries tended to become monopolies he proposed that they should come under public control.[92] He also emphasized the need for rigorous population control to keep down the demand for such routine goods.[93] Provided this was done, Hobson expected that the share of mass-produced commodities in national income would fall. As industrial society progressed and as consciousness of social purpose increased, redistribution of income through taxation of rent, together with better education and welfare, would release individual creativity. The attention of consumers would shift from mass-produced to individually produced goods that would satisfy the aesthetic impulses of men and

---

[90] *Confessions*, 37. Clarke comments that *Evolution* marked the point at which Hobson acquired a 'distinctive voice'. *Liberals and Social Democrats*, 49.

[91] *Evolution of Modern Capitalism*, 355.

[92] Ibid. 381–2.

[93] Ibid. 378–9. Hobson may have taken this on board via Robertson, who was strong on the subject and who was clearly influenced by Ruskin. See *The Fallacy of Saving*, ch. 8.

women both as producers and consumers, reducing costs and increasing utility as assessed by Hobson's new welfare standard. The emergent society would thus temper and reshape capitalism by setting up demands for activities that reduced division of labour and were products of the 'whole man' of Ruskin's dream.[94] But Hobson was also keen to distance himself from Ruskin on some vital matters. Countering Ruskin's own hostility to Darwinism, he cast his Ruskinian vision in an evolutionary mould: society's idea of the good life was not static and backward looking but dynamic and necessarily changeful.[95] Similarly, he attacked Ruskin's view that society should be run by its traditional elites, arguing instead for a frank acceptance of democracy. Yet the New Liberal society Hobson envisaged was not egalitarian but one based on equality of opportunity and accepting differences in ability and reward.[96] It was also intrinsically capitalist: he rejected Ruskin's attack on interest as usury, insisting that it could be a legitimate payment for abstinence.[97] Hobson's Ruskinite society had a much bigger role for the state, as an operator of routine industries and provider of welfare services, than Gladstonian liberalism could live with. Yet outside that state arena, Hobson envisaged the growth of a business sector very like the small-scale capitalist society beloved of traditional liberalism, though one in which artistic accomplishment and personal industrial creativity had a much bigger role to play than perhaps Smiles, Cobden, and Spencer had ever imagined.

Hobson set up his New Liberal-Ruskinite utopia in conscious opposition to three competing visions of the future. The first was the existent laissez-faire capitalist society which still had a wide acceptance in liberal circles and in the Liberal party, where fear of the state remained strong. The second was that championed by the Fabians and by popular writers such as Edward Bellamy in *Looking Backwards* (1888). Here, utopia was seen in terms of taking over existing industrialism by the state and making it work more fairly

[94] For a similar approach to the future of industrial civilization see William Clarke, 'The Limits of Collectivism', in *William Clarke*, ed. Burrows and Hobson. Clarke first published this article in 1893.
[95] J. A. Hobson, *John Ruskin: Social Reformer* (3rd edn. 1904), 101–6. The book was first published in 1898.
[96] Ibid. 176–209.
[97] Ibid. 143–52.

and efficiently. Hobson despised a great deal of current industrialism and wished to see it vanish rather than be sanctified through state control. He also thought that such model societies had too little understanding of the need for individual expression and creativity. The third alternative was Morris's arresting vision, best expressed in *News from Nowhere* (1890) In reaction to Bellamy, Morris had merged Marx with Ruskin, positing a revolutionary abolition of capitalism followed by the rise of spontaneously artistic, egalitarian society. Hobson believed that Morris's new society would be anarchic and unstable; that its noble ideal of making all work artistic was impossible, an opinion he shared with Ruskin; and that only in a capitalist society, modified by the state in the manner he had suggested, would dull or disagreeable work get done effectively.[98]

INDIVIDUALISM, SOCIETY, AND THE STATE

Hobson's *via media* between private and state provision had emerged almost completely by 1898 and it was a sometimes uneasy compromise between the claims of the individual and those of society.[99] Unearned incomes would disappear under progressive taxation, bringing about a rather speedier 'euthanasia of the *rentier*' than Keynes later envisaged.[100] The state would take over the running of large industries producing standardized commodities and eliminate the monopoly rents they generated under private ownership. Yet his was still basically a capitalist society based on inequalities in income and wealth, one where someone with rare abilities and energies could exact higher payments than the average. Hobson expected that increased economic opportunity would

[98] J. A. Hobson, 'Edward Bellamy and the Utopian Romance', *Humanitarian*, 13 (1898), 179–89. See also *John Ruskin*, 306–7. As justification for talking of Hobson as a utopian, I am indebted to K. Kumar, *Utopianism* (1991), 29–30. See also F. D. Curtin, 'Aesthetics in English Social Reform: Ruskin and his Followers', in H. Davis, W. C. DeVane, and R. C. Bald (eds.), *Nineteenth Century Studies* (Ithaca, NY, 1940) for discussion of Hobson, Morris, and Patrick Geddes as interpreters of Ruskin.

[99] On this theme see J. Allett, 'The Conservative Aspect of Hobson's New Liberalism', in Freeden (ed.), *Reappraising J. A. Hobson*; J. Townshend, 'Hobson and the Socialist Tradition', in Pheby (ed.), *J. A. Hobson after Fifty Years*.

[100] Keynes's famous phrase was almost invented by the remarkable Robertson, who in 1892 looked forward to 'the complete euthanasia' of 'the idle class'. *The Fallacy of Saving*, 142.

eventually reduce inequalities markedly[101] and he hoped that the more work became a utility rather than a cost the more those with special skills would concentrate on enjoying their lives on fairly modest incomes rather than fighting for the highest pay they could get.[102] But he did not expect all inequalities to be eliminated: he took it for granted, for example, that 'brainworkers' had greater needs than their horny-handed brethren and should therefore get higher pay.[103] In many ways, his New Liberalism was a return to the vision of a 'mixed' economy to be found in the second part of Paine's *Rights of Man* and in his *Agrarian Justice*, though it is doubtful if either Hobson or his colleagues were fully aware of the parallels between Paine's thinking and their own.[104]

Hobson hoped that both the man of ability and the manual worker toiling for the state in what he admitted would still be boring, mechanized industries would, as the public sector expanded, become increasingly aware of themselves as cogs in a social machine whose good it was their main business to foster.[105] In this, he was aligning himself with that long tradition of liberal thinkers, including Mill, Green, and Spencer, who expected altruism to grow as society developed. He made no apology for the teleology implicit in this evolutionary perspective, arguing that the only way to make sense of the mass of social data was to have some conception of the ends of existence.[106] However, Hobson tended to think of 'Society' not simply as an organic entity but as one with a distinct personality, capable of inspiring devotion and sacrifice in the same way that religion had done in the past. He wanted to encourage individual flourishing not just for its own sake but because he believed that it contributed to the richness and variety of that society. He did worry sometimes that a large public sector would become bureaucratic and oppressive and might need to be limited[107] but he did believe that, ultimately, the individual was

[101] J. A. Hobson, *The Social Problem: Life and Work* (1902 edn.), 166 ff.

[102] Ibid. 169–73.

[103] Ibid. 164–5.

[104] Hobson's celebration of Paine in *A Modern Outlook* (1910) is rather superficial and his reference in *The Social Problem* (21) is equally unrevealing. The Rainbow Circle showed no insight into Paine's revolutionary economic proposals. Freeden (ed.), *Minutes of the Rainbow Circle*, 96–8.

[105] *The Social Problem*, 220.

[106] Ibid. 66–8.

[107] Ibid. 243–7.

subordinate to Society.[108] It is not easy to reconcile this with the pluralism at the heart of the liberal tradition. Yet Hobson's position was only a development of the widespread belief among liberals that there was such a thing as the common good and was a very able attempt to deal with the immensely difficult task of reconciling social action with individual liberty.[109] Moreover, although he occasionally supported attitudes and programmes which today seem highly illiberal, Hobson proved to be a keen champion of individualism on a number of occasions when he felt that the state power was becoming too great, as was the case during the First World War.

PARASITISM AND INDUSTRY

An important element in Hobson's writings from the mid-nineties was his increasingly confident use of the language of evolutionary biologism that characterized the work of Spencer and became immensely popular through such works as Benjamin Kidd's *Social Evolution* (1894). One feature of this, illustrating his shift towards New Liberalism, was his evolving sense of the notion of parasitism. He had, of course, suggested in 1891 that the poor in London were parasitic on society (though he had not used the word)[110] and he sometimes demonstrated a fierce illiberalism subsequently in arguing that the 'unfit' should be socially controlled and even prevented from marrying or producing children[111] since they were incapable of becoming 'autonomous self-developers'.[112] But by the late 1890s he was more likely to use the language of biology as a weapon against the rich and their unearned incomes. The use of the word 'parasite' to describe the idle rich was well established in the

---

[108] See the discussion ibid. 87–94. The transition from 'society' to 'Society' first took place in 'The Rights of Property'. I have benefited a great deal here from Collini, *Hobhouse*, and Freeden, *New Liberalism*.

[109] See here the illuminating discussion in Freeden, *New Liberalism*, 110–16.

[110] See *supra*.

[111] *The Social Problem*, 214–17.

[112] The phrase is Bellamy's (*Liberalism and Modern Society*, 32), which he applies to Mill but which can equally be applied to Hobson. For the coercive aspects of New Liberalism in this regard see Freeden, *New Liberalism*, 177–94. Hobhouse was much more cautious on the matter than was Hobson. Collini, *Liberalism and Sociology*, 201–2, 205–6. Note that Hobson wrote an approving review of E. S. Talbot, *Degeneracy: Its Causes, Signs and Results* (1898), where criminals were described as parasitic, in *Ethical World*, 27 May 1899, 329–30. On Talbot see Pick, *Faces of Degeneration*, 23.

early 1890s and it was a key part of the vocabulary of the Fabians.
In *Fabian Essays* Sydney Olivier spoke of a 'class or society—not
dependent on its own industry but feeding like a parasite upon
another society or class', and Shaw later used the word to describe
absentee landlords.[113] Hobson also insisted that, because it was
not worked for, such income was debilitating to recipients who were
thus 'parasites' and inevitably subject to atrophy: the 'logical
end of a society living on unearned incomes would be death by
overfeeding, or the inability to digest and assimilate their food'.[114]
Sport could ward off the evil hour but the wealthy were subject
eventually to the same intellectual and physical degeneration as
were the poor. The Fabians had recognized that poverty and crime
in urban Britain were the mirror image of the parasitism of its propertied elites.[115] Hobson took a similar line: 'the convex congested
paunch of the torpid plutocrat who consumes without effort of
producing, implies the concave anaemic body of the inefficient
starveling as its equal and opposite'.[116] One consequence of living
off unearned income was, of course, oversaving and underconsumption that, in this context, become examples of a biological
malfunction: Hobson was writing about a capitalist society as an
organism that was diseased. Despite the rich crop of evolutionary
metaphors that littered his pages, Hobson was keen to avoid the
biological determinism that underlay many popular works of the
time.[117] Like Ritchie, Hobson believed that the trend of evolution
was away from the 'lower' struggle for mere material survival and
towards the 'higher' one where competition was expressed through
the clash of ideas and institutions.[118] In the process, mankind was

---

[113] Lawrence, 'Popular Radicalism and the Socialist Revival in Britain', 176,
181–3; S. Olivier, 'The Moral Basis of Socialism', in Shaw and Bland (eds.), *Fabian
Essays*, 116; Bernard Shaw, 'Socialism for Millionaires', *Contemporary Review*, 69
(1896), as repr. in id., *Essays in Fabian Socialism* (1932), 106–7.

[114] *The Social Problem*, 118.

[115] Olivier, 'The Moral Basis of Socialism', 122–3.

[116] J. A. Hobson, 'The Rights of Property', *Free Review*, 1 (1893), 139.

[117] The dangers of basing sociology on biology were well recognized at the time.
See, for example, the views of Richie and Henry Sidgwick in den Otter, *British
Idealism*, 127–33. For a wider survey see Freeden, 'Biological and Evolutionary
Roots of the New Liberalism in England'.

[118] Hobson, *The Social Problem*, 76–7, 81. The justification for using this source
at this stage in the argument is that it was largely made up of articles written for
Ethical World in 1898 though not printed as a book until 1901. For Ritchie's antici-
pation of this idea see his *Darwinism and Politics* (1889) and den Otter, *British
Idealism*, 92–8. Hobhouse's approach to evolution was very similar to Hobson's.
Collini, *Hobhouse*, esp. ch. 5.

becoming more conscious of itself and, therefore, more capable of directing its own future. Capitalism was subject to many maladies but, with proper treatment, they could be cured and the application of the right medicine was, he insisted, a matter of political and social choice.

Another pronounced feature of Hobson's early work was his deep suspicion of the economic and social efficacy of large parts of the service economy. The south, or rather the south-east, of England was the most rapidly developing part of the kingdom and its growth was largely driven by services with the City of London as a central feature: but Hobson complained that the 'greater part of the South of England [is] degenerating into a mere playground for the "classes".'[119] In the *Physiology* the authors implicitly adopted the Smithian distinction that characterized industry and agriculture as productive, or adding value to the economy, and services as unproductive.[120] Such distinctions had been slowly eroded in later classical thinking and they disappeared from neo-classical economics.[121] Yet they remained popular not just amongst Marxists, who embraced them with enthusiasm, but also amongst provincial, liberal businessmen and the working class who voted for Gladstone.[122] Hobson recognized that the share of services in national income was rising and that of manufacturing falling: but he often thought of the former as a refuge for those thrown out of industry by machinery, or driven by chronic underconsumption into 'dealing' and 'trading' because unable to find work in 'making', adding little to the economy in the process.[123] Although he later repudiated the Smithian distinction[124] it is evident that he thought much of the service economy was dependent on the rich and would disappear with them, an attitude he shared with William Clarke and other New Liberal thinkers.[125]

[119] *The Social Problem*, 119–20, 251–2.

[120] Backhouse. 'Mummery and Hobson's *The Physiology of Industry*', 88.

[121] For a brilliant survey see H. Boss, *Theories of Surplus and Transfer: Parasites and Producers in Economic Thought* (Cambridge, 1990). Unfortunately Hobson receives no attention in this work.

[122] Cain, 'Hobson, Wilshire and the Capitalist Theory of Capitalist Imperialism', 457–8.

[123] J. A. Hobson, 'Occupations of the People', *Free Review*, 1 (1894), 520–40. Cf. *The Physiology of Industry*, ch. 5.

[124] *The Social Problem*, 27–8.

[125] William Clarke, 'The Social Future of England', *Contemporary Review*, 78 (1900).

In taking this stance, Hobson was reflecting a tradition that could be traced back to Paine and to Cobbett and the attack on 'Old Corruption', that pre-1815 alliance between land and finance in which the Bank of England and the monopoly chartered companies based in the City had played a conspicuous part. John Bright's contemptuous reference to the City of London in 1865 as 'steeped to the lips sometimes in perilous speculations' was one manifestation of that tradition; Gladstone's hostility to the Bank of England, a survivor of this era, and his attempt to curb its powers in the 1860s was another.[126] Hobson despised much of modern industry and feared the growth of big business and the enhanced industrial power it might bring with it. He also attacked the narrow 'muck and brass' economism of modern 'Manchesterism' which he felt still dominated business attitudes in Britain. In tones reminiscent of Arnold Toynbee's famous critique of the Industrial Revolution and anticipatory of the massively influential social history of the Hammonds,[127] he also declared that the result of such thinking in the nineteenth century was that the destinies of society had fallen into the hands of 'millowners, financiers and their intellectual henchmen' and resulted in 'despotism and degradation' for the mass of workers. Like William Clarke, whose view of the effects of the Industrial Revolution was even more scathing than his own, he believed that this narrow-minded business class had hijacked liberalism and the Liberal party and provoked social division and class hostility as a result.[128] He also argued that orthodox economic thinking was, in large part, an apologia for the prejudices of this 'Manchesterism'.[129] Nonetheless, in his new moral world a virtuous, beautified, harmonious, but still market-driven industry would be one of its vibrant cores. In that sense, Hobson's natural links were with those, including Joseph Chamberlain, who still

---

[126] *Speeches on Questions of Public Policy by John Bright, M.P.*, ed. J. E. Thorold Rogers (1868), 129; Cain and Hopkins, *British Imperialism*, 138.

[127] For the Hammonds' connection with the New Liberal movement see Clarke, *Liberals and Social Democrats*, esp. 74–82.

[128] *The Social Problem*, 21. Clarke, 'The Industrial Basis of Socialism', 6–7; id., 'Political Defects of the Old Radicalism', *Political Science Quarterly*, 14 (1899); both repr. in *William Clarke*, ed. Hobson and Burrows,. The *PSQ* paper had its origins in a talk given to the Rainbow Circle in 1894. See Freeden (ed.), *Minutes of the Rainbow Circle*, 19–20.

[129] *The Social Problem*, 25. Hobson was systematically unfair to Mill in this regard as a reading of this chapter will make plain. He was probably reading Mill through Ruskin's eyes.

thought in terms of an alliance of producers, of combining industrial capitalists and workers against landlords and rentiers. As
befitted his own provincial origins, Hobson's radicalism was, in fact,
a highly intellectualized version of the popular 'master narrative' of
the English provinces, recently revealed by Patrick Joyce, which saw
worker and small capitalist as 'the people' united in battle against
privilege and fighting to recover their birthright from idle aristocrats and, increasingly, from the plutocrats of the City of London.
It was a narrative that was still alive and well in the writings of
J. B. Priestley in the 1930s and 1940s.[130]

New Liberal and Fabian rent analysis had, of course, deliberately
shifted the focus of attention from land to capital as the largest
source of unearned increment. Hobson himself noted that many
radicals and liberals were Georgeites and obsessed by the land question, failing to recognize that free trade 'clips the wings of English
landlordism' by encouraging cheap imports and that the 'manufacturing and commercial classes' were now at the forefront of
wealth creation.[131] But like many other liberal thinkers and politicians, Hobson was reluctant to believe that Britain must forgo its
agricultural heritage and commit itself to an ever-extending urbanism and his concerns reflected the persistence of the land issue in
Liberal politics. Thinkers such as Green and practical politicians
like Chamberlain agreed that one major cause of urban poverty was
excessive migration from rural areas and that stemming the flow
through land reform would go some way towards solving urban
problems.[132] Hobson's interest also chimed in with the 'back to the
land' movements of the time that expressed a deep sense of yearning
for a disappearing rural culture.[133] He was deeply impressed by
Ruskin's passionate conviction that all 'true and worthy' ideas, all
that was noble in life, came from the contemplation and study of
nature and that great art was an expression of these ideas.[134] In
Ruskin's eyes, agriculture was the foundation stone of the good life

[130] P. Joyce, *Visions of the People* (1991). On Priestley as carrier see J. Baxendale,
'"I Had Seen a Lot of Englands": J. B. Priestley, Englishness and the People', *History
Workshop Journal*, 51 (2001), 102–6.
[131] 'The Influence of Henry George in England', 840–1.
[132] Chamberlain, *The Radical Programme*, pp. xvi–xxii; C. Harvie, *The Lights of
Liberalism: University Liberals and the Challenge of Democracy* (1976), 162–6.
[133] See J. Marsh, *Back to the Land: The Pastoral Impulse in England from 1880
to 1914* (1982).
[134] *John Ruskin*, 29 ff.

and urbanism was itself good only insofar as it was a natural extension of it. Modern urbanism, driven on by machines, was intrinsically evil since it encouraged unhealthy luxury and illth, and poverty and degeneration amongst the masses. Ruskin's agrarianism had its intellectual roots in his study of classical civilization: but it was also a late emanation of the civic humanist tradition of the seventeenth and eighteenth centuries in England where the land was associated with virtue and independence and towns with luxury, corruption and loss of autonomy.[135] Indeed, Ruskin argued that a society whose wealth was based on manufacturing and which had to import supplies of food was not only making itself politically vulnerable to other nations but was also demonstrating moral weakness because it had become too dependent on industry with all its attendant evils.[136] In the mid-1890s Hobson came to agree with Ruskin, though he translated the latter's concern with virtue into a language which had a greater resonance among contemporary Liberal elites when he spoke of the degradation of 'physique and character' in modern towns and of a 'base, ugly and depressing environment' which, in corrupting and stifling the sense of beauty, inevitably undermined morality.[137] He also gave a radical twist to the discussion when he claimed that, with land reform, Britain would be able to supply most of its own food, halt the drift of population to the towns, and create a 'restored yeomanry' in the process.[138]

CONCLUSION

In 1889, when he co-wrote *The Physiology of Industry*, Hobson was still at heart a free market liberal of the old school. It was only

[135] On civic humanism in its nineteenth-century guise see Burrow, *Whigs and Liberals*. For Ruskin's own experiments in land restoration and those of his followers see W. H. G. Armitage, *Heavens Below: Utopian Experiments in England 1560–1960* (1961), 289–304.

[136] See John Ruskin, *Fors Clavigera*, vol. iv, letter 44, Aug. 1874 and letter 67, July 1876, in *Works*, ed. Cook and Wedderburn, xxviii (1907), 132–6, 653–4. There are strong parallels between Ruskin's ideas on the question of agricultural self-sufficiency and those of Malthus.

[137] *John Ruskin*, 230, 257.

[138] See J. A. Hobson, 'The Decay of English Agriculture', *Commonwealth* (Mar. 1896), 85–8; id., *Co-operative Labour on the Land* (1894), pp. vii-xii. He did, however, recognize that there were limits to this process since agriculture was ultimately subject to diminishing returns and too much emphasis upon it was incompatible with 'the higher life'. Hobson, *The Social Problem*, 205–13.

from 1893–4 onwards that he could be reasonably described as a 'progressive' and as a 'New Liberal' in the making though his coercive attitudes towards the 'unfit' and his dependence on Ruskin's thought has raised questions as to whether his thinking was truly within the liberal tradition. Yet, as we have seen, Hobson can lay claim to have made a successful attempt to reconcile individualism with a new role for the state as society's representative. By 1898 the main process of development of his ideas was largely complete even though his most enduring economic and sociological writings were still to come: in that year he wrote the essays which made up *The Social Problem*, his first outstanding work of social philosophy. As we shall see in the next chapter, his ideas on international relations and imperialism went through a similar process of transformation in the 1890s, though at a slower pace. It was only on the eve of the Boer War that Hobson brought his ideas on the evolution of capitalism and capitalist society in the most advanced countries into line with his increasingly radical views on overseas expansion to create the theory of economic imperialism for which he is justly famous.

CHAPTER THREE

Becoming an Anti-imperialist, 1887–1898

In his mature writings on imperialism, Hobson was drawing on a
rich tradition of radical protest going back to the eighteenth
century that he inherited and to some extent transformed. Given
his upbringing and initial assumptions, it took him a long time
to connect with this tradition. His emergence as a radical anti-
imperialist took rather longer than his appearance as a New Liberal
on the domestic front and he did not bring together his thinking on
domestic and imperial matters until 1897–8. Moreover, as we shall
see, his attempt to weld together his arguments about underconsumption with a condemnation of imperial expansion supposedly
derived from Cobden created unresolved tensions and contradictions in his argument which were to be carried into *Imperialism:
A Study*.

THE RADICAL TRADITION

In radical discourse, the most fundamental political battle was the
one fought out between a 'natural' society, made up of small-scale,
competitive capitalist businesses in agriculture, commerce, and
industry, and an unnatural one based on aristocracy and its control
of the land and the state. Overseas expansion of territory was seen
in this light, as one of a number of devices used by the aristocratic
'Few' to enhance its power and prestige at the expense of the 'Many'.
It involved the extension of the state and thus brought extra employment to the clients of the aristocracy; it was associated with warfare
and thus gave succour to the military interests lying at the centre of
aristocratic life; it also excused higher taxation including indirect
taxation which, in the early nineteenth century, meant the hated

Corn Laws, the most visible sign of aristocratic privilege. And, as Paine graphically expressed it, 'in reviewing the history of the English Government, its wars and its taxes, a bystander, not blinded by prejudice or warped by interest, would declare that taxes were not raised to carry on wars but wars were raised to carry on taxes'. Overseas conquests, like war, great armaments, and an adventurous foreign policy, were thus a means of maintaining the status quo, of 'conquering at home'[1] or, in Bright's most famous words, of maintaining 'a gigantic system of out-door relief for the aristocracy of Great Britain'.[2] Nonetheless, radicals were always careful to distinguish colonialism based on emigration from additions to territory in heavily populated foreign countries. The former were extensions of Britain's free societies and capable of self-development: the latter could only be ruled autocratically and were sources of war and of exploitation which deranged the economy and polity of Britain.[3]

It is important to recognize that the City of London and metropolitan finance were long thought of as a part of the complex of interests behind colonialism and aggression overseas. Hostility towards aristocracy was firmly tied in with antagonism to the growth of the national debt, in the eighteenth century and during the French wars of 1790–1815, and to the rise of what Cobbett dubbed the 'paper aristocracy'.[4] Landed and financial wealth were intermingled to a marked extent within the system of 'Old Corruption'—the manipulation of taxation and state patronage through an aristocrat-dominated Parliament.[5] Radical thinkers regarded monopoly corporations such as the East India Company, the Bank of England, large parts of the City fed on government stock and the rentier populations living upon it (mainly in the south of England), as 'outworks' of the system, elaborate extensions of a governmental machine intent on amassing unproductive wealth. Such was the growth of the national debt by the early part of the nineteenth century that John Wade, the radical publicist, could

---

[1] Thomas Paine, *The Rights of Man* (Everyman edn. 1966), 55.
[2] *Speeches on Questions of Public Policy by John Bright, M. P.*, ed. J. E. Thorold Rogers, vol. ii (1868), 382.
[3] Taylor, 'Imperium et Libertas?
[4] *The Opinions of William Cobbett*, ed. G. D. H. Cole and M. Cole (1944), 68–9.
[5] P. Harling, *The Waning of 'Old Corruption': The Politics of Economical Reform in Britain, 1779–1846* (Oxford, 1996); P. Harling and P. Mandler, 'From "Fiscal-Military" State to Laissez-Faire State, 1760–1850', *Journal of British Studies*, 32 (1993).

argue that Britain was faced with an attempt to replace 'the feudal aristocracy from which Europe has suffered so much, with a monied aristocracy more base in its origins, more revolting in its associations and more inimical to general freedoms and enjoyment'.[6] Richard Cobden also saw 'the bankers and moneymongers' of the City as an extension of the aristocratic system and condemned the loans floated there to prop up feudal regimes in Europe which, he claimed, were used in 'obstructing industry'.[7] The link made between the City of London and aristocracy in radical thinking highlights the fact that, across Europe, anti-imperial sentiment was frequently a protest against the persistence of 'the two primal forms of exploitation, both with deep roots in the Middle Ages, that of the feudal lord and the usurer'.[8]

The Gladstonian state, under which the forces of liberalism gathered from the 1850s onwards, was the culmination of a long process, whose origins can be traced back to the 'economical reform' movement of the 1780s, which severely undermined the governmental arm of aristocratic power. In curbing government expenditure and reducing the national debt, Gladstonianism also forced the City to shift its interests from government stock to the running of a more open international economy; and as the power of the great chartered companies declined, the City became an even stronger devotee of free trade and the nightwatchman state in the later nineteenth century than the radical forces which had originally promoted it.[9] In radical eyes, however, free trade was not just a way of extending business or a method of preventing aristocracy from using the state to protect its private interests. It was also a means of spreading international co-operation and of spreading prosperity, thus undercutting the forces of war and colonialism that aristocracy thrived upon. Paine believed that commerce was 'a pacific system, operating to cordialise mankind, by rendering Nations, as well as individuals, useful to each other' and that, if 'it were permitted to act to the universal extent that it is capable, it would extirpate war, and produce a Revolution in the

---

[6] J. Wade, *The Extraordinary Black Book* (1831), 377.
[7] *Speeches on Questions of Public Policy by Richard Cobden, M. P.*, ed. J. Bright and J. E. Thorold Rogers, vol. ii (1870), 193–4.
[8] Semmel, *The Liberal Ideal and the Demons of Empire*, 12.
[9] The difficult transition in the City is documented in A. C. Howe, *Free Trade and Liberal England* (1997), ch. 2.

uncivilised state of Governments'.[10] For Cobden, the leader of the Anti-Corn Law campaign in the 1840s, the hope that free trade would further the cause of international peace was the chief energizing force in his political life.[11] In this he was the most potent carrier of the tradition dating back to David Hume and Montesquieu who, although they recognized that 'commerce' did not encourage the heroic virtues favoured in the civic humanist tradition, lauded it as the carrier of civility and peaceful interdependence. Those who were busy making money would have less time for making war.[12]

Nonetheless, despite free trade, the Reform Acts, the installation of the Gladstonian minimalist state, and the triumph of 'industrialism' and of 'voluntary co-operation' there was still the fear that old elites could use their remaining authority and wealth to turn Britain back into a 'militant' society where 'compulsory co-operation' was the rule.[13] It was that fear which underlay the vehement reaction of Gladstone and other liberals and radicals to Disraeli's policy of 'imperialism' in the 1870s when that word was beginning to take on its modern meaning of domination over non-European peoples. Disraeli's declaration that Queen Victoria was Empress of India and his use of Indian troops in the Russo-Turkish crisis of the late 1870s reminded radicals forcibly that despotic rule abroad could be used to undermine liberty at home.[14] Tory imperialism, it was argued, meant an alliance between the 'Upper Ten Thousand' and the unorganized labouring masses—a little later characterized as the degenerate 'residuum' of London and other major cities and towns—who were easily dazzled by talk of glory and roused by 'jingoism' (a word invented in 1878).[15] Together, they were seen as a threat to the 'higher order of working men and the middle

---

[10] See *The Rights of Man*, 214-15.

[11] P. J. Cain, 'Capitalism, War and Internationalism in the Thought of Richard Cobden', *British Journal of International Studies*, 5 (1979).

[12] A. Hirschman, *The Passions and the Interests: Political Arguments for Capitalism before its Triumph* (Princeton, 1977).

[13] For the distinction between 'industrial' and 'militant' societies see H. Spencer, *Principles of Sociology* (1876), vol. i, Pt. II, 576-96; J. Y. D. Peel, *Herbert Spencer on Social Evolution* (Chicago, 1972), has useful extracts at 149-66.

[14] A good introduction is C. C. Eldridge, *Disraeli and the Rise of a New Imperialism* (Cardiff, 1996). See also P. J. Cain (ed.), *Empire and Imperialism: The Debate of the 1870s* (South Bend, Ind., 1999).

[15] W. R. Greg, 'Foreign Policy of Great Britain: Imperial or Economic?', *Nineteenth Century*, 4 (1878), 398-9.

class' who were the backbone not only of industry and commerce but also of liberalism and the Liberal party. The historian Goldwin Smith also gloomily surmised that the richer manufacturers and businessmen were buying land, marrying into the aristocracy, and joining the 'classes' against the 'masses'.[16] He believed that, if allowed to run its course, the revival of imperialism would halt or reverse economic progress and even threaten political liberty.[17] Other radicals feared the eventual collapse of capitalism and the advent of socialism as war taxation drained away the nation's savings, industrial employment was lost, and the working class were reduced to the status of a 'mob'.[18]

The fervour of Gladstone's Midlothian campaign of 1879–80 is understandable in this context but it disguised the fact that Conservative and Liberal governments were both susceptible to pressure from numerous forces making for expansion, including provincial industrialists and commercial men clamouring for new markets because of 'overproduction'[19] as well as investors anxious for the safety of their assets abroad. Gladstone's own decision to occupy Egypt in 1882, only four years after he had condemned the project as unnecessary and unjust, graphically illustrated the problem.[20] Over the next two decades the boundaries of the empire were extended enormously in Africa and Asia under both Liberal and Conservative administrations. Henry Richard, Welsh Liberal MP and leading member of the Peace Society, had pointed the finger of suspicion at City financiers in the Egyptian crisis,[21] and the idea that imperialism was a necessary part of capitalist expansion began to make some headway. In the mid-1880s, via the Socialist League, William Morris had come to the conclusion that the partition of

---

[16] Goldwin Smith, 'The Greatness of England', *Contemporary Review*, 34 (1878), 7–8. Gladstone used the 'classes and masses' terminology in a famous speech in 1886. Matthew, *Gladstone, 1809–1898*, 348–9.

[17] Smith, 'The Greatness of England', 18.

[18] F. Seebohm, 'Imperialism and Socialism', *Nineteenth Century*, 7 (1880) as reprinted in Cain (ed.), *Empire and Imperialism*, esp. 298–9, 301–2; D. A. Hamer, *John Morley: Liberal Intellectual in Politics* (Oxford, 1968), 131–3.

[19] W. G. Hynes, *The Economics of Empire: Britain, Africa and the New Imperialism* (1979).

[20] Gladstone's denunciation of the idea that Britain should occupy Egypt in order to protect the Suez Canal can be found in his 'Aggression on Egypt and Freedom in the East', *Nineteenth Century*, 2 (1877) as reprinted in Cain, *Empire and Imperialism*, esp. 200 ff. For the Egyptian crisis itself see Ch. 8 *infra*.

[21] H. Richard, *Mr. Chamberlain's Defence of the War* (1882?).

Africa between the European powers was 'prompted solely by the desire to exploit the country in the interests of capitalists and stockjobbers . . . who could not exist as a class without the exploitation of foreign nations to get new markets'.[22] By 1890, in fact, it was something of a commonplace on the left of politics that imperial expansion was driven by economic motives and that 'the flag follows the filibuster and trade follows the flag, with the missionary bringing up the rear'.[23] The growing conviction on the left of British politics that profit was the guiding principle behind imperialism was hardened by Parliament's acquiescence in the creation of City-financed chartered companies—such as Rhodes's British South Africa Company and McKinnon's Imperial East Africa Company—which promised to promote British interests in their chosen regions without direct involvement by the state.

Pressure certainly grew within the Liberal party for a frank acceptance of the need for expansion as international economic rivalry increased. Rosebery, who was Prime Minister in 1894–5 when the final decision was taken to incorporate Uganda as a British protectorate in the wake of the bankruptcy of the Imperial East Africa Company, was an avowed 'free trade imperialist'.[24] Rosebery was leader of the Liberal Imperialist group within the party and, though it was relatively small in numbers, it had a disproportionate share of the party's front-bench talent.[25] By the late 1890s, the Liberal party was bitterly divided on imperial expansion, with the Cobdenites condemning Rosebery's strategy as the antithesis of liberalism because it was a sure recipe for massive state expenditures and because it would increase the pressure to raise revenue through tariffs. But though often opposed to expansion, very few liberals were willing to accept Cobden's belief that the best thing Britain could do for its existing empire was to withdraw from it.[26] Most

---

[22] Quoted in E. P. Thompson, *William Morris: Romantic to Revolutionary* (1977), 387. A similar analysis came from Belfort Bax. Porter, *Critics of Empire*, 99–101.

[23] G. B. Shaw, 'The Transition to Social Democracy', in Shaw and Bland (eds.), *Fabian Essays* 199. Cf. Clarke, 'The Industrial Basis of Socialism', 82.

[24] For Rosebery's views see Bennett, *The Concept of Empire*, 296–7, 302–4, 310–11. For the provenance of the term 'free trade imperialism' see J. Gallagher and R. E. Robinson, 'The Imperialism of Free Trade, 1815–1914', *Economic History Review*, 5 (1953–4), 1–15.

[25] H. C. G. Matthew, *The Liberal Imperialists* (Oxford, 1973).

[26] For Cobden's forthright view on Britain in India see J. Morley, *The Life of Richard Cobden*, ii (1881), 207.

assumed that Britain had a duty to bring civilization and good government to Africa and Asia and few questioned its ability or right to do so. Gladstone regretted that Britain had taken control of India but, once there, he was convinced that it had a duty to bring the benefits of its own energy in the pursuit of liberty and progress— based on that 'industry' which Smiles had seen as central to the British character—to the native population. Indians had no 'general inferiority of mind' which could justify British rule nor was their 'civilisation less matured by time'. What distinguished the British was 'comparative force of manhood and faculties of action' and this made their supremacy over India not only possible but was enough to 'invest it with a humane and beneficial aspect'.[27]

HOBSON'S EARLY WRITINGS

A close reading of his early writings indicates that Hobson often supported policies which fit the description 'free trade imperialist'. His opinions were certainly much closer to those of Rosebery and the emergent Liberal Imperialists than to Gladstone's or to the radical anti-imperialist tradition just outlined. Hobson also showed strong sympathy with Chamberlain's brand of Liberal Unionism. Chamberlain broke with Gladstone over the issue of Irish Home Rule and empire unity in 1886 and in the following decade he tried to combine his long-standing social radicalism with enthusiasm for empire by claiming that imperial expansion and imperial economic unity were vital to employment and to the welfare of the working man. Indeed, in the early 1890s, Hobson occasionally went beyond the free trade imperialist position and showed some sympathy for protection. In doing so, he was anticipating the kind of policies which Chamberlain adopted from the late 1890s onwards. However, during the key years of the mid-1890s when he was acquiring his New Liberal philosophy, Hobson wrote very little on overseas issues except for his father's newspaper. Whether because of a lack of interest or because he was constrained by his dependence on his father, his writing on imperial matters then did not rise much

---

[27] W. E. Gladstone, 'England's Mission', *Nineteenth Century*, 4 (1878), as repr. in Cain (ed.), *Empire and Imperialism*, 253. Bright had similar views: see Bennett, *The Concept of Empire*, 172–3.

beyond the conventional wisdom. After the death of his father in 1897, Hobson's views shifted rapidly leftwards and, by 1898, he had already sketched out the position for which he later became famous and which, he claimed, was in a direct line of descent from Cobden.

Hobson's early conservatism in social matters was reproduced in the wider arena of international affairs. He supported Union with Ireland and the Unionist cause partly because he believed that Home Rule was 'disintegrating the Empire'[28] and partly because its leaders 'represent the force of solid intelligence and respectability which has given firmness to our constitution and order to her progress'.[29] His views on the broader issues of foreign and imperial policy were no less sound. In 1888, he took issue with the ageing radical hero John Bright, supporting imperial federation because 'it was the only sure protection against the otherwise inevitable decay which history teaches us is the lot of nations which have reached the proud position England now occupies'. Empire unity was necessary to forestall the expansionary ambitions of France and Russia: we should also stay close to Germany and Austria in order to restrain them.[30] Three years later, when noticing a meeting of the United Empire Trade League, he added that 'the establishment of an Imperial Zollverein is one of the great possibilities for the future, although hardly more than a remote possibility at present'.[31] In the same year he could be found arguing that the 'prime principle' of our foreign policy was that Russia was to be kept out of Constantinople and that, in this context, 'our interests in holding fast Egypt' were obvious.[32] Hobson also showed a keen appetite for 'informal' imperial expansion in the interests of export industrialism. In 1887, for example, he was advocating 'commercial advances' on China. 'The opening of the vast Chinese Empire to European trade would be the greatest event since the discovery of America . . . Think what a market for English manufactures if it could be opened!'[33] It may

---

[28] 'A London Letter', *Derbyshire Advertiser*, 2 Dec. 1887, p. 8. It must be remembered that support for the Union with Ireland was sometimes combined with a resolute determination to oppose every attempt to extend the empire, a position exemplified by two leading Liberal Unionists, Leonard Courtney and Goldwin Smith. See Harvie, *The Lights of Liberalism*, 222.

[29] *Derbyshire Advertiser*, 16 Dec. 1887, p. 8.

[30] Ibid. 7 Apr. 1888, p. 8.

[31] Ibid. 10 Apr. 1891, p. 2.

[32] Ibid. 18 Sept. 1891, p. 6.

[33] Ibid. 21 Oct. 1887, p. 8.

also be worth noting that, in 1889, Hobson and Mummery pointed out that, where there was underconsumption, war could give employment to otherwise underutilized capital assets. Of course, they also insisted that it was better to solve the underconsumption problem by increasing demand in other ways: but their position was perfectly compatible with the common business argument, strongly supported by Chamberlain, Rosebery, and others, that 'overproduction' made it imperative to extend British markets overseas by aggressive imperial methods if necessary.[34]

There is no doubt either that Hobson's growing concern with poverty sometimes led him to adopt positions on international economic matters which conflicted with established Liberal policy and came close to the kind of solutions advocated by protectionists. In the late 1880s he warned against the 'economic fallacies'[35] of the fair trade movement as a good Liberal should, and declared that 'Free trade stands on precisely the same basis of certainty as mathematical demonstrations', though he also warned against 'mere unintelligent fetish worship' in this context.[36] His interest in imperial federation suggests, indeed, some flexibility on the issue and his attitude to free trade certainly became more pragmatic. In 1889, in *The Physiology of Industry*, Hobson and Mummery claimed that, at a time of acute commercial depression, imposing tariffs would not further reduce output as free traders always insisted. In their view, during a slump when selling was difficult, labour and capital would shift from production to distribution; a tariff would simply encourage some factors to return to production by increasing the inputs necessary to maintain the same output.[37] Also, when faced with the question of raising the consumptive power of the working classes, the authors argued that this would be simpler if the immigration of cheap labour from the Continent were restricted or prevented because otherwise the average wage would be forced down and demand curtailed: 'the instinct which has led Americans and Australians to refuse to permit immigration of Chinese was a true instinct.' It followed that 'it is clearly for the interest of English labourers to prevent', by legislation if necessary, 'such free influx of foreign labour as shall enable the quantity of

---

[34] *The Physiology of Industry*, 161–3.
[35] *Derbyshire Advertiser*, 2 Dec. 1887, p. 8.
[36] Ibid. 16 Dec. 1887, p. 8; 4 Nov. 1887, p. 8.
[37] *The Physiology of Industry*, 205–9.

labour demanded to be supplied at an unduly low price'.[38] Two
years later, in *Problems of Poverty*, Hobson repeated his concern
about immigrant labour, pointing out that the problem would
become more acute as international factor mobility increased. Now
he added that free entry for foreign goods could have the same effect
on the living standards of the poor as free immigration even though
free trade increased total national income.[39] Hobson expected the
pressure for both an Alien Law and protection to grow as workers
became more conscious of their interests: if a 'few shiploads'[40] of
Chinamen were to arrive in east London, he argued, legislation
of this kind would be inevitable unless some other remedies for
poverty could be found, and:

it seems not unlikely that a democratic government will some day decide
that such artificial prohibition of foreign labour, and the foreign goods
which compete with the goods produced by low-skilled English labour, will
benefit the low-skilled workers in their capacity as wage-earners, more than
the consequent rise in prices will injure them in their capacity as
consumers.[41]

Hobson moved furthest away from a free trade stance in 1891 when
he considered the British social problem in the context of a developing world economy more fully than in *Problems of Poverty*. He
repeated his argument about the need for restriction of immigrants
but this was now regarded as only a short-term palliative.[42] In the
longer term, the main problem was that, while capital was rapidly
becoming more cosmopolitan, labour could be expected to move
more sluggishly in response to widening economic opportunity in
the world economy. Hobson expected that capital would soon begin
to flow from Britain to countries such as India and China where

[38] Ibid. 212–13.
[39] *Problems of Poverty* (1891 edn.), 59–62, 90–2.
[40] Ibid. 125.
[41] Ibid. 126–7. Cf. Hobson, *Evolution of Modern Capitalism* (1894 edn.), 355.
It should, however, be noted that the Fabians were also hostile to free immigration
of labour. See G. Wallas, 'Property under Socialism', in Shaw and Bland (eds.), *Fabian
Essays*, 137–8. Eugenicists also saw alien immigrants as adding to the problem of
degeneracy in towns. See Searle, *Eugenics and Politics in Britain*, 39–41. For the
context of these ideas see C. Holmes, *John Bull's Island: Immigration and British
Society, 1871–1971* (1988), esp. Pt. II.
[42] J. A. Hobson, 'Can England Keep her Trade?', *National Review*, 17 (1891), 5,
10. This article is reprinted in *Hobson: Writings on Imperialism and Internationalism*
ed. Cain.

there were vast supplies of cheap but skilful craft labour which could easily adapt to modern industrial conditions. He recognized that the productivity of Indian and Chinese labour was lower than that of the English worker but the difference in wage levels was, he believed, more than enough to compensate for the productivity gap. As a result, 'we must be content to look forward to a not too distant future when this capital will find its most profitable investment outside England, leaving English labour to starve and, driven by starvation, to follow reluctantly in the track of migrating capital'.[43]

This outcome would be the inevitable result of supporting 'the ideal of free trade in capital and labour' which 'would ride roughshod over all the higher purposes of life, distributing mankind not according to the requirements of moral or intellectual advance, or even of physical wellbeing, but according to the method of division which was conducive to the largest nett aggregate of wealth'.[44] Hobson expected that these changes would happen with great speed and that English capital could be 'drained' in a generation. He inferred from this that England needed protection. By this he did not mean protection against foreign imports, which he claimed would simply lead to a fall in the rate of return on investments and give further encouragement to the export of capital. Instead, he suggested that foreign investment could be prohibited or heavily penalized through taxation.[45] Otherwise, if these tendencies were allowed to work themselves out,

another century may see England the retreat for the old age of a small aristocracy of millionaires who will have made their money where labour is cheapest and return to spend it where life is pleasantest. No productive work will be possible in England, but such labour as is required for personal service will be procurable at a cheap rate, owing to the reluctance of labour to keep pace with the migration of capital. Thus, without any wild stretch of the imagination, we may look forward to a revived feudalism in which the industrial barons will rule, with that absolute sway which wealth must exercise over poverty, the more sentimental or less adventurous menials who shall cling to their own country, in preference to following into India, China, or Heaven Knows where, the march of emancipated capital.[46]

Hobson's concern with the fate of the working man and with the future of industry and democracy is plain here but his stance at the time was closer to the developing Conservative anti-cosmopolitanism, which flowered into the tariff reform movement

---

[43] Ibid. 9. [44] Ibid. 8. [45] Ibid. 10. [46] Ibid. 11.

after 1903, than it was to radicalism or socialism. It may well have been the concerns expressed here which inclined him to consider some kind of imperial tariff union with a degree of sympathy. In 1891 he hinted that the international mobility of capital would be less of a worry within the empire:

if by this time the unity of the British Empire has become so vigorous a reality to us that we view the shift of trade and population from England to India or Egypt with the same indifference with which we have seen the rise of Lancashire and the decline of Huntingdonshire, we may await with philosophical complacency this marking out of economic forces.[47]

The *National Review* article reveals fairly nakedly the bias against 'unproductive labour' and its relationship to financial wealth which was a marked feature of the liberal tradition as it came through from Cobden and Bright. But that bias was also carried by Chamberlain into the Conservative party from the mid-1890s and became a staple ingredient of the tariff reform campaign as the protectionists struggled to put industry at the centre of the party's concerns. In questioning free trade in this way, Hobson was distancing himself from the policy which more than any other distinguished liberals from their opponents.[48]

After 1891, as his New Liberalism began to take shape, Hobson did not make a case for protection in any new writing, though *Problems of Poverty* was republished in 1896 and 1899 without the statements in question being omitted or modified. However, his growing horror at the condition of urban England often made him, in common with other progressives, hostile to free trade as an aspect of that 'Manchesterism'[49] which he believed had dominated economic policy in the nineteenth century. Free trade encouraged international competition, which stimulated the development of machinery and big business and was therefore forwarding the march of a civilization which had no answer to the problems of poverty and unemployment[50] and which Hobson, now under

---

[47] Ibid. 9.

[48] For Chamberlain's tariff campaign see *infra* Ch. 6. William Clarke had recognized the threat of Asian competition to British industry but did not attack free trade. 'The Industrial Basis of Socialism', 73.

[49] 'Manchester' was the subject of critical debate at the Rainbow Circle very early in its history. Freeden (ed.), *Minutes of the Rainbow Circle*, 5 Dec. 1894, pp. 17–19.

[50] *Evolution of Modern Capitalism*, 352–5.

Ruskin's tutelage, also condemned as ugly and depressing. The effect of free trade was 'to remove workers from good air, ample space, sunshine and other bounties of nature and place them in circumstances where they can produce a larger quantity of industrial wealth'.[51] As a true Ruskinian, one of his cherished ideas as a reformer from the mid-1890s was to see more people settled on the land while, under free trade, the drift to the towns was accelerating because imports of food were destroying agricultural business. In 1894 he lamented the 'domination of such narrow 'economic' considerations as should break up our country life and transfer an increasing proportion of our workers to a life of physical deterioration'. He did not advocate protection but he did want to see reforms which would 'reduce the alarming dependence of England upon foreign nations for her means of physical subsistence'.[52]

HOBSON, RHODES, AND THE JAMESON RAID

As we saw in the previous chapter, Hobson's New Liberal reformism was well developed on the domestic front by 1895. However, he wrote very little about imperialism in the mid-1890s except for his father's newspaper. It was not at the forefront of his mind most of the time and so his thoughts on the subject changed more slowly. Some shift in his opinions is evident, however, in a long review of Benjamin Kidd's *Social Evolution* he published in 1895 attacking Kidd's Social Darwinism and the aggressive imperialism to which it gave support. To Kidd's vision of continuous warfare in pursuit of efficiency, Hobson opposed Spencer's conviction that altruism would eventually overcome antagonism: throughout his years of maturity Hobson was keen to stress that Darwinism emphasized the importance of co-operation and community just as much as conflict in describing successful evolution.[53] He also resisted Kidd's assumption that the struggle between the great powers for global domination was inevitable. Kidd, declared Hobson, wanted 'quantitative' progress while he emphasized the importance of

---

[51] *The Social Problem*, 19.
[52] Hobson (ed.), *Co-operative Labour on the Land*, pp. ix, xi.
[53] Which was why he became an enthusiast for Kropotkin's views. On Kropotkin see D. Miller, 'Peter Kropotkin (1842–1921): Mutual Aid and Anarcho-communism', in J. A. Hall (ed.), *Rediscoveries* (Oxford, 1986).

'qualitative' change. The first was 'measured in square miles of territory, bales of cotton goods and millions of low-class English lives
which are engaged in cut-throat competition of military and
commercial rivalry',[54] whereas what was wanted was to limit quantity in order to improve quality. Kidd also failed to understand the
'evolutionary character of socialism'. What was needed was
equality of opportunity on a global scale. Socialism, he declared,
'achieves this equalisation of opportunity by putting down some
lower forms of struggle, in order that the struggle may take a higher
and intenser form. When all mankind was placed upon absolute
equal terms of competition in the rivalry of life, the ideal of
socialism would be attained.'[55] Here Hobson was extending to the
international arena his evolutionary organicism supported by
Ritchie's argument that the battles of the future were more likely to
be between ideas than armies,[56] but at no point in his article did he
attack imperial expansion *per se*.

Hobson's strong aversion to the Jameson Raid of late 1895 also
marked some change in his perspective. The association between
Jameson's vain mission and the desire of mining capitalists such as
Cecil Rhodes to be rid of Kruger's Afrikaner government in the
Transvaal, which the mine owners saw as dangerously obstructive
of their operations, caused uproar in Britain and was certainly a key
moment in the emergence of the idea of 'financial imperialism'.[57]
Hobson recognized that Rhodes had instigated the Raid, that it was
an obvious example of 'stock-jobbing imperialism',[58] and that
Rhodes had tried 'to upset the Government of a peaceful state in
order to grab gold'.[59] He also anticipated some of his own later
thinking when he analysed the list of shareholders of Rhodes's
British South Africa Company. He noted its strong aristocratic and
City of London connections and concluded that 'most of these
people are in a position to bring political influence to bear in favour
of a business undertaking in which they were personally interested,
and the aggregate power of so large a body of shareholders must

[54] J. A. Hobson, 'Mr Kidd's "Social Evolution"', *American Journal of Sociology*,
2 (1895), 309.
[55] Ibid. 308.
[56] Den Otter, *British Idealism*, 97.
[57] Porter, *Critics of Empire*, 60–2.
[58] *Derbyshire Advertiser*, 22 May 1896, p. 8.
[59] Ibid. 7 Aug. 1896, p. 8.

be very large indeed'. He also pointed out that about one-quarter of the shareholders were foreigners and that this was an illustration of the cosmopolitan nature of modern commercial enterprise.[60]

Hobson even went so far at that time as to describe Britons as 'a go-ahead people given to annexing territory which belongs to other people',[61] but it would be hasty to infer that his views on imperialism had undergone radical change. Some of Hobson's anger at Rhodes may have been due to his belief that the Colossus's inept policy towards Kruger had alienated the Dutch population in the Cape Province and thus had, at the least, delayed a federation of the South African states under British leadership which was evolving naturally before his interference.[62] Hobson certainly never turned his fire on his favourite apostle of imperial unity, Chamberlain, talking instead of the latter's 'dignified repudiation' of the Raid as Colonial Secretary.[63] Moreover, as he recognized, there were many Liberal Unionists and Conservatives who were also 'disgusted' with Rhodes's action, 'which, if it makes for an England large in acreage, certainly makes for an England small in honour'.[64] Moreover, in his more casual writings, he was still inclined to offer some support for imperial expansion rather than condemn it outright when opportunity arose. In 1895, for example, he could be found arguing that Britain ought to ensure 'her share' of the trade when China was opened and secure herself another treaty port.[65] His respectful attitude towards Chamberlain, now Colonial Secretary in a Conservative administration, was also still strongly evident in the same year when he commented on the latter's pursuit of imperial federation. He reminded his readers that Cobden 'was no doubt carried away by Utopian visions when he contemplated the cessation of wars' if free trade were widely adopted: but he did believe that 'commerce was indisputably the chief guarantee of peace between nations' and that it had been a key factor in preventing war with the United States. Despite this, he was still tempted by the idea of empire economic unity which was 'a taking one and is in harmony with a strong national sentiment'. Even though 'the practical difficulties were very grave' he was clearly willing to contemplate imperial preference in some circumstances

---

[60] Ibid. 1 May 1896, p. 8.   [61] Ibid. 15 Jan. 1897, p. 8.
[62] Ibid. 21 Aug. 1896, p. 8.   [63] Ibid. 24 Jan 1896, p. 8.
[64] Ibid. 22 May 1896, p. 8.   [65] Ibid. 22 Mar. 1895, p. 8.

and recognized that trade federation would be the prelude to closer political and military ties.[66]

Such views were very different from the more thoroughgoing anti-imperialism of colleagues such as Clarke.[67] Even in 1896 Hobson's position still had affinities with Conservative and Liberal Unionist thinking, some of it influenced by Ruskin. Ruskin was a persistent advocate of colonization which he thought of as a natural extension of the vigour of a dynamic agrarian society.[68] Indeed, he thought that one advantage of colonialism was that Britain could export some of its industrialism to the periphery whilst remaining itself primarily agricultural.[69] Ruskin had a profound influence on J. A. Froude's attitude to colonialism. Froude had a more pessimistic vision of British industrialism than Ruskin since he considered it irreversible. He thought of the white colonies as the advancing agricultural frontier where British civilization could renew its strength, provided that governments could overcome their natural inclination towards free trade cosmopolitanism and actively promote migration to British lands, rather than acquiescing in the flow of British population to its potential enemy the United States.[70] Froude quite consciously connected his own colonialism with that seventeenth- and eighteenth-century tradition which linked together virtue, independence, and landownership: his book *Oceana* (1886) was named after a utopian colonial project imagined by Sir James Harrington two centuries before.[71] His ideas became part of a wider current of interest in 'Greater Britain' beginning in the mid-1870s, flowing through Sir John Seeley into the imperial federation

[66] Ibid. 4 Oct. 1895, p. 8.

[67] Clarke had a long history of opposition to imperial federation schemes. See, for example, W. Clarke, 'The Future of the Canadian Dominion', *Contemporary Review*, 38 (1880).

[68] His most famous plea for colonization was made in his inaugural lecture as Slade Professor of Art in Oxford in 1870. *Works*, ed. Cook and Wedderburn, xx, 42–3.

[69] See 'The Future of England', in *The Crown of Wild Olive*, para. 159, in *Works*, ed. Cook and Wedderburn, xviii.

[70] J. A. Froude, 'England and Her Colonies', *Fraser's Magazine*, 81 (1870) and 'The Colonies Once More', ibid. 82 (1870). Both essays are reprinted in Cain, *Empire and Imperialism*.

[71] On Harrington see J. G. A. Pocock, *The Machiavellian Moment: Florentine Political Thought and the Atlantic Republican Tradition* (Princeton, 1975), esp. 510 and also the introduction to J. A. Froude, *Oceana: or England and her Colonies* (1886). See also the perceptive comments by J. W. Burrow, *A Liberal Descent: Victorian Historians and the English Past* (Cambridge, 1981), 284–5.

movement of the 1880s and beyond. And, as industry came under pressure from foreign competition, it was not surprising that a 'Greater Britain' movement intent on preserving both industry and agriculture should emerge. In that sense, the Chamberlainite imperial federation movement that received Hobson's qualified support was a natural development of the Greater Britain idea, though Froude and Ruskin would have found its emphasis on preserving British industry repugnant.[72] What they all shared was a sense of empire as an expanding British society: Froude and Seeley were both dubious about the long-term value of Britain's control of India because the latter was not a natural extension of the nation.[73]

New Liberalism and the 'Progressive Review'

Hobson had been an active member of the Rainbow Circle since its inception in 1894 and was closely associated with the *Progressive Review* from 1896 onwards.[74] He was thus exposed to the anti-imperialist radicalism of Clarke, G. H. Perris, and others who were becoming involved in the bitter battle within the Liberal party and other progressive groups over the significance of imperialism. The *Progressive Review* was emphatically radical in its attitude to imperialism from the beginning.[75] It reacted to the growing imperial fervour in Britain in the late 1890s, which was associated with the reconquest of the Sudan, Anglo-French antagonisms in both East and West Africa, Queen Victoria's diamond jubilee celebrations, and the stand-off between the Transvaal republic and the British government, by reasserting a Cobdenite perspective tempered by recent events in South Africa.

Although in its essence capitalism is international, and although it will prove in the long run one of the leading factors in breaking down nationalism, for

---

[72] Julius Vogel, 'Greater or Lesser Britain', *Nineteenth Century*, 1 (1877) marks a point at which Froude's vision was expanded to include industry. The essay is repr. in Cain (ed.), *Empire and Imperialism*.

[73] J. A. Froude, 'England's War', in *Short Studies on Great Subjects* (1907), iii. 276; J. R. Seeley, *The Expansion of England* (1883), 304.

[74] Hobson advertised the first edition of the *Progressive Review* in his father's newspaper though without mentioning his own association with it. (*Derbyshire Advertiser*, 25 Sept. 1896, p. 8).

[75] Porter, *Critics of Empire*, 177 ff.

the present it is accustomed to find in exaggerated forms of nationalism its most potent ally. The music hall patriot is encouraged to howl for Jameson, or any other hero of the hour, when in reality he is howling for the financiers who are making Jameson their tool.[76]

Clarke, the editor of the *Review*, linked the newer forms of financial capitalism associated with foreign investment with the older forces of militarism fuelled by jingoistic nationalism thus bringing together 'old' and 'new' liberal thinking,[77] though it is clear that finance was now beginning to be thought of as a central rather than a subsidiary feature of imperialism.[78] Clarke accused 'the financial class, that sinister class' of encouraging imperialism and an armed peace in Europe for its own benefit. As nations became more entangled in debt as a result, the hold of finance over governments and peoples would become greater and the hold of the military in society would increase. Clarke's conclusion that 'everything in Europe makes day by day for financial despotism' reinforced the idea that the anti-liberal forces were changing in composition though still an outgrowth of traditional enemies.[79]

Under Clarke's influence, Hobson did begin to shift in a more radical direction, though he persisted in his interest in imperial federation in ways which were possibly connected with Ruskin's influence upon his thinking. Writing under the pseudonym 'Nemo' in 1897, he began by assuming that nations had ends or ideals and asked how imperialism might contribute towards them.[80] Just as individuals in a society had to adjust their aspirations and energies to serve the good of the nation, so national claims to a right to expand had to fit in with 'a rational cosmic plan' which Nemo assumed would involve qualitative improvement rather than merely quantitative growth.[81] He accepted that no nation had an inalienable right to a territory simply because of long occupation: if that

[76] William Clarke, 'The Genesis of Jingoism', first published in the *Progressive Review* 1 (1897); repr. in *William Clarke*, ed. Burrows and Hobson, 108–17.

[77] See also William Clarke, 'The Curse of Militarism', in *William Clarke*, ed. Burrows and Hobson, 118–26. John Morley, Cobden's biographer, also spoke of the 'money interest' in imperialism. Collini, *Liberalism and Sociology*, 87.

[78] Porter, *Critics of Empire*, 57–70; G. Searle, *Corruption in British Politics* (Oxford, 1987), 65–9.

[79] 'Is Democracy a Reality?', *Progressive Review*, 2 (1897), 26–7.

[80] Nemo, 'Ethics of Empire', *Progressive Review* (Aug. 1897). Hobson did not acknowledge authorship of the article in his autobiography but the language of the piece is remarkably similar to that employed in his major writings on imperialism.

[81] Ibid. 450–1.

occupation blocked world progress then others could justly colonize such lands.[82] However, colonizing nations like Britain had asserted themselves through brute force not reason. In practice, there were no accepted rational criteria for judging who was fit for the role of world civilizer: why should Britons alone decide whether 'the slow going civilisation of the Transvaal Boer' was better for the world than the one the British wished to foist upon it?[83] Certainly Britain could not simply assume its civilization was the best and, anyway, the existence of a wide variety of civilizations probably offered the maximum evolutionary possibilities. In practice, Nemo felt that the Anglo-Saxon development of North America, Australia, and 'some parts of South Africa' which was based on 'prior rights of occupation' had been for the 'good of humanity'.[84] But the British occupation of India failed to meet this standard, despite the fact that it had brought better government and better economic management than its predecessors. Nemo assumed that, through emigration and colonization, places like North America were extensions of our civilization and thus organic growths. Britons could not colonize India in this way and, using the language of biologism which became a marked feature of Hobson's writing in the later 1890s, he claimed that Britain could only fix itself upon the subcontinent as a parasite. As such, it could not guide India's destiny properly and the latter needed freedom to develop more naturally. This parasitism was also harmful to the 'self-realization' of England which was corrupted by the unearned wealth drawn from India. England was also harmed by the authoritarianism of Indian life and government which was exported back to Britain in the form of ex-imperial servants who often dominated the south of England and were 'anti-democratic by conviction'.[85] Indeed, Nemo argued, if societies were judged by their contribution to world civilization in a dispassionate manner, it was possible that, like the New Zealand Maori, 'the Southern Englishman might find himself served with a writ of ejectment by the High Court of Humanity'.[86] He concluded by asserting that further external expansion was largely unnecessary. It absorbed resources badly needed for domestic affairs and it served to distract

---

[82] The idea that the more civilized had a right to occupy the land of those less advanced can be found in Thomas More, with whose work both Ruskin and Hobson were familiar. See More's *Utopia* (Cambridge, 1989), 56.

[83] Nemo, 'Ethics of Empire', 454.

[84] Ibid. 455.   [85] Ibid. 455–9.   [86] Ibid. 453.

the nation from its own ills and to preserve an undesirable status quo. The argument that new territories were necessary for exports ignored the lessons of free trade and gave 'active support [to] that very Militarism which is the arch-enemy of Industry'.[87] The Idealist element in Hobson's thinking is evident here and the article also ends with a strong radical flourish, adopting Spencer's language as well as his ideas, though no attempt was made to introduce finance as an agent of imperialism in the manner of Clarke or other radicals.

What is also noticeable—despite the dismissive attitude to the aboriginal peoples of white settled territories, a blind spot Hobson shared with other radicals—was his emerging cultural relativism. This was a brave position to adopt at a time when European imperialist passions were becoming more and more inflamed and a crude Darwinism informed the language of even cautious politicians like Lord Salisbury, who spoke of a world divided between 'living and dying' nations.[88] Even so, imperialist sympathies of a rather surprising kind remained a part of Hobson's intellectual baggage. Early in 1897 he praised Alfred Milner's appointment as High Commissioner in South Africa: no one 'sounder' or 'more solid' could have been found.[89] Milner had been an enthusiastic follower of Ruskin when at Oxford and he became a firm supporter of imperial federation, so there was an affinity with Hobson. Moreover, the latter could not of course anticipate that Milner would soon show such a determination to eliminate the independence of the Afrikaner republics and push them into war with Britain. But it is still surprising to hear such a strident imperialist commended for his 'brilliant work' in reorganizing Egyptian finance, and his book *England in Egypt* (1892), with its built-in assumptions about British superiority and right to rule, given such a good press at this stage in Hobson's intellectual progress.[90]

---

[87] Ibid. 460–2. For a very similar argument see *The Social Problem*, 272–9.

[88] B. Porter, *The Lion's Share: A Short History of British Imperialism* (3rd edn. 1996), 127.

[89] *Derbyshire Advertiser*, 18 Feb. 1897, p. 8.

[90] Hobson did object to Britain's aggressive policy in the Sudan because he felt that it reinforced the idea that they were intent upon staying in Egypt, a policy he believed might lead to war with France. Ibid. 20 Mar. 1896, p. 8.

FREE TRADE AND FOREIGN POLICY

Nonetheless, Nemo had ended by associating imperialism with militancy and accounting it subversive of industry. In 1898 the Cobdenite and Spencerian note became the dominant one in Hobson's writing on imperialism because he now began to see it, for the first time, as *the* threat to democracy, to the possibilities of social reform, and to the emerging programme of New Liberalism. Hence he felt an urgent need to combat the claim that trade followed the flag and that imperial expansion was necessary to furnish markets for British goods—made with increasing stridency by major and minor political figures, journalists, and the massed ranks of Britain's Chambers of Commerce—and to resist strongly the rising clamour for protectionism. As for the latter, there was a widespread feeling in liberal ranks that free trade could soon be lost, and the morale of Cobdenites was at a very low ebb[91] when Hobson enlisted himself to the cause. Exactly why Hobson made such a decisive intellectual leap at the time is not obvious. A Pauline conversion cannot be ruled out—Hobson was apt to change his views quite abruptly—and the death of his father in 1897 may have been a significant moment.[92] Whatever the stimulus, it took him well beyond the thinking of his radical colleagues and inaugurated a new era in anti-imperial thought.

The specific events which heralded Hobson's conversion was the heated debate over the 'scramble' for spheres of interest in China, which had been precipitated by China's defeat at the hands of Japan in 1895.[93] There was a strong feeling in Britain, as in other parts of Europe and in America, that the opening of the Chinese market would offer unrivalled opportunities for export growth and that any developed nation which commanded China's economy would leap decisively ahead of its rivals. Such speculations imparted a feverish sense of urgency to the debate about spheres of interest. Holt S. Hallett, a spokesman for British economic interests in China, was representative in declaring that 'trade is the lifeblood

[91] A. C. Howe, 'Free Trade and the Victorians', in A. Marrison (ed.), *Free Trade and its Reception, 1815–1960* (1998), 177.

[92] His father's death made him financially independent and he never wrote for the *Derbyshire Advertiser* again. It is possible that he felt intellectually completely independent for the first time as well.

[93] For British imperialism in China see *infra*, Chs. 5 and 8.

of manufacturing nations, and increased trade they must and will have, even if they have to parcel out China and tumble down its dynasty to obtain it'.[94] After commenting on a number of minor breaches of free trade including 'attacks on the free entry of aliens',[95] Hobson objected to this policy of forcing open markets in China in the name of free trade which was, he declared, 'the thin end of the wedge of empire as India, Egypt and Africa testify'.[96] Cobden's free trade policy was based on peace and was an attempt to unite mankind: he had never intended that the British 'should seek to impose it by kicks and blows upon others'.[97] Grabbing spheres of interest was also incompatible with free trade: the British claimed to be countering the monopolistic policies of other powers but a sphere 'will be virtually under the British flag and we are convinced that trade follows the flag'. Whatever the British government might say, the policy was designed to create a monopoly of trade and industrial development in parts of China which 'is itself "Protection" of a most insidious and dangerous character'.[98] Hobson also lamented the fact that so many in the Liberal party supported such a policy 'which is in effect nothing else than a direct repudiation both of the logic and the utility of free trade'.[99]

However, although this argument established his free trading credentials, it did nothing in itself to counter his previous worry— widely shared among social reformers as well as pro-imperialists— that the importance of foreign trade to England's prosperity and the growth of competition for markets made imperialism or protection, or both, unavoidable. As recently as 1896, for example, Hobson had admitted that attempts to counter underconsumption by raising wages or shortening hours in trades subject to foreign competition could result in unemployment of both capital and labour.[100] Hobson now had to show that improvements in Britain's economic

---

[94] Holt S. Hallett, 'British Trade and the Integrity of China', *Fortnightly Review*, NS 63 (1898), 679.

[95] J. A. Hobson, 'Is England a Free Trade Country?', *Reformer*, 15 Sept. 1898, 173–4.

[96] Ibid. 176.

[97] Ibid. 177; J. A. Hobson, 'Free Trade and Foreign Policy', *Contemporary Review*, 74 (1898), 168; repr. in *J. A. Hobson: Writings on Imperialism and Internationalism*, ed. Cain.

[98] 'Is England a Free Trade Country', 176.

[99] 'Free Trade and Foreign Policy', 167.

[100] *The Problem of the Unemployed*, 108–9.

welfare, more especially the welfare of its working class, were compatible with a 'pure' free trade policy. The result was his seminal article 'Free Trade and Foreign Policy', where he tried to demonstrate that the drive for foreign markets was caused by oversaving and that the national interest was not served by it. In doing so, he applied the analysis of Britain's internal capitalist crisis he had developed throughout the 1890s to its external relationships for the first time.

In the *Problem of the Unemployed*, published in 1896, Hobson had recognized that any particular nation might solve its oversaving problem by capital export: but he then contented himself with arguing that, whatever the status of individual nations, there remained a general oversaving problem amongst advanced industrial countries which had to be dealt with and he made no attempt to take the analysis of capital export further.[101] It was only in 'Free Trade and Foreign Policy' that Hobson made the critical theoretical move by arguing not only that the oversaving which was endemic in industrial societies found an outlet in foreign investment but that one of the consequences of this was a competition between the powers for new fields for financial expansion.[102] Moreover, he was now trying to construct a general theory of imperial expansion as a product of a malfunctioning global capitalist system rather than simply offering an explanation for British imperialism—though, as will become apparent later, the peculiarities of the British experience did have a strong influence on the nature of the explanation.

Hobson began by highlighting the three interlinked economic arguments which, he believed, imperially minded politicians and businessmen used most frequently to justify imperial expansion. First, there was the claim that the British economy could only grow and prosper, and living standards for the common man improve, if its foreign trade expanded continually. Following on from this, it was frequently asserted that, in the face of a 'pushful' policy by Britain's rivals, the growth of foreign trade could only be secured

---

[101] Ibid. 86–8.

[102] The first historian to recognize the significance of Hobson's 1898 article was Bernard Porter. See his *Critics of Empire*, 194. Similar arguments linking foreign investment and imperial expansion with domestic crises can be found in North America. See C. A. Conant, 'The Economic Basis of "Imperialism"', *North American Review*, 167 (1898), and H. Gaylord Wilshire, 'The Significance of the Trust', *Wilshire's Magazine* (Nov. 1901).

by adopting an aggressive policy of expanding imperial territory and by increasing naval and military spending significantly. Finally, the proponents for a 'forward' policy were convinced that the costs involved in the naval and military build-up they advocated were outweighed by the resulting trade gains. The new military expenses of imperialism were a kind of 'insurance premium' and well worth paying.[103]

Hobson responded not by assaulting the first, most important, strand of the argument, but by assuming for the moment that there might be some truth in it and concentrating on the two subsidiary arguments.[104] The notion that foreign trade could only be secured by aggression was disposed of in true Cobdenite fashion. If, for example, Russia, France, and Japan occupied China, and we were excluded from the territorial division, the development of China undertaken by the other powers would stimulate their own growth, increase foreign trade in general, and thus bring benefits to Britain.[105] Moreover, Britain would make direct as well as indirect gains from occupation by the powers because its competitiveness in some areas such as shipping would ensure that business came its way. As for the question of military expenditure as an insurance premium needed to ensure the safety of overseas trade, Hobson flatly denied that it was necessary. He examined the trade statistics between Britain and its empire and showed that the rate of increase in trade over the previous generation had been considerably less than the rate of growth of military expenditure. Moreover, the new empire, especially the African territories occupied since 1880, did a pitifully small trade with Britain which hardly justified the cost of its acquisition. Even if it were true that growth and welfare depended on increasing exports, imperialism was too expensive a way of obtaining them.[106]

Although Hobson's points, especially the second, appeared to be telling, his position was vulnerable to the common argument that,

---

[103] 'Free Trade and Foreign Policy', 169–76.

[104] Ibid. 169.

[105] For a similar argument by a cautious Tory imperialist see Henry Birchenough, 'Do Foreign Annexations Injure British Trade?', *Nineteenth Century*, 41 (1897), 994–5.

[106] This echoes the views of the Cobdenite Lord Farrer, 'Does Trade Follow the Flag?', *Contemporary Review*, 74 (1898), 810–20. See also A. G. Hertzfeld, 'Our Falling Trade', *Westminster Review*, 150 (1898), 622.

although the new territories had produced little advantage up to the present, they would one day be a valuable resource which had to be kept out of the hands of foreign protectionist powers. So, in order to prove that imperialism was unnecessary, he had to attack the initial argument in favour of expansion and deny that an expanding foreign trade was essential. In 1896, in *The Problem of the Unemployed*, when discussing ways of increasing agricultural output and employment, Hobson had met the claim that reducing agricultural imports would also reduce exports and cause unemployment by pointing out that, as domestic agriculture grew, so would demand for home manufactures.[107] Now he generalized this argument dramatically, using some of Adam Smith's reasoning in his attack on mercantilism, and at one point employing the same language as the *Wealth of Nations*.[108]

Smith was somewhat ambivalent about the importance of foreign trade in commercial society. In one place in the *Wealth of Nations* he spoke of foreign trade as a 'vent for surplus' produce and, as such, important in maintaining full employment levels of output in Britain.[109] It was this version of free trade as an engine of growth that Cobden implicitly adapted to his own purposes in his free trade campaigns and propaganda. It had wide popularity among the business class who had supported Cobden in the 1840s. Unfortunately, it could easily be turned into an argument that imperial expansion was necessary to the health of the British economy: Edward Gibbon Wakefield, for example, had argued that underconsumption existed in Britain and had then used the 'vent for surplus' hypothesis to justify his colonial land and emigration schemes in the 1830s and 1840s.[110] Many businessmen and politicians in the 1880s and 1890s also inferred that imperial markets were vital to national economic prosperity. But Smith had also attacked the idea that the continued expansion of foreign trade, and the colonialism it provoked, were

---

[107] *The Problem of the Unemployed*, 152.

[108] Hobson used *The Wealth of Nations* as one of his texts on his University Extension course in economics. See *Oxford University Extension Seventh Summer Meeting* (Aug. 1895), which is in the Bodleian Library shelfmark 26269 e44.

[109] Adam Smith, *An Inquiry into the Nature and Causes of the Wealth of Nations*, i (Oxford, 1976), 372.

[110] B. Semmel, *The Rise of Free Trade Imperialism: Classical Political Economy, the Empire of Free Trade and Imperialism, 1750–1850* (Cambridge, 1970), chs. 4 and 5. D. Winch, *Classical Political Economy and the Colonies* (1965), ch. 7.

vital to the prosperity of the nation, and this was the dominant theme in the *Wealth of Nations*.[111] Making an implicit assumption of what later became known as Say's Law—that all that was supplied necessarily also created its own demand and that full employment was the norm within any free economy—Smith felt that, in a world free of mercantilist attempts to boost foreign trade artificially, the ratio of foreign trade to national income would fall significantly. Smith also claimed that exchange between two points within the domestic economy was of greater benefit to the nation than exchange involving foreigners. The home trade 'generally replaces by any such operation two distinct capitals that had both been employed in the agriculture and manufactures of the country' whereas foreign trade 'will give but one half the encouragement to the industry or productive labour of the country'.[112] The belief in Say's Law prompted James Mill to argue later that foreign trade was a 'mere auxiliary' to domestic growth and that if the former were to disappear altogether national income might be lower but that 'every labourer would find work, and every shilling of capital would find employment'.[113] Later economists were more nuanced in their approach but broadly accepted the Say's Law argument which gave some radical thinkers and politicians a powerful means of denying that overseas expansion and imperialism were necessary to economic health.[114] There was, in fact, an unresolved tension within radicalism between those, like Cobden, who equated the extension of economic interdependence with the evolution of a peaceful internationalism and those who feared that dependence on international trade made advanced industrial nations vulnerable to calls for imperial expansion and, therefore, reinforced or reactivated the power of aristocracy and of militancy.

In 'Free Trade and Foreign Policy', Hobson ignored 'vent for surplus' and seized on Smith's demonstration that foreign trade was not a critical factor in economic growth. Some foreign trade was obviously necessary because there were important commodities

[111] For a discussion of Smith's complex view of foreign trade see C. E. Staley, 'A Note on Adam Smith's Version of the "Vent for Surplus" Model', *History of Political Economy*, 5 (1973), 438–48.

[112] Smith, *Wealth of Nations*, i. 368.

[113] James Mill, *Commerce Defended* (1805), in *James Mill: Selected Economic Writings*, ed. D. Winch (Edinburgh, 1966), 150, 155.

[114] For a detailed exposition see Cain, 'International Trade and Economic Development in the Work of J. A. Hobson before 1914', 420–3.

Britons could only acquire from abroad and some commodities had to be exported to pay for them. Generally speaking, however, 'it is a grave error to regard increase of foreign or colonial trade as an index of the real prosperity of the nation' because 'there is no advantage in an increase of foreign, as distinct from home, trade'. Furthermore, the latter provided 'a more solid and substantial basis for industrial prosperity' partly because it was more secure but, more significantly, because 'the gain arising from home trade is double instead of single, the full advantage which both parties obtain from exchange being kept within the nation'.[115]

Smith's own reasoning depended on the Say's Law assumption that all resources could be employed domestically, and Hobson went on to make a similar claim. It was unnecessary to 'spend our energy . . . in wrangling with other nations for markets in Africa and Asia' when there was an 'immense potential market for the conveniences and comforts of life' among the mass of people in Britain. He went on:

With each increase of production is created a corresponding power of consumption vested in the owners of productive factors. If these owners of consuming power exercise it in such a way as to make the standard of national consumption rise with every increase of producing power, no such pressure of the needs of foreign markets would be felt.

In other words, Say's Law would work provided that income was well distributed. The difficulty in practice was that income was very badly distributed and domestic consumption did not rise at a sufficient rate to match increased production because underconsumption, and its corollary oversaving, occurred.

Though a potential market exists within the United Kingdom for all the 'goods' that are produced by the nation, there is not an 'effective' demand, because those who have the power to demand commodities for consumption have not the desire, since their material needs are amply satisfied, while those who have the desire have not the power. Stated otherwise, the working classes of this country possess an insufficient proportion of 'effective demand'; the actual rise in their standard of comfort, though in some cases considerable, has not been at all commensurate with the growth of productive power of the nation, especially in manufactures.

[115] 'Free Trade and Foreign Policy', 177.

As a result, the 'upper class and a large section of the middle classes, who own an excessive proportion of the goods that are produced' tried to find markets for the surplus abroad and clashed with other nations with similar problems.

If direct testimony to this fact and its consequences is desired, it is found in the large surplus of our national income which, being needed neither for home consumption nor for capital in home industries, seeks foreign investments,—a sum which though it admits of no precise computation, must far exceed a total of two thousand million pounds sterling. It is possible, indeed, that the growing pressure of the need for foreign investments must be regarded as the most potent and direct influence on our foreign policy. Our surplus products, which the working class cannot buy and the wealthier classes do not wish to buy, must find customers among foreign nations, and since those who sell them do not even desire to consume their equivalent in existing foreign goods, they must lie in foreign countries as loans or other permanent investments. A portion of the yield of these investments is represented in the excess of our import over export values, but only a portion, a large part going to swell the sum of the investments. Thus, in the first resort, it is the excessive purchasing power of the well-to-do classes which, by requiring foreign investments, forces the opening up of foreign markets, and uses the public purse for the purposes of private profit-making.[116]

Hobson was claiming that, in a well-regulated, healthy economy with a better distribution of income, foreign trade and foreign investment would be of much more marginal significance.[117] In a diseased capitalist world on the other hand, with its extremes of wealth and poverty, they were essential to survival and imperialism was the inevitable outcome. Lurking behind this argument is, of course, the extended bio-sociological analysis he had developed in the 1890s and which was summed up in *The Social Problem*. In a world where there was an imbalance between productive effort and consumption, oversaving was inevitable: when the balance was corrected, Say's Law would work and the problem of imperialism would be solved. Using language that was consciously Spencerian, he pointed out that the nation had a choice

---

[116] Ibid. 177–9.

[117] For a similar emphasis on the need to boost the home market—by land reform in this case—in order to reduce dependence on foreigners see Hertzfeld, 'Our Falling Trade', 623–4.

between external expansion of markets and territory on the one hand, and internal social and industrial reforms upon the other; between a militant imperialism animated by the lust for quantitative growth as a means by which the governing and possessing classes may retain their monopoly of political power and industrial supremacy, and a peaceful democracy engaged upon the development of its natural resources in order to secure for all its members the condition of improved comfort, security, and leisure essential for a worthy national life.[118]

Imperialism was not only unnecessary, it was positively harmful. In adopting this analysis, Hobson at last aligned himself closely with the radical tradition of anti-imperialism and anti-colonialism. While he believed that maintaining a high level of foreign trade was essential to the welfare of the average man, Hobson was always to be tempted by some form of imperialist solution to the problem of rising foreign industrial competition and to have some sympathy with free trade imperialism, which Liberal Imperialists such as Rosebery espoused, or with the 'social imperialism' eventually embraced by Cecil Rhodes and Chamberlain. But once he had convinced himself that the existing international economic system begat imperialism and had begun to see the latter as *the* great barrier to social progress, Hobson recognized the affinity between his own ideas and those of the radical anti-imperialists. He then went on to claim that the 'New Liberalism' was a natural development of the older variety. His progress in this regard was similar to that of another leading prophet of New Liberalism, L. T. Hobhouse, whose violent opposition to imperial expansion opened his eyes to the value of the 'Manchester School' though their free market views had hitherto made them objects of suspicion.[119] In claiming kinship with Cobden and other traditional anti-expansionist liberals Hobson and Hobhouse were in effect asserting that they, as New Liberals, were the direct heirs of what Clarke had called 'Old Radicalism'. In practice, however, Hobson's position was not truly Cobdenite: the particular Smithian approach to foreign trade he adopted put a very different stress on the importance of international commercial relations than did Cobdenism. Although Hobson was happy to agree that free international trade encouraged harmony among nations, in 'Free Trade and Foreign Policy' he was implicitly arguing

---

[118] 'Free Trade and Foreign Policy', 179.
[119] Collini, *Liberalism and Sociology*, 85–8.

that trade would only be truly free when social reform and redistribution of income within nations had taken place. He was also making a case for a reduction in the importance of the international dimension in Britain's economic life, one that made social progress much more a domestic matter. In taking this stance, Hobson perhaps deserved the epithet 'Little Englander', hurled at the anti-imperialists by the supporters of the Boer War, rather more than most.

RECONCILING FREE TRADE AND
ANTI-IMPERIALISM

The extent of the tranformation in his views which had taken place—and of the intellectual difficulties embedded in them—is also evident in another long article, written in 1898 for the Co-operative Wholesale Society (CWS), where he again addressed the widespread fear that Britain's foreign trade was being undermined by international competition and that a grave national crisis was at hand. He admitted, as he had done in 1891, that European and American competition was likely to increase and also that 'not only England but Western Europe may lose in large measure the position of the workshop of the world, which may be transferred to ... Asiatic areas with their huge, cheaply subsisted, and submissive populations'. He also recognized that loss of markets and the increasing penetration of the home market by foreign goods was 'driving us back to the protective policy from which we emerged in the middle of the century'.[120] In contrast to the position he had adopted in the early 1890s, however, he now claimed that the problems could be met without recourse to imperial expansion and war. International competition was a good thing in itself because it extended the international division of labour for everyone's ultimate benefit. As for Britain, measured in real terms, trade had doubled in thirty years and, if its imports of goods had risen much faster than exports, service exports, especially returns on foreign investment which he estimated at £120 million per annum, had more than compensated.[121] If imports from abroad displaced home production

---

[120] J. A. Hobson, 'Foreign Competition and its Influence on Home Industries', *Co-operative Wholesale Societies Annual* (1899), 198–200.

[121] Ibid. 201–4.

then resources would move to other areas in which Britain had an advantage over rivals: 'When foreign goods compete with and displace British goods in the British market, though they injure a particular trade, they do not in any way reduce the aggregate of trade or employment in Britain.' Losing foreign markets might be more of a problem in terms of lost output but even that would be countered by 'a gradual transference of capital and labour to other more thriving trades'.[122]

An imperial *Zollverein* no longer appealed to him because its advocates were 'strong supporters of a pushful foreign policy directed at the continual enlargement of the Empire and the consequent acquisition of new markets . . . supported by powerful and expensive armaments'. Besides, trade did not follow the flag: Britain's trade had increased faster with its supposed rivals than with its empire.[123] Finally, losing markets abroad did not matter because the British could live more from their own resources. To prove this he repeated his Smithian analysis. 'Trade is what we want, not foreign trade; other things equal, domestic trade is preferable to foreign trade, for, as in trade both parties must make a profit, home trade keeps both profits within the nation.'[124]

Much of what Hobson wrote in the CWS article would have seemed no more than common sense to orthodox free traders, though some might have dissented from his stress on the importance of the domestic market. It seems strange, at first blush, to find Hobson arguing that the loss of foreign markets could not cause unemployment when he was already well known for arguing that unemployment was an endemic feature of modern capitalist society. What is implied here was something which became plain only at a later stage of Hobson's intellectual development: his firm belief that unemployment existed and Say's Law did not function because of a maldistribution of wealth and income in modern societies and for that reason alone. Moreover, Hobson believed not only that changes in foreign transactions could not cause unemployment but that, since they tended to reduce income inequalities by widening the market, such transactions reduced the tendency to underconsumption, oversaving, and unemployment.[125] Holding such beliefs, Hobson was enabled to combine domestic social radicalism with

[122] Ibid. 205–9.   [123] Ibid. 217–19.   [124] Ibid. 222.
[125] See *infra*, Ch. 6.

orthodox opinions on matters of international trade. The attempt to reconcile his domestic heresies and his anti-imperialism with free trade orthodoxy had its price. It was difficult, for example, to reconcile his arguments about the benefits to the nation of income from foreign investments in the CWS article with his position in 'Free Trade and Foreign Policy' where foreign investment is categorized as the product of a diseased capitalism and the direct outcome of massive inequalities in wealth distribution. If foreign investment emanated from the wealthy would not the return income merely add to the problem of maldistribution rather than reduce inequalities?

Coming closer to Cobden and free trade orthodoxy also meant distancing himself somewhat further from Ruskin. Although Hobson did not mention Ruskin's attitudes to colonization in his biography of the latter published in 1898 he did devote an appendix to Ruskin's stance on war and warfare. Ruskin's position was broadly civic humanist since he called for a citizen's army or militia and saw war as essentially chivalric and heroic. Only heroic societies resting on military virtues produced great art, and the luxury and corruption of modern capitalism destroyed both.[126] Hobson described these 'as the pages we would most willingly delete from his works' and pointed out that Ruskin was not consistent in his views and had at times recognized that modern wars were not only horrific but actually fed the capitalist machine system he loathed so much by encouraging the armaments industries. More fundamentally, Ruskin's position implied that 'the transition from a military to an industrial organization of society, which Herbert Spencer regarded as a distinctive mark of civilisation, is really a matter of degradation', a position Hobson was bound to deny strongly. Ruskin looked to the re-creation of a pre-capitalist society: Hobson was committed to a reformed capitalism, one which combined free market internationalism with a liberalized Ruskinite organicism in the hope of establishing a new industrialism that was peaceful and prosperous but also capable of heroism of a different kind and of artistic achievement.[127]

---

[126] Ruskin, *Crown of Wild Olive*, esp. paras. 89, 99, 116, in *Works*, ed. Cook and Wedderburn, xviii.

[127] *John Ruskin*, 321–5.

Conclusion

Despite the tensions about the status of foreign trade lurking in the background of his thought, 'Free Trade and Foreign Policy' is undoubtedly one of Hobson's finest achievements, combining theoretical insight with economy and clarity of argument to an unusually high degree. But though Hobson had produced an impressive outline theory of economic imperialism, he still had to demonstrate that the theory illuminated reality. The connection between underconsumption, foreign investment, and imperialism, which was at the core of the analysis, was no more than a hypothesis, if a brilliant and exciting one. The sketch of 1898 also left a number of other important issues unresolved. Hobson had given finance the starring role in driving forward imperialism but he had not given any clear indication of how in practice foreign investors influenced imperial policy. His analysis at this point was not much more sophisticated than that of the liberal financial journalist A. J. Wilson, who saw 'the all-pervading army of the international usurers' as dominating the economic policies of increasingly warlike and imperialist great powers and warned that their exactions might one day cause national bankruptcies and a 'revolt of the masses'.[128] There were other problems. It was clear that foreign investment and exports of goods and services went together since the former could only be transferred by means of the latter. Manufacturers were often vocal supporters of imperialism and, in *The Social Problem*, Hobson indicted the manufacturing interest for pursuing an export-driven policy in order to avoid a high-wage/domestic growth strategy.[129] What was the relationship between these powerful forces of finance and industry? Over the next few years, spurred on by his experience of the South African war, Hobson strove to answer this and many other key questions about the causes of imperial expansion. He also took the subject much further than his predecessors had done. Between 1899 and 1902 he attempted nothing less than to tie together more firmly than ever before the economics, politics, and ideology of imperialism and to provide an explanation of the phenomenon that would apply to all advanced industrial countries.

[128] A. J. Wilson, 'The Immorality and Cowardice of Modern Loan-Mongering', *Contemporary Review*, 73 (1898), 326–34. Hobson noted Wilson's article in *John Ruskin*, 325.

[129] *The Social Problem*, 22–3.

Between 1889 and 1891, Hobson's position on imperialism oscillated between free trade imperialism and the social imperialism of the later Chamberlain. After that time, Hobson never objected to free trade in this way again but he remained concerned about the impact of a loss of international trade on the welfare of the masses. These concerns either inclined him to argue for more agricultural self-sufficiency or kept alive his interest in finding new markets for British goods even when this meant imperial expansion. Along with his Ruskinian ideas, his assumption that international trade was crucial to prosperity probably also explains his continued concern with schemes of imperial consolidation: even in 1896 he had a lingering feeling that imperialism and empire unity were compatible with a radical social programme. All this was swept aside from 1897 onwards as Hobson unveiled a penetrating critique of imperial expansion. But given his particular history, it may be that some of the virulence of his subsequent opposition to imperial expansion in general, and to Chamberlain and the protectionist movement in particular, sprang from a desire to hide a guilty past.

CHAPTER FOUR

The Economics of Imperialism, 1899–1902

Introduction: The Origins of 'Imperialism: A Study'

Hobson became joint editor, with Stanton Coit of the London Ethical Society, of *Ethical World*, a weekly magazine, in 1898. In the next few years he also worked for the *Speaker*,[1] did a stint in South Africa for the *Manchester Guardian* in the summer of 1899 just before the South African war began, and contributed to a number of other newspapers and weeklies. During the war, his journalism, political activism, and more considered writings lived in a sometimes uneasy relationship. He gathered much valuable material especially from the South African trip: but he had to write speedily, often in response to fleeting events and sudden crises, and to face the difficulty of handling the passionate feelings, his own as well as those of others, aroused in the very heated debates on the rights and wrongs of imperialism. Sometimes this undoubtedly reduced the coherence of his work and obscured the big picture of imperialism he was trying to construct. During 1899–1901, for example, when he was active in anti-war bodies such as the International Arbitration and Peace Association and the League of Liberals against Aggression and Militarism,[2] the argument about underconsumption, which was a vital part of his case as presented in 'Free Trade and Foreign Policy' in 1898, fell from view when he was writing on imperialism. His attention became fixed on finance itself, and on

---

[1] The *Speaker* was transformed into an anti-expansionist organ with New Liberal sympathies in 1899 under the editorship of J. L. Hammond. Emy, *Liberals, Radicals and Social Politics*, 133; Clarke, *Liberals and Social Democrats*, 76–7.

[2] P. Laity, 'The British Peace Movement and the War', in Omissi and Thompson (eds.), *The Impact of the South African War*.

financiers and their role in politics, in a way that made it more difficult to distinguish his own position from that of mainstream anti-imperial liberalism.

Imperialism: A Study was also put together partly from diverse pieces written in 1901 and 1902, some in heavyweight academic journals but most placed in less exacting liberal and radical weeklies like the *Speaker*, and was not as well-organized or co-ordinated a work as could be wished. As Bernard Porter has noted, the systemic theory of 1898 and the more conspiratorial elements introduced by his experience in South Africa lay uneasily together in *Imperialism*[3] and led to ambiguities and sometimes outright contradictions. Nonetheless, although he made some rash statements, took up unnecessarily extreme positions, and was sometimes inconsistent, he did slowly put together a more complex theory of imperialism, and one in closer touch with current evidence, than he had managed in 'Free Trade and Foreign Policy'. Certainly *Imperialism* was Hobson's most sustained and successful attempt to assimilate the phenomenon of imperialism into his broader stream of thinking about capitalist society and its future and it was much more comprehensive in its coverage than any previous radical attempt to assess contemporary European and American expansion overseas: it was noteworthy, for example, for the fact that Hobson took a far more sustained interest in the question of how overseas territories should be governed than previous radical thinkers, most of whom had been interested in imperialism solely from a domestic standpoint. In a favourable review of *Imperialism*, one leading American political scientist thought that it contained no new evidence and that 'the principles considered are fairly familiar' but that 'the groupings of considerations are nevertheless very original and constitute a most striking representation of the anti-imperialist position'.[4] This may do insufficient justice to Hobson's originality but it does point to one of the great strengths of the book. *Imperialism* also contains some of Hobson's finest writing. It can be read today for pleasure as well as for instruction and it still conveys something of the emotional intensity of the crisis which gave it birth.[5]

---

[3] Porter, *Critics of Empire*, 214–30.

[4] P. S. Reinach in *Political Science Quarterly*, 18 (1903), 531.

[5] For an excellent introduction to the debate on the meaning of imperialism at the time see A. S. Thompson, 'The Language of Imperialism and the Meanings of Empire: Imperial Discourse in British Politics, 1895–1914', *Journal of British Studies*, 36 (1997).

THE BOER WAR AND FINANCIAL IMPERIALISM

The reasons why Britain went to war with the Transvaal[6] and its sister state the Orange Free State in 1899 and eventually absorbed both into the empire are complex and are dealt with elsewhere.[7] What is noteworthy here is that, guided by Chamberlain as Colonial Secretary and Alfred Milner the High Commissioner in South Africa, the British government claimed that its intervention in Transvaal politics was undertaken to ensure political representation for British and other immigrants, known as 'Uitlanders', who had emigrated to the Transvaal in large numbers after gold was discovered there in 1886. This was certainly an issue capable of rousing the support of the British public. Many liberals, and a considerable part of the Liberal party, were uneasy with the government's aggressive pursuit of Uitlander rights. However, since the Transvaal actually made the first military move, most liberals felt obliged to support the war once it had begun. Nonetheless, the military humiliations of the war, its length and its cost, together with the hostility of most other great powers during the conflict, added to the already widespread feeling that Britain's day as a great economic and political force might be soon over.

Fears about Britain's long-term economic viability certainly reached a new pitch of intensity around 1900. The slow growth of exports, the decline of agriculture under free trade, and the rapid rise of manufactured imports in the 1890s meant a considerable widening of the balance of trade gap, stimulating a clamour for new markets, on the grounds that 'trade followed the flag', and for protection and for imperial consolidation. In some circles, the import gap was regarded as a clear sign that Britain was actually 'living off capital' and that when that capital was exhausted the country would be bankrupt and ruined.[8] This in turn prompted a response, led by such eminent figures as Sir George Giffen, the Board of Trade statistician, who estimated that the trade gap was not only filled by income from services—insurance, short-term credits, shipping—and from returns on foreign investment but that

---

[6] The Transvaal was also known as the South African Republic.

[7] The origins of the Boer War are examined in Ch. 8.

[8] 'The Author of "Drifting"' [Ellis Barker], 'The Defence of the Empire: An Open Letter to Lord Salisbury', *Contemporary Review*, 79 (1901); id., 'The Economic Decay of Great Britain', ibid. 79 (1901). Barker published a series of articles under the latter title in *CR* volumes 79 and 80.

we earned enough from these activities to ensure a handsome surplus on the balance of payments as a whole. Such evidence suggested that Britain was responding positively to international competition and that it was in good economic health.[9] Nonetheless, there was widespread unease about the rise of services, and of the City of London in particular, to such prominence, and fears about the long-term consequences of relying on foreign investments were as strong amongst pro-imperialists as they were amongst radicals. Perhaps inspired by the Hooley company-promotion scandals of the late 1890s,[10] there was much talk at the turn of the century about 'shareshufflers' and 'speculative financiers' who were 'parasitical' on industry and cosmopolitan (that is, Jewish) rather than patriotic.[11] Some on the right of politics also exhibited an obvious producer bias and some equated industry with Britishness and virtue as well as power.[12] Henry Birchenough, silk entrepreneur, Conservative Member of Parliament and a man of Chamberlainite sympathies, declared that 'the true business of an imperial people is production not finance. Money-finding may be a sign of prosperity but it may also be a sign of decadence.'[13] Benjamin Kidd was equally alarmed that the British had 'begun to be less of an industrial people and more of a people living by waiting on, and catering for, a rich and pleasure-seeking population'.[14] After 1903, Chamberlain's tariff reform movement owed some of its support to this strong feeling on the right of politics that free trade and foreign investment were together undermining the manufacturing and agricultural sectors that were the true sources of Britain's economic and military strength. Chamberlain himself feared that, in relying more

[9] Sir G. Giffen, 'Are We Living off Capital?' (1901), in his *Economic Inquiries and Studies* (1904); id., 'Our Trade Prosperity and the Outlook', *Economic Journal*, 10 (1900). Barker's statistics and conclusions were directly contested by H. Morgan-Browne, in 'But Are We Decaying?', and 'Is Great Britain Falling into Economic Decay?', *Contemporary Review*, 79 (1901), and ibid. 80 (1901); and by W. H. Mallock, 'The Alleged Economic Decay of Great Britain', *Monthly Review* (Sept. 1901).

[10] D. Kynaston, *The City of London: Golden Years, 1890–1914* (1995), 179–83.

[11] Barker, 'The Economic Decay of Great Britain', 637; W. S. Lilly, 'Collapse of England', *Fortnightly Review*, NS 72 (1902), 779; J. W. Cross, 'British Trade in 1898: A Warning Note', *Nineteenth Century*, 45 (1899), 854.

[12] Cross, 'British Trade in 1898', 854–6.

[13] H. Birchenough, 'Lord Rosebery on the Dangers to British Trade', *Nineteenth Century*, 48 (1900), 1069.

[14] B. Kidd, 'Imperial Policy and Free Trade', *Nineteenth Century*, 54 (1903), 40.

and more on services, many Britons were become wealthier but that the nation itself was becoming weaker and more vulnerable.

The sharpest intellect amongst the contemporary diagnosticians of financial imperialism is forgotten now and was only a shadowy figure even to his contemporaries to whom he presented himself under the apparently impenetrable disguise of 'Ritortus'.[15] Ritortus was proud of the British Empire, showing a Kiplingesque delight in the innate qualities of the English character and in English [*sic*] 'pluck'[16] which would not have been out of place in the contemporary *Daily Mail*. Yet he was hostile to the jingo strain in imperialism, sceptical even about the value of going to war in South Africa, and, via his command of international trade theory derived from John Stuart Mill and Robert Torrens, painted a more sophisticated picture of financial imperialism than even Hobson achieved and one which also brutally exposed the weakness in the position of those who advocated either free trade imperialism or imperial economic unity.

Like the tariff reformers a few years later, Ritortus believed that Britain's commercial and industrial supremacy had been carefully fostered by the state under a protectionist regime and that free trade only became a plausible option once that supremacy had been established. However, the acceptance of unilateral free trade had been a profound mistake because it had shifted the terms of trade against Britain, opened up its market to competition from abroad without reciprocity, and, by lowering profits, had stimulated the export of capital. This flow of capital overseas had built up the power of our rivals, particularly the United States. It had also engendered an economic imperialism which went far beyond the boundaries of constitutional empire: as his comments on Argentina's and China's relations with Britain showed, Ritortus had a remarkable understanding of the financial basis of what has been called in modern times 'informal empire' and 'the imperialism of free trade'.[17] Capital rather than trade was, he insisted, the basis of

[15] There appears to be no exact Latin equivalent: but *retortus* means 'twist round to face in the opposite direction' or 'reverse the course of', which would make sense in the context of Ritortus' argument, as readers will see.

[16] Ritortus, 'The Imperialism of British Trade—I', *Contemporary Review*, 76 (1899), 133.

[17] He was also well aware of the importance of British direct investment and the extent to which 'England is no longer a mere creditor who draws interest but also a landlord and a proprietor who draws rent and profits', though he exaggerated the

Britain's global domination, and 'this point is often forgotten by our modern Imperialists, who talk so grandiloquently of the extension of our Empire, and yet narrow its limits to the red lines on the world's map'.[18] But, in his opinion, the price paid for the invisible empire of finance was high. British capital abroad, in helping to open up new territory and bring it into the world economy, had now turned the terms of trade dramatically back in Britain's favour and led to a flow of cheap commodity imports in payment of interest and dividends. This flow had undermined British agriculture and made Britain much more strategically vulnerable than hitherto. Now, as Europe and America industrialized behind carefully erected tariff barriers of their own, the maintenance of a free trade–foreign investment regime meant that much of industry was also in danger of destruction.[19] Britain was becoming an economy dominated by services or, as Ritortus dramatized the matter, 'the balance of power removes from Manchester and Birmingham to St Swithins Lane and Lombard Street'.[20] He warned that

> The gain which the moneyed classes draw from their investments abroad, and the temporary golden rain which through them falls at present on that part of the community which is in their pay or ministers to their luxuries, cannot possibly last for ever, and cannot compensate us for the misfortune which will overtake us if we allow our great national industries to be sacrificed.[21]

Should this trend continue, Ritortus argued that Britain would suffer the fate of imperial Rome and lose the industrial capability and the power to hold on to the formal empire it had acquired over the centuries.[22]

Whereas Hobson, like other radicals, wanted to solve the problem of financial imperialism through social reform under free

extent of total British capital abroad, estimating it at £4–5 bn. whereas it only reached about £4 bn. in 1913 after a prolonged Edwardian boom ('The Imperialism of British Trade—I', 149, 152). For informal empire and free trade imperialism see J. Gallagher and R. E. Robinson, 'The Imperialism of Free Trade, 1815–1914', *Economic History Review* 2nd ser., 6 (1953–4).

[18] 'The Imperialism of British Trade—I', 145.
[19] Ritortus, 'The Imperialism of British Trade—II', *Contemporary Review*, 76 (1899), 286–92.
[20] 'The Imperialism of British Trade—I', 143.
[21] 'The Imperialism of British Trade—II', 285.
[22] Ibid. 295–7.

trade, Ritortus was a conservative in social policy, and despite being an old-fashioned believer in sound money and Gladstonian finance, deviated sharply from the classical liberal position by arguing that salvation lay in protection for domestic agriculture and industry. However, despite his stress on the importance of industry in maintaining both Britain's status as a great power and its internal cohesion, Ritortus had no faith in the movement for imperial economic unity. The supporters of Chamberlain looked to the possibility of creating a 'Greater British' industrial giant across the white empire: but Ritortus felt that Britain had little to gain from such a strategy and was sure that 'if we must get rid of the Manchester school we must certainly not replace it by a Birmingham school'.[23] Emerging Dominions such as Canada and Australia were heavily indebted to Britain and forced to sell their produce cheaply in British markets to pay their debts, thus undermining the prosperity of British agriculture. In order to amass the sterling to make the payments they also restricted their industrial imports from Britain through protection and encouraged import substitution, building up, in the process, industrial structures that would one day be directly competitive with the mother country's. Since the white empire's competition had helped to undermine the mother country's agricultural base and it would soon threaten its industry and would do little to halt the shift to finance and services, it should be subject to tariffs also.[24] In arguing in this manner, Ritortus was offering a form of 'Little England' imperialism based on 'pluck, enterprise and business capacity'[25] which differentiated him sharply from Chamberlain.[26]

RADICALISM IN WAR

In the run-up to the Boer War and during it, liberal protests were often carried on in language inherited from earlier struggles. For the aged Spencer, the war was one aspect of a revived imperialism that was leading to the 're-barbarization' of society.[27] John Morley,

---

[23] Ibid. 282–3.   [24] Ibid. 301–2.   [25] Ibid. 294.

[26] Ritortus was writing when Chamberlain's proposal for an imperial *Zollverein* was still on the table and before the latter switched to a policy of preference as from 1903. But his critique was equally effective against either policy.

[27] Peel, *Herbert Spencer*, 259–60; H. Spencer, *Facts and Comments* (1902), 112–33.

Cobden's spiritual heir, also carried into the South African war most of the ideas that had led him to support Gladstone against Disraeli in the 1870s.[28] Other veterans such as William Harcourt, a former Chancellor of the Exchequer, chiefly lamented that the expense of war would undermine the economic foundations of the Gladstonian state and jeopardize free trade.[29] Even more adventurous critics did not distinguish too clearly between finance and other forms of capitalist business as the villain of the piece; and many were still keen to load most of the blame on traditional elites. In some cases, 'pro-Boer' Liberals merely added financiers, almost casually, to a list of the usual suspects. In attacking the Liberal Imperialists in 1899, A. R. Wallace, MP and member of the South Africa Conciliation Committee, made the time-honoured claim that 'every triumph of expansionism is a rebuff to Democratic Liberalism. Expansionist Imperialism means more despotism abroad and more Aristocratic Recrudescence at home' and diverted attention from the need for domestic reform.[30] He also added that it let loose 'a thousand firms, financiers, adventurers and company promoters' but left the impression that the latter played a subordinate part.[31] Even L. T. Hobhouse, who had read Hobson's 1898 article and was instrumental in sending him to report on the South African crisis for the *Manchester Guardian*,[32] was still writing in 1899 in mainly Spencerian terms of a return to militarism. He did, however, mark out the 'commercial Jingo' and the 'investing Jingo' as pushing for expansion and went on to argue that British governments in conquered lands like Egypt were often no more than debt-collecting agencies for financiers and investors.[33]

Other analyses which extended traditional radical discourses on imperial expansion emphasized industry as much as finance. G. H. Perris, the crusading liberal journalist and peace campaigner was

---

[28] Hamer, *John Morley: Liberal Intellectual in Politics* (1968), 310–28.

[29] Porter, *Critics of Empire*, 84–7.

[30] A. R. Wallace, 'The Seamy Side of Imperialism', *Nineteenth Century*, 75 (1899), 799.

[31] Ibid. 792. For a similar approach see the speeches of the radical MP F. A. Channing as reported in S. Maccoby (ed.), *The Radical Tradition, 1763–1914* (1952), 213–14.

[32] P. M. Krebs, *Gender, Race and the Writing of Empire: Public Discourse and the Boer War* (Cambridge, 1999), 23.

[33] L. T. Hobhouse, 'The Foreign Policy of Collectivism', *Economic Review*, 9 (1899), 203–4, 208. For a similar analysis see A. J. Wilson, 'The Art of Living on Capital', *Contemporary Review*, 75 (1899), 870.

much more inclined to blame the former for imperialism though it is not clear whether he was including commerce and services in his indictment. He claimed that industry had once promised to abolish privilege but had become 'plutocratic' and was now allied with aristocracy against democracy. We were, he declared, at 'the definite transition point between feudalism and industrialism'.[34] Desperate to avoid attack on its privileges at home, property had turned to imperialism which fostered an armed peace good for the armaments business and which brought new conquests where capital could be a law unto itself. Empire was 'a dumping ground for the greedy plutocrats, the decrepit aristocracy, the parasitic official and military classes who feel their supremacy in British life gradually slipping away'.[35] And he went on to warn that 'Caesarism and Plutocracy abroad mean Caesarism and Plutocracy at home'.[36] Industry had turned predator and, together with aristocracy, was intent on a new career of plunder. William Clarke appeared to agree with Perris. He reiterated the standard view that industrialism was vital to liberalism and to the progress of democracy: but went on to say that, with the rise of big business, 'it is quite conceivable that the industrial movement which determines our political evolution may draw society into the clutches of an oligarchy'[37] intent on imperialist exploitation which would destroy both liberalism and democracy.

The most comprehensive radical analysis of imperialism in the run-up to the Boer War was made by J. M. Robertson, Hobson's colleague and friend. Robertson's work betrays some of the uncertainties among radicals about the capitalist origins of imperialism. Though he felt that the economic pressures behind imperialism were growing stronger by the year, Robertson believed that 'the passion for nation and race'[38] was still the chief motive for imperialism as it had been in Disraeli's day, and that these psychological drives reinforced the power of aristocracy and militarism. The end result was 'to set up unity for [the] clashing classes of parasite and drudge by making them collectively parasitic upon other communities'.[39]

---

[34] G. H. Perris, 'The New Internationalism', in S. Coit (ed.), *Ethical Democracy* (London, 1900), 47.

[35] Ibid. 55.   [36] Ibid. 58.

[37] W. Clarke, 'The Social Future of England', *Contemporary Review*, 78 (1899), 658.

[38] J. M. Robertson, *Patriotism and Empire* (1898), 173.

[39] Ibid. 148.

The notion of parasitism, which Hobson had himself used in 1897, ran all through the book with finance emphatically linked to it.[40] Robertson came near to a financial theory of imperialism when he claimed that 'imperial expansion is substantially a device on the part of the moneyed class primarily to further their own chances secondarily to put off the day of reckoning between capital and labour'.[41] But he had spoken earlier of the 'primary desire of the commercial classes to buy cheap and sell dear'[42] as the main motive for imperialism, and also argued that 'the only interests really furthered by fresh expansion are those of the speculative capitalist class, the military and naval services, the industrial class which supplies war material, and generally those who look to an imperial civil service as a means of employment for themselves and their kin'.[43] In Robertson's analysis, finance was very prominent in the discussion but it did not bear quite the weight of responsibility for imperialism that Hobson had accorded it in 1898 or the weight that the latter was to place on it in his work in 1899–1901.

From 'Ethical World' to 'The War in South Africa'

Hobson's visit to South Africa in the summer of 1899 was certainly very important in colouring his views and also gave him the means to add politics and personalities to the rather abstract approach to imperialism he had adopted in 1898. Yet the line of argument he adopted in his writings on South Africa was already evident earlier in that year in articles written while he was still actively editing *Ethical World*. Commenting on the recent occupation of the Sudan and the Anglo-French crisis on the Nile at Fashoda which followed it, he claimed that Rhodes's scheme for a Cape to Cairo railway was 'the animating motive of our movement to Khartoum' and that the British government was in danger of becoming 'the catspaw of financial schemers' who wished to use it 'to fleece the public'. He also accused Rhodes of using expansion as a means of finding

---

[40] Robertson had used the word earlier in his career. See *The Fallacy of Saving* (1892), 125. For a detailed analysis of its use by Hobson, see Ch. 5 *infra*.

[41] *Patriotism and Empire*, 188. Cf. the claim that 'the investing and exporting interests at present rule our counsels' (185).

[42] Ibid. 177.   [43] Ibid. 187.

cheap labour to be enslaved in South African mines.[44] Soon after, he poured scorn on Kipling's 'White Man's Burden', pronouncing the latter's claim that imperialism was not essentially about gain as 'simply one of those stupendous feats of mendacity which seek credence by staggering the critical faculties of the reader'. Taking Egypt as a representative case of expansion, he admitted that British rule had done some good there but argued that even the government which occupied Egypt in 1882 had admitted to the primacy of strategic motives—the defence of Suez and India—in determining the occupation. Hobson dismissed this explanation as a fiction since the Cape route was the key to Indian security: 'the actual impelling force [was] the interest of investors in Egypt, who, having put their money in a risky enterprise, desired to use the power and the money of the public to protect them against these very risks, and to make their private ventures securely profitable.' And such imperialism if unchecked led on to autocracy, to 'the dominance of militarism, financial magnates and a small inner cabinet'.[45] The editors of *Ethical World* also lambasted Rosebery for spending his time at the races with Cecil Rhodes and Leopold Rothschild, arguing that he was bound to be corrupted by the company of 'financial Jews and the filibustering speculators of South Africa'.[46] They went on to claim that 'the growing influence of financiers in foreign politics is notorious' and 'a great source of danger' and that 'a statesman, who is suspected of being in very great intimacy with financiers is, as a matter of fact, prejudicing his reputation for political impartiality'. But they could not offer concrete proof of the connection between finance and imperialism and their protest, in response to readers' complaints, that the emphasis on Jews simply reflected their importance in international finance and was not anti-Semitic does not read very convincingly.[47] Hobson said nothing at this time about underconsumption or the relation between the domestic economy and imperialism and his position in these articles was not greatly different from that of many other Liberals scandalized by Rhodes's

[44] J. A. Hobson, 'What Peace?', *Ethical World*, 28 Jan. 1899, p. 51.
[45] J. A. Hobson, ' "The White Man's Burden" ', ibid., 18 Feb. 1899, p. 105.
[46] Leading article, ibid., 27 May 1899, p. 323.
[47] See the letters from readers under the headings 'Jewish Financiers' and 'Financial Jews', and the editors' responses, ibid., 3 June 1899, p. 350; 10 June 1899, p. 366. See also J. Allett, 'New Liberalism, Old Prejudices: J. A. Hobson and the "Jewish Question" ', *Jewish Social Studies*, 49 (1987).

actions in South Africa and the rather abject failure of Parliament to bring him to book.[48]

Hobson's experience as a journalist in South Africa in the summer of 1899 simply gave additional confirmation to what had already become a settled conviction.[49] In justifying a forward policy against the Boer republics of the Transvaal and the Orange Free State, the British government claimed to be acting to defend the political rights of the unenfranchised non-Boer immigrants and, more generally, to be upholding the cause of civilization against Boer obscurantism, inefficiency, and abuse of human rights. There were also widespread fears that the Boer republics were determined to use the power given them by mining revenues to overturn British supremacy in the region. In his travels in South Africa, Hobson concluded that the immigrants or 'Uitlanders' were uninterested in getting the vote; that the fear of a Boer takeover was unfounded; and that, while the government of the Transvaal was backward and sometimes oppressive, its shortcomings were wildly exaggerated and that, left to themselves, the Boers would eventually come to terms with modernity. On his return, and when the war had broken out, he once again accused Rhodes of plotting 'to use the armed forces of the British Crown and the money of the British taxpayer to obtain for himself and his fellow capitalists . . . political control of the Transvaal' with the aim of changing policies on African labour, customs duties, mineral rights, railway rates, and many other matters, in order to raise the profits of mining capitalism.[50] What South Africa added to his experience was, first, a strong sense of the international, cosmopolitan nature of financial capitalism. He claimed that 'there is good reason to suppose that the French and German holdings, taken together, largely outweigh the English interest in Rand mines'.[51] Moreover most of this foreign interest was Jewish in origin. Whilst he protested against the 'ignominious passion of Judenhetze' he felt it important to point out that the South African economy as a whole was dominated by 'a class of financial capitalists of which the foreign Jew must be taken as the leading type' and they were the most powerful element in the series of interlocking directorships through which the mines were

[48] J. Butler, *The Liberal Party and the Jameson Raid* (Oxford, 1968).
[49] I agree here with Allett, *New Liberalism*, 26, 131.
[50] Hobson, *The War in South Africa*, 196, 207.
[51] Ibid. 193.

controlled.[52] The future of the Transvaal was, therefore, in the hands of 'this small ring of financial foreigners' who would 'simply add to their other businesses the business of politics'. Hobson drew the ironic lesson:

We are fighting in order to place a small international oligarchy of mine-owners and speculators in power in Pretoria. Englishmen will surely do well to recognise that the economic and political destinies of South Africa are and seem likely to remain, in the hands of men most of whom are foreigners by origin, whose trade is finance, and whose trade interest is not British.[53]

Secondly, Hobson also became convinced that the mine owners owed a critical part of their success to the fact that they controlled the South African press and that they could thus ensure that the British press also disseminated their views.[54] He also endowed the mining capitalists with an unusual capacity for clear-sighted action as well as ultimate control of policy:

If this war can be successfully accomplished and a 'settlement' satisfactory to the mine owners can be reached, the first fruits of victory will be represented in a large, cheap, submissive supply of black and white labour, attended with such other economies of 'costs' as will add millions per annum to the profits of the mines. The men who, owning the South African press and political organisations, engineered the agitation which has issued in this war, are the same men whose pockets will swell with this increase; open-eyed and persistent they have pursued their course, plunging South Africa into temporary ruin in order that they may emerge victorious, a small confederacy of international mineowners and speculators holding the treasures of South Africa in the hollow of their hands.[55]

Writing soon after his return, Hobson's analysis followed that laid out in *The War in South Africa* but extended the political dimension of the argument. Now he claimed that Rhodes had entered politics to enhance his financial interests and had sometimes opposed the extension of British imperial power when he felt his own position was threatened. On the other hand, he admitted that Rhodes had developed wider ambitions though he was unwilling to grant them too much influence on policy.

[52] Ibid. 189–92.   [53] Ibid. 196–7.

[54] Ibid. 110–16. The idea that the press was used by interested parties to deliberately inflame imperialist passions was hardly new. See Clarke, 'The Genesis of Jingoism', 115, for a recent example. Cobden had recognized the power of the press in encouraging support for Palmerstonianism in the 1850s.

[55] *The War in South Africa*, 240.

I am very far from believing that Mr. Rhodes has been moved exclusively or chiefly by financial considerations in his politics: it is quite likely that some large, indefinite desire to express his personality in what is termed 'empire building' may have fused with, and at times overpowered, the narrower financial aims. But two facts stand out clearly in his career: first, that he and his confederates have systematically used politics to assist their business projects; second, that in politics they have adopted 'Imperialism' as a last resort.[56]

Hobson was convinced that the Transvaal government had good reason to arm itself after the Jameson Raid, which wrecked any immediate possibility of liberal reform in the republic, confirmed Kruger as President, and gave new life to 'the blind, fanatical obstruction of the old Boer party'.[57] Indeed, he was convinced that the Raid had sabotaged 'the peaceful competition of social ideas, customs, languages, which was readily assimilating the two peoples in the Colonies' and which 'brought home a genuine identity of interests and the need of growing federation of states, for economic and social, if not for definitely political purposes'.[58] The Transvaal's suspicion of British intentions was inevitably confirmed by High Commissioner Milner's bellicosity. Milner had strong imperialist views of his own but he 'fell quickly under the control of politicians, financiers and journalists whom [the Transvaal government] knew to be their enemies'.[59] Milner, he believed, had been 'the easy instrument of political partizans and business men whom he has thought to use for purposes of information but who have used him for more practical purposes'.[60] Similarly, Chamberlain 'possibly imagined himself a free agent' but was in practice the 'instrument' of South African finance.[61]

In 1900, Hobson made some important steps forward in generalizing from recent events, arguing that 'the full significance of this evil business in South Africa is only understood when it is recognised as a most dramatic instance of the play of modern forces which are worldwide in their scope and revolutionary in their

---

[56] J. A. Hobson, 'Capitalism and Imperialism in South Africa', *Contemporary Review*, 77 (1900), 7; repr. in *Hobson: Writings on Imperialism and Internationalism*, ed. Cain.

[57] Ibid. 13–14.

[58] J. A. Hobson, 'The Inevitable in Politics—II', *Ethical World*, 15 Sept. 1900, p. 580.

[59] 'Capitalism and Imperialism in South Africa', 14.

[60] J. A. Hobson, 'The Pro-consulate of Milner', *Contemporary Review*, 78 (1900), 553.

[61] 'Capitalism and Imperialism in South Africa', 16.

operations' and as the result of the 'interplay of two sets of forces
. . . International Capitalism and Imperialism'. He argued that the
rise of foreign investment was transforming international politics:

The growing tendency of modern civilised communities to stake large
portions of their property in foreign lands runs counter to all past traditions of nationalism, and sets up an antagonism between the political and
economic structures of the modern world. As long as the intercourse
between nations was wholly or chiefly confined to trade or exchange of
commodities, nationalism could still express the economic as well as the
political status of the citizen. But the large establishment by members and
classes belonging to one nation of permanent investments of capital in
another country is a patent breach of the old order, destroying the very
roots of the national sentiments.

In theory, national governments could simply repudiate all responsibility for the fortunes of their investors overseas; in practice, they
were under heavy pressure to bring these expanding economic interests under their political control. The latter was difficult to avoid
because investors 'have often secured the protection of the British
State by screening themselves behind the more consistently admitted
rights of British subjects to personal protection against dangers and
grievances incurred in foreign countries'. Of course, investments in
'powerful civilised states' such as the United States could hardly
prompt imperialism: it was in 'small, decadent, or new countries'
that financial imperialism was possible. These included 'Turkey,
Egypt, China, the South American States' besides South Africa.[62]
Hobson admitted that the stress on financial capitalism was over-
simplified: 'no play of historic forces is so simple as this has been
represented to be.' Imperialism was driven by high motives in some
cases such as the desire to civilize and to spread Christianity.
Nonetheless, the justification for such abstraction from reality was
that finance, 'though it never acts alone, is the most powerful
guiding force, co-operating with and moulding for its own purpose
other weaker forces with purer, but less definite aims'. And around
'this nucleus of economic forces' other economic interests gathered:
industries that benefited from the arms trade; exporters who
believed the 'fallacious' idea that trade follows the flag; professional
men looking for careers in the public services.[63]

[62] Ibid. 1–3.
[63] Ibid. All quotes are from 15–17.

It is noticeable, however, that Hobson did not mention the connection between underconsumption and foreign investment at this time and his stress on the evils of finance could be assimilated easily enough into the broad current of opposition to the Boer War amongst 'Little Englanders'. His experiences in South Africa dovetailed neatly with the thinking of F. W. Hirst, a fervent anti-imperialist in the Cobden–Gladstone tradition who later became editor of *The Economist*, and the writer who came closest to Hobson in isolating finance as the *causa causans* of the Boer War. What chiefly concerned Hirst was the collapse of Gladstonian finance as a result of expenditure on the war which, he believed, redounded to the benefit of the City of London and its cosmopolitan financial connections. He had read Hobson's *War in South Africa* and had no hesitation in branding the war an episode in 'Financial Imperialism' which was 'impure, corrupt and degrading'.[64] The financiers of South Africa had fooled the British government into acting on their behalf, he declared: 'ministers are a row of puppets and a board of international financiers sitting in Paris or Berlin or London pull the wires'.[65] Empire policy was being dictated 'by foreigners for foreigners' and, following in Hobson's footsteps, Hirst's analysis also took a frankly anti-Semitic turn when he suggested that the changing fortunes of war caused fluctuations in London securities and that the effects 'reverberate in every synagogue of Europe and America'.[66] He also took from Hobson the view that South African finance controlled the press and had used it to incite jingoistic passions.[67] Like many other radicals, Hirst poured scorn on the idea that Britain needed new export markets or that the markets made available by imperialism could possibly justify the huge cost of acquiring them.[68] He did recognize the interests of the armaments trade, however, and went on to suggest that some of the richer manufacturers, those who had given up active management in the new, large, joint stock enterprises which provided their incomes, had lost touch with their roots and were mistakenly following the imperialist trail:

The sons of the shrewd manufacturers who followed Cobden are sleeping partners in limited companies and supporters of Mr. Chamberlain. Their

---

[64] F. W. Hirst, 'Imperialism and Finance', in *Liberalism and the Empire* (1900), 63. Cf. 43.
[65] Ibid. 59.   [66] Ibid. 44. Cf. 30.   [67] Ibid. 63 ff.
[68] Ibid. 72–4. Cf. Robertson, *Patriotism and Empire*, 174–9.

concerns are controlled by managing clerks. Useless in their industrial sleep, they are dangerous in their political dreams. They will wake up with a shock to find that the vulgar idols of Imperialism have ruined their fortunes without improving their stations.[69]

Hirst went on to insist that 'vast fortunes accumulated by monopoly and stockjobbing arouse hatred, malice and disgust. Riches so acquired are seldom usefully employed.' Like many anti-war protestors of provincial background (his father had made his money in Yorkshire wool) Hirst automatically associated finance with speculation, gambling, luxury, and corruption.[70] And in his hatred of the emerging plutocracy, 'a rule of rich men and their instruments', he was, like Hobson, registering the claim that a new class of financiers now had a determining influence on policy. But in warning of a revival of aristocracy, he was also linking new enemies with more traditional ones and with an earlier radical-liberal discourse.[71]

Hobson's *War in South Africa* undoubtedly played a part in confirming the suspicions of many radicals that the war was being fought at the behest of 'alien financiers' who had hijacked the British state to serve their purposes. Such notions became a commonplace among 'pro-Boer' Liberals such as G. K. Chesterton, a frequent writer for the *Speaker*, and Hilaire Belloc.[72] Under Hobson's influence, it was echoed by Christian Socialists such as Scott Holland for whom the South African conflict was 'a sinister capitalist plot, engineered by international mining interests', an example of 'fat City men gone mad'.[73] The Labour party's anti-war activists like John Burns, Hardie, and Carpenter also used Hobsonian arguments though it must be said that trade unionists opposed to the war were mainly concerned that mine owners' control of black labour would lead to a fall in employment and wages for white workers.[74]

---

[69] Hirst, 'Imperialism and Finance', 75.

[70] See H. J. Ogden, *The War against the Dutch Republics in South Africa: Its Origins, Progress and Results* (Manchester, 1901), 72–3.

[71] Hirst, 'Imperialism and Finance', 113–14.

[72] M. Ward, *Gilbert Keith Chesterton* (1944), 119; J. P. McCarthy, *Hilaire Belloc: Edwardian Radical* (1978), 61–3.

[73] P. D. Jones, *The Christian Socialist Revival, 1877–1914: Religion, Class and Social Conscience in Late Victorian England* (Princeton, 1980), 199–205.

[74] S. Koss, *The Pro-Boers* (Chicago, 1973), 55–7, 94–5. Ogden, *The War against the Dutch Republics*, 79–93; Porter, *Critics of Empire*, 103–4, 126–34. Porter highlights the frequent use of Hobson's *War in South Africa* by the Labour press.

J. L. Hammond, a passionate Gladstonian and future historian of
the British working class,[75] also brandished Hobson's *War in South
Africa* as an authority in claiming that South Africa was run by
'a motley group of marauding financiers who measure civilisation by their fortunes, and select their fatherland as others select
their banks' and who, 'having no patriotism of their own . . . make
it their business to exploit the patriotism of others'.[76] Campbell-
Bannerman, the Liberal party leader, recognized that those in his
party opposed to the war were largely divided between a group
who attributed the outbreak of war to bungled diplomacy by Milner
and Chamberlain and another who saw it as 'a scandalous plot of
money-seekers using the British Government as a catspaw backed
by the pure Jingo piratical spirit'.[77] Even the veteran radical
Goldwin Smith was won over to the financial explanation. Writing
during the war, he was sure that the mining capitalists were respon-
sible for it and that 'Rhodes was the soul of the whole business'.[78]
Looking at the imperial process in general, he wrote of British policy
as 'impelled not more by the lust of empire than by commercial
greed' and of a 'party of Imperial aggrandizement in alliance with
the craving of capital for new markets'.[79] His analysis also had a
marked anti-Jewish flavour.[80] Also, although Shaw's *Fabianism and
the Empire* (1900) sided with the pro-imperialists in that he believed
that expansion was inevitable given great power competition, there
was a considerable minority within the Fabian Society, led by S. G.
Hobson, who wanted to condemn outright the 'Imperialism of
Capitalism' in South Africa. Shaw dealt with this by demanding
state control of the mining industry to prevent it from becoming
'a prey of commercial speculators of all nations and races'. He also
warned that if Britain did not adopt Fabian socialism and left
development to market forces it would export too much capital
and take to living as a parasite off the work of less developed
nations. 'Already our imports exceed our exports . . . and the day is
coming when it will be possible for all England to live barrenly on

[75] On Hammond, see Clarke, *Liberals and Social Democrats*, 74 ff.

[76] J. L. Hammond, 'Colonial and Foreign Policy', in *Liberalism and the Empire*,
184, 191.

[77] J. S. Galbraith, 'The Pamphlet Campaign on the Boer War', *Journal of Modern
History*, 24 (1952), 118–19.

[78] Goldwin Smith, *In the Court of History: An Apology for Canadians who are
Opposed to the Boer War* (1902), 26.

[79] Ibid. 8, 61.   [80] Ibid. 66–7.

unpaid-for imports representing rent, dividends and tribute from without, as it was for Rome, or as it is for Eastbourne at present'.[81]

'THE PSYCHOLOGY OF JINGOISM'

Once back in England, Hobson spent a great deal of his time explaining how it was that that this small knot of financiers could influence British policy in their favour. In *The War in South Africa*, Hobson pointed to the 'all-important' role of the press.[82] The British press was only partly under the direct control of the South African mining magnates but the rest depended for their copy on South African newspapers owned by financial capitalists. It was the press, he believed, that had convinced the British public of a Boer conspiracy to throw Britain out of South Africa, of the supposed inefficiency of the Transvaal government, and of the legitimacy of the grievances of the Uitlanders, all of which Hobson thought was manifestly nonsense.[83] The result was that 'the powerful English press of South Africa, thus owned and controlled by closest financial bonds succeeded first in inflaming the public in South Africa and afterwards in communicating the passion to the minds of the British public'.[84] Hobson frankly recognized that the press in the Transvaal and in the Orange Free State, the smaller Afrikaner state, was equally under the thumb of their governments and that the aims of the mine owners had been materially aided by the 'stupid Jingoism of the British public'.[85] What he failed to note was that,

[81] G. B. S. Shaw, *Fabianism and the Empire* (1900), 53. On Fabian imperialism see A. M. McBriar, *Fabian Socialism and English Politics*, 119–25, 130; and Porter, *Critics of Empire*, 109–22.

[82] One should note that journalists have a natural tendency to boost the importance of their own trade and Hobson may well have been influenced by this consideration at least subconsciously. I do, however, generally subscribe to the view that the press had a critical role to play in activating popular support for the war. See Krebs, *Gender, Race and the Writing of Empire*, ch. 1.

[83] *The War in South Africa*, 206–8.

[84] Ibid. 227.

[85] Ibid. 217. He recognized later that the press of Holland, where there was intense sympathy for the plight of their Dutch cousins in South Africa, was similarly biased. J. A. Hobson, *The Psychology of Jingoism* (1901), 107. For studies of the press during the war, see Krebs, *Gender, Race and the Writing of Empire* and H. J. Field, *Towards a Programme of Imperial Life: The British Empire at the Turn of the Century* (Oxford, 1982), esp. chs. 4 and 5, which has a brilliant portrait of the flag-waving journalism of G. W. Steevens of the *Daily Mail*. See also A. J. Lee,

even though they continued to support the imperial cause, most newspapers became increasingly critical of the management of the war and that an elite newspaper like *The Times* often felt obliged to give coverage to pro-Boer opinions despite its own vigorous support for the annexation of the Boer republics.[86]

Hobson had been interested for some time in trying to understand the roots of the imperial fervour that gripped the nation before and during the war. In articles written for *Ethical World* before he visited South Africa he had investigated two leading ideas, those of 'Destiny' and 'Mission', which informed much imperial propaganda. Destiny, as in the notion of 'manifest destiny' invented in America, was often invoked as an excuse for expansion and it had the advantage of absolving a nation from guilt feelings. But it also implied inevitability, itself an uncomfortable idea, and was often supplemented by the, implicitly contradictory, one of Mission which suggested choice. Mission was a powerful guiding notion in imperialist countries. 'For certain sections of modern peoples the idea of a collective duty of a nation to aid the civilisation of the world has assumed a real validity.'[87] After his return from South Africa, he used the work of the Frenchman Desmolins, to illustrate how ideas such as these could be used to justify expansion illegitimately.[88] Desmolins had cloaked destiny in Darwinian garb when arguing that, because the British were racially superior to the Boers, the extension of British power into the Transvaal was inevitable and empire justified. Hobson described this as 'a formula which relieves him of the necessity of even touching in a single page any of the actual concrete issues that have arisen between the Transvaal and Great Britain' and went on to show how Desmolins's approach justified, as an inevitable law of the universe, any amount of horror inflicted and gave Britons an excuse not to face up to the fact that the war had begun because they had willed it so.[89] Similarly, Hobson

'The Radical Press', in A. J. A. Morris (ed.), *Edwardian Radicalism, 1900–1914: Some Aspects of British Radicalism* (1974).

[86] See J. Beaumont Hughes, 'The Press and the Public during the Boer War 1899–1902', *Historian*, 61 (1999).

[87] J. A. Hobson. 'Issues of Empire', *Ethical World*, 1 July 1899, pp. 404–5; 8 July 1899, pp. 419–20.

[88] M. Desmolins, *Boers or English: Who are in the Right?* (1900).

[89] 'The Inevitable in Politics—II', *Ethical World*, 8 Sept 1900, p. 580. Religious leaders who opposed the war or the imperial project in general were few in number. See G. Cuthbertson, 'Preaching Imperialism: Wesleyan Methodism and the War', in Omissi and Thompson (eds.), *The Impact of the South African War*.

castigated those churchmen who defended and even exulted in the war. Hobson put this down to the predominance of Old Testament notions rather than those derived from the gentler teachings of Jesus. Beating the Boers was a sacred duty that became mixed with the long-held notion that the British Empire was God's chosen instrument and Britain a modern Israel. This in its turn was often transmuted into the vaguer idea of a 'Providence' who watched over Britain and which even decreed that British power should be spread as far as possible, an idea even the ultra-cautious Lord Salisbury was not averse to uttering.[90]

Behind these relatively sophisticated ideas lay more basic and frightening emotions summed up in the word 'jingoism' or mob enthusiasm for imperial war and expansion. Using the work of the French sociologist Gustave le Bon,[91] Hobson saw jingoism as 'primitive passion, modified and intensified by certain conditions of modern civilisation'.[92] It was given particular virulence in modern times, he thought, by the mass urban civilization he had, as we have seen,[93] long distrusted. Like other reform-minded liberals,[94] Hobson was convinced that modern town life, besides spawning the degenerate underemployed population who were the usual targets of jingoistic propaganda, also lowered vitality generally through repetitive machine work. It increased nervous strain and produced weak characters who were almost infinitely suggestible and desperate for sensation and excitement, whether it was provided by a football match or an imperial war.[95] It was the perfect setting for the emergence of the 'mob mind' with its 'lust for race domination' which could overcome even education and intelligence and led people to hate, and to wish to destroy, peoples with whom they could have no serious quarrel in everyday life. It was essentially 'the passion of the spectator, the inciter, the backer, not the fighter',[96] but it could be put to good use by those for whom war

---

[90] *The Psychology of Jingoism*, 41–62.

[91] Le Bon's fluence on Hobson in discussed by Freeden, 'Hobson's Evolving Conceptions of Human Nature', 60–2; J. A. Hobson, 'The Psychology of the War Spirit', *Ethical World*, 9 Dec. 1899, p. 769.

[92] *The Psychology of Jingoism*, 2, 12.

[93] See *supra*, Ch. 2.

[94] See the remarkably similar analysis of urban man provided in C. F. G. Masterman (ed.), *The Heart of the Empire* (1901), 4 ff.

[95] *The Psychology of Jingoism*, 6–8.

[96] Ibid. 9.

and imperialism was a profitable business. In arguing thus, Hobson was following in the footsteps of Max Nordau who had recently argued that the pace and frenzy of modern life was destroying both bodily and mental health. But there is also no doubt that, like Masterman, who took an equally dim view of urban man, Hobson was building on a tradition of radical thinking about the dangers of an alliance between the rich and 'the mob'.[97]

Indeed, what primarily interested Hobson about all these ideas and emotions, whether primitive or sophisticated, was that they could be used to serve economic interests of a sinister kind. He noted, for example, how some commercial men professed Christian motives in trade in order to make their activities more acceptable.[98] What was more important, however, was how imperialist and warlike impulses could be harnessed by financiers with an interest in extending the frontiers of British control abroad. The press was the critical agent. For the average citizen with a limited education, 'the appearance of hard truth imparted by the mechanical rigidity of print possesses a degree of credit which, when the statement is repeated with sufficient frequency, becomes well nigh absolute', and the 'terse, dogmatic, unqualified, and unverifiable cablegram is the most potent form of this emotional explosive'.[99] Even 'educated Jingoes', those with beliefs in the civilizing mission or the justice of Britain's cause in South Africa, believed what they read in their particular newspaper.[100] Hobson then laid out in more detail how the financier-dominated South African press was the key source of information about the war for most British newspapers. He also charged financiers with the crime of splitting the Liberal party, describing how they had 'visibly corrupted' the *Daily News*, a prominent British liberal paper, 'and reduced to Jingoism a large section of Liberals throughout the country, breaking the party of effective criticism of Government policy in parliament and in the country'.[101] The result was that anti-

---

[97] Pick, *Faces of Degeneration*, 24–5, 222–3; Stedman Jones, *Outcast London*, 151; Masterman, *The Heart of the Empire*, 7–9. For radical thinking in the 1870s, see *supra*, Ch. 3.

[98] *The Psychology of Jingoism*, 55.

[99] Ibid. 10–11.

[100] Ibid. 100. A little later, however, Hobson accused them of knowing rather more than this but refusing to make the effort to educate themselves properly (pp. 101–2).

[101] Ibid. 114.

war sentiment had been largely suppressed and 'mineowners and politicians . . . have succeeded in impressing the public mind with the idea of this conflict as a "sacred war" undertaken in the interests of Christianity and civilisation'. Patriotism was a screen behind which businessmen worked, 'seeking their private gain under the name and pretext of the commonwealth',[102] using honestly held moral ideas for immoral purposes. Hobson was convinced that the manipulation of the press had made imperialism so popular that even so-called independent newspapers were forced to toe the line for fear that opposition would lead to the withdrawal of vital advertising revenue.[103]

The Emergence of 'Imperialism: A Study', 1901–1902

Hobson did not finally bring together the skeleton outline of his economic theory as first presented in 1898 and his subsequent journalistic and political experiences until late in 1901. Then he wrote the series of six articles for the *Speaker* that, together with an article printed in the *Contemporary Review* early in 1902, became, with some important additions and corrections, the bulk of the matter printed in Part I of *Imperialism: A Study* under the title 'The Economics of Imperialism'. However, in *Imperialism* the argument was contained within an overarching framework emphasizing the burgeoning conflict between nationalism and imperialism, which he had already highlighted in 1900, and was one that had strong affinities with earlier radical thinking. He declared that the main foundation of human progress amongst advanced nations in the early nineteenth century had been nationalism defined, using J. S. Mill's criteria, as unity based on race, descent, geographical propinquity, and, above all, a shared history. Colonialism, the spread of nationality abroad through settlement, as in the case of

---

[102] Hobson had taken this phrase from Sir Thomas More's *Utopia* and had also used it at the end of 'Free Trade and Foreign Policy', 178.

[103] *Imperialism: A Study*, 216. Most of the Liberal press was in favour of the war except the *Manchester Guardian*. The *Daily News* was captured for the 'pro-Boer' cause in 1901. Koss, *The Pro-Boers*, p. xxx.

Australia or Canada, was a legitimate extension of nationalism. Moreover, nationalism in that form was 'a plain highway to internationalism'. A 'true strong internationalism in form and spirit would . . . imply the existence of powerful, self-respecting nationalities which seek union on the basis of common national needs and interests'. Trade was one of the most important of these common interests and Cobdenites had recognized free trade as a means to the 'quick growth of effective, informal internationalism by peaceful, profitable intercommunication of goods and ideas among nations recognising a just harmony of interests in free peoples'. The growth of imperialism had blasted these hopes. Imperialism, now the chief policy aim of all the great powers, was a debased form of nationalism. It encouraged territorial expansion beyond the natural boundaries of a healthy nationalism, fostered antagonism between nations, and threatened the peace and progress of the whole world. His intention in the rest of the book was, he declared, to lay bare the economic foundations of this 'anarchic cosmopolitanism' and its ideological support system.[104] Hobson followed this with a geographical survey of world empires which illustrated the rapid expansion of British, European, and American control over Africa and Asia since 1870 and particularly since the mid-1880s. All the territory occupied was in tropical or subtropical areas where extensive white settlement was not possible and where the native population was 'incapable of exercising any considerable rights of self-government, in politics or industry'.[105] In the list of territories acquired by Britain he included some not technically part of the Queen's dominions, such as Egypt, thus indicating that economic imperialism sometimes overstepped the bounds of formal empire.[106]

Chapter 2 of Part I of *Imperialism* was a revised and extended version of the first of the *Speaker* articles, 'The Commercial Value of Imperialism'. The original article was designed to counter two imperialist claims: that expanding foreign trade was vital to the economic health of the nation and that imperialism was necessary to ensure trade expansion.[107] The main counter-claim was that

[104] *Imperialism* (1988 edn.), 3–13. All references in the chapter are to this edition unless otherwise stated.

[105] Ibid. 15–27. Quote at p. 27.   [106] Ibid. 17.

[107] J. A. Hobson, 'The Commercial Value of Imperialism', *Speaker*, 2 Nov. 1901, pp. 124–6.

foreign and colonial trade 'plays a very small part in furnishing the income of the nation'. He came to this conclusion by assuming that only the profits from overseas trade represented value added, calculating them as equivalent to one-fortieth of national income. Hobson then produced a table showing that the money value of external trade per head was slightly lower in the late 1890s than it had been in the 1870s and went on to make the stronger claim that internal trade had developed faster than overseas trade in both volume and value in that period.[108] He also denied that trade followed the flag: the share of the empire in British trade at the end of the century was, he declared, less than that of the much smaller empire of the mid-nineteenth century.[109] Moreover, within the empire, growth in trade with 'our genuine colonies' such as Canada, Australasia, and the Cape Colony had been much stronger than with the dependencies, especially those in Africa and Asia which had been acquired under the 'new Imperialism'. Hobson admitted that Egypt 'yields a trade of some magnitude': but trade with the rest, especially those acquired from the mid-1880s onwards, was worth less than £10 million altogether. It was 'the smallest, least progressive and most fluctuating in quality, while it is the lowest in the character of the goods which it embraces'.[110]

Chapter 2 of the first edition of *Imperialism* reproduced most of this with some minor changes and additions to the statistics, but the original was also expanded in ways which complicated and, to some extent, undermined the argument. A reader in the columns of the *Speaker* attacked Hobson's claim that the value of foreign trade arose only from the profits earned. In response, Hobson reinforced his position by arguing that most of the goods entering overseas trade could be sold at home: consequently the true value of the former was its greater profitability and it was not essential to prosperity. This argument, along with an estimate of the profits on external trade as £38 million per annum or one-forty-fifth of national income, was added to the *Speaker* article when it appeared in *Imperialism*. He also conceded there that the income derived

---

[108] Foreign trade did decline as a proportion of national income between 1870 and 1900. F. Crouzet, *The Victorian Economy* (1982), 112.

[109] The first of the two tables Hobson used to demonstrate this gives the empire a much higher share of British trade than does the second. 'The Commercial Value of Imperialism', 125.

[110] Ibid. 126.

from external trade should include the salaries of commercial clerks and income from some other sources while insisting that this made little difference to his central thesis.[111] It has been argued that Hobson's gloss on his original statement represented a retreat from an untenable position. However, he had put forward a similar thesis in 'Free Trade and Foreign Policy' and, as we have seen, it had an impressive pedigree.[112] However, at this point in *Imperialism*, he did not attribute Britain's high trade ratio to domestic underconsumption as he had in 1898.

In chapter 2, Hobson also printed a table taken from A. W. Flux, the economic statistician, reinforcing the argument that trade with the white-settled, self-governing, 'genuine' colonies was more dynamic than with other parts of the empire.[113] He then immediately cast doubt on Flux's conclusion by noting that Cape Colony and Natal could easily be classed as tropical because of their vast black populations who had no political rights. British trade with these two colonies had risen rapidly since the 1880s while that with the remaining white settlements had languished.[114] Hobson seems not to have noticed that this conclusion undermined his general assertions, reprinted from the *Speaker*, about the unsatisfactory nature of tropical trade and the weak association between that trade and imperial expansion.[115]

In effect, Hobson's recognition that exports to the Cape and Natal had increased from £4 million in 1884 to £12 million in 1898 subverted his general thesis that trade expansion and imperialism did not go together since trade with the landlocked Boer republics, annexed in 1900, was included in the figure and was the most dynamic element within it. His position was further undermined by a new table printed near the end of the chapter that he appeared to believe supported his case.[116] This table indicated that, although

---

[111] *Speaker*, 16 Nov. 1901, pp. 186–7; *Imperialism* (1902 edn.), 31–3.

[112] Clarke, 'Hobson, Free Trade and Imperialism', 309–10. For 'Free Trade and Foreign Policy' see *supra*, Ch. 3. Hobson's argument was also remarkably similar to that put forward by the businessman and philanthropist Andrew Carnegie in 'British Pessimism', *Nineteenth Century*, 49 (1901), 908–9.

[113] A. W. Flux, 'The Flag and Trade', *Journal of the Royal Statistical Society*, 62 (1899), 496–8.

[114] Hobson does not mention it, but the sluggishness of trade with the emerging Dominions was chiefly the result of the length and severity of the depression in Australia in the 1890s.

[115] *Imperialism* (1902 edn.), 39–42.   [116] Ibid. 43.

trade with many new acquisitions since 1870 was very small, the amount done with Egypt (which Hobson noted in the textual gloss) and the Malay States was much more considerable. Hobson could not include the recently annexed Boer republics in his table because their trade was listed in that of the Cape and Natal. However, if it is assumed that the republics accounted for half of the trade done with the latter, then exports and re-exports to Egypt (£6.2 m.) the Malay States (£6.8m.),[117] and the Transvaal and Orange Free State (£7 m.) were worth £20 million in 1900. Hobson also listed about £3.3 million of exports to other recent acquisitions, bringing the total to roughly £23 million or about 6.5 per cent of British exports. Moreover, using the same criteria, imports from the new possessions were worth £29–30 million in 1900.[118] Trade followed the flag to a greater extent than Hobson was willing openly to admit. The economic case for imperialism could also be strengthened by rejecting Hobson's marginalist approach to the value of foreign trade and also by pointing out that some of the new territories which produced poor trade results in 1900 might become more important markets under British control in the future.

Hobson went on to argue that Britain had vastly increased its armaments and antagonized the other great powers (its best customers) for a very small return in trade terms. He made the drastic assumption that 'it is not unreasonable to saddle the New Imperialism with the whole of the increase' in the expenditure on armaments since 1884. According to his own figures, expenditure rose from £28 million per annum in 1884 to £64 million in 1899 before rising sharply to £124 million in 1902 as a result of the war in South Africa.[119] Not surprisingly, he concluded that Britain would have been wiser to have left these new areas for other imperial powers to develop, trusting that its own competitiveness and the effects of multilateralism would bring it some of the trade benefits even if tariffs were raised against Britain.[120] Clearly, Hobson did

---

[117] Hobson gives figures for the 'Malay Protectorate States' in 1899 whereas the *Annual Statement of Trade of the United Kingdom with Foreign Countries and British Possessions*, Cd. 549 (1901), lists only 'Straits Settlements' and gives export figures to them of £3.2 m.

[118] Imports as listed in Hobson's table on p. 43 total to £25.94 m. £3.7 m. has been added to represent the Boer republics' share of imports from the Cape and Natal which was £7.4 m. in 1900. The latter figure is from the *Annual Statement of Trade*.

[119] *Imperialism*, 64–5.

[120] Ibid. 65–9. The original of this section was in the *Speaker*, 7 Dec. 1901.

not consider that the new imperial territories were likely to become important markets in the future as Rosebery and others averred. He spoke, rather, of each new territory 'yielding smaller and more precarious increments of trade to a larger outlay of material and intellectual capital'.[121] Hobson also poured cold water over the 'widely prevalent belief that imperial expansion is desirable, or even necessary, in order to absorb and utilise the surplus of our ever-growing population'.[122] There was no danger of population in Britain outrunning the means of its subsistence: its rate of growth was slowing down and it would be stationary by 1950 if present trends continued into the future. Emigration was always a small proportion of population and only a tiny proportion of it went to the new empire acquired in Africa and Asia after 1870 because geography and climate made settlement largely impossible. Consequently, 'the new Empire was even more barren for settlement than for profitable trade'.[123]

Three of the articles in the *Speaker* series were brought together to form the critical chapter 4 of the first part of *Imperialism* entitled 'Economic Parasites of Imperialism'.[124] The central question at issue in the chapter was: if imperialism brought only very small trade gains, increased the chances of disastrous wars with other great powers, and cost the nation far more than it received, was it simply irrational? Hobson answered that it was irrational from the national standpoint but that various 'well-organised business interests' gained from it and had the power to enforce it; and he tried to introduce evidence to show that this was true not only of Britain but of other imperialist nations. Among the obvious beneficiaries were the armaments manufacturers who covered a range of industries, including metals and shipbuilding, and were supported by the soldiers, sailors, and diplomats whose careers were dependent on armaments and by the shipping industry. But the range of industrial interests supportive of imperialism was greater than this. With the armaments trades

[121] *Imperialism*, 69.
[122] Ibid. 41. The original article is J. A. Hobson, 'Imperialism as an Outlet for Population', *Speaker*, 9 Nov. 1901, pp. 154–5.
[123] *Imperialism*, 45. For Hobson's anti-Malthusianism see Wood, *British Economists and the Empire*, 245–6.
[124] The *Speaker* articles were 'Economic Parasites of Imperialism', 16 Nov. 1901, pp. 179–81; 'Imperialism, the Policy of Investors', 23 Nov. 1901, pp. 210–11; and 'The Financial Direction of Imperialism', 30 Nov. 1901, pp. 245–6.

stand the great manufacturers for export trade who gain a living by supplying the real or artificial wants of the new countries we annex or open up. Manchester, Sheffield, Birmingham, to name three representative cases, are full of firms which compete in pushing textiles and hardware, engines, tools, machinery, spirits, guns, upon new markets. The public debts which ripen in our colonies, and in foreign countries which come under our protectorate or influence, are largely loaned in the shape of rails engines, guns, and other materials of civilisation made and sent out by British firms. The making of railways, canals, and other public works, the establishment of factories, the development of mines, and improvements of agriculture in new countries, stimulate a definite interest in important manufacturing industries which feeds a firm imperialist faith in their owners.[125]

Those manufacturers pushing for imperial expansion had political clout via Chambers of Commerce and other pressure groups based in parts of Africa and China. Nonetheless, he appeared to think that the interest of these industrialists was based on false expectations and ignorance: 'the manufacturing and trading classes make little out of their new markets paying, *if they knew it*, much more in taxation than they get out of them in trade.'[126] To these industrial interests Hobson added the colonial civil service as an important middle-class concern, commenting that the additional employment created was 'inconsiderable, but it arouses that disproportionate interest which always attaches to the margin'.[127] As Etherington has noted, many of the interests mentioned by Hobson were the usual suspects cited by earlier radicals, though the emphasis given to industry was now more marked.[128]

However, Hobson went on to insist that foreign investment was the crucial element in understanding modern imperialism. Using current estimates of the growth of foreign investment, he concluded that British assets held abroad were worth £2 billion, that the income derived from them was at least £100 million per annum, and that it had risen sharply since the mid-1880s when the modern phase of imperialism had begun.[129] Income from investments abroad enormously exceeded the profits on foreign trade; and he was sure that the foreign investors were the only group whose

---

[125] *Imperialism*, 49.   [126] Ibid. 53. My italics.   [127] Ibid. 51.
[128] Etherington, *Theories of Imperialism*, 64–7.
[129] *Imperialism*, 52–3, 61–3. His main sources were Sir G. Giffen, 'The Excess of Imports', *Journal of the Royal Statistical Society*, 62 (1899), 35, and C. A. Harris, 'Foreign Investments', in R. Inglis Palgrave (ed.), *The Dictionary of Political Economy*, ii (1900), 62.

returns outweighed the taxes they paid to promote imperial expansion and that British foreign and imperial policy reflected their power.[130] At this point, Hobson distinguished between investors in general and 'the financier, the general dealer in investments' in particular, designating the former the 'catspaw' of the latter. Such financiers were the creators of new capital and the main determinants of the value of existing stocks. They were largely 'men of a single and peculiar race' who formed the 'central ganglion of international finance' and who were in 'a unique position to manipulate the policy of nations'. Should anyone have failed to divine which race was in question, Hobson then rhetorically asked: 'Does anyone seriously suppose that a great war could be undertaken, by any European State, or a great State loan subscribed, if the house of Rothschild and its connections set its face against it?' Not just British but also American and European expansion had brought 'grist to the financial mills'. Financiers gained from new loans but also because they were in a position to make speculative gains from the oscillation in stock values which always accompanied imperial conflict, as the South African crisis from the Jameson Raid onwards testified.[131] Hobson was, however, keen to stress that 'where war would bring about too great and too permanent a damage to the substantial fabric of industry', the financial power would draw back from it.[132] But his conclusion was that these international financiers 'have the largest definite stake in the business of Imperialism, and the amplest means of forcing their will upon the policy of nations'.[133]

Up to this point in the argument Hobson had indicted finance as the main culprit but he had said little about the state of the economy on which it rested. He rectified this in chapter 6 of the first part of *Imperialism*,[134] where he began by reiterating the standard argument for imperial expansion: overproduction of goods and capital, exacerbated by the growth of international competition, made new markets essential. Any nation standing aloof from this would be

[130] *Imperialism*, 53–4. Hobson reinforced the point by quoting the Italian economist Achille Loria, who saw imperialism in Mexico, Egypt, and Tunis as a means of ensuring debt collection. A. Loria, *Economic Foundations of Society* (1902), 273.
[131] *Imperialism*, 56–8.
[132] Ibid. 58.   [133] Ibid. 59.
[134] A reprint with minor changes of 'The Economic Taproot of Imperialism', *Contemporary Review*, 81 (1902).

excluded by the protectionism of competitors from markets which, if they were small to begin with, would grow rapidly as the new colonies were developed on Western lines. To underline how widespread these views were, Hobson showed their strength in the newest recruit to imperial expansion, the United States. Here, the growth of trusts and cartels behind protectionist barriers had produced enormous productivity gains which went to big business leaders in the form of enhanced profits. Such surpluses could not find sufficient outlets internally: hence American imperialism in the Pacific and Cuba which was a mere starting point for much bigger claims to come in China and South America.[135] This was the first time that Hobson had made an explicit link between the rise of trusts, oversaving, and overseas expansion, and he was indebted to the American Marxist Gaylord Wilshire for helping him to understand American experience.[136] But Hobson emphasized that capital oversupply was a common problem involving most advanced European states as well as Britain.

This problem was the 'taproot' of imperialism: but Hobson now declared, rather late in the argument, that it was the result of underconsumption which was itself the fault of a maldistribution of wealth. While income remained badly distributed the rich had to oversave and they could find no profitable outlet for their savings other than abroad. A redistribution of income would divert most of these savings back to the domestic market and drastically reduce the pressure for imperial expansion. Firmly yoking together his earlier analysis of the defects of capitalism with his work on imperialism, he proposed that the poor distribution of income and wealth had forced on Britain

the unnatural and unwholesome specialisation . . . which has induced an overgrowth of certain manufacturing trades for the express purpose of affecting foreign sales. If the industrial revolution had taken place in an England founded upon equal access by all classes to land, education and

---

[135] *Imperialism*, 73–80.
[136] Hobson acknowledged Wilshire's work ibid. 84. On Wilshire see N. Etherington, *Theories of Imperialism*, 25–37. Etherington also claims that Hobson got the main elements of his theory from Wilshire, but this ignores the fact that Hobson's own thinking about financial imperialism began before Wilshire had published his own ideas. See Etherington, 'The Capitalist Theory of Capitalist Imperialism', 46, 59, 61; and Cain, 'Hobson, Wilshire and the Capitalist Theory of Capitalist Imperialism', 455–7.

legislation, specialisation in manufactures would not have gone so far . . . foreign trade would have been less important, though more steady; the standard of life for all portions of the population would have been high, and the present rate of national consumption would probably have given full, constant, remunerative employment to a far greater quantity of private and public capital than is now employed.[137]

Higher wages and social reform were necessary to transform capitalism and to end imperialism. 'Trades Unionism and Socialism' were the natural enemies of Imperialism because they removed the surplus income which stimulated it.[138] Britain should now turn from the 'extensive' and 'quantitative' growth path towards the 'intensive' and 'qualitative' one, exhibited by countries like Denmark and Switzerland, where better land and income distribution had created a much more self-contained and contented population.[139] In a Hobsonian universe, each nation would rely much less on the international economy while still retaining free trade.

In the last chapter of Part I of *Imperialism*, Hobson turned to the relation between imperial expansion and government spending and taxation. Imperialism meant high military spending and war loans but the capitalists who benefited resisted direct taxation because it fell on themselves and they proposed increases in indirect taxes, including tariffs on imports, instead. More traditional liberals also feared that free trade was under serious threat. A. J. Wilson felt that that protection was inevitable if 'militarism' continued and that it would include agricultural protection because of the importance of the rural interests of the ruling Conservative party.[140] F. W. Hirst also prophesied that, as taxes rose to pay accumulating war debts, the pressure to abandon free trade and introduce protection might become irresistible. Moreover, although tariffs would be introduced first for revenue purposes, he believed they would soon be used to shelter agriculture and to revive the landed interest at the expense of industry. 'What is mere loss of trade compared with a restoration to power of a landed interest?' he asked rhetorically.[141] Hobson's position was very similar though he argued that, to be politically acceptable, the policy would have to be dignified as part of a crusade for imperial unity or as a military necessity. Agricultural

---

[137] *Imperialism*, 88–9.   [138] Ibid. 90.   [139] Ibid. 91–3.
[140] A. J. Wilson, 'Trade Prosperity and Government Waste', *Contemporary Review*, 75 (1899), 480.
[141] Hirst, 'Imperialism and Finance', 110.

protection would be presented as a policy for maintaining secure food supplies and the rural population who, Hobson agreed, made the best soldiers; the industrial classes would be reconciled by tariffs of their own.[142] A new alliance of propertied interests, with its political centre in the Conservative party, was being forged and the Liberals, infected with imperialism themselves, were in no position to oppose it.[143]

However, the argument as presented in *Imperialism* was subtly different from the one Hobson had put forward earlier that year in the *Fortnightly Review*. In that article, Hobson had admitted, first, that protectionism had done no obvious harm to Germany or the United States and that the connection between economic growth and free trade had been much exaggerated; secondly, that, given underconsumption and overproduction, the free trade argument that imperialism was unnecessary to domestic prosperity inevitably looked weak. Perhaps in response to criticism, he left both of these confessions out of *Imperialism* because they appeared to suggest that free trade was unnecessary or impossible to defend.[144] Hobson also had to guard himself against those who, while supporting the New Liberal demand for higher levels of domestic consumption, believed that it could be enhanced by getting rid of free trade. Just after Hobson had published his gloomy assessment of the future of free trade in the *Fortnightly*, J. B. Crozier hailed Hobson as 'the most subtle, clear-sighted and penetrating of living economists' and declared himself a strong believer in 'Hobson's law of the dependence of production of wealth on its consumption'. But he went on to argue that, under free trade, the high level of imports was reducing income and consumption and harming the productive economy. Protection was thus necessary to maintain internal demand and prevent economic collapse.[145] To counter such arguments Hobson stressed, in *Imperialism*, that fiscal policy was dictated largely by financial interests. Their main

---

[142] *Imperialism*, 103–6.   [143] Ibid. 101.

[144] J. A. Hobson 'The Approaching Abandonment of Free Trade', *Fortnightly Review*, NS 71 (1902), 435–7. He was taken to task by the economist H. W. Macrosty, who complained that Hobson's gloomy forecast of doom was doing a disservice to the free trade cause 'by minimising the resources at its disposal and the public resolution to apply them for the public good'. H. W. Macrosty, 'Organisation or Protection?', *Fortnightly Review*, NS 71 (1902), 876.

[145] J. B. Crozier, 'How to Ruin a Free Trade Nation', *Fortnightly Review*, NS 71 (1902), 33, 36, 39, 43 ff.

concern, in limiting imports and pushing exports through imperialism, was not to develop trade *per se* but to increase the export surplus and allow greater foreign investment to take place. Protection, he insisted, was 'a serviceable instrument' of 'a creditor or parasitic nation' not of a productive one which would be harmed by the process.[146]

FINANCE THE 'GOVERNOR OF THE IMPERIAL ENGINE'?

Hobson is famous for the idea that finance and financiers were the main orchestrators of imperial expansion in his time. He made his most emphatic statement of the matter when explaining why, if 'the non-economic factors of patriotism, adventure, military enterprise, political ambition and philanthropy' were so obviously present in imperialism, finance should be accorded greater significance. Finance, he admitted, did not supply most of the 'motor power' of imperialism. Instead

finance is rather the governor of the imperial engine, directing the energy and determining its work: it does not constitute the fuel of the engine, nor does it directly generate the power. Finance manipulates the patriotic forces which politicians, soldiers and philanthropists generate; the enthusiasm for expansion which issues from these sources, though strong and genuine, are irregular and blind; the financial interest has those qualities of concentration and clear-sighted calculation which are needed to set Imperialism to work. An ambitious statesman, a frontier soldier, an overzealous missionary, a pushing trader, may suggest or even initiate a step in imperial expansion, may assist in educating patriotic public opinion to the urgent need for some fresh advance, but the final determination rests with the financial power.[147]

Financiers did not invent imperialism but they conspired to channel imperial fervour in the directions which best suited their own ends. As Allett put the matter, Hobson was arguing here that 'a well-organised clique of financiers would experience little difficulty in manipulating the various "non-economic" forces so as to tailor events to their private advantage'.[148] They were able to do this

[146] *Imperialism*, 106–7.   [147] Ibid. 59.
[148] Allett, *New Liberalism*, 163.

because they were the only interest with a coherent idea of what they wanted and had the power to shape policy. There is no doubt that this remained Hobson's most enduring conviction and was repeated frequently over the years. Yet it was heavily qualified, even subverted, on a number of occasions in *Imperialism*.

The first shift in the argument took place when discussing the links between trusts and imperialism in the United States. Imperialism was now defined as 'the endeavour of the great controllers of industry to broaden the channel for the flow of their surplus wealth by seeking foreign markets and foreign investments to take off the goods and capital they cannot sell at home', an emphasis rather different from his previous one in giving industry priority over finance.[149] The change could be explained as a simple slip of the pen by a writer in a hurry. Alternatively, the difference might have been based on the fact that the relations between industry and finance were very different in the USA (and Germany) from those in Britain he had previously been discussing. In analysing trusts, Hobson was describing the interlocking of emerging corporate industry and giant banks that were the bases of the 'finance capitalism' described later by Hilferding and by Schumpeter.[150] Nearly all Hobson's material on trusts came from the United States,[151] a reflection of the fact that big business was much less well developed in Britain than in America or Germany. Hobson knew that there were a great many price-fixing agreements across British industry and obviously regarded such restraints on competition as normal business practice: but a combination was a much looser, less effective, and more easily disrupted business weapon in Britain than elsewhere.[152] He would also have been aware that relations between finance and industry were much more indirect in his native country than in its major industrial competitors. Foreign investment raised in the City had to be transferred by exports, often the products of northern industry: but City money did not flow into investments in the industrial provinces. The two business communities were far apart, ignorant

---

[149] Imperialism 85. Hobson also betrayed some uncertainty about the priority of finance over industry later in the argument (221).

[150] R. Hilferding, *Finance Capital: The Latest Stage of Capitalist Development* (1910; repr. 1981); J. A. Schumpeter, *Imperialism* (1919) reprinted in R. Swedberg (ed.), *Joseph A. Schumpeter: The Economics and Sociology of Capitalism* (Princeton, 1991).

[151] See the first edition of his *Evolution of Modern Capitalism*, chs. 5 and 6.

[152] Ibid. 122–5.

of each other, and mutually suspicious.[153] Moreover, although there were considerable holdings of foreign assets in industrial districts such as Lancashire, a very high proportion of foreign investments were held by 'peers and gents' and represented a new and powerful link between government, London society, the traditional landed interest, and the City, a combination recently described as 'gentlemanly capitalist' and much stronger in its influence in the service sector-driven south-east of England than in the industrial provinces of Britain.[154] In liberal and radical circles associated with industry, such differences and divisions provoked exaggerated fears of London finance and its influence on policy. Hobson's own attitude to finance reflected this long-standing provincial-radical distance and anxiety. When discussing Britain, his emphasis was on conspiracy and was often detached from fundamental issues such as oversaving and underconsumption. No serious attempt was made to define the nature of financial capitalism in Britain beyond some suggestive remarks about the emergence of the south of England as a rentier society feeding on the returns from foreign investment.[155] Hobson thus hovered between a traditional radical view of finance as conspiratorial and a more systemic one treating imperialism as a function of developing finance-capitalist structures. The tension between the two was reflected most obviously in the contrast between his treatment of the economic motivation behind imperialism in Britain and in America.

In Part II of *Imperialism* the argument took other directions, and far more subtle ones than in Part I. At one point, instead of reasserting the primacy of finance in Britain, Hobson offered a list of the 'vested interests' who protected themselves from domestic upheaval and attack by supporting imperialism, declaring that:

the city ground landlord, the country squire, the banker, the usurer, and the financier, the brewer, the mine-owner, the ironmaster, the shipbuilder, and the shipping trade, the great export manufacturers and merchants, the clergy of the State Church, the universities, and the great public schools,

---

[153] P. J. Cain, 'Tradition and Innovation: The City of London, 1870–1914', in J.-P. Dormois and M. Dintenfass (eds.), *The British Industrial Decline* (1999), 195–9.

[154] For 'gentlemanly capitalism' see Cain and Hopkins, *British Imperialism*, esp. 38–50. See also L. E. Davis and R. A. Huttenback, *Mammon and the Pursuit of Empire: The Political Economy of British Imperialism, 1860–1912* (Cambridge, 1986), ch. 7.

[155] *Imperialism*, 314, 364–5.

the legal trade unions and the services have, both in Great Britain and on the Continent, drawn together for common political resistance against attacks upon the power, the property, and the privileges which in various forms and degrees they represent.[156]

The list was Hobson's updated and amended version of the 'few' or the 'classes' of traditional radical discourse. It contained all the forces traditional radicals could identify as the enemy although there was also a novel emphasis on industrial interests. Finance, though well represented, was given no special priority. It is also possible to see the list as an exercise in primitive Gramscianism with established and parvenu propertied interests coalescing into a new 'historical bloc' and coming together to exercise a 'hegemony' which rested as much upon cultural foundations as upon crude economic imperatives or overt political coercion.[157] From this perspective, imperialism was the 'first defence' of all of the parasitic elements in the propertied structure. Many of these interests received a wide range of benefits from imperialism in terms of jobs and markets, but even those receiving no direct stimulus gained from the powerful brake which it put upon the process of liberal reform.[158] Imperialism was the best answer current elites could find for the problem of oversaving: in more Gramscian terms, it was also the chief support for existing hegemonic structures not only because of its direct benefits but, more importantly, because of its power in co-opting both the educated part of the nation and the masses into support for unreformed capitalism.

As for the educated, Hobson, like Gramsci, was well aware of the role of intellectuals in supporting the power structure. For example, with the rise of the new 'redbricks' in mind, Hobson commented that universities were hardly likely to challenge existing orthodoxies because of their dependence on 'the charity of millionaires': 'philosophy, the natural sciences, history, economics, sociology are to be employed in setting up new earthworks against the attack of the disinherited masses upon the vested interests of the

---

[156] Ibid. 142. Allett's argument that Hobson was identifying a 'military/industrial' complex at the heart of imperialism is interesting in this context. See *New Liberalism*, 149–51.

[157] A. Gramsci, *Selections from the Prison Notebooks*, ed. Q. Hoare and G. Nowell Smith (1971).

[158] *Imperialism*, 220.

plutocracy'.[159] In the circumstances, there was little chance, for example, that 'a political economist with strong views on controlling capital [would] be elected to a chair in economics'. Arts and social science teaching was 'selected and controlled' in the service of imperialism even though its university practitioners were usually trying to act in a disinterested way.

For these business politicians biology and sociology weave thin convenient theories of race struggle for the subjugation of the inferior peoples, in order that we, the Anglo-Saxon, may take their lands and live upon their labours: while economics buttresses the arguments by representing our work in conquering and ruling them as our share in the division of labour among nations, and history devises reasons why the lessons of past empire do not apply to ours while social ethics paints the motive of 'Imperialism' as the desire to bear the 'burden' of educating and elevating races of 'children'. Thus are the 'cultured' or semi-cultured classes indoctrinated with the intellectual and moral grandeur of Imperialism.[160]

The particular animus against universities was undoubtedly a result of Hobson's personal history: but this passage in particular is testimony to his recognition that the defence of imperialism rested on impressively wide intellectual supports. Many, if not most, educated Britons believed that the extension of empire was a means of spreading freedom and justice; they were convinced that Britain had entered Egypt, India, and tropical Africa on a mission to bring Christianity and civilization rather than for any interested motive. They also genuinely believed that the independent Transvaal, small as it was, posed a threat to the existence of the empire and that defeating it in war was necessary to preserve the empire and all it stood for; and they also believed that the military action necessary for control and expansion was a price worth paying to achieve a noble end.[161]

The controllers of finance were also susceptible to the allure of such elevated arguments. As early as 1903, Norman Angell was attacking Hobson's assertion that financiers approached imperialism

---

[159] Ibid. 218–19. Compare Gramsci's description of the power of civil society in advanced industrial countries and his argument that the state was 'only an outer ditch, behind which there stood a powerful system of fortresses and earthworks'. *Prison Notebooks*, 238.

[160] *Imperialism*, 221–2.

[161] Ibid. 196–206.

in a coldly rational way. Angell argued instead that 'the intensity of feeling which embraced . . . the whole nation—a feeling which in every characteristic was non-rational—precludes the idea that it had its origins in or is mainly animated by a limited clique whose motives are intensely rationalistic'. Financiers might use this sentiment for economic ends but they were also victims of it.[162] What Angell did not appear to notice was that Hobson undermined his own position in *Imperialism* to some extent because he had to admit—as he had done, grudgingly, when discussing Rhodes's motives in 1900—that even businessmen, like most of the politicians directly involved, often believed in the imperial mission themselves. As he put it, 'the politician always, the business man not seldom, believes that high motives qualify the political or financial benefits he gets', and he even allowed that 'it is quite likely that Earl Grey thought that the Chartered Company [the British South Africa Company] which he directed was animated by a desire to improve the material and moral condition of the natives of Rhodesia, and that it was attaining this objective'.[163] In Part I, when discussing how financial interests in Britain had supported increases in military spending, he had hinted that they might also share the delusions of other imperialists when he wrote about the 'financial and industrial capitalists who have mainly engineered this policy, employing their own genuine convictions to conceal their ill-recognised business ends'.[164] Later on, and equally revealingly, he confessed that 'most of those men who have misled [Britain] have first been obliged to mislead themselves'.[165] So, it appears, it was with a good conscience that, largely through the press, financiers encouraged those 'primitive lusts' among the degraded masses of urban Britain which inspired jingoistic imperialism, that remnant of an ancient militarism industrialism had so far failed to wipe from the soul of modern man.[166] As Porter has noted, Hobson was a rationalist. Faced with the conclusion that imperialism was irrational from the national standpoint, he tried to rescue a rational approach by showing that some people benefited from the process based on a rational calculation of their own interests in deluding the rest of the nation: hence the argument for financial conspiracy.[167] What is suggested here, however, is that Hobson's

[162] N. Angell, *Patriotism and Three Flags: A Plea for Rationalism in Politics* (1903), 24 as quoted in Porter, *Critics of Empire*, 221.
[163] *Imperialism*, 197–8.   [164] Ibid. 96.   [165] Ibid. 211.   [166] Ibid. 212–16.
[167] Porter, *Critics of Empire*, 216 ff.

description of the power of imperialist ideology in *Imperialism* was so compelling that, despite himself, he came close on occasion to accepting Angell's view that all those involved in the process, including the most obvious beneficiaries, were driven by irrational desires. For all participants, imperialism was to some extent an act of faith, a leap into the unknown.

When discussing the beliefs of imperialists, Hobson did try to rescue his original argument by insisting that the economic motives for imperialism were stronger than others. There was, he claimed, a 'blending of strong interested with weak disinterested forces' and 'when business is harnessed with benevolence the former is commonly allowed to determine the direction and to set the pace'.[168] He tried to convince himself and his readers that the educated imperialist could only hold on to his or her beliefs through denial and 'the power of self-deceit', a weakness to which he believed the British were particularly susceptible.[169] They could fool themselves by refusing to delve too deeply into the evidence and by hiding behind a carefully constructed language of imperialism that masked the brutalities and exploitation on which it was based. He described the 'verbal armoury of Imperialism' thus:

Paramount power, effective autonomy, emissary of civilisation, rectification of frontier, and the whole sliding scale of terms from 'hinterland' and 'sphere of interest' to 'effective occupation' and 'annexation' will serve as ready illustrations of a phraseology devised for purposes of concealment and encroachment. The Imperialist who see modern history through these masks never grasps the 'brute' facts but always sees them at several removes, refracted, interpreted, and glozed over by convenient renderings.[170]

In such Orwellian passages analysing the language of power, Hobson can sound as if he were making a contribution to modern discourse analysis or to post-colonial studies. It takes some effort to remember how astounded and indignant he would have been had

---

[168] *Imperialism*, 200–1.   [169] Ibid. 209–11.

[170] Ibid. 207–8. Hobson drew here on Ruskin's analysis of 'masked words'— 'There are masked words—which nobody understands, but which everybody uses, and most people will also fight for, live for, even die for, fancying they mean this or that—There never were creatures of prey so mischievous, never diplomatists so cunning, never poisoners more deadly, than these masked words; they are the unjust stewards of all men's ideas: whatever fancy or favourite instinct a man most cherishes, he gives to his favourite masked word to take care of for him'. (*Sesame and Lilies*, para. 16, in *Works*, ed. Cook and Wedderburn, xviii).

his own language of liberal progressivism been dissected in a similar manner. Also, he offered no evidence, other than assertion, for the primacy of economic motives. Despite his own attempts to manipulate the reader's response, the vivid and compelling way in which he wrote of imperial fervour was as likely to lead that reader to deduce that the economic forces which backed imperialism did so just as much for moral or patriotic reasons as for the more cynical motives which Hobson wishes to press upon his or her attention.[171] What is presented in Part II is not just an ignorant and self-deluded nation manipulated by clear-eyed, amoral, selfish financiers. Rather, Hobson sometimes depicted imperial expansion as the result of a wide range of propertied interests coming together 'instinctively'[172] to support a policy of expansion that welded them emotionally to the bulk of the nation and, by creating cross-class solidarities not evident otherwise, served their interest in maintaining the status quo while bringing direct material gains to some of them.[173]

This, of course, was not the message Hobson wished to convey and he continually tried to recover the simplicity of the original argument. Near the end of the book, for example, he referred to the influence of 'investors and financial managers' that 'secures a national alliance of other vested interests which are threatened by movements of social reform'.[174] Yet even here the phrasing suggests a toning down of the conspiratorial element in his thinking. Overall, there were enough variations on the theme in *Imperialism* to show that Hobson was not absolutely certain about the matter and that his uncertainty sometimes led him away from the conspiracy theory he had announced early in the book and towards different and more subtle attempts to unravel the links between the structures

[171] The call to imperial patriotism was critical to the Conservative victory at the 1900 election. See P. Readman, 'The Conservative Party, Patriotism and British Politics: The Case of the General Election of 1900', *Journal of British Studies*, 40 (2001). On this theme see also J. Schneer, *London 1900: The Imperial Metropolis* (New Haven, 1999), ch. 10.

[172] *Imperialism*, 197.

[173] 'If the relationship between intellectuals and people-nation, between the leaders and the led, the rulers and the ruled, is provided by an organic cohesion in which feeling-passion becomes understanding and thence knowledge (not mechanically but in a way that is alive) then and only then . . . can there take place an exchange of individual elements between the rulers and the ruled, leaders and led, and can a shared life be realised which alone is a social force.' Gramsci, *Prison Notebooks*, 418.

[174] *Imperialism*, 361.

of capitalist society, the ideologies of imperialism, and imperial policy-making. The complexity of the evidence often forced him to abandon simplicity, with the result that his answers to questions about the chief motivators and beneficiaries of imperialism occasionally turned out to be rather more ambiguous—and probably more interesting—than he originally intended.

HOBSON'S ECONOMICS OF IMPERIALISM: A CRITICAL APPRAISAL

Hobson's conclusion that finance was 'the governor of the imperial engine' rested on a number of assumptions, none easy to defend. He had argued: first, that the value of foreign trade to the nation was small and that it was unnecessary to the prosperity of advanced industrial countries;[175] secondly, that not only was the trade gained from imperial expansion in tropical and subtropical lands very limited but the benefits were much outweighed by the costs of their acquisition; thirdly, that the power of finance was indicated by the immensity of the returns on foreign investment compared with those on foreign trade. The first proposition, though coming from a respectable intellectual tradition, was extremely contentious and was heavily criticized.[176] His second rested on trade statistics that to some extent undermined his own argument and upon the remarkable assumption that all increases in military spending over the previous twenty or thirty years were directly attributable to imperial expansion. The third was seriously flawed. His assertion that foreign investment was a much more lucrative business than foreign trade did not compare like with like. In assessing the value of foreign trade he assumed that, if consumption patterns were changed, most could be diverted to the home market and that, therefore, only the extra profit gained in foreign trade should be counted as a gain to the nation. This was contentious enough, but to be consistent he should have made similar assumptions about foreign investment and given some estimate of the difference in income arising from investing abroad rather than at home. Instead, what he offered was a comparison between the *net* value of foreign trade and the *gross* value of returns on foreign investment, inevitably inflating the importance

---

[175] A point reiterated ibid. 81.   [176] See *supra*, Ch. 3.

of the latter and, by implication, that of the financiers who controlled it. Another weakness in Hobson's analysis of the link between the expansion of the imperial frontier and foreign investment was that he did not discuss the distribution of the latter. He was well aware how much of it went to foreign countries, quoting statistics indicating that only about a third of all British overseas investments in government loans and railways had been placed in the empire.[177] Judging from his remarks on the marginal importance of new acquisitions as sources of employment and of export markets it can be inferred that he thought only a small proportion of foreign investment was directly involved in imperial expansion in tropical Africa and Asia, especially since he was well aware that capital could only be transferred abroad via the export of goods and services. But no explicit statement was made in *Imperialism* and a reader could easily come away with the impression that a substantial amount of British capital was involved in all recent acquisitions, especially when faced with statements such as:

Aggressive Imperialism, which costs the taxpayer so dear, which is of so little value to the manufacturer and trader, which is fraught with such grave incalculable peril to the citizen, is a source of great gain to the investor who cannot find at home the profitable use he seeks for his capital, and insists that his Government should help him to profitable and secure investments abroad.[178]

It may, however, be significant that this statement comes directly after a brief mention of the occupation of Egypt (1882). Hobson had recognized the significance of Egypt in British foreign trade. Egypt was also, for him, a clear example of investor imperialism, and the British capital involved was much greater than in tropical Africa, a fact Hobson must have known but did not discuss. Moreover, the implication of the whole argument, and of his work over the previous three years, was that South Africa had recently absorbed a much larger share of British overseas capital than had tropical Africa though, again, no precise evidence was offered.[179] The end result was that his failure to discuss the distribution of foreign investment made it difficult to distinguish between those

[177] *Imperialism*, 62. Compare 'Capitalism and Imperialism in South Africa', 2.
[178] *Imperialism*, 55.
[179] For a discussion of Hobson's thesis in the context of present-day discussions of the costs and benefits of empire see Ch. 8 *infra*.

areas where British capital investments loomed large in the process of expansion and those where they did not.

Hobson's fourth major contention was that the great international financiers had power over the politicians of the imperialist nations and were the true guides of their foreign policies. Fifthly, he claimed that they could manipulate public opinion in these nations through control of the press;[180] and, finally, he argued that financiers possessed a singleness of purpose and a clarity of vision accorded to no other body of men involved in imperial endeavour. There was some truth in the fifth proposition, though the picture was more complex than Hobson painted it, but he supplied no direct evidence for either the fourth or the sixth other than certain inferences drawn from the relations between South African mining magnates and politicians. Moreover, both of these claims were nuanced, and to some extent subverted, as the argument proceeded. In Part I, the American evidence suggested a different kind of finance capitalism existed there, one where industry had equality, if not priority, over finance. Then in Part II, Hobson developed his Gramscian argument about the complicity of propertied interests as a whole in imperialism in a way which accorded finance no special place; and he went on to present a sketch of the ideological foundations of imperial endeavour which, whatever his original intentions, sometimes hinted that financiers were as likely to be as ideologically blinkered as the populace they were supposed to manipulate.

[180] *Imperialism*, 60.

CHAPTER FIVE

Imperialism: A Study:
Parasitism and Industry

In Part II of *Imperialism*, Hobson set out to defend in more detail the major propositions he had laid down in Part I. This involved him in an extensive survey of the impact of imperialism in Britain, in the empire, and in those territories such as China that seemed about to fall under European control. In his endeavour, he made extensive use of the terms 'parasite' and 'parasitic' to describe the imperialist process, following the lead of fellow anti-expansionists such as J. M. Robertson. The use of these metaphors marked a development in radical thinking as radicals attempted to come to terms with financial imperialism (as a relatively new element) in ways strongly influenced not only by the biologism of contemporary discourse but also by recent medical discoveries.[1] They played a crucial explanatory role in Part II of *Imperialism* in conjunction with what Hobson conceived as their polar opposite, 'industry'. Indeed, *Imperialism* was written in terms of a confrontation between parasitism and industry, a confrontation that would determine the future of humanity for generations to come yet one where outcomes were uncertain. The clash between good and evil and the anxiety about who would be the victor imparted a dramatic quality and an excitement to *Imperialism* that distinguish it from most of his other works and from others in the radical canon. Nonetheless, Hobson was clearly developing an already existent radical discourse, not breaking away from it, as we shall see.

---

[1] See M. Worboys, 'The Emergence and Early History of Parasitology', in K. S. Warren and J. Z Bowers (eds.), *Parasitology: A Global Perspective* (New York, 1983).

The Ethics of Industrialism

In the traditional antithesis in radical thinking between industrial and militant societies, 'industry' reflected the moral and intellectual qualities of the skilled artisan and the small entrepreneur, the core of the 'producers' alliance', rather than the unskilled mass of labourers, casuals, and 'loafers' whose ignorance and moral frailty made them easy prey for the 'classes'.[2] Thus industry was associated with energy, creativity, manly independence, peace, and civic virtue—indeed all the qualities which went to make up moral health or 'good character'—while militancy produced the corresponding vices associated with authoritarian rule.[3] Finance had originally been accorded a minor role in defining militancy when the British aristocracy was in the ascendent. Its rise, by 1900, into a leading force behind imperial expansion required some parallel evolution in the radical discourse, though one which never lost its connection with the world of Spencer and Cobden. J. L. Hammond, for example, could still associate industry and commerce with 'spreading enlightened notions', 'distributing knowledge more widely', and 'extending respect for humane and honourable ideas'.[4] He also believed that industrial competition engendered in people an 'active sense of responsibility', gave them a concern for 'great and vivifying principles', and promoted 'an idealism [which] belongs to all robust and virile natures', all qualities essential to a true liberalism. Imperialism, by contrast, was a product of moral decline that, in the shape of Rosebery's Liberal Imperialism, was shaming the party of Gladstone, inducing in it a 'temper of fatalism', a 'moral somnolence', and 'a listless indifference'.[5] Hammond left his readers in no doubt that this imperialism was driven essentially by finance and by the 'civilisation of De Beers'.[6] The fact that Chamberlain, once a radical himself, was an instigator of the South African war made him an awful warning of how financial imperialism led to 'degradation of character'.[7] Imperialism was turning 'a strenuous, virile, self-respecting, and honourable England' into 'a tumid, plethoric, dissipated England, big at the expense of her greatness

[2] See in particular Smith, 'The Greatness of England'.
[3] See John Morley's speech at Falkirk in November 1901 as reported in Koss, *The Pro-Boers*, 239–41.
[4] Hammond, 'Colonial and Foreign Policy', 173.
[5] Ibid. 163–4.   [6] Ibid. 192.   [7] Ibid. 182.

. . . an England swollen and bloated out of recognition'.[8] There is not much distance between this association of financial imperialism with unhealthy, slovenly obesity and Robertson's use of the word 'parasitic' to describe the nature of British expansion noted earlier.[9]

As we have seen, Hobson had taken up the idea of parasitism in the late 1890s to describe the activity of 'living off the energy of other people through rent, dividends, inheritance or gift'; in short, it was applied to those in receipt of unearned income. In the long term, he believed, parasitism 'saps all the roots of active energy' both physical and mental. At that time, Hobson spoke of the 'torpid plutocrat' and his main examples were absentee landlords and the directors of large joint stock companies whom he thought of as sinecurists.[10] It was his interest in imperialism that led him to think of finance as the key to parasitism.[11] On the other side, his idea of industry developed upon lines clearly derived from Smiles, Spencer, and Cobden and was very similar to Hammond's in directly associating earnest economic activity with high-toned morality and freedom. This is evident from a remarkable, if little known, article that Hobson published two years before *Imperialism*, where he declared that 'modern industrialism' and 'moral advance' went broadly together. Industry 'requires large numbers of men to work in close co-operation . . . with instruments which they utilize in common, for the production of commodities in which they have a common interest' and thus served that common good which liberal intellectuals such as Hobson so eagerly sought. Commerce subserved this common interest by uniting 'in ever closer bonds groups of workers over the constantly-widening area of the world market'. Between them they were 'laying a firm basis of solidarity of interests upon which may be built a true temple of humanity. The industrial world thus regarded is a vast mutual benefit society, a continual education in the paths of peace and practical brotherhood.'[12]

So the Industrial Revolution had been a 'great liberating force' and industry was still largely devoted to tasks that 'exercise qualities

---

[8] Ibid. 186–7.   [9] See *supra*, Ch. 2.

[10] Hobson, *The Social Problem*, 114–18.

[11] For early references to parasitism by Hobson in connection with imperialism see 'Issues of Empire—III', *Ethical World*, 15 July 1899, pp. 437–8, and *The Psychology of Jingoism*, where he spoke of a Britain 'enfeebled by a parasitic life of Empire' (p. 96).

[12] J. A. Hobson, 'The Ethics of Industrialism: A Diagnosis', in Stanton Coit (ed.), *Ethical Democracy* (1900), 81. For an earlier version see 'The Ethics of Industrialism', *New Age* (1898), 468–9, 487, 503, 519, 554, 585.

of ingenuity, courage, perseverance and forethought, self-restraint and harmonious co-operation'.[13] Yet the economic and moral benefits of that revolution had been perverted by the inequalities in wealth and power which had produced big business and monopoly, given machinery such prominence in industrial life, and produced monotonous exhausting work in 'unsanitary, ugly and congested towns'.[14] Modern capitalist industry was also too much pervaded by a spirit of unhealthy competition. It encouraged people to get the better of each other and was based on unfair bargaining due to inequalities between the parties concerned that distributed the gains from trade inequitably, fostering immoral relationships that 'degrade the character'. As a result, he concluded that present-day industrialism 'does not differ essentially from militarism. It is still the game of war played upon a different plane'.[15] To produce the true, small-scale, organic industrialism would require the drastic reforms he had already outlined in the 1890s in *The Evolution of Modern Capitalism* and in *The Social Problem*. In 1900 he was particularly concerned to emphasize that proper industrialism could not be achieved by encouraging class division 'under the cloak of social justice' because that produced 'envy, hatred, malice and all uncharitableness' and, in denying the possibility of a common good, undermined character. 'Both concrete reforms, and the methods of obtaining them, must strengthen the moral character of individuals, and must be direct feeders of a spirit of ethical democracy, which shall bind individuals and classes by a conscious bond of moral fellowship.'[16]

Although he continued to describe big industrial businesses which exercised monopoly powers as parasitic, Hobson still believed that small-scale industry, similar to that of Cobden's time, could be revived under a social reforming government; that the producers' alliance could still flourish; and that a reformed industry was the key to a morally healthy, liberal future otherwise threatened by the rise of parasitism and the militancy it bred. Indeed, these two

[13] 'The Ethics of Industrialism', 92.
[14] Ibid. 83.
[15] Ibid. 92–4. On inequalities in bargaining and the forced gains he thought resulted see J. A. Hobson, 'The Economics of Bargaining', *Economic Review*, 9 (1899), 20–41 and repr. in *Hobson: Writings on Distribution and Welfare*, ed. Backhouse,
[16] 'The Ethics of Industrialism', 98.

complex and competing ideas of 'industry' and 'parasitism' and the antagonism between them are the crucial underpinning for his attack on the political and ideological props of imperialism and on imperial policy overseas which occupied most of Part II of *Imperialism*. In these pages—occupying twice the space devoted to explaining the economic basis of imperialism—Hobson demonstrated most obviously that he was amending and adding to a long-running radical discourse rather than adopting any revolutionary new approach to the problem of imperial expansion.

LIBERALISM AND IMPERIALISM

In Part II, Hobson was determined to hammer home the message that the new financially driven imperialism was a threat to every kind of liberal value in Britain, to 'peace, economy, reform, and popular self-government',[17] because it supported militarism and parasitism. Despite the widespread assumption that Britain was diffusing its own governing institutions abroad, Hobson pointed out that in 1902 only about 11 million of the 367 million peoples in the British Empire had real self-government and that the vast extension of empire that had taken place since 1880 had simply added to the area despotically controlled.[18] He recognized that British rule had brought some benefits to the dominated lands. In the case of India, for example, although he denied that the standard of living of the masses had risen under imperial rule he mentioned improved law and order, lower taxation, and the provision of a railway network as definite gains.[19] But he claimed that no prominent civil servant or minister charged with imperial responsibilities expected the area under forms of self-government to increase; and he held up Milner's statement in *England in Egypt* that 'I cannot shut my eyes to the fact that popular government, as we understand it, is for a longer time than anyone can foresee at present out of the question' as representative of elite opinion in general.[20] Colonialism—the planting of British settlements abroad in sparsely inhabited lands—was a natural extension of a vigorous and growing society,[21] an organic extension of the mother country. But

---

[17] *Imperialism*, 126. [18] Ibid. 113–22. [19] Ibid. 287–90.
[20] Ibid. 123. Milner, *England in Egypt* (1892), 378–9.
[21] *Imperialism*, 6–7.

imperialism meant the conquest of peoples Britons could neither supplant nor assimilate and where the few British residents were merely the top-dressing on an alien civilization they could not change fundamentally, as in India.[22] Nor was colonialism a 'drain upon our material and moral resources' since it led to 'free white democracies': but imperialism was a dangerous means of spreading autocratic rule which was bound to infect British society with anti-liberal sentiments and institutions.[23] It is noticeable that although, as we shall see, Hobson was much concerned about the fate of indigenous peoples under imperial control in Africa and Asia he said nothing in *Imperialism* about the suppression and ill-treatment of the aboriginal peoples of Australasia and Canada as the latter became the 'free white democracies' he lauded.

Imperial expansion had brought Britain into conflict with a range of European powers and had inexorably led to increased international tension and warfare which was pushing the country back towards militancy. Hobson was convinced that the '*Pax Britannica*, always an impudent falsehood, has become a grotesque monster of hypocrisy', and that competitive expansion in Africa and Asia 'implies militarism now and ruinous wars in the future'. Britain was plunging into an armaments race that could derange the public finances (leading to the protectionism he had warned against earlier in the book) and undermine the economy because competing cliques of businessmen in each imperialist country were determined to 'spend the blood and money of the people . . . feigning national antagonisms which have no basis in reality'.[24] Increased aggression meant a large increase in the cost of the army and the wages of recruits would be forced up as demand rose. Hobson believed that there would be demands for conscription as conflicts with other powers escalated, though he felt that the 'slumdwellers and weedy clerks' who were amongst the main products of large towns and of the diseased industrialism they contained would hardly make an effective fighting force. They lacked the quality of 'brute endurance'

---

[22] Ibid. 294–304. Hobson was able to call here on the testimony of Sir John Seeley, an advocate of Greater Britain who in his best-selling book *The Expansion of England* (1883) contrasted the natural affinity between the white parts of the empire, based on race and religion, with the artificial assimilation that had to be practised as regards India.

[23] *Imperialism*, 124–5.

[24] Ibid. 124–30. The quotations are from pp. 126, 130, and, 127.

that hardy peasants possessed.[25] Moreover, every soldier recruited was one fewer person able to keep the economy going; diverting resources to the army was bound to reduce national output over time and limit the amount of skill available to industry and commerce.[26] Given the difficulties of recruiting suitable cannon fodder at home and the political problem of selling conscription to an unwilling public, Hobson thought that Britain might slip easily into employing huge mercenary armies culled from the cheap labour of their dependent territories. Britain had already adopted such a policy in India, and, as in the later Roman Empire, it meant that 'a metropolitan population entrusts the defence of its lives and possessions to the precarious fidelity of "conquered races" commanded by ambitious pro-consuls'. This increased the risks of war and made war more barbarous. If widely adopted by imperial powers, it could turn Africa and Asia into 'huge cockpits for the struggles of black and yellow armies representing the Imperialist rivalries of Christendom . . . involving in their recoil a degradation of Western States and a possible *debacle* of Western civilisation'.[27]

Hobson felt that the self-governing white colonies had enhanced the cause of liberty in Britain by their 'practical successes in the arts of popular government'. By contrast, the extension of despotic empire had not only increased the secrecy of government, strengthened cabinet government at the expense of Parliament, and increased support for the idea of national governments which would do away with healthy party conflicts: it had also 'served to damage the character of our people by feeding the habits of snobbish subservience, the admiration of wealth and rank, the corrupt survivals of the inequalities of feudalism'. Following faithfully in the footsteps of Cobden, Gladstone, and other radical critics of empire, Hobson also indicted imperialism for diverting funds and energies from social reform and of holding back the liberal progress that had been the foundation of Britain's long-standing eminence in the world. It was, he said, 'a commonplace of history how Governments

---

[25] Here Hobson's argument was similar to that of the supporters of conscription who were alarmed by the poor health and fitness of army recruits during the Boer War and who were instrumental in persuading the government to set up the Interdepartmental Committee on Physical Deterioration, which recommended that the state take steps to ensure better feeding of the nation's youth. See G. R. Searle, *The Quest for National Efficiency: A Study in British Politics and Political Thought* (Oxford, 1971), ch. 3.

[26] *Imperialism*, 130–2.   [27] Ibid. 136–8.

use national animosities, foreign wars and the glamour of empire making, in order to bemuse the popular mind and divert rising resentment against domestic abuses'.[28] The extent to which imperialism helped to consolidate the power of the controllers of wealth over the political process in Britain was vividly illustrated for Hobson by the way in which the Liberal party had been infected with the virus and compromised. Like Hobhouse, who dated the beginning of the problem to the Home Rule crisis of 1886 that split the party, he thought that imperialism had taken the party away from its true mission—domestic reform.[29] In a bitter attack on Liberal supporters of imperialism, he claimed that, 'having sold their party to a confederacy of stock gamblers and jingo sentimentalists [they] find themselves impotent to defend Free Trade, Free Press, Free Schools, Free Speech or any of the rudiments of ancient liberalism'. They had followed 'their business interests and prepossessions', taken refuge in 'patriotism', surrendered real two-party government, and thus betrayed their heritage. (Hobson no doubt had in mind here Rosebery's role in trying to forge a government of national unity during the war crisis.)[30] He was convinced that the only hope for the future was if the Liberal party co-operated with the rising Labour party to forge a new progressive alliance.[31]

The vital link between autocratic tendencies at home and the extension of empire was brought vividly home in Hobson's description of men who

trained in the temper and methods of autocracy as soldiers and civil officers . . . reinforced by numbers of merchants, planters, engineers and overseers, whose lives have been those of a superior caste living an artificial life removed from all the healthy restraints of ordinary European society, have returned to this country, bringing back the characters, sentiments, and ideas imposed by this foreign environment.

Some of these ex-colonials, who were 'openly contemptuous of democracy', became MPs or were influential in local government and were a powerful brake on reform. According to him, they were particularly influential in the south and south-west of England. There is no doubt that Hobson saw them as parasitic on the territories they

[28] Ibid. 142.
[29] L. T. Hobhouse, *Democracy and Reaction* (1904; 1909 edn.), 67–8.
[30] Searle, *The Quest for National Efficiency*, ch. 4.
[31] *Imperialism*, 143–9.

had once dominated, living on pensions and other investment inflows from the dependent empire.

Could the incomes expended in the Home Counties or other large districts of Southern Britain be traced to their sources, it would be found that they were in large measure wrung from the enforced toil of vast multitudes of black, brown and yellow natives, by arts not differing essentially from those which supported in idleness and luxury imperial Rome.[32]

The militancy that this class of men supported was a direct outcome of a newer form of imperialism: the exploitation of non-Western territories through foreign investment that now formed one of the main source of parasitism in Britain.

THE FUTURE OF IMPERIALISM: CHINA

Hobson supported his claims about the imperial origins of parasitism in his chapter 'Imperialism and the Lower Races' which concentrated upon Britain's recent acquisitions in central and southern Africa.[33] As the amount of Western capital invested in such places grew, the more likely were Western governments to establish formal control. Yet, despite this, the extension of Western economic power into tropical Africa was largely unsupervised and meant that the local populations fell under the control of white businessmen who were often interested in the exploitation of native land or of mineral deposits without any thought for the long-term viability of the areas they had invaded. The great drawback to profitable development of mining enterprises was the shortage of local labour that was reluctant to leave its traditional occupations. Hobson listed the brutal methods, such as violence, fraud, hut taxes, and various methods of conscription and expropriation including indentured labour, whereby entrepreneurs like Rhodes forced labour off the land and into the mines, often imposing inhuman conditions of living on the recruits.[34] In these circumstances, imperialism was little

---

[32] Ibid., 150–1.
[33] This chapter was composed of a series of articles written originally in the *British Friend* (1902), 53–5, 81–3, 129–32.
[34] *Imperialism*, 247–72. In the 1902 edition, Hobson added an appendix to this chapter on methods of labour recruitment by the Rand mining magnates of South Africa that was omitted from later editions (*Imperialism*, (1902), 298–304).

more than an engine for the extraction of unearned income: 'the stamp of "parasitism" is upon every white settlement' because 'nowhere are the relations between white and coloured people such as to preserve a wholesome balance of mutual services'. The small white populations 'remain an alien body of sojourners, a "parasite" upon the carcase of its "host", destined to extract wealth from the country and retiring to consume it at home'. The work done by the whites, even by Boer farmers, was minimal and their society exhibited 'laxity and torpor, the brief spasmodic flares of energy evoked by dazzling prospects among small classes of speculators and businessmen in mushroom cities like Johannesburg serving but to dazzle our eyes and hide the deep essential character of the life'.[35] He also feared that, without control, parts of Africa might fall into chaos, with private economic interests raising private armies and instituting 'personal despotisms', 'instilling civilised vices and civilised diseases', as in the Congo Free State under King Leopold's personal rule. And it might end 'in some terrible *debacle* in which revolted slave races may trample down their parasitic and degenerate slave masters'—a thought perhaps inspired by his knowledge of the Roman Empire.[36]

Britain's long-standing control of India had also resulted in parasitism though of a more complex kind. Although Hobson admitted that the statistics emerging from India were often unreliable, he was concerned that a considerable part of the revenues gathered through taxation in India went to recipients in Britain, that the Indian taxpayer was supporting an army used for general imperial purposes, and that 'nearly the whole interest on capital invested in India is spent out of the country'.[37] He also condemned the imposition on India of free trade in the interests of British textile

---

[35] *Imperialism* (1988 edn.), 282–3.

[36] Ibid. 230. In this chapter, Hobson quoted from Gilbert Murray's 'The Exploitation of Inferior Races in Ancient and Modern Times: An Imperial Labour Question with a Historical Parallel', in *Liberalism and the Empire* . For an earlier liberal/radical warning that imperialism might produce a Roman-style collapse in British civilization see Seebohm, 'Imperialism and Socialism', in Cain (ed.), *Empire and Imperialism*, 303–4. See also R. H. Betts, 'The Allusion to Rome in British Imperial Thought in the Late 19th and Early 20th Centuries', *Victorian Studies*, 15 (1971).

[37] *Imperialism*, 288. For a modern assessment of the importance of the 'drain' of Indian income to Britain in the nineteenth and early twentieth centuries see A. K. Banerji, *Aspects of Indo-British Economic Relations, 1858–1898* (Bombay, 1982), chs. 4, 8, and app. II.

exporters.[38] However, there is no doubt that Hobson saw the long-settled British relationship with India and the newer form in Africa as the forerunners of a much more epic and world-turning set of events about to unfold in China, where 'the spirit and methods of Western Imperialism in general are likely to find their most crucial test',[39] with massive consequences for the distribution of political and economic power across the globe in the twentieth century. Hobson had, of course, put China at the centre of the picture in his first attempt to predict the future of the world economy in 1891, and it had also inspired his first great breakthrough in understanding imperialism in 1898, so his concern now was no great surprise. But to understand why Hobson took China so seriously and fully to appreciate the argument he developed, it is necessary first to take a brief look at some aspects of the debate on China's future going on in Britain around the turn of the century.

The publication of Charles Pearson's remarkable *National Life and Character* (1893) marked the moment when the China question, or what was otherwise known as the 'Yellow Peril', first became a matter of widespread attention amongst elites of all political colourings in Britain. Pearson, a former academic historian who had had a successful career as a politician in Australia, came to believe that the laissez-faire/free trade world in which British character and enterprise had flourished was destined to destroy its founders and the industrial civilization they had built upon it. Pearson's central economic argument was remarkably similar to Hobson's of two years earlier though Pearson was unaware of it. He, too, argued that the growth of the global economy under the umbrella of imperial expansion was releasing an increasing flow of capital to the less developed parts of the world. The latter, especially China where labour was abundant, cheap, and highly skilled, would soon industrialize and begin to undermine the economic basis of white civilization. Reflecting his Australian experience and antipodean fears of Chinese immigrants, Pearson's vision of the future was drenched in a mixture of racial arrogance and fear. He expected that an industrialized Asia would throw off imperialist control and create a hostile, militaristic civilization which would put Europe and America on the defensive, forcing the latter back to their pre-imperial geographic limits. The one-time imperial powers would be

---

[38] *Imperialism*, 292–3.   [39] Ibid. 304.

forced to arm themselves against their resurgent former dependants, making the rise of the state inevitable; and the latter's role would also be much enlarged because, as industry declined and emigration ceased, heavy tariffs would have to be reintroduced and income redistributed in favour of the poor to prevent crisis and social break-down. Pearson's gloomy Spencerian conclusion was that industrial society would give way again to militancy and socialism, and the energetic, self-improving characters who had created, and been sustained by, liberal globalism would disappear.[40]

If Pearson's pessimism undermined the Cobdenite vision of a world of peaceful, mutually beneficial free trade[41] it was equally challenging to many imperialists. They supported the scramble for 'spheres of interest' in China for reasons most graphically illustrated by the American imperialist Brooks Adams. According to Adams, the great industrial nations had increased productivity to the point where they must export or die, and control of the huge China market was the key to survival. Nations left out of the scramble would fall into economic stagnation and would be forced into collectivism to curb unrest among the masses.[42] If, however, Pearson was right, the Brooks Adams solution to the coming crisis was unworkable because the extension of imperialism in China would reawaken the sleeping giant and produce precisely those outcomes imperialists wished to avoid. Of course, some fervent imperialists refused to accept Pearson's logic. To many of them, the Chinese were simply a 'backward' people quite incapable of matching Western technological skill and productivity.[43] Imperialists who did feel the force of Pearson's prophecies responded by arguing that this was the best reason for abandoning free trade and retreating into a protected empire that would also regulate 'unfair' competition

[40] C. H. Pearson, *National Life and Character* (1893), esp. 122–33. See also his 'The Causes of Pessimism', *Fortnightly Review*, NS 54 (1894), 441–54. There is a fine biography by J. Tregenza, *Professor of Democracy: The Life of Charles Henry Pearson, 1830–94* (Cambridge, 1968).

[41] Pearson's argument impressed some liberal thinkers such as James Bryce and Henry Sidgwick. Harvie, *The Lights of Liberalism*, 232–5.

[42] Brooks Adams, 'The Commercial Future, I—The New Struggle for Life among Nations (from an American Standpoint)', *Fortnightly Review*, NS 65 (1899), 274–83. On Adams see Semmel, *The Liberal Ideal and the Demons of Empire*, 96–8. For a very similar British argument about the vital future importance of the China market see Hallett, 'British Trade and the Integrity of China', 664–79.

[43] See W. S. Lilly's review of Pearson in *Quarterly Review*, 177 (1893), 126; S. Walpole's review in *Edinburgh Review*, 178 (1893), 285–6.

within its boundaries and do its best to ensure that the dependencies did not industrialize.[44] Otherwise, Britain would face 'international industrial warfare of the most savage intensity' with living standards reduced to a bare minimum.[45]

Fear and loathing of China reached a peak of intensity during the Boxer rebellion in 1900, the Chinese national response to foreign intrusion. The ferocity of the Chinese reaction prompted some knowledgeable Britons to forecast that the time would soon come when 'the Yellow Peril will be beyond ignoring'. Sir Robert Hart, the former Inspector-General of the Imperial Maritime Customs, predicted that the descendants of the Boxers would soon 'carry the Chinese flag and Chinese arms into many a place that even fancy would not suggest today, thus preparing for future upheavals and disasters never even dreamt of'. If the imperialist intruders could unite, disarm China, and subject it to the peaceful work of Christianity and industrialism for some generations, this outcome could be avoided. But Hart believed that this was unlikely and that European rivalry would most probably lead to the militarization of China.[46] Such arguments were countered by those who believed that the Chinese lacked 'the comprehensiveness of brain' to organize themselves for foreign conquest or to use modern mechanized means of warfare accurately.[47] Yet even those who disparaged China economically and militarily detected a more insidious menace: the real 'Yellow Peril' for them was the threat of mass migration of Chinese to Europe. The 'hideous possibility' was that Chinese competition would reduce wages drastically 'until the poorest white had become more degraded, because less abstemious, than the yellow alien'. Rigorous exclusion, as practised in Australia, was the only remedy for this imminent attack on the character of Western civilization that would realize Pearson's nightmare through the back door.[48]

---

[44] B. Kidd, *The Principles of Western Civilisation* (1902), esp. 21–9. On Kidd see P. Crook, *Benjamin Kidd: Portrait of a Social Darwinist* (Cambridge, 1984).

[45] J. B. C. Kershaw, 'The Future of British Trade', *Fortnightly Review*, NS 62 (1897), 749.

[46] Robert Hart, 'The Peking Legation: A National Uprising and International Episode', *Fortnightly Review*, NS 68 (1900), 735–9. *The Times* correspondent A. R. Colquhoun, whose book *China in Transformation* (1898) influenced Hobson's own thinking on China, shared Hart's apprehensions.

[47] L. Sanders, ' "The Yellow Perils" ', *Anglo-Saxon Review* (Dec. 1900), 97.

[48] Ibid. 100–2. The explicit racism of many British responses to their Chinese 'Other' is discussed in R. Bickers, *Britain in China: Community, Culture and Colonialism* (Manchester, 1999), ch. 2.

On the radical side, William Clarke and J. M. Robertson both bent Pearson's predictions to suit their own agendas. Clarke, who before his death in 1900 despaired of the reform process in Britain, thought that Western industrialism would be destroyed by Chinese advance but that Western financiers would stay in charge of Chinese industrialization. Europe would become the leisure centre of the new wealthy made fat through profits made in Chinese industry, plutocracy would undermine democracy as industry declined in Europe, and the continent would enter its 'epoch of rest'. Robertson agreed in part, arguing that Britain might become a 'deserted dustheap' unless the process was halted and the domestic market boosted by social reform and redistribution sufficiently to counteract Chinese industrial advance.[49] For the Fabians, Shaw recognized some potential benefits of Chinese development under Western capitalism. Assuming that 'foreign imports cannot harm English industry as a whole' he argued that, under free trade, sweated industries would be eliminated by Chinese competition and, provided the state organized Britain's resources efficiently, resources would flow into more capital- and knowledge-intensive goods to everyone's benefit.[50] But he also recognized the possibility that unregulated Chinese development could undermine Europe's industry and standards of living.

Clearly, if we meddle with China, and our interference does not relieve the poverty that produces emigration, we shall find ourselves in a Yellow Muddle that may bring the Chinese War to our own streets. If the Powers, to avert this danger, agree to deny to the Chinaman the international rights they force him to concede to Europe, competitive capitalistic exploitation of Chinese cheap labour on the spot will lead to a clamor [*sic*] in this country for protection against imports from China. On this point Imperialist statesmen must make up their minds promptly; for imports produced by foreign sweated labour have been in the past the most potent instruments of the downfall of Empires through Imperialism.[51]

Shaw then went on to claim that cheap imports of this kind could cause widespread unemployment in Britain, leading either to a 'bread and circuses' policy *à la* Rome or revolution.[52] 'The practical

[49] Clarke, 'The Social Future of England'; Robertson, *Patriotism and Empire*, 188.
[50] Shaw, *Fabianism and the Empire*, 51–2.
[51] Ibid. 49.   [52] Ibid. 53.

moral is that Empire will ruin us, as it ruined earlier civilisations, unless we recognise that unearned income, whether for British individuals living unproductively on British labor [*sic*] or British Islands living unproductively on foreign labor, is a cancerous growth in the body politic.'[53] His solution was a socialist reorganization of industry with minimum standards and wages set throughout the area of Western control to cut out unfair competition.

Hobson's own stance on China in *Imperialism* reflected the complexity of the debate, and though it incorporated much of the thinking of his article of 1891 it did so in a very different political context and one now influenced by the discourse of parasitism. The world, he argued, was on the brink of 'the most revolutionary enterprise that history has known' as capital export from the industrial countries began to penetrate China. He went on to examine a number of possible outcomes. First, China could soon then develop to the point where she might

turn upon her civiliser untrammelled by need of further industrial aid, undersell him in his own market, take away his other foreign markets and secure for herself what further developing work needs to be done in the other undeveloped parts of the earth ... reversing the earlier process of investment until she gradually obtained financial control over her quondam patrons and civilisers.[54]

This was the position adopted by Pearson but Hobson was not content to rest there. A second possibility was that China might initially be developed by the Japanese, who had already made great strides towards emulating Western industrial might, rather than by Western capital and enterprise, because of the cultural affinity between China and Japan. Then, provided that both countries could avoid becoming the financial clients of Europe or America, they could together become successful competitors with the older industrial centres 'swamping the markets of the West and driving those nations into a still more rigorous Protection with its corollary of diminished production'.[55] However, Hobson thought the most likely outcome of the development of a global economic imperialism was not the dominance of the great Asian nations over their original patrons, but rather a vast growth in the wealth and power of the finance capitalist class in the West and their subordinate clients

[53] Ibid. 54.   [54] *Imperialism*, 308.   [55] Ibid. 317–18.

in the East.[56] The losers would be the exploited masses in China, whose traditional way of life would be destroyed by Western-style industrialization, and the working masses of Europe and America, whose hard-won standards of living and democratic aspirations would be fatally undermined by the growth of Asiatic industry. The result—already forecast in 1891—would be a rentier economy in the West, in which the wealthy few would be served by

a somewhat larger body of professional retainers and tradesmen and a large body of personal servants and workers in the transport trade and in the final stages of production of the most perishable goods; all the main arterial industries would have disappeared, the staple foods and manufactures flowing in as tribute from Asia and Africa.[57]

China's industrial prospects were, Hobson thought, 'so enormous and expansible as to raise the possibility of raising whole white populations in the West to the position of "independent gentlemen" living, as do the small white settlements in India or South Africa, upon the manual toil of these laborious inferiors'. As living standards in the West declined, refractory elements could be quelled either by importing labour from the East or by the menace of an Asian mercenary army.[58] The West was already parasitic on its empires and the income flowing back from them was already transforming parts of it, such as Switzerland and the south of England, into societies dependent on imperial exploitation. The subjection of China would allow a 'vast extension of such a system . . . draining the greatest potential reservoir of profit the world has ever known in order to consume it in Europe'.[59]

Economic penetration of China had been slow in the recent past because the great industrial powers were in competition for stakes in China's future with all the dangers of war this had brought in its train. The disunity of the West had allowed the Chinese to play one nation off against another, putting off the evil day of Western dominance. However, Hobson expected that the great powers would soon learn 'the art of combination' and, under the sway of their dominant, cosmopolitan interest groups, join together to exploit China. For 'a parasitic exploit so gigantic' it was important to avoid war, which in modern times was becoming too costly, but to maintain militarism as a useful way of keeping social order.

---

[56] Ibid. 323.   [57] Ibid. 314.   [58] Ibid. 313–14.   [59] Ibid. 364–5.

Then would begin in earnest the exploitation of 'a mine of labour power richer by far than any of the gold or other mineral deposits which have directed Imperial enterprise in Africa and elsewhere'. The task would occupy the surplus capital of Europe and the United States for a generation as traditional society in China and industrial life in the West collapsed.[60] Unless drastic social reform in the West destroyed imperialism by cutting off the financial flows which sustained it, the world could be soon be dominated by parasitic finance capitalists exercising their power through 'inter-Imperialism'.[61] Having made his forecast, Hobson admitted that it might never materialize: but he believed that 'the influences which govern the Imperialism of Western Europe today are moving in this direction, and, unless counteracted or diverted, make towards some such consummation'.[62]

THE FUTURE OF IMPERIALISM: THE WHITE EMPIRE AND EMPIRE UNITY

Near the end of *Imperialism*, in what must be the least-read chapter in the book, Hobson went on to examine what might happen to the relations between Britain and its white-settled empire—the emerging Dominions of Canada, Australia, New Zealand, and South Africa—in the age of financial parasitism. His chapter reflected not only his long-running concern with the white empire but a general upsurge in interest in the idea of imperial unity fostered not only by the Boer War but by increasing anxieties about Britain's ability to survive as a great power in the twentieth century.[63] As already noted, some imperialists responded to the predicted rise of China as a competitor by calling for imperial unity. For others, the rise of big business in America and on the Continent, the sharp increase in global competition for markets in the 1890s, and the growing military power of Britain's rivals seemed to open

---

[60] Ibid. 310–13.

[61] Hobson uses this phrase on p. 332 of *Imperialism* to describe a world divided peacefully between a few great empires.

[62] Ibid. 365.

[63] The only historian who has recognized Hobson's interest in the white-settled parts of the empire is Wood, 'J. A. Hobson and British Imperialism', 491–5, and id. *British Economists and the Empire*, 253–5.

the possibilities for some dramatic *bouleversement* in world power that could only be contained effectively by a united British Empire. The recent loss of the remnants of the Spanish Empire in the Caribbean and the Pacific to the United States seemed an awful portent to many. The coming struggle to 'redivide the world' was often seen in stark terms. As one popular journalist put it in 1901, the struggle for existence was getting much tougher: he looked to 'the dangers of impending, national, if not racial, wars, wars on the most pressing economic grounds, wars for existence rather than for expansion or for national vanity, wars of hitherto undreamed of magnitude and undreamed of consequences'.[64]

Most crystal-ball gazers recognized that the empire's position was threatened most by Russia, Germany, and the United States. The fear of Russian imperialism in the Middle and Far East was strong and Germany was emerging at the beginning of the nineteenth century not only as an economic but also as a naval rival. But it was the United States whose progress was watched with most unease. Even in the 1870s and 1880s there were prominent voices calling for imperial unity and 'Greater Britain' with the newly forged Union offering both a stimulus and a warning.[65] By 1900 the latter's future dominance was beginning to seem irresistible. Lord Rosebery tacitly accepted this when, in his rectoral address at Glasgow University, he admitted that, had the American Revolution not taken place, then the centre of gravity of the empire would be moving from London to New York.[66] J. L. Garvin, prominent journalist and enthusiastic imperialist, recognized that 'America cannot be prevented . . . from attaining at some period during the twentieth century the industrial leadership of the world'. Whether the empire survived depended on whether Britain had the economic vigour to beat Germany for second place. If it failed, then it would face a 'dispeoplement like that of Ireland on a greater scale'.[67] W. T. Stead was more emphatic about the American challenge. He offered the British people two stark choices. They could join the United States, bringing their empire with them, to create an English-speaking

[64] Barker, 'The Economic Decay of Great Britain', 610.

[65] The power and example of the United States after the Civil War were crucial factors shaping both Froude's 'England and her Colonies', written in 1870, and Seeley's *The Expansion of England* (1883).

[66] W. T. Stead, *The Americanisation of the World* (1902), 152.

[67] Calchas, 'Will England Last the Century?', *Fortnightly Review*, NS 69 (1901), 25–6, 34.

union. If so, 'they may continue for all time to be an integral part of the greatest of all World-Powers . . . capable of wielding irresistible influence in all parts of the planet'. The alternative was 'the acceptance of our supercession by the United States . . . the loss one by one of our great colonies and our ultimate reduction to the status of an English speaking Belgium'.[68] In the face of this apparently inevitable transformation, there were many who believed that Britain's only hope of surviving as an imperial power was as 'Greater Britain', an economic union of the white parts of the empire which would be populous enough and strong enough to keep the non-white empire together and fend off the challenge of America and Germany.[69] The impetus to unity was also strengthened at this time by the direct participation of the white colonies in the war in South Africa. Empire unity posed a threat to free trade: many supporters of unity argued either for a *Zollverein* or for preferential tariffs within the empire as a means of bringing its parts closer together and encouraging ultimate political union.

The position adopted by Hobson had strong affinities with traditional radical thinking.[70] He objected to protection of any kind because he now believed that it aggravated maldistribution of income and stimulated foreign investment and because it would antagonize Europe and America: free trade was 'the most potent guarantee of peace which we possess'.[71] In any event, he expected the settlement colonies to reject a *Zollverein* because it would force them to replace customs revenue with a hated income tax. Moreover, they would only accept preferences if they could raise tariffs on foreign goods rather than reduce them on imports from Britain and this would inevitably harm their growing trade with foreign nations. Preferences would also raise prices in Britain and disrupt natural channels of trade.[72] On the wider front, he felt

---

[68] Stead, *The Americanisation of the World*, 151.

[69] Ogniben, 'The United States of Imperial Britain', *Contemporary Review*, 81 (1902); E. R. Faraday, 'Some Economic Aspects of the Imperial Idea', *Fortnightly Review*, NS 64 (1898). For the popularity of the 'Greater Britain' notion, see A. S. Thompson, *Imperial Britain: The Empire in British Politics c1880–1930* (1999), ch. 1.

[70] See Cain (ed.), *Empire and Imperialism*, 1–19.

[71] *Imperialism*, 106–7, 343.

[72] The argument in the first edition was slightly different here from that in later ones. See *Imperialism: A Study* (1902), 359–65. For changes in later editions see *supra*, Ch. 6.

that the settlement colonies had little to gain from political union
and that this would become obvious once the fervour of the Boer
War had passed. In any imperial assembly, their voices would be
swamped by that of the mother country and their freedoms
curtailed. In the present dangerous world they would also be
deterred from union for fear of finding themselves embroiled in
European and imperial wars.[73]

Nonetheless, Hobson was worried that the colonies could still be
tempted to become partners in the parasitic process. They contained
within themselves the same forces that impelled imperialism in
Britain and might therefore follow the same path.

The same conspiracy of powerful speculators, manufacturing interests and
ambitious politicians, calling to their support the philanthropy of missions
and the lust for adventure which is so powerful in the new world, may plot
the subversion of honest, self-developing democracy, in order to establish
class rule, and to employ the colonial resources in showy enterprises of
expansion, for their own political and commercial ends.[74]

Most white colonies had already embarked on sub-imperialist
expansion in their immediate neighbourhoods. The danger was
that they might be tempted into a federation if, under some future
Chamberlainite government, Britain offered to put the power of
the whole empire at their disposal thus giving additional impetus
to these local imperialist energies. The businessmen who supported
imperialism in Britain were already heavily involved in much private
and public investment in the colonies and might see it as in their
interests to push for a similar policy on the periphery of empire
just as they had done at home. Moreover, large business interests
in Australia or Canada might want to use the power of the
metropolis to further their own sub-imperialist designs. Indeed,
Hobson felt that that was what had happened in South Africa when
Rhodes and company, unable to carry out their expansion plans
on their own, had called in the support of Britain and plunged
the country into the Boer War as a result. If federation came about
on these terms, democracy in the colonies would be badly wounded.
Britain itself would be exposed to more risks as its junior partners
brought it into conflict with other great powers on distant imperial

[73] *Imperialism* (1988 edn.), 333–40, 351–2.
[74] Ibid. 345.

frontiers, and its own militancy would be exacerbated. Hobson did not think that this unholy alliance of metropolitan and white settler imperialism was the most likely outcome of present trends. He also believed that even if it came to pass it could only delay, not prevent, the fragmentation of the empire: once secure in their own imperial careers the colonies would find the link with Britain irksome and restricting.[75] His Gladstonian conclusion was that the colonies would become increasingly distant and independent and that this was for the best. South Africa apart, they would maintain ties with Britain because there would still exist the 'moral bonds of community of language, history and institutions, maintained and strengthened by free social and commercial intercourse'.[76] Nonetheless, vestiges of his old interest in imperial unity remained. He had suggested earlier in *Imperialism* that 'a voluntary federa-tion of free British States, working peacefully for the common safety and prosperity, is in itself eminently desirable, and might indeed form a step towards a wider federation of civilised states in the future'.[77] Nor did he rule out 'a possible future re-establishment of loose political relations in an Anglo-Saxon federation', thus linking himself with a long line of radical thinkers who saw the United States as a sister state rather than an enemy.[78]

INDUSTRY, DEMOCRACY, AND INTERNATIONALISM

At the beginning of Part II, when discussing the evils of militarism, Hobson had declared that military discipline might have its uses for 'clodhoppers' but that it harmed skilled labouring men by taking away their initiative. He saw the soldierly character as a 'degraded' one: the 'order and progress' which Britain had attained over the centuries had been achieved not by militarism, which could only impose a conformity in mediocrity, but 'by the cultivation of the

[75] Ibid. 345–9.
[76] Ibid. 354, 350. For Gladstone's position see Bennett (ed.) *The Concept of Empire*, 153–7.
[77] *Imperialism*, 332.
[78] Ibid. 351. Anglo-Saxonism was evident in, for example, Charles Dilke's *Greater Britain: A Record of Travel in English-Speaking Countries during 1866 and 1867* (1868).

ordinary civic and industrial virtues'[79] which now had to be reasserted in view of the dangers of imperialism. As we have already seen, 'industry' and 'industrialism' and other closely associated terms such as 'work' and 'co-operation' were key words for Hobson, their intricate meanings defined within an ongoing radical discourse he had connected himself with in the mid-1890s. They were words with hard, practical applications but they also had strong moral, imaginative, and even poetic overtones. Protean and multifaceted, they evolved in meaning over time and their meanings were always contestable as well as expansible even within the radical tradition itself, partly because of their implied connection with other contestable words such as 'liberty', 'character', and 'community' which were equally liable to redefinition. One of the important, if little noticed, aspects of *Imperialism* is that it contained an implicit, extended, and intricate definition of 'industry' and of 'industrialism', one rooted in the tradition best represented in the immediate past by Spencer but one developed beyond that level to account for changing times and for Hobson's own idiosyncratic 'take' on the modern world.

This definition began to unfold most obviously in Part II, chapter 2 'The Scientific Defence of Imperialism', where Hobson considered the validity of a cluster of contemporary biological and bio-sociological justifications for imperial expansion. The first of these was the claim that imperialism was a vital part of an evolutionary battle amongst nations to see who was the most efficient and thus the fittest to survive.[80] In *Imperialism*, this stance was associated with the biologist and eugenics expert Karl Pearson,[81] but it was very similar to the position of 'some liberals with socialistic leanings' whom Hobson had confronted elsewhere.[82] One of these was undoubtedly D. G. Richie, former Fabian and author of some foundational New Liberal philosophical texts. Responding partly to Hobson's reports of his visit to South Africa, Richie scorned the 'anecdotal historian, the gossipy journalist and the political

---

[79] *Imperialism*, 132–5.   [80] Ibid. 153–5.

[81] Hobson refers to Pearson's *National Life from the Standpoint of Science* (1901). For Pearson see Searle, *Eugenics and Politics*, *passim*. Hobson also mentions the American sociologist Giddings and he could also have included Benjamin Kidd, whose *Principles of Western Civilisation* was printed in the same year as *Imperialism*.

[82] J. A. Hobson, 'Socialistic Imperialism', *International Journal of Ethics*, 12 (1901), 44. The context is well described in P. Crook, *Darwinism, War and History* (Cambridge, 1994).

partizan' who thought wars originated in blundering statesmanship or the 'interested schemes of some self-seeking financiers'. War had always been 'the great maker of nations', part of the struggle for social progress: 'military success, in the long run does prove the possession of certain moral and intellectual excellences.' From Richie's perspective, the Boer War was part of a process which was dividing the world up between a few great empires which 'represent a higher stage' of civilization. These empires were more likely 'to be stable, less exposed to war' and were 'preparing the way for a federation of the world'. Vigorous and enterprising white races would inevitably overflow into backward lands like water flowing downhill, so responsibilities had to be recognized and authority imposed to prevent either 'black anarchies or white tyrannies'. If, he went on, all conquests were wrong, we would be obliged to hand back America to its native inhabitants.[83]

Hobson confessed that this provided one of the most popular and appealing arguments for imperialism, but he felt that it was logically flawed. From asserting that a people had a right to expand because they were militarily stronger, it was an easy but illegitimate step to claim that the winners were also morally superior and that it was their destiny, or even their duty, to civilize the world. It was faulty reasoning such as this, Hobson thought, which justified imperialism in the eyes of statesmen such as Chamberlain and Rosebery and inspired hordes of gallant young men, such as the late Hubert Hervey of the British South Africa Company, to give their lives to the cause. It was comforting, even uplifting, to believe that the struggle for imperial territory increased the vigour of the human race, gave control into the hands of those 'representing the highest standard of civilisation or social efficiency', and, by either eliminating or subjugating the 'inefficient', raised global standards of life and government.[84] Another flaw in the Pearson position, and by

[83] D. G. Richie, 'War and Peace', *Studies in Political and Social Ethics* (1902), esp. 136, 154, 158, 164, 168. The essay was first published in the *International Journal of Ethics* 11 (1901), and set off a furious and inconclusive debate with J. M. Robertson that spilled over into vol. 12. See also Richie's letters to *Ethical World* disparaging Hobson's position on 17 Feb. 1900, p. 110, 3 Mar. 1900, p. 142, and 29 Sept. 1900, p. 613. See also Hobson's response to the latter, *Ethical World*, 6 Oct. 1900, and p. 639.

[84] *Imperialism*, 155–61. Hobson quotes from Earl Grey's *Memoir of Hubert Hervey* (1899). Hervey and Grey's memoir are briefly discussed in Field, *Towards a Programme of Imperial Life*, 84–6.

implication that of Richie, as Hobson saw it, was that the former had admitted that, in order to make the imperialist nation stronger in the face of its enemies, the economic and social struggle within the nation had to be mitigated because this would produce social solidarity, raise the efficiency of the race, and preserve unity. If this was so, why not take the argument further and recognize that, by suppressing conflict amongst nations, some form of international government could make for a more efficient world order? Hobson admitted that a positive answer to his question presupposed that there was some emergent community of humanity, some embryonic society beyond the confines of nationalism and reflecting a 'certain homogeneity of character, interests, and sympathies' throughout the globe. Its existence was denied by some powerful figures, such as Richie and the Idealist philosopher Bernard Bosanquet, who were convinced that it was impossible to find 'the common experience necessary to found a common life' outside national boundaries, and by the prominent American sociologist Giddings, who saw 'like-mindedness' as similarly limited in scope.[85] Hobson had, therefore, to prove that international community and harmony was possible while distinguishing his idea of internationalism from the imperialist version proposed by Richie and others. The manner in which he did so indicated most clearly how he associated 'common life' and 'community' with industrialism in the complex and highly charged sense given it by Cobden, Smiles, and Spencer.

Most European states had a much 'larger community of experience' than a century before, based on 'direct intercommunication of persons, goods and information', which was laying the foundations for internationalism and a future federation of states who were increasingly 'like-minded':

The most potent and pervasive forces in the industrial, intellectual, and moral life of most European races, so far as the mass of the peoples are concerned, have so rapidly and closely assimilated during the last century as of necessity to furnish a large common body of thought and feeling, interests and aspirations which furnish a 'soul' for internationalism.

And Hobson made it plain in his concluding chapter that, in a world free of vested interests, internationalism would display itself, first, as an extension of national industry. The latter was critical in

[85] *Imperialism*, 161–7.

providing 'improved intercommunication of persons, goods, and information', out of which would grow the 'courts and congresses' and the 'intellectual internationalism' that would 'contribute to the natural growth of such political solidarity as was required to maintain this real community'.[86] Indeed, 'the main economic conditions affecting . . . working life' together with the process of education had already ensured that peoples were 'far closer akin in actual interests' than were their governments, who were still dominated by parasitic forces that needed hostile nationalism and imperialism to survive.[87] Industrialism bound peoples together in community and co-operation at both the national and international level: militarism, driven by imperialism, enslaved and divided them. But Hobson also wanted to redefine industrialism in a New Liberal fashion: the action of the state in equalizing opportunities actually increased the amount of competition in the nation, made it more vigorous in itself, and made external aggression redundant. As competition for land and resources was suppressed, the struggle between individuals shifted to 'higher planes' and 'ever higher forms of self expression'. And, within the widening circle of people with whom men identified themselves as growth proceeded, they also provided services for each other that were a part of 'that expanded individuality we term altruism or public spirit'.[88]

Hobson's interest in expanding and updating the idea of industrialism becomes clearer in his response to the second of the 'scientific' arguments he felt obliged to confront. How far was imperial expansion made necessary by a Malthusian imperative to command new land and resources? To respond to the question by saying that nations could export manufactured goods in return for food and raw materials was insufficient. Competition in manufactures was getting fiercer and international markets were overstocked: the terms of trade were likely to turn against industrial nations in the future and imperialism was one way to counter it.[89] Hobson's

---

[86] Ibid. 363.   [87] Ibid. 167–71. The longer quote is on p. 170.

[88] Ibid. 171–4. The quotations are from p. 172.

[89] Ibid. 174–6. The source used by Hobson, which he described as 'brilliant', was E. van D. Robinson, 'War and Economics', *Political Science Quarterly* 15 (1900). Robinson's argument has affinities with Ruskin's that Hobson does not mention (see *supra*, Ch. 3). Alfred Marshall was also concerned that the terms of trade would shift against Britain in the twentieth century as population began to press upon food supplies. See W. H. B. Court, *British Economic History, 1870–1914: Commentary and Documents* (Cambridge, 1965), 320–5.

answer was that the human species had now evolved sufficiently to allow conscious control of population increase—including the weeding out of the degraded and 'unfit'—and the reorganization of its economic life in ways that reduced dependence on foreign supplies of basic commodities. Every advanced nation now had the technological ability to raise enough food for its people provided that there was wholesale reform of land use allowing for 'intensive cultivation'. Hobson wanted to reverse the trend to urbanization with the dependence on foreign supplies of food and the degeneration of the population that entailed and spoke of a 'moral and aesthetic revolt against the life and work of towns'. Clearly, in his new moral universe, 'industry' ought to have greater place for agriculture and for the 'skilled, competent farmer'.[90]

The stress on agriculture had been part of Hobson's vision of a new economic society, and a new industrialism, since the mid-1890s. That vision, combining radicalism with Ruskin and outlined in *The Evolution of Modern Capitalism*, *The Social Problem*, and other major writings, was fully in evidence as Hobson met the third of the bio-sociological excuses for imperialism attributed to Charles Pearson in his *National Life and Character*. Would not the cessation of the struggle for food and resources produce a form of luxurious living that would weaken the nation and make it prey to more primitive but more aggressive enemies? But Hobson did not envisage a future industrialism based on material luxury. The intensive cultivation he had in mind required 'peaceful, steady, orderly co-operation', thus releasing much more 'freedom, energy and initiative'. For all its virtues in comparison with the militarism preceding it, industrial civilization had hitherto been of a 'rude' kind.[91] It was based on inequalities in income and wealth that had spawned machinery, crude standardization, the degradation of modern urbanism, and the struggle for overseas markets. It had been formative in the creation of that regime of underconsumption, oversaving, and foreign investment that spawned parasitic imperialism and which was pushing humanity back towards militancy. Indeed, Hobson thought of the early stages of industrialism as merely an advanced form of militancy, since he believed that with the coming of the New Liberal stage 'the lower military and industrial struggle

---

[90] *Imperialism*, 174–82.   [91] Ibid. 186.

ceases'.[92] Thereafter, mankind would devote 'a larger and larger proportion of energy to struggles for intellectual, moral and aesthetic goods rather than for goods which tax the powers of the earth'.[93] The new economy would be much more domestically based than the old, thus reducing the openings for international conflict and removing the need for the present armoury of tariffs and other obstructions to international intercourse. In future, under universal free trade, international competition would take place not with 'guns and tariffs' but with 'feelings and ideas' in what would be 'none the less a national struggle for existence, because in it ideas and institutions which are worsted die, and not human organisms'.[94] That open international environment would be the basis of a self-renewing, vigorous nationalism whose 'value and character are expressed through work', which was the foundation of all 'that is really great and characteristic in national achievements of art, literature and thought'. It would, in its turn, breed a healthy international competition in 'languages, literatures, scientific theories, religious, political, and social institutions, and in all the arts and crafts' while simultaneously creating the common life which would be the future basis for international government and for a federation of civilized nations.[95]

Yet one question remained to trouble him. If the Western nations developed on these lines they would be vigorous and inventive still: their purified industrialism would continue to encourage that energy which lay at the heart of their success in the past while allowing them to enter a federal union. But if they shed their own military might not they be ripe for defeat by more primitive but more militaristic nations? Hobson acknowledged the problem: 'we cannot get the whole world to the level of civilisation which will admit it into the [federation].'[96] He then pointed out that the non-Western world would most certainly be provoked to attack if it were subject to

---

[92] Ibid. 188. In this regard, Hobson's thinking is much closer to that of Schumpeter than has hitherto been recognized.

[93] Ibid. 183.   [94] Ibid. 186, 188.

[95] Ibid. 186–7. See also pp. 192–3 for a similar discussion where he declared that: 'Only by raising the crude, fragmentary, informal, often insincere beginning of international government into stronger, more coherent, and more complex authority can the struggle for life proceed upon the highest arena of competition, selecting the finest forms of social efficiency.'

[96] Ibid. 193.

parasitic imperialism and if Western nations put themselves at its mercy by recruiting huge mercenary armies amongst its peoples. He also clearly implied, however, that some level of armaments would be required to defend advanced countries against less advanced ones and he ended somewhat uncertainly, with a question of his own rather than with a confident answer: 'Is it possible for a federation of civilised States to maintain the force required to keep order in the world without abusing her power by political and economic parasitism?'[97]

IMPERIALISM AND THE 'LOWER RACES'

Hobson's vision of the relationship between industry, community, liberty, and progress strongly influenced his approach to the management of territories already brought under imperial control or threatened with intrusion by the imperial powers. It also led him to suggest very different solutions to the problems of the 'lower races' in black Africa on the one side and India and China on the other.[98] Despite his harsh critique of European capitalist activities in Africa, he was sympathetic to arguments about the necessity for the opening up of 'backward' areas in Africa to Western economic intrusion and for the extension of European political power in tropical parts of Africa and Asia. He agreed with Benjamin Kidd[99] that, given the rising demand for tropical goods, the need for the opening up of new areas of supply was growing and that they could legitimately be brought under the control of Europe in order to stimulate their development even if establishing a Western-style government involved some display of force. Hobson's justification for imperialism in Africa derived from a line of thinking that Montesquieu could have approved. The climate in the tropics bred 'indolence and torpor': as a result the 'arts of industry' were hardly cultivated there and it followed, naturally, that Africans were 'unprogressive peoples' stuck at a very low level of civilization. Intervention was, therefore, reasonable because 'there is no inherent natural right of a people to refuse that measure of compulsory

---

[97] Ibid. 195.
[98] Hobson seems never to have considered the plight of aboriginal peoples in white-settled communities.
[99] See Benjamin Kidd's influential book *The Control of the Tropics* (1898).

education which shall raise it from childhood to manhood in the order of nationalities' and it was justifiable 'not only on material but on moral grounds'. European government was necessary to organize the native populations and show them how to work effectively. Exposure to European civilization would then 'stimulate in them a desire for material and moral progress, implanting new "wants" which form in any society the roots of civilisation'.[100] Hobson's Ruskinian organicism led him to believe that, just as individuals within a nation had to act for the common good, so nations had to work for the good of mankind and no nation or race had the right to isolate itself from what was generally deemed to be progressive.[101] At the same time, it must be recognized that his interventionism was also based on a concept of industrialism that was in a direct line of development from earlier radical thinking.

Hobson was not, of course, advocating a capitalist free-for-all: that had led in the recent past to brutal exploitation of local labour, to expropriation of native land, and to economic parasitism.[102] The purpose of good government in Africa was to restrict capitalist intervention and to subject it to very strict rules. Economic development was to be carefully monitored and controlled to ensure that it was a natural outcome of African society and not some 'mechanical' imposition from outside which would destroy traditional civilization.[103] But, given what had happened in the recent past in South Africa and with the horrors of the Belgian Congo in mind, Hobson did not trust any particular European nation to

[100] *Imperialism*, 223–9.

[101] See Porter, *Critics of Empire*, 334. For a similar argument see Hobson, 'Socialistic Imperialism', 45–7. Given his strictures about the 'unfit' in Britain it is not surprising that, when discussing international governments of the future, Hobson should have considered 'a rational stirpiculture' which might 'require a repression of the spread of degenerate or unprogressive races', though he thought it very unlikely in practice.

[102] It should be noted that although he thought that all chartered companies were 'private despotisms', they could be nakedly exploitative, as in the case of the British South Africa Company, or they could be run in a 'scrupulous and far-sighted way' as by Sir George Goldie and his Royal Niger Company. His thinking here has some connection with that of Mary Kingsley in her *West African Studies* (3rd edn. 1964). On Kingsley, see Porter, *Critics of Empire*, esp. 149–55, 240–53.

[103] For 'mechanical' here see Hobson, 'Socialistic Imperialism', 54. Hobson's Rainbow Circle associate Ramsay MacDonald also feared that imperialism substituted the mechanical for the organic. See his 'The Propaganda of Civilisation', *International Journal of Ethics*, 11 (1900–1), 463–5. On MacDonald see Porter, *Critics of Empire*, 157–68, 185–90.

practise good government. What was required was international government, 'some organised representative of civilised humanity' which recognized the 'organic unity' of the world. Such a government would develop Africa for the benefit of all and would also ensure 'an improvement and elevation of the character of the people who are brought under its control'.[104] Like Ramsay MacDonald who also adopted an organic approach to the question of African development, Hobson insisted that any such government could only rule out exploitation by preventing European ownership of land, mining operations, or the forcing of labour. It would preserve as much of traditional society as possible while exposing it to the ideas and enterprise of Europe.[105] Hobson recognized that local labour was often reluctant to work in European capitalist enterprise: but local peoples should be left to move naturally, in response to over-population on the land or because 'the pressure of new needs and a rising standard of consumption' led them to look for new work opportunities. Wise imperial control would thus stimulate growth and change but only such as arose naturally out of existing society. 'Natural growth in self-government and industry along tropical lines would be the end to which the enlightened policy of civilised assistance would address itself' because, he argued, it was beginning to be recognized that there are 'many paths to civilisation' and 'liberty of self-development' was essential to avoid the imposition of an alien capitalism.[106] He summed up the matter:

So far as Imperialism seeks to justify itself by sane civilisation of lower races, it will endeavour to raise their industrial and moral status on their own lands, preserving as far as possible the continuity of the old tribal life and institutions . . . If under the gradual teaching of the industrial arts and the general educational influences of a white protectorate many of the old political, social, and religious institutions decay, that decay will be a whole-some process, and will be attended by the growth of new forms, not forced upon them, but growing out of the old forms, and conforming to laws of natural growth in order to adapt native life to a changed environment.[107]

This mixture of conservatism and liberalism arose naturally out of Hobson's blending of radical industrialism with Ruskin's more

---

[104] *Imperialism*, 229–32. Hobson, 'Socialistic Imperialism', 47–8.

[105] MacDonald, 'The Propaganda of Civilisation', 466.

[106] *Imperialism*, 243–5, 254–6. Hobson thought that the British government in Basutoland was beginning to operate on the right lines and MacDonald agreed. See 'The Propaganda of Civilisation', 466.

[107] *Imperialism*, 279–80.

conservative organicism and his own Idealist commitment to the common good. He agreed with MacDonald when the latter wrote that it was wrong to assume that Africans were 'doomed to go through an industrial revolution precisely the same as ours'.[108] Like the latter he believed that their progress depended upon creating an industrial culture of their own but he never doubted that it would be one that would ensure that they evolved as primary producers rather than as modern manufacturing nations.

INDIA, CHINA, AND INDUSTRIALISM

Hobson saw India and China in a rather different light, exhibiting little of that negative 'orientalism' which Said has argued blighted Western understanding.[109] Both were already industrial societies in Hobson's definition of that term and had built impressive civilizations that, in his view, were far more venerable and well rooted than those in Europe or America. Their industrialism, based on agriculture and a host of rural crafts that grew out of agriculture, was the key to the survival of the village communities that were the bedrock of those civilizations, of their religion, their arts, and their morality. They were functioning, complex, organic communities whose future would be put in jeopardy by the thoughtless imposition of Western capitalism. They were also societies from which Europe and America, 'the mushroom civilisations of the West',[110] could learn much. Indeed, he wanted to capture some of the essential spirit of Indian industry and incorporate it into the new industrialism he advocated. As his long quotation from Birdwood indicates, Hobson was among those who wanted to praise traditional, unmechanized Indian industrialism, with its natural artistic beauty and its freedom from ugly urbanism and pollution, in order to damn the distorted version which he believed had arisen in the West.[111] He felt that the recent advent of European-

---

[108] MacDonald, 'The Propaganda of Civilisation', 462–3.

[109] E. W. Said, *Culture and Imperialism* (1993), 12, 290–1, for comments on Hobson which are unravelled and unpicked below.

[110] *Imperialism*, 326.

[111] Ibid. 290–1. Hobson quotes here from Sir John Birdwood, *The Industrial Arts of India*, (1880). On Birdwood see J. M. McKenzie, *Orientalism: History, Theory and the Arts* (1995), 121–4. An appreciation of Eastern art often became a weapon in the hands of those in Britain with an anti-imperial agenda (McKenzie, *Orientalism*, 211–12).

type industrialism in India under free trade was disastrous both economically and morally: 'all who value the life and character of the East deplore the visible decadence of the arts of architecture, weaving, metal work and pottery, in which India has been famed from time immemorial.'[112] If Western capitalism were allowed unhindered access it would not only destroy the best of Indian industry but also undermine the village community on which civilization depended.

An industrial system, far more strongly set and more closely interwoven in the religious and social system of the country than ever were the arts and crafts in Europe, has been subjected to forces operating from outside, and unchecked in their pace and direction by the will of the people whose life they so vitally affected. Industrial revolution is one thing when it is the natural movement of internal forces, making along lines of self-interests of a nation and proceeding *pari passu* with advancing popular self-government; another thing when it is imposed by foreign conquerors looking primarily to present gains for themselves and neglectful of the deeper interests of the country.[113]

Hobson feared the same fate would befall China. He was not uncritical of Chinese society but he had a somewhat romantic vision of its strengths.[114] These, he believed, rested as in India upon an intricate intertwining of agriculture and on rural crafts supporting stable, long-lasting village communities. In the latter, all active members were roughly equal: they were largely free of government interference, had a strong moral base, and their citizens admired scholars and manual labours more than soldiers.[115] Western intrusion had disrupted this peaceful life through its militarism in China, by inveigling Chinese governments into an indebtedness that led them to increase taxes on local communities and by attracting labour into towns with a rapidity that threatened to undermine the communal land systems of rural areas. Capitalism would also impose 'a new system of industrial caste' upon China and, as the villages collapsed and urban society grew up, morals would decay also. 'The changes of external environment which have come with dangerous rapidity in Europe during the nineteenth century, forced

---

[112] *Imperialism*, 290.   [113] Ibid. 292.

[114] He did not assume, as the Fabians did, that the Chinese, like Africans, had a 'lower civilisation'. Shaw, *Fabianism and the Empire*, 45–7.

[115] *Imperialism*, 319–23.

still more rapidly on China by foreign profit-seekers, would produce reactions of incalculable peril upon the national life and character'.[116]

As in Africa, Hobson wanted to preserve as much as possible of the historic civilization of Asia. In India he was thus aligning himself with those British forces, from Metcalfe onwards, who wanted to protect the traditional institutions of India if only to ensure stability, a movement that had gained in strength after the Mutiny of 1857. His sympathy with India's artistic heritage was an echo of Morris's Ruskinian conviction that the spread of capitalism into the underdeveloped world was having almost wholly destructive effects: 'whatever romance or pleasure or art existed there is trodden down into a mire of sordidness and ugliness'.[117] His concerns were also similar to Gandhi's, whose exposure to Ruskin made him a passionate defender of the historical industry and crafts of his country.[118] Hobson's own respect for Asian tradition arose from a powerful sense of Western ignorance. As he wrote elsewhere, he was struck by 'how utterly all European nations fail to understand the delicate multiform thing which is rudely generalised as "the Oriental mind"'.[119] Despite this, Hobson was not an altogether conservative voice on Asia any more than he was in the African context. Although he argued that the West had much to learn from Asia[120] he insisted that the reverse was also true. 'Some strange fiat of arrest, probably due to mental exhaustion, has condemned the brown men and the yellow men to eternal reproduction of old ideas.'[121] Like

---

[116] Ibid. 324.

[117] William Morris, 'How we Live and how we might Live' (1884), in *Political Writings of William Morris*, ed. A. L. Morton (1973), 140. Morris was, of course, implicitly dissociating himself here from his other great mentor, Marx, who had a much more robust and optimistic view of the spread of capitalism in India.

[118] On Gandhi's use of the argument that Indian 'primitivism' made it unamenable to British control see McKenzie, *Orientalism*, 35–6. Ironically, Ruskin himself, at least after the Mutiny, disparaged Indian handicrafts as not based on natural models and took his inspiration from medieval Europe instead. Partha Mitter, *Much Maligned Monsters: A History of European Reactions to Indian Art* (Oxford, 1977), 239–47.

[119] Hobson, 'Socialistic Imperialism', 53. For a confident and patronizing attempt by an avowed imperialist to see into this 'mind' see J. L. Gorst, 'The Oriental Character', *Anglo-Saxon Review*, 2 (Sept. 1899).

[120] Cf. MacDonald, 'The Propaganda of Civilisation', 459–60.

[121] *Imperialism*, 325. This is a direct quotation from Meredith Townsend, *Europe in Asia* (1901), 9. Olivier also described Indian civilization as 'arrested'. 'The Moral Basis of Socialism', 123.

Mill and Gladstone before him, Hobson saw true industrialism as resting on powers of never-ending activity, powers vital to liberty and thus to both moral and material progress. The East had to be aroused from its 'sleep of many centuries' so that it might appreciate Western science, liberty, and literature.[122] Like African society, it needed to be exposed to the West in ways that would stimulate organic change. In its turn, the West could learn valuable lessons in attempting to overcome the perversions of its own over-mechanized and degrading form of capitalism. Yet while parasitic financial imperialism was the order of the day, neither side could learn from the other. 'What Asia has to give, her priceless stores of wisdom garnered from her experience of ages, we refuse to take; the much or little that we could give we spoil by the brutal manner of our giving. That is what Imperialism has done, and is doing, for Asia.'[123]

HOBSON, THE RADICAL TRADITION, AND IMPERIALISM

Hobson ended the book—the most eloquent and impassioned he ever wrote—by warning that 'Imperialism is only beginning to realise its full resources, and to develop to a fine art the management of nations.'[124] If it continued then the world was faced with a parasitism of the kind that eventually brought the ruin of the Roman Empire. What his discussion of China in particular revealed was Hobson's fear that, in the near future, imperialism would absorb a much greater share of Western trade and investment with all the possibilities for war and the destruction of European industry, liberalism, and democracy thereby implied. That analysis forecast the possibility of a huge transformation in the nature of global capitalism—and global political and social relations— comparable with the predictions of an imminent 'redivision of the world' made later by Hilferding, Bukharin, and Lenin and, in less structured form, by many of Hobson's contemporaries in Britain at the turn of the century. In that sense, what had happened in South

---

[122] How misleading this characterization of the Asian past was is evident in, for example, H. van der Ven, 'The Onrush of Modern Globalization in China', in A. G. Hopkins (ed.), *Globalization in World History* (2002).
[123] *Imperialism*, 327.
[124] Ibid. 361.

Africa was more significant to Hobson as an indicator of what was to come than it was in itself.[125]

The only sure way to forestall such a dreadful future was to undertake drastic measures of social reform in Europe and America that would remove the chief source of the problem, the unequal distribution of wealth and income in the advanced nations. Reform would revolutionize social and economic relations in the imperialist countries: it would also, by reducing international transactions to a much lower level, transform relations with the backward nations of the earth. Once the pressure for new markets and new outlets for capital was cut down, African and Asian societies would be left to develop naturally with international contacts under free trade being large enough to be a spur to development but not so large as to swamp, exploit, or destroy the indigenous economies and cultures. These societies would, in other words, be left free to take their own path towards modernity and to the freedoms that it brought in its train.[126] Cobdenism was thus approved: but, in Hobson's new moral world, it could work only in a very attenuated form. Nonetheless, the fact that Hobson's main economic inspiration at this time was derived from Adam Smith rather than Cobden does not vitiate the argument that his work is best seen as a sustained attempt to bring up to date a long radical tradition of criticism of empire and imperialism.

In immediate, practical terms, the key problem was the one he had identified in 1900: the British policy of going to the rescue of their citizens in trouble overseas which unfortunately allowed 'the most reckless and irresponsible individual members of our nation to direct our foreign policy'.[127] Unscrupulous politicians had often used this national predilection for their own ends. What made it a real danger to the nation now, however, was its use by those investors overseas who called upon governments to aid them when they were aggrieved even though the returns they received on their

---

[125] This approach to understanding Hobson can be found in Etherington, *Theories of Imperialism*, which deserves much more attention than it has received.

[126] Readers will recognize the affinity between Hobson's thought and that of E. F. Schumacher, *Small is Beautiful: A Study of Economics as if People Mattered* (1973). In thinking of international trade as a way of stimulating new wants and encouraging change, Hobson was also following in the footsteps of T. R. Malthus in his *Principles of Political Economy* (1820), though he was probably unaware of this.

[127] *Imperialism*, 357.

investments reflected the extra risks they were taking in putting their assets abroad. Hobson was sure that the biggest problem was not from 'genuine' investors but from the financiers who made their money out of fluctuating stock prices. He wanted to curb the risk that these people could use the power of the state to achieve their private ends through 'an absolute prohibition of the right of British subjects to call upon their Governments to protect their persons or property from injury and dangers incurred on their private initiative'.[128] This, he recognized, was a 'counsel of perfection' requiring the advent of a real democracy; and 'whether this or any other nation is yet competent for such a democracy may well be a matter of grave doubt'.[129]

Hobson's analysis in *Imperialism* is shot through with the mixture of radical and Ruskinian ideas that underlay his diagnosis of domestic maladies in *The Social Problem*. Those who lived on unearned income were parasites who harmed themselves and their host society and were agents of degeneration not progress. Imperialism, that 'depraved choice of national life',[130] was the ultimate parasitic activity, drawing rentier fortunes from the poor in the underdeveloped world in order to undermine true industry and the industrial foundations of modern civilization. It had no constructive role to play in shaping the world economy or world culture: its impact was negative for both conqueror and conquered. Empires were mere 'mechanical' contrivances imposing a false unity upon territories the imperialist nation could never assimilate. They were preventing the growth of vigorous nationalities based on organic industrial progress who would eventually provide the basis for a genuine future internationalism while preserving the genuine particularity of each of the parts. Yet, as he recognized, imperialism could call on an impressive range of intellectual and moral support and it provided the gravest challenge to radicals and liberals who cherished the cause of reform at home or in the empire. Since he saw it as *the* danger to the future world civilization in which he had invested so much intellectual and emotional capital, it is no wonder that Hobson was so bitterly hostile to imperialism and that he put so much of his energy at this time into combating it.

---

[128] Ibid. 359.   [129] Ibid. 360.   [130] Ibid. 368.

The Reception of 'Imperialism: A Study'

Imperialism was a seed that initially fell on rather stony ground even amongst some of the liberals and radicals who agreed with Hobson that imperial expansion was an evil to be avoided and even though a financial interpretation of the South African crisis was, of course, widely accepted on the left of politics. Older Cobdenite radicals such as Morley, and younger ones like Hirst, were happy to enlist New Liberal support in defence of free trade and anti-imperialism. Yet they retained a deep suspicion of the state as economic actor and were not keen to embrace the New Liberal reformism that was emblazoned across imperialism.[131] Such traditional Gladstonian thinking remained deeply embedded in the Liberal party until 1914 and even beyond.[132] Moreover, most mainstream liberals at this time were hostile to general theories of financial imperialism whether New Liberal in origin or not.[133] Many also thought that Hobson had absurdly overstated the harm done by imperial expansion. In a long discussion of imperialism, the *Edinburgh Review* accepted that the economic benefits brought by the new acquisitions in Africa were small, that they were 'an expansion of autocracy', and that imperialism could prove harmful to domestic prosperity.[134] They also agreed with Hobson about the importance to the economy of foreign investment and were even willing to believe that financial considerations had loomed large in the occupation of Egypt and in bringing the South African crisis to a head.[135] Yet they still felt that he had badly exaggerated his case in condemning imperialism so vehemently and that 'the economic danger we should

[131] See, generally, Howe, *Free Trade and Liberal England*, ch. 7. On Hirst see Emy, *Liberals, Radicals and Social Politics*, 104–5. For Morley's praise of Hobhouse's anti-imperialism and suspicion of his social remedies, see Collini, *Liberalism and Sociology*, 101.

[132] G. L. Bernstein, *Liberalism and Liberal Politics in Edwardian Britain* (Winchester, Mass., 1986), esp. 79–82, 101–3, 120–6; M. Dawson, 'Liberalism in Devon and Cornwall, 1910–1931: "The Old Time Religion"', *Historical Journal*, 38 (1995). See also Emy, *Liberals, Radicals and Social Politics*, 78–9.

[133] Some peace activists accused Hobson of forgetting that commerce was essentially peaceful. P. Laity, 'The British Peace Movement and the War', 153.

[134] 'Expansion and Expenditure', *Edinburgh Review*, 197 (1903), 357. The *Edinburgh* was Liberal Unionist in sentiment but it had a wide appeal amongst Liberals because it was against both 'obstructive Toryism' and 'reckless Radicalism'. W. E. Houghton (ed.), *Wellesley Index of Victorian Periodicals*, i (Toronto, 1966), 421.

[135] 'Expansion and Expenditure', 353–4, 362–3.

deplore is rather the waste and misapplication of capital resources than either their too rapid increase or their concentration, too great as it is for political stability, in the hands of a small minority of the population'.[136] Nor did the *Edinburgh* accept the underconsumptionist analysis on which Hobson's theory rested. They thought that his claims about the declining importance of foreign trade under a new economic regime were grossly inaccurate[137] and that the analysis was far too hostile to capital:

> Speaking, as he does, with Cobden's voice of free trade, of armaments, of internationalism and of empire, he yet turns his back on the most essential part of Cobden's teaching, the reliance on the free play of economic forces, and discards the solution of the social problem offered by a policy of free exchange in favour of the methods of socialism. Both in his hostility to capital and in his theories of taxation, he foreshadows the development which the free trade school expected and feared when they set their face against imperial expansion.[138]

Commenting a little later on Hobson's call for greater state intervention in the economy they wrote that 'Taxation is, of course, the engine which is to be employed for this purpose, and we arrive at a direct opposition to the free trade policy, for protection and socialism are but forms of the same economic heresy, and socialism, as Mr. Bernard Shaw reminds us, is the true alternative to free trade.'[139] Hobson did not go so far as Cobden in repudiating empire outright and he recognized that Europeans had a part to play in civilization: but he was far adrift of those liberals, most probably the majority, who still had a confident belief in Britain's 'civilizing mission' and looked forward to some form of white imperial unity.[140] Those few who supported a pro-Boer position were accused of making an unfair comparison of the British Empire, which was bringing the rule of law to large parts of the world, with Roman militarism and the exploits of Napoleon and Russian tsars. *Au fond*, the liberal faithful were assured, the empire was not

---

[136] Ibid. 368.   [137] Ibid. 348.   [138] Ibid. 361.

[139] Ibid. 364. Elsewhere it was argued that Hobson's book was not one 'to dismiss with ridicule or contempt because, in the eyes of most men, the author seems absurdly to overstate his case'. 'Foreign Politics and Commonsense', *Edinburgh Review*, 197 (1903), 269.

[140] On this theme, see the interesting articles 'The Paradox of Imperialism', *Monthly Review* (Oct. 1900), and 'The Empire and Militarism', ibid. (Nov. 1900); also [Arthur Elliot], 'The English Radicals', *Edinburgh Review*, 191 (1900), 222.

militaristic but commercial, though commercial expansion sometimes led to problems that had to be resolved by arms. In fact, it
was argued, it was precisely because the British Empire was imbued
with the ideas of liberalism that it was such a success.[141] Not
many liberals would have disagreed, nor did they repudiate the idea
of imperial unity that was supported by a number of liberal
thinkers.[142]

Even among the New Liberal fraternity, there were serious rifts
over imperialism and imperial policy. Richie had exposed these
differences in his response to Hobson's writings on South Africa and
they were in plain view at the meetings of the famous Rainbow
Circle that was at the heart of the progressive movement in Britain
at the turn of the twentieth century. The fervent anti-war views of
members such as Hobson, Clarke, Robertson, Perris, and Olivier[143]
were strongly contested by Samuel, Morrison, and Murray
MacDonald. MacDonald, a founder member of the Circle and a
strong believer in underconsumption, attacked Jingoism but felt
also that expansion 'has brought to birth the idea of the Empire as
a real community of interest'. He looked to imperial federation
under free trade as a step forward in world civilization.[144] Samuel,
despite his closeness to Hobson on questions of social reform, was
a supporter of Rosebery's ideas, which he called a 'rational patriotism', and he believed that, although the Boer War was the result of
diplomatic bungling, it had to be supported once it had begun.[145]
In a paper read to the Circle in 1900, he admitted that extending
the empire was an expensive business but insisted that it brought
new markets and, by contributing to economic progress, helped to
provide the funds for social reform. The 'average elector', he
claimed, wanted imperialism and social reform and both were

[141] Hobson was accused by a Fabian reviewer of confusing imperialism with
jingoism. *Fabian News* (1903), 7–8.
[142] Including, for example, J. H. Muirhead, 'What Imperialism Means', *Fortnightly Review*, NS 68 (1900), 181.
[143] Olivier, who was an original Fabian as well as a Rainbow Circle member,
supported a Hobsonian position on imperialism and was angrily opposed to the qualified approval of policy offered in Shaw's *Fabianism and Empire*. F. Lee, *Fabianism
and Colonialism: The Life and Thought of Sydney Olivier* (1988), 70, 77–8.
[144] Freeden (ed.), *Minutes of the Rainbow Circle*, 68–78; J. A. Murray MacDonald,
'The Imperial Problem', *Contemporary Review*, 80 (1901), esp. 486, 489–91; and id.,
'The Liberal Party', ibid., 79 (1901). For MacDonald see Emy, *Liberals, Radicals and
Social Politics*, 49.
[145] B. Wasserstein, *Herbert Samuel: A Political Life* (Oxford, 1992), 40–1.

attainable: the 'Little Englandism' of many progressives got in the way of reform, partly because the unpopularity of their views meant that few were elected to Parliament and the reform cause was thus under-represented in politics.[146] In his book *Liberalism*, published in the same year as *Imperialism*, Samuel conceded much of the Cobdenite case against empire—its high defence cost, its attraction of foreign hostility, its diversion of political energy.[147] On the credit side, though, he set empire trade, which he expected to grow enormously; the empire's role in fostering emigration without loss of nationhood; its vital place as a source of men and supplies in war; its civilizing and liberalizing role in the world; and its ennobling qualities for the average man since it strengthened in him 'the qualities of foresight, persistency, self-sacrifice and restraint'. This last he thought the 'richest gift' of empire.[148] Although some of the rhetoric could easily have come from a speech by Chamberlain, Samuel was keen to steer a course between 'Little Englanders' and 'Jingoes' and repeated his belief that failure to come to terms with empire had cost the Liberal party dear at elections.[149]

Whatever its subsequent fame, *Imperialism*'s lack of faith in the ability of Britons to run an empire, and in the possibilities of empire unity, undermined its influence in the early days of its publication. Hobson's drastic position on Britain's role in the international economy and his dire predictions about the outcomes of present policies also spoke to only a small fraction of Britain's liberal elites, new or old style, when first published and for many years afterwards.

---

[146] Freeden (ed.), *Minutes of the Rainbow Circle*, 73–4. For liberal attacks on Samuel's imperialist views, see Wasserstein, *Herbert Samuel*, 51.

[147] H. Samuel, *Liberalism: An Attempt to State the Principles and Proposals of Contemporary Liberalism in England* (1902), 301–10.

[148] Ibid. 310–25.

[149] Ibid. 338. See also H. Samuel. 'The Cobden Centenary', *Nineteenth Century*, 55 (1904), 905–7. Charles Trevelyan, another New Liberal sympathizer, also distanced himself from the Hobson position. See A. J. A. Morris, *C. P. Trevelyan, 1870–1956: Portrait of a Radical* (1976), 33, 36–7.

CHAPTER SIX

Dilemmas of a New Liberal: Free Trade, Foreign Investment, and Imperialism, 1903–1914

INTRODUCTION: HOBSON'S CONTRADICTIONS

Between writing *Imperialism: A Study* and the outbreak of the First World War, Hobson's thinking on imperialism presented a challenge for any serious reader of his works. In many ways, the Edwardian period was his most productive time as an economic theorist. During it, he developed his analysis of the concept of surplus to its most refined point, producing the outstanding statement of his position in *The Industrial System* in 1909 and successfully popularizing his findings in *The Science of Wealth* (1911) where he was careful to distinguish between the elements of income that were necessary to provide for future growth and those which were unearned and unnecessary and could be taxed away and redistributed socially.[1] Hobson's mature economics became a fundamental part of New Liberal thinking.[2] Hobson also incorporated this newer version of his theory into his Ruskinian vision of welfare with maximum effect in *Work and Wealth*, published in 1914, setting the themes outlined in *The Social Problem* in a more rigorous frame.

On the other hand, his writings on imperialism offer a much less clear and consistent picture. He repeated what he had said in

---

[1] The best introduction to this aspect of Hobson's thought is Allett, *New Liberalism*, ch. 3.

[2] It informs the economic analysis in L. T. Hobhouse's famous *Liberalism* (1911) in which New Liberalism is presented as a natural development of the nineteenth-century liberal tradition.

Imperialism on a number of occasions, issuing a second edition of the book in 1905 and developing some of the themes therein in new and sometimes fascinating ways. Much of this material, whether recycled or fresh, was written in response to the crises facing the Liberal governments after 1906. Hobson had hopes that these governments, which laid the foundations for what was later called the welfare state, were the true beginnings of industrial democracy in Britain. Inevitably, the forces of tradition and conservatism represented chiefly by the Unionist party assailed them. Especially during the battle over the budget of 1909, the constitutional crisis of 1909–11, and the Ulster crisis of 1914, Hobson felt the need to remind his readers of the precariousness of the new order in politics and of how parasitic imperialism was still the main force threatening its continuance, using language which would have been familiar to any student of *Imperialism*.[3] He also became heavily engaged in defending free trade after the launch of Chamberlain's tariff campaign in 1903. Hobson always thought of protection as a policy which could only benefit vested interests: but he recognized Chamberlain as a serious competitor for the working-class vote and one who had to be strenuously opposed. However, in the process of lauding free trade as an ally of industrial democracy, he sometimes took up positions which were at odds with arguments he had advanced in *Imperialism* and even put a question mark against his status as an economic heretic. Hobson was also caught up in explaining the reasons for the huge boom in British foreign investment of 1906–14. Protectionists claimed that free trade undermined British industry and forced capital out of the country. In opposing such claims, Hobson also moved a long way from the kind of reasoning which informed *Imperialism*. Overall, his writings on international trade, foreign investment, and imperialism appear to have a peculiarly schizophrenic quality at this juncture, offering visions of a new world of democracy and internationalism on the one hand, while almost simultaneously presenting dramatic insights into the strength and depth of the forces making for imperialism on the other. Indeed, the strain of trying to reconcile the view that imperialism was *the* force for evil with his increasing triumphalist

---

[3] For Hobson's own role in the context of this Liberal revival see Clarke, *Liberals and Social Democrats*, chs. 4 and 5; Emy, *Liberals, Radicals and Social Politics*, esp. ch. 4.

notions about the beneficial effects of international trade and factor movement on the progress of nations, eventually led to him to repudiate some of the key doctrines of *Imperialism* in a strange book, *An Economic Interpretation of Investment* (1911) which was never reprinted and is not mentioned at all in his autobiography. By this time, Hobson was no longer thinking of imperialism as a tragic outcome of a diseased capitalist system. Rather, he categorized it as a stage, probably an inevitable one, in a process of world development and one broadly beneficial to all participants.

FROM FINANCIERS TO FINANCE CAPITALISM

Hobson's commitment to the views he had expressed so trenchantly at the end of the Boer War was reaffirmed when he issued a second edition of *Imperialism* in 1905 with a few alterations to the text, some of which reinforced the argument. One of his main contentions in *Imperialism* was that imperial expansion in Africa and Asia, especially expansion into tropical areas, had brought minimal benefits in trade terms. However, some of the evidence he had produced in the first edition undermined rather than strengthened his case.[4] In chapter 2 of Part I of the revised edition, Hobson tried to strengthen his claims about the weak association between foreign trade growth and recent imperial expansion. He not only omitted to mention the importance of trade with the recently annexed Boer republics but also cut out the sections that had considered South Africa as a tropical rather than a white-settled territory. Moreover, Egypt was now omitted from the table that showed trade with recent acquisitions. He was thus able to conclude that the export trade with new territories amounted to about £9 million and imports from them were worth only £8 million. Britain's Malayan acquisitions accounted for more than half of all this trade and Hobson played down its significance by emphasizing that it was largely 'through traffic with the Far East'.[5]

A year later, he also took the opportunity provided by a new edition of his best-known book, *The Evolution of Modern Capitalism*, to extend his analysis of finance capitalism, an analysis only briefly undertaken in *Imperialism* and which had strong

---

[4] See Ch. 4, *supra*.   [5] *Imperialism* (1988 edn.), 36–40.

similarities to that produced later by Marxist thinkers and by Schumpeter. Again, most of his evidence on the rise of the corporate economy and monopoly practice came from the United States but, using the recent work of British analysts,[6] Hobson was able to show the emergence of a rash of new combinations and amalgamations in iron, steel, engineering, and chemicals at the turn of the century though nearly all were more loosely structured than were the leading American combines. He also noted that monopoly in British business did not just occur in industries where there were economies of large-scale production but was also related to other factors such as successful branding, or the influence of the state as was the case with the armaments companies.[7]

In a new chapter 10 he also gave, for the first time, a thorough account of the role of the financier as the key element in emergent big business, using his own experience in the United States and his reading of Veblen[8] and other contemporary American economists to add to the position taken up in *Imperialism*. Hobson did not simply condemn finance and financiers: he recognized that they had a part to play in promoting new enterprise and in marketing stock in existing companies. In performing these tasks, financiers enhanced the efficiency of the system.[9] At the same time, he emphasized the control exercised by the relatively few financial establishments and their dominance of the small stockholders who were a mere 'capitalist proletariat'.[10] Financial power was so concentrated and so unregulated that it was often a force for evil, due especially to the financier's ability to control the market speculatively through his manipulation of information and to combine industrial units into trusts and cartels which raised prices and profits by restricting output.[11] Using Standard Oil as his main example, Hobson argued that such monopolies created excess profits that were used to extend

[6] H. W. Macrosty, 'Business Aspects of British Trusts', *Economic Journal*, 12 (1902); E. Hubbard, 'American "Trusts" and English Combinations', ibid., esp. 169–72.

[7] J. A. Hobson, *The Evolution of Modern Capitalism* (1906 and subsequent edn.), 205–7, 208–9. For the 1897–1902 merger boom see L. Hannah, *The Rise of the Corporate Economy* (2nd edn., 1983), 21–3.

[8] Thorstein Veblen, *The Theory of Business Enterprise* (1904). A product of Hobson's visit to America was his 'The American Trust', *Economic Review*, 14 (1905).

[9] *Evolution of Modern Capitalism*, 245.

[10] Ibid. 242.   [11] Ibid. 235–55.

market control by buying in other companies in allied fields, the whole being controlled via a network of interlocking directorships. These combines, he believed, tended 'more and more to assume the shape of a purely financial power'. Moreover, as trusts became dominant in the economy, the excess profit generated had to be invested abroad. Trusts gave rise to oversaving and thus to foreign investment and an imperialist drive for markets, 'primarily markets for investment, secondarily markets for surplus products of home industry'. He concluded that concentration of capital, aided crucially by protectionist policies, was the chief reason for the recent conversion of the United States to imperialist adventure and for the pressure there for larger defence expenditure. The latter provided big business with lucrative contracts and helped to 'forward the aggressive political policy imposed on the nation by the economic needs of the finance capitalists'.[12] Clearly, the relationship between industry, finance, government, and imperialism was looser in Britain because big business was less in evidence: but, as one of the leading British analysts had noted, the combination movement there was only in its infancy and could be expected to grow to the point where serious state intervention might be necessary to control it.[13]

What is of particular interest here is that Hobson saw South Africa as a prime example of this new form of capitalism adapted to local circumstance. The South African economy was dominated by a small group of financiers whose power rested on diamonds and gold. They had used the wealth generated there to control most other major investment outlets and to wield political power. 'In new unsettled countries the financier is in constant need of political assistance' and, to achieve their end of maximizing profits, they had 'worked' the political process. 'The newness of the country and the absence of any earlier growth of strong vested interests have enabled these financiers, drawn from all the European countries, to develop the latent powers of pure finance more logically than elsewhere.' These men were also 'financial intellects of the highest order' who had bought the press, subsidized and flattered politicians in Britain as well as South Africa, and finally provoked the recent war. Adventurers and 'concession mongers' such as

---

[12] Ibid. 259–64.
[13] H. W. Macrosty, 'The Growth of Monopoly in British Industry', *Contemporary Review*, 75 (1899), 377–8.

Jameson and Rhodes were necessary to the success of capitalist schemes in South Africa and aristocratic members of the board of the British South Africa Company and other concerns were also useful for political purposes. To Hobson, however, the key figures were the pure financiers—Beit, Wernher, Eckstein, Barnato. Rhodes, he now thought, had been particularly helpful to them because his political genius and his imaginative flair gave 'a temporary cloak of political significance to adventures which were *au fond* operations of the stock market. His disappearance has exposed to plainer view the actual mechanism of South African finance.' Hobson supported his argument with tables showing how a group of twenty-four men controlled the major firms through interlocking directorships and that six of these made up the 'small inner ring of South African finance'.[14] It is also clear that he thought the concentration of capital was much greater, and the links between capitalism and politics much stronger, in South Africa than they were in Britain itself. Hobson had already suggested in *Imperialism* that South African capitalists had turned to Britain to help them achieve their imperialist goals only when they could not be reached by purely local means.[15] It would not be difficult to infer from what Hobson wrote in 1906 that the South African war and the conquest of the Transvaal were examples of a successful attempt by a highly concentrated and unusually influential sub-imperialist capitalism to impose its policies on the metropolis where the forces of finance were more loosely tied both to the press, to other sectors of the economy, and to government.

His analysis of South Africa was developed in other ways. In the second edition of *Imperialism*, Hobson also took account of Milner's attempt to draft in Chinese labour to reactivate the Rand mines after the war. He saw this simply as an attempt to restore profits by undercutting the wages of white labour. Such exploitation could not, in his view, stimulate the demand necessary for long-term industrial or agricultural development in South Africa:

upon such an economic foundation no secure fabric of industrial and political civilisation can be erected: after a single generation of feverish gold-getting, in which British supremacy is maintained by a constantly changing majority of temporary town residents, the industrial strength of the country

---

[14] *Evolution of Modern Capitalism*, 265–72.
[15] Hobson, 'Capitalism and Imperialism in South Africa', 5–9.

must steadily and surely decline, returning not to the more primitive condition of wholesome agriculture from which it temporarily emerged, but to a prolonged miserable struggle of trade and manufactures in a country strewn with the decaying wreckage of disused mines and rotting towns. Hebrew mining speculators, American and Scotch engineers, Chinese miners, German traders will evacuate the country they have sacked, leaving behind them a population of Boers spoiled in large part by their contact with a gambling and luxuriant European civilisation, and a host of Kaffirs broken from the customary life of agriculture and hanging around the cities of South Africa—a chronic pest of vagabonds and unemployed.[16]

Under the hammer of parasitic capitalism, South Africa would degenerate in a more spectacular fashion than had London in the late nineteenth century.[17] Imperialist exploitation could not act to bring to South Africa the kind of industrial civilization that Hobson thought was the foundation for widespread prosperity, liberty, and democracy.

Hobson had previously argued that the controllers of the South African economy would abandon the British connection when it had served their purpose in uniting South Africa under a government sympathetic to capitalism. Writing in 1909 of the coming Union of South Africa eventually created a year later, he claimed that the Union would be dominated by the Boers who had only accepted the imperial connection out of temporary necessity. There were those in Britain who argued that the war of 1899–1902 was justified by the Union but, consistent with his earlier ideas, Hobson denied this: unity was coming anyway because South African economic development was creating an irreversible dependence amongst the states. Without the war, unity might have come sooner and been less dominated by the Dutch nationalism the war had inflamed. He also poured scorn on the idea that union in South Africa was a step in the direction of imperial federation. In the second edition of *Imperialism*, Hobson had strengthened his claims that imperial federation was impossible by emphasizing that each of the Dominions had a vested interest in boosting its own industrial development and that this would make economic union, the

---

[16] *Imperialism*, 277.
[17] Put into more modern language, Hobson was arguing that the linkage effects of mining development on the internal economy would be very small. See also his article 'The Industrial Future of South Africa' in *Co-operative Wholesale Societies Annual* (1901).

basis of imperial federation, very unlikely.[18] A trip he made to Canada around this time confirmed his view of Dominion economic development. It convinced him that Canada was moving towards effective independence and that, insofar as it was willing to let foreigners into its markets, it would favour the United States as least as much as Britain in the future.[19] In 1909 he went further, arguing that all the Dominions were moving away from Britain even on foreign policy matters and that they would not fight to preserve the empire in the event of a European war. Beyond this, federation was impossible because the empire was half independent, half slave, with South Africa a particular problem because it was both. British control of India made it tolerant of the colour bars that disfigured South Africa and made the latter unjust, undemocratic, and unstable. His conclusion was that South Africa was more like the southern United States than Australia or Canada and would be a source of unrest and division in the empire rather than unity.[20]

IMPERIALISM AND THE NORTH–SOUTH DIVIDE

The advent of the Liberal government and the beginnings of what was later called the welfare state certainly heartened Hobson considerably. But he remained acutely aware of the power of vested interests within the Liberal party itself as well as those massed together in the Conservative party. His fears were at their height in the years 1909–10. Given the constraints of free trade and the need to raise revenue for social reform and for rearmament, the Chancellor of the Exchequer, Lloyd George, introduced his super-tax proposals. They were deliberately intended to provoke the Conservative-dominated House of Lords, which had already put the brake on several Liberal reforms, and they succeeded brilliantly.[21] The Lords threw out the budget, precipitating a constitutional crisis that was only resolved, after two elections in 1910

[18] *Imperialism*, 341–2.

[19] J. A. Hobson, *Canada Today* (1906), esp. 65–9, 99–105, 134–42.

[20] J. A. Hobson, 'South Africa as an Imperial Asset', *English Review*, 3 (1909), 324–34. This essay was reprinted in his *The Crisis of Liberalism* (1909) and in Hobson, *Writings on Imperialism and Internationalism*, ed. Cain.

[21] See A. K. Murray, *The People's Budget, 1909–10: Lloyd George and Liberal Politics* (Oxford, 1980).

had returned the Liberals to office with a reduced majority, in the Parliament Act of 1911 which restricted the Lords' veto. Hobson thought that the budget had been forced on the Liberals by rearmament and the 'Dreadnought' crisis it provoked with Germany and that there was no real democratic conviction behind it. But the budget did threaten 'unearned income' and the mass ranks of conservatism were thrown against it lest the idea of progressive taxation should become accepted by the mass of the electorate. In 1909, he assessed the interests lined up against reform in one of his most Gramscian passages.

The forces of Conservatism must use every weapon in their armoury, constitutional, electoral, educational; every art of menace, cajolery, misrepresentation and corruption, which the control of the party machinery, landlordism, 'the trade', finance, the Press, the Church, 'Society', 'sport', the 'services', place at their disposal, will be plied with unexampled ardour. The House of Lords only forms the first line of the trenches. Behind it lies a whole row of defences, represented by the laws and the judiciary, the bureaucracy, the Court, the electoral machinery (favouring at every turn the power of the purse), the secret unrepresentative character and working out of Cabinet government, the manipulation of public opinion through the public house, the Press, the pulpit and those other instruments of popular instruction which depend for their financial support upon the charity of the propertied classes.[22]

These were the sources of 'Oligarchy, Protection, Militarism, Imperialism'[23] and the latter was one of the main weapons 'exploited by Conservatism to break and dissipate the new forces of social reform which were beginning to assert themselves in Liberalism'.[24] In warding off attacks on economic privilege, the vested interests relied mainly on the call to individualism, supported by orthodox political economy, and on fostering that competitive instinct in men that led to foreign rivalry and imperialist exploit.[25] Hobson, along with other radicals, was particularly upset by the Liberal government's commitments to rearmament and its alignment with France and Russia against Germany. Apart from the enormity of siding with the Tsar, the suppressor of democratic institutions in his own country, radicals also drew the lesson that such militaristic policies were a clear indication of the hold which vested

---

[22] Hobson, *The Crisis of Liberalism*, p. x.
[23] Ibid. 188.   [24] Ibid. p. viii.   [25] Ibid. 183–4.

interests still had over the formation of policy.[26] As Hobson put it, 'for some time to come high officials in this country will, by their economic interests, their upbringing and their social habits, be in most imperfect sympathy with the aspirations of democracy'.[27] This was particularly dangerous in relation to foreign and imperial policy where the House of Commons was not traditionally much consulted and where the diplomats and politicians involved were, even during Liberal administrations, very much of the old school. 'Since foreign policy determines in the main our naval and military expenditure and policy, the aristocracy in foreign affairs virtually restricts the powers of the [House of] Commons over finance and through finance over the whole range of domestic policy.'[28]

Hobson's strong awareness of the fragility of the radical cause and the strength of the forces of reaction was evident even in his more academic work. In 1910 when analysing the outcome of the first election of that year, Hobson built upon some scattered remarks he had made in *Imperialism* to produce a pioneering piece of electoral sociology. The Liberal and the Labour vote was, he noted, largely concentrated in the Celtic fringes and in the north of England, or in 'Producer's England' where industry set the tone of modern life. On the other hand, the south of England, the Conservative party's stronghold, he labelled 'Consumer's England' and claimed that there it was the leisured class, living on unproductive surplus, who dominated attitudes and expectations. This leisured class, he explained in language clearly influenced by Veblen, was also a rentier class.

The Home Counties, the numerous seaside and other residential towns, the cathedral and University towns, and in general terms the South, are full of well-to-do and leisured families, whose incomes, dissociated from any present exertion by their recipients, are derived from industries conducted in the North or in some oversea country. A very large share, probably the major part, of the income spent by these well-to-do residential classes in the South, is drawn from investments of this nature. The expenditure of these incomes calls into existence and maintains large classes of professional men, producers and purveyors of luxuries, tradesmen, servants and

[26] J. A. Hobson, 'England's Duty to the Russian People' *South Place Magazine*, 12 (1907), 147–8; id., 'The Art of Panic Making', ibid., 14 (1908), 118–20.
[27] *The Crisis of Liberalism*, 14. For the context see Morris (ed.), *Edwardian Radicalism*.
[28] *The Crisis of Liberalism*, 10.

retainers, who are more or less conscious of their dependence on the will and patronage of persons 'living on their means'. This class of 'ostentatious leisure' and 'conspicuous waste' is subordinated in the North to earnest industry: in the South it directs a large proportion of the occupations, sets the social tone, imposes valuations and opinions. This England is primarily regarded by the dominant class as a place of residence and playground in which the socially reputable sports and functions (among which church-going, the theatre, art, and certain mild forms of literary culture are included) may be conducted with dignity and comfort. Most persons living in the South certainly have to work for a living, but much of their work is closely and even consciously directed by the will and demands of the moneyed class . . .[29]

Hobson was well aware that 'unproductive surplus' was gathered from northern industry through various kinds of monopoly but he was also aware that unearned income came from rentier sources, often in foreign lands, and that the south of England was its main destination. It was this income—called 'surplus' in *The Industrial System*—which formed the backbone of the forces of 'Imperialism, Militarism, Protection, Oligarchy'. They dominated a huge class of unorganized and deferential labour and relied upon the Conservative party to defend their interests against the 'intelligent artisans' who formed the backbone of Liberalism. These latter were often trade unionists 'whose conditions of employment and of living evoke energy of mind and educate them in habits of co-operative action towards common ends'.[30] They were the major force behind the social reform movement.

Hobson made the link between foreign investment, imperialism, and southern England plainer in another article in the same year when he reinvoked the 'parasitism' that had occupied such an important place in his analysis in *Imperialism*. After discussing the parasitic nature of 'Brighton, Bournemouth, Eastbourne, Tunbridge Wells' and declaring that 'an enormous proportion of the work of the Metropolis is predatory activity fraught with no net social utility' he broadened the analysis.

---

[29] J. A. Hobson, 'The General Election: A Sociological Explanation', *Sociological Review*, 3 (1910), 113. Reprinted in *Hobson: Writings on Imperialism and Internationalism*, ed. Cain. For a modern analysis see G. Blewett, *The Peers, the Parties and the People: The General Elections of 1910* (1972).

[30] 'The General Election', 113–17. For a similar analysis, see J. A. Hobson, 'The Two Englands', in *A Modern Outlook* (1910).

What the pleasure centres of the south are to the rest of England, England herself is becoming to the Empire . . . A certain self-continence of England has kept her within moderation in the treatment of dependencies. For the most part, she has eschewed the direct methods of plunder adopted by great empires of the past. But indirectly and surely parasitic habits are growing upon her. Our treatment of India best illustrates our more subtle modes. Not by direct extortion of tribute do we suck advantage out of her; trade, officialism, and investments are the modern methods, more effective for the very reason that they retain the semblance and to some extent the reality of mutualism. Some work we do for India, but nothing at all commensurate with the large sums we draw from her as expenses of government, pensions, profits on trading monopolies and other investments. It seems probable that in the not remote future both England and other highly developed industrial nations of West Europe will, through the economic suckers of investment, live to a larger and larger extent a parasitic life, exploiting under a system of economic serfdom or unequal exchange the lower races of the earth . . .[31]

The City of London had been much alarmed by Lloyd George's supertax proposals which they claimed trenched on the investment capital of the nation.[32] Hobson reacted to this by examining the City for the only time in his career, albeit briefly. To do so, he drew a contrast between 'proprietary' parasitism, where the receivers of income were entirely passive, and 'predatory' parasitism which required a certain skill and effort in drawing sustenance from the victim. Landlords and the directors of industrially based joint stock companies were often examples of the former while the City exhibited many examples of the latter. 'Under a thin cloak of social service and genuine utility it covers a great predatory system.' Hobson acknowledged that City financiers had a role to play in 'directing large currents of capital into serviceable channels' and were 'a necessary instrument in this important work of distribution'. Yet 'enormous abuses are commingled with these uses'.

. . . the bigger financier, by speculating in fictitious stock or fictitious goods, creates artificially the fluctuations in price from which his profits are derived; the promoter, by false valuations and specious advertisement, deceives investors and cancels the value of their savings: the princes of

---

[31] J. A. Hobson, 'Social Parasitism', *English Review*, 4 (1909–10), 357–8.
[32] On the City's views see Kynaston, *The City of London*, 494–502. For a wider view of elite reaction to the budget see H. V. Emy, 'The Impact of Financial Policy on English Party Politics', *Historical Journal*, 15 (1972).

finance mould politics and public opinion, raise national crises and sway the destinies of empires for the benefit of their pockets. The very difficulty, perhaps the impossibility, of separating legitimate from illegitimate finance is the protection and encouragement of financial parasitism.[33]

If there was a strain of uncertainty in Hobson's assessment of the utility of the City it is clear that he had a very strong sense of how deeply embedded in British economic life and culture were the forces of conservatism and how difficult it would be to eliminate them. Indeed, although he had no doubt that, in the long run, the new moral world which he hoped for would eventually appear, Hobson was also constantly warning the faithful about the enormous strength of the vested interests, ideological as well as material, and of their ability to slow down or even reverse the tide of reform. Financial parasitism and imperialism were still dominant themes in his writing. He never made a more concerted attempt to describe the peculiarities of the British capitalist structure and the role of finance within it than at this time; and the roots of his own thinking in the radical industrialism of the provinces—the provinces of Paine, of Bright, of Cobden, and of Spencer—was never more evident than it was in 1909–10. His picture of southern Britain as a paradise for parasites is, of course, hugely overdrawn and completely misses the economic dynamism which made London and the south-east corner of England the most complex, wealthy, and fast growing part of the national economy. Yet he was right to stress that in economic structure and political affiliation it was sharply different from the industrial provinces and that its economy depended far more on traditional sources of wealth and the returns on foreign investment than did other parts of the economy.[34]

DEFENDING FREE TRADE

Hobson's deepening understanding of the nature and the strength of the interests supporting British imperialism revealed in his writings on domestic politics contrast rather starkly with the more optimistic

[33] 'Social Parasitism', 353–4.
[34] The best introduction to the regional economic differences in Britain is C. H. Lee, *The British Economy since 1700: A Macroeconomic Survey* (Cambridge, 1986). See also id., 'The Service Sector, Regional Specialisation and Economic Growth in the Victorian Economy', *Journal of Historical Geography*, 10 (1984).

note which he struck in his writings on foreign trade and foreign investment, most of which was produced in the context of the debate over tariff protection. One year after *Imperialism* was published, Chamberlain launched the tariff reform campaign, his answer to the complex of domestic and international issues facing the British voter. Chamberlain hoped, through a system of mutual preferences, to begin the long process of uniting the empire, reversing the perceived decline in Britain's status as a great power in the twentieth century, and safeguarding British industrial development in the face of fierce and growing foreign rivalry. He also promised to bring full employment and, by raising tariff revenues, to provide funds for measures of social reform such as old age pensions. The campaign was a frontal attack on Liberalism as a political force, an attempt to head off the Liberal party's post-Boer War challenge by attracting the mass vote for a rival conception of welfare based on imperial foundations.[35] Tariff reform was a serious threat to Liberal domination of industrial Britain and the ideologues of 'Constructive Imperialism'—Ashley, Cunningham, Mackinder, Hewins, and others—also presented a formidable intellectual challenge to the New Liberal philosophy of Hobhouse and Hobson. For the Constructive Imperialists were also champions of industry, suspicious of the City and finance and believers in organic community—though one forced to fight for its life in an amoral Darwinian universe of competing empires.[36]

In *Imperialism*, Hobson had looked at protection and preference almost entirely from the point of view of government finance and war, but now he had to broaden his analysis to meet the new menace, becoming an active propogandist for the free trade cause. Hobson had to attack protection because free trade was a matter of entrenched belief in the Liberal party and because it was so

[35] For an introduction to the campaign see P. J. Cain, 'Political Economy in Edwardian Britain: The Tariff Reform Controversy', in A. O'Day (ed.), *The Edwardian Age: Continuity and Change* (1979). For a more detailed treatment see A. Marrison, *British Business and Protection, 1903–1932* (Oxford, 1996).

[36] E. E. H. Green, *The Crisis of Conservatism: The Politics, Economics and Ideology of the Conservative Party, 1880–1914* (1995). See also P. J. Cain. 'The Economic Philosophy of Constructive Imperialism', in C. Navari (ed.), *Politics and the Spirit of the Age* (Keele, 1996). For an instructive comparison between Mackinder's and Hobson's views on the international order see J. Kearns, '*Fin-de-Siecle* Geopolitics: Mackinder, Hobson and Theories of Global Closure', in P. J. Taylor (ed.), *Political Geography in the Twentieth Century: A Global Analysis* (1993).

popular with the urban working-class electorate.[37] But he was also genuinely convinced, as were most other New Liberal and Labour activists, that protection was a policy designed to aid the rich and privileged and that it would aggravate economic and social divisions in Britain. In his immediate response to Chamberlain's campaign in 1903, he admitted—as he had done earlier[38]—that, although world wealth would be maximized under free trade, there was no guarantee that any particular industry would always flourish in Britain. This led to a tension between national aspirations and the relentless pressures of the international economy. Imperialism and Protection were, he argued, two interrelated ways of trying to cope with the problem.

Imperialism represents a more or less conscious and organised effort of a nation to expand its old political boundaries and to take in by annexation other outside countries where its citizens have acquired strong industrial interests. Protection represents the contrary tendency, an effort to prevent industrial interests from wandering outside the political limits of the nation, to keep capital and labour employed within the political area, confining extra-national relations to commerce within the narrower limits of the term.

Chamberlain's campaign was an attempt to do both, 'expanding political control, contracting industrial life' because free trade was seen as a threat to national prosperity and social order.[39] But, as he had done since the late 1890s, Hobson denied that, even under existing conditions of trade, there was any real possibility of Britain losing her industrial strength. Instead, he claimed that protection would diminish national wealth by reducing allocative efficiency. If the demand for protection came from a difficulty in selling goods then this could be remedied by redistribution of income and wealth: but, he was sure, this was exactly what tariff reform was designed to avoid. Protection was, in fact, the policy of just those parasites who stood to lose most from social reform.

---

[37] On the popularity of free trade and the revival of free trade interests after Chamberlain's commitment to preferences see Howe, *Free Trade and Liberal England*, ch. 7.

[38] *Evolution of Modern Capitalism* (1894 edn.), 110.

[39] J. A. Hobson, 'The Inner Meaning of Protectionism', *Contemporary Review* 84 (1903), 366–7; repr. in *Hobson: Writings on Imperialism and Internationalism*, ed. Cain.

Like Mill and Cobden before him, Hobson was as concerned by the moral implications of protection as he was by the economic. It 'would kill off part of the intercourse with other nations on which the growth and enrichment of our nationality depends'. 'Free Trade', he concluded, 'is the expression of national self interests through the intercourse of nations and is thus the foundation of internationalism'. It had become essential to the evolution of man to the position where he could control himself and his environment rationally. Protection and imperialism would exist so long as unreformed capitalism produced maldistribution, monopoly, and the search for exclusive markets. Once it was reformed, and industrial democracy set in its place, internationalism would flourish. 'The chain of logic runs thus: without economic justice there can be no democracy; democracy is the essence of true nationalism. Free Trade is the expression of national self interests through the intercourse of nations and is thus the foundation of internationalism'.[40]

All this was compatible with what he had written in *Imperialism*. But he also wrote in the same article that the 'civilisation of the future' depended upon nations 'entering into ever closer commercial intercourse with one another' and that Britain was too committed now to international trade for a policy of imperial agricultural self-sufficiency to work.[41] Such sentiments did contradict the message of *Imperialism*. Therein, Hobson had argued that foreign trade was not essential to Britain's future and that a radical redistribution of income and wealth would lead to a marked shrinkage in overseas transactions whether in trade or capital. Hobson's attitude to foreign trade in *Imperialism* in 1902 got him into trouble with some reviewers, including those sympathetic to his general argument, and his opponents found him easier to dismiss because of this particular doctrine as well as his underconsumptionist heresy. Leonard Courtney, a Gladstonian liberal who had been one of the leaders of the 'pro-Boer' movement during the war, praised the book and thought it provided conclusive proof of the conventional liberal notion that trade 'flows along currents of cheapness rather than in sequence to the national flag'.[42] Hobson's attempt to belittle the importance of foreign trade was, on the other hand, nothing more

[40] 'The Inner Meaning of Protectionism', 373–4.
[41] Ibid. 374, 368.
[42] L. Courtney, 'What is the Advantage of Foreign Trade?', *Nineteenth Century*, 53 (1903), 806–7.

than 'an extravagant reaction against the error of idealizing foreign trade'; it would be impossible to support Britain's population at their existing standard of living without extensive international specialization. Courtney also brought up the interesting point that Hobson's own position might be used as an excuse for a protectionist policy.

> If an equivalent home trade could with only a transitory dislocation of usage take the place of foreign trade, why should we not make ourselves independent or indeed, why should we not, dispensing with the co-operation of foreigners, call into existence an additional industrial population at home?[43]

Perhaps in response to criticisms like Courtney's, Hobson did modify the section on foreign trade in the second edition of *Imperialism*. The passage arguing that foreign trade only contributed one-forty-fifth of national income was omitted. He also conceded that some overseas markets were an 'economic necessity' for Britain. Exports were important to purchase food and raw materials unobtainable at home or only attainable at great cost and that made 'a considerable external market a matter of vital importance'. But 'outside the limit of this practical necessity' he reiterated the claim that domestic trade could replace foreign without much loss of income and that foreign trade was a less important element in economic life than generally assumed.[44] Hobson's analysis in the first edition of *Imperialism* had a paradoxical air: free trade was vital to the flourishing of internationalism but trade between nations would diminish rapidly as industrial democracy advanced. In the second edition, the argument shifted, with the emphasis now laid upon the tendency among advanced nations for foreign trade to grow more slowly than national income. This position was based on detailed study of census data. From this he drew the conclusion that, as living standards rose, consumer demand was becoming more refined, individual, and non-material, and that most of these demands would inevitably have to be met internally. International trade might increase in absolute terms but relative to national income it would decline.[45]

---

[43] Ibid. 809–10.   [44] *Imperialism*, 28–30.
[45] Ibid. 30–1. See also J. A. Hobson, *International Trade: An Application of Economic Theory* (1904), ch. 1; id., 'Occupations of the People', *Contemporary Review*, 88 (1905), 200–1.

Despite this refinement, it is evident that, in his writings on international trade after 1903, Hobson steadily abandoned the 'marginality' approach to foreign trade he had accepted in *Imperialism*. Implicitly in his article on protection in 1903, and more explicitly in *International Trade*, he adopted the 'vent for surplus' hypothesis which assumed that foreign and domestic exchange were closely connected.[46] From this perspective, foreign transactions were an important rather than a peripheral element in growth; capital and labour flows were key elements in the working of the international economy; and these factors of production were often more mobile internationally than domestically.[47]

Explaining the relation between trade and growth in 1904, Hobson was quite explicit about the connection. In dismissing Chamberlain's dream of a self-sufficient empire, he wrote that 'when we regard the amount of our dependence upon the United States and other foreign countries for our food and other necessaries of life, we shall perceive that we have gone too far in our international reliance for any such reversion to Imperial self-sufficiency to be efficacious'.[48] Commitment to overseas markets had led to an international division of labour that was irreversible; and one crucial corollary of this, had Hobson followed the 'vent for surplus' analysis rigorously, was that adverse changes in Britain's foreign trade could lead to structural problems and unemployment. But Hobson could not accept that conclusion. Because Chamberlain's protectionism was politically so closely associated with imperialism, Hobson wanted to show free trade in its best light and to argue that it could bring only benefits to the nation. To prove this, he argued that, although the market segmentations and class divisions within Britain that created the problem of surplus, underconsumption, and unemployment could not be cured by free trade, the latter did alleviate them. If internal markets were inflexible and distorted by social, educational, and other barriers, trade in goods and international capital flows helped to open them up by breaking down

---

[46] In his preface to *International Trade*, Hobson explicitly abandoned the comparative cost theory on which the 'marginality' approach rested, arguing for 'a simplification of the theory of foreign trade by the extension to it of the same laws as govern the rates of exchange between commodities within a single nation' (p. vi).

[47] On a 'vent for surplus' or 'factor endowment' approach to international trade see D. P. O'Brien, *The Classical Economists* (Oxford, 1975), 170–2; J. H. Williams, 'The Theory of International Trade Reconsidered', *Economic Journal*, 39 (1929).

[48] *International Trade*, 175.

local monopolies: 'free exchange always tends to equalise the costs of production and so to enforce a better division of labour'.[49] Hobson now expected foreign investment and migration to increase considerably in the future.[50]

Having dissociated free trade from unemployment, Hobson then declared that 'unemployment can arise *only* from bad distribution of income, and can be cured *only* by a better one'.[51] He then considered two possible exceptions to this generalization. First, protection might be justified if, as some tariff reformers alleged, the highly cartelized industries of foreign countries such as Germany used protection as a device to 'dump' their produce on British markets at low prices with the long-run aim of undermining the profitability of British industry.[52] But Hobson denied that this was so, and spoke of dumping as a short-term expedient adopted by foreign industrialists in slumps that brought some benefits to British consumers and producers in terms of cheapness.[53] Secondly, he considered the protectionists' claim that, if there was considerable unemployment of resources, tariffs could encourage increases in output in Britain, albeit at the expense of employment elsewhere but without diverting resources from other domestic areas. Hobson accepted this as theoretically sound but denied that there was any scientific way of nicely adjusting tariffs to the needs of particular industries. In practice, tariffs would be applied indiscriminately and through political pressure: inefficient and naturally decaying industries would be kept alive and resources seriously misallocated.[54] He went on to insist that, whatever the impact of tariffs on specific firms and industries, any general scheme of tariffs would encourage cartels, distort the allocation of resources, reduce productivity, and raise prices. It would, therefore, enhance the maldistribution of income, raise unemployment and oversaving, and encourage a forced export

[49] Ibid. 97. International trade encouraged convergence: it was 'helping to raise the economic conditions of the more backward European nations to the level of the more forward ones' (ibid. 49).

[50] Ibid. 46–9. See also pp. 106–12 where Hobson writes of foreign investment as an important element in equilibrating imports and exports.

[51] Ibid. 151. My italics.

[52] The most sophisticated analysis of dumping by a convinced protectionist came from W. G. Ashley, *The Tariff Problem* (1903). See also L. L. Price, 'The Economic Possibilities of an Imperial Fiscal Policy', *Economic Journal*, 13 (1903), 502–3.

[53] International Trade, 154 and ch. 10.

[54] Ibid. 152–62.

of capital, labour, and goods rather than a natural one.[55] Protection, he concluded, sheltered the parasites of the nation, the large landowner and the big capitalist, at the expense of the smaller businessman and trader and the working masses.[56] It also fomented hostility between nations and was the enemy of peaceful internationalism.[57] It was a policy 'instinctively' adopted by vested interests, encouraging imperial adventure and favouring the few at the expense of the many.

A couple of years later, Hobson made a study of the American tariff that came to exactly the same conclusion. Until the Civil War, he claimed, the United States was headed for free trade. The expense of war had then induced governments to introduce tariffs for revenue purposes. Behind the tariff had grown the trusts that, by distorting the distribution of income, had produced oversaving and forced the search for export markets and new outlets for capital that lay behind American imperialism.[58] The gainers were a small fraction of the community, its leading financiers and industrial employers: the losers were the rest of the nation, business and workers alike. The same was true, he thought, of Canada where the chief beneficiaries of protection were said to be 'the little group of railroad men, bankers, lumber men, and manufacturing monopolists who own the country'.[59] Hobson was also very aware of the fact that the growth of monopoly in Britain had been curtailed by free trade that had undermined some ambitious merger projects and limited the scope of others.[60] He agreed emphatically with Macrosty when the latter argued that 'it is a plain necessity that if trusts are going to dominate industry free trade is an indisputable safeguard to consumers'[61] especially since, in establishing monopoly at crucial points in the market, big business in Britain was cutting into the profits of small firms as well as inhibiting consumption.[62] Hobson was convinced that, unwittingly or not, protectionists were intent on a policy that would consolidate and strengthen those business elements with the most obvious interest in foreign investment and imperial expansion.

---

[55] Ibid. ch. 11.   [56] Ibid. 166–7, 170.   [57] Ibid. 179–80.
[58] J. A. Hobson, *The Fruits of American Protection* (1907).
[59] Ibid. 42; *Canada Today*, 47 and also 110–12.
[60] *Evolution of Modern Capitalism*, 207–8.
[61] Macrosty, 'Business Aspects of British Trusts', 366.
[62] *Evolution of Modern Capitalism*, 212–15.

In *Imperialism*, as we have seen, Hobson was not very clear about how much foreign trade and investment was actively involved in new imperial expansion. Nonetheless, he was sure that imperialism would absorb a much greater share in the near future and, despite his commitment to free trade and internationalism, he felt that industrial democracy and an extensive international trade were incompatible. In contrast, in *International Trade*, foreign trade and international factor movements were both treated as natural extensions of the domestic economy, necessary to growth and beneficial to all at home or abroad.[63] The benign effects of international economic relations were emphasized though his discussion was tempered by a few hints about exploitation. At one point he did recognize that trade with 'savage or backward' countries was biased in favour of rich countries by force and fraud.[64] Generally speaking, however, he played down the fact that some trade and foreign investment was based on imperialism, was exploitative, and brought in income which widened class divisions in the receiving country rather than narrowed them. Even if he had taken care to make this distinction explicit in *International Trade*, he would not have erased all the inconsistencies between his new position and the one he had upheld in *Imperialism*. His arguments in the former book about the increased role for international factor movement in the future was just about compatible with the idea that the ratio of foreign trade to national income would fall over time.[65] It was not possible, however, to reconcile the extreme 'marginalist' thesis, repeated in the second edition of *Imperialism*, with the 'vent for surplus' approach of *International Trade*.

'AN ECONOMIC INTERPRETATION OF INVESTMENT'

International Trade offered an optimistic perspective on the future of the global economy and, after it, Hobson continued to take a much more positive view of the outcome of the effects of overseas transactions on welfare. By 1906 he was certainly looking at the

---

[63] Trade was said to be raising income in the poorer parts of Europe towards the levels of the better-off. *International Trade*, 49.

[64] Ibid. 73.   [65] Ibid. ch. 1.

global economy through spectacles altogether more rose-tinted than would have been conceivable at the turn of the century. It would be wrong to say that he was ignoring his earlier opinions totally; he still recognized that 'we have the struggle for spheres of influence amongst nations, the struggle for greatness, for national self-assertion in various forms and in various parts of the world, that struggle which on the political and military side takes the title of imperialism'.[66] By this time, nonetheless, he was very sure that these admittedly pervasive phenomena of conflict and oppression would soon disappear as internationalism brought peace and equality for all. Referring to the great increase in international commerce in the preceding generation, he stressed that 'this is the great thing which is happening from the standpoint of the material development of the earth, the flow of capital and labour, drawn primarily by the self interest of its owners to combine in method and at places which are most effective for production of wealth for the world— not of wealth for any individual nation'.[67] Tariffs and other hindrances to trade were now seen as 'small and comparatively trivial barriers set up against the majestic world-flow of capital and labour. What is aimed at is a levelling process throughout the world, a levelling of economic and ultimately of social conditions between one part of the world and another.'[68]

By the time he published this, Hobson was confident that the Chamberlainite programme of imperial federation was doomed because the voters in Britain had decisively rejected it. Nonetheless, he was still reminding his readers that social reform was important in realizing the anti-imperial project. Cobden, he argued, had been on the right lines in seeing commerce as a peacemaker: but he had failed to realize that class differences in each nation would lead to imperialism and he relied too much on purely commercial contacts to bring peace. 'We now understand that nations, like individuals 'cannot live by bread alone' but by every sound feeling that comes from the heart of humanity.'[69] It followed that 'effective democracy is essential to the achievements of peaceable relations between the nations of the world.'[70]

[66] J. A. Hobson, 'The Ethics of Internationalism', *International Journal of Ethics*, 17 (1906), 19; repr. in *Hobson, Writings on Imperialism and Internationalism*, ed. Cain.
[67] 'The Ethics of Internationalism', 20.
[68] Ibid. 21.   [69] Ibid. 23.   [70] Ibid. 28.

There is no doubt that this position made much more sense if it was assumed that foreign trade was, and would remain, an important element in the economic life of nations rather than an unimportant or declining one. In a laudatory review of foreign trade in *The Science of Wealth* he wrote about the 'growing relative importance of that trade for every country'.

Though Great Britain and a few of the continental countries are in advance of the rest, the inhabitants of every country are becoming more dependent upon the inhabitants of other countries for things they want to sell and buy. Every year larger and larger quantities of goods flow across the national frontiers and seek purchasers in foreign markets.[71]

The analysis followed that outlined in *International Trade* closely. In discussing foreign investment, Hobson spoke of it giving nations a 'powerful interest in the peace, well-being and prosperity' of each other and added that 'this is not rendered less significant by the knowledge that the great bulk of this income [from foreign investments] is enjoyed by a very small class of well-to-do people'.[72]

Hobson adopted a similar line of reasoning when discussing foreign investment during the budget crisis of 1909.[73] Protectionists had long insisted that free trade, by reducing the profitability of British industry, encouraged foreign investment.[74] In 1909 they joined with some of the great financiers of the City to complain that Lloyd George's budgetary radicalism was scaring capital away from Britain and reducing output and employment.[75] These claims duly produced their counter-claims from journalists, industrialists, and even the youthful Keynes, all of whom denied any shortage of capital for industry and insisted that foreign investment represented a surplus that boosted foreign trade and Britain's national

---

[71] J. A. Hobson, *The Science of Wealth* (1950 edn.), 240.

[72] Ibid.

[73] For an excellent introduction to what follows see A. Offer, 'Empire and Social Reform: British Overseas Investment and Domestic Politics, 1908–14', *Historical Journal*, 26 (1983).

[74] Cain and Hopkins, *British Imperialism*, 190.

[75] See *Parliamentary Debates* (Lords), iv (1909), 22 Nov. 1909, cc. 745, 890–2 (Lansdowne) and 24 Nov. 1909, cc. 967–8 (Milner) for Conservative party claims. For City voices see cc. 796–7 (Revelstoke); 25 Nov. 1909, cc. 899, 904 (Avebury); 29 Nov. 1909, cc.1155–6 (Rothschild), cc.1297–8 (Denbigh). On City attitudes to the Budget see also Kynaston, *The City of London*, 494–502.

income.[76] The latter view was strongly reinforced by the work of the economist Sir George Paish, whose statistical study of foreign investment gave a detailed picture both of its extent and distribution for the first time.[77] Paish convinced Lloyd George that it would be counter-productive to tax foreign investment because it was helping to cheapen overseas supplies of food and raw material and encouraging British exports.[78] Thereafter, Liberal politicians attacked tariff reformers by associating the free trade–foreign investment regime with the prosperity of industry and of the nation in general.[79]

Fearing that Conservatives might panic working men into associating free trade and supertax with unemployment, Hobson responded to the crisis by reiterating his view that 'nothing will increase the volume and steady the course of employment but an improved distribution of wealth'. At present, because of a faulty distribution of income, there were plenty of surplus savings about which could find no outlet at home. Stopping foreign investment by taxing it would only increase the problem of excess capital; and 'since international commerce makes every nation to share to some extent the resources of the others, every nation would be a loser'. Exports of capital increased world wealth, enhanced internationalism, and, by cheapening imports, raised living standards in Britain.[80]

Apart from his chapter in *The Science of Wealth*, Hobson's positive approach to international trade reached its most potent expression in *An Economic Interpretation of Investment*, which was based upon a series of articles written in 1910 in a monthly guide to

[76] *Parl. Deb.*, 23 Nov. 1909, cc. 843–4 (Pentland); 24 Nov. cc. 959–64 (St Davids); 29 Nov. 1909, cc. 1285–7 (Grimethorpe). See also F. W. Hirst, *British Capital at Home and Abroad* (1911) and J. M. Keynes, 'Great Britain's Foreign Investments' *New Quarterly* (1910); repr. in *The Collected Works of John Maynard Keynes*, xv (Cambridge, 1971), 44–59.

[77] Sir George Paish, 'Great Britain's Investments in Other Lands', *Journal of the Royal Statistical Society*, 72 (1909); id., 'Great Britain's Capital Investments in Individual Colonies and Foreign Countries', ibid., 74 (1911).

[78] The importance of foreign investment also convinced Lloyd George of the need for more naval rearmament. Offer, 'Empire and Social Reform', 126–7, 129.

[79] W. S. Churchill, *The People's Rights* (1909; repr. 1970), 104 ff. For the investors' view see Investment Critic, 'Prejudices of Investors', *Financial Review of Reviews* (Dec. 1912), 37.

[80] J. A. Hobson, 'The Investment of British Capital Abroad: Does it Injure the British Worker?', *Labour Leader*, 12 Feb. 1909, 105.

investors, *The Financial Review of Reviews*, and published in book form in 1911. The book benefited from the evidence which Paish had unearthed and which showed that the bulk of British overseas capital went to push back the agricultural frontiers and to open them up to trade in white-settled migrant areas such as the United States, the British settlement colonies, and parts of South America. Hobson used these and other statistics with skill: but his tone was frequently indistinguishable from that of the average financial journalist whose only interest was in showing his readers how to make a quick profit. The Hobson of the *Economic Interpretation* bore very little relation to the Hobson who wrote *Imperialism*. To begin with, his attitude to financiers was very different from that in 1906 or 1909. Good promoters were important because they could pick winners. Their function was 'indispensable' and, although fraud sometimes occurred, they possessed 'a really serviceable skill of a high intellectual order'.[81] Prospectus writers also had crucial parts in the drama of investment. His general conclusion was that

> however large the allowance for fraud and overreaching on the part of skilled middlemen, the delicacy and importance of the services they render . . . are undeniable. A delay of half a century in the development of a whole country as big and rich as Great Britain, or the fate of a whole series of industrial inventions, may sometimes hinge upon the exact selection of time and method in the issue of a prospectus, the names of the directors, the nature of the information given or withheld, the apportionment of the capital assigned to different classes of bonds or shares, or any one of a series of such determinant details.[82]

And, though he described the London Stock Exchange as 'a private club' and a 'close monopoly', he still saw it and other Exchanges as critical to the proper allocation of investment worldwide.[83]

In the *Economic Interpretation*, Hobson again adopted a Smithian 'vent for surplus' approach to foreign transactions to show their vital economic importance and then used this as a basis from which to talk of the 'coming internationalism'. At one level, the export of capital was now seen as something that followed naturally when a country reached a certain stage in its economic evolution. So we find Hobson writing, in language reminiscent of J. S.

---

[81] J. A. Hobson, *An Economic Interpretation of Investment* (1911), 9.
[82] Ibid. 10.   [83] Ibid. 12–13.

Mill, that 'when the safest, most fundamental and upon the whole, most profitable employments for capital at home have been already amply furnished by our saving and investing classes, it is natural, desirable, and even necessary, that large quantities of the fresh capital should be placed further afield'.[84] And he went on to say that:

foreign investment does not injuriously compete with home investments robbing the latter of capital which it could put to advantageous use in employing British labour but . . . they represent a use found abroad for a surplus quantity of British saving which otherwise would either not exist at all or would represent a wasteful oversupply of home capital . . . Foreign investments, then, form in the first instance a safety valve against excessive gluts of capital at home. They find a profitable use for capital which otherwise could not economically fructify at all.[85]

Any attempt to prohibit capital export would simply mean that some countries would be choked with capital while others did not receive enough for development and world production would be reduced. In *An Economic Interpretation of Investment*, although he still recognized a maldistribution problem in industrial countries, Hobson claimed that a policy of redistributing income through, for example, increasing the share of wages in national income would enhance growth, increase savings and *also* foreign investment.[86] As he put it, he expected that in the future 'international will continue to gain on purely national finance';[87] an argument which implicitly contradicted the idea put forward in *International Trade* that, as national income increased, foreign transactions would decline in relative importance.

Foreign investment had been condemned in *Imperialism* as destructive of the culture of the receiving nations but now it was the beneficial effect on the latter that was emphasized. Hobson was, by this time, in no doubt that the flow of capital from the West was good not only for all classes in the creditor country but also for the nations who received it, whatever stage of development they might have reached. Its general effect was to diffuse world

[84] Ibid. 66. Cf. J. S. Mill. *Principles of Political Economy*, in *Collected Works of John Stuart Mill*, vol. iii (Toronto, 1965), 745–6.
[85] *Economic Interpretation*, 89. Pages 79–124 of the book are reprinted in *Hobson: Writings on Imperialism and Internationalism*, ed. Cain.
[86] This is the implication of the argument at 37.
[87] *Economic Interpretation*, 132.

wealth.[88] Similarly, immigration of labour did not reduce living standards or displace native labour but elevated wages and increased employment opportunities.[89] Surveying the whole process, he declared roundly that 'The development of a backward country by foreign capital is always beneficial to the country itself, to the industrial world at large (by increasing world trade) and to the investing country in particular.'[90] Developments of this kind would create a world of wealthy nations mutually beneficial to each other and part owners of each other's assets. Newly developing countries would begin to compete in industries in which Britain was now dominant, but the only effect would be to encourage Britain to move 'gradually out of those branches of production into others that yield products which enable us to buy from them upon terms advantageous to us, the goods we formerly produced'.[91]

Hobson did not altogether abandon the position that foreign investment was a source of imperialist exploitation, but his attitude to it was now very different from that of 1902. He was ready to believe that 'the cosmopolitan investor' had the same interest as the domestic businessman in 'good order, education and improved efficiency of labour', but his inability easily to influence the governments of those areas in which he had placed his funds often led him into conflict with these governments and induced him to call on his own state to help him out in crises. And, 'as foreign trade and foreign investment advance it becomes a more important and more useful function of every government to try to secure for its citizens new markets for their goods and for their capital, and to employ public diplomacy and force to improve the markets already got and the capital already invested'.[92]

When the borrowing country was unstable or otherwise insecure and the lender was a more powerful military entity, the result was often imperialism. Hobson had no doubt that the prime cause of imperialism was 'the pressure of the investing class for larger and safer areas of profitable investment', pressure which often led to wars which were beneficial to certain interests within each nation, as in the case of the South African war. While each government tried to keep exclusive control of particular areas for investment, Hobson

---

[88] *The Science of Wealth*, 239.
[89] Ibid. 243.
[90] *Economic Interpretation*, 100–1.
[91] Ibid. 98.   [92] Ibid. 106–7.

admitted that conflict was inevitable.[93] On the other hand, he did not believe that this exclusiveness would prove possible in the future. He was impressed by the growing 'cross-ownership' of capital especially in Latin America and the Far East. Given the enormous potential of China and the sheer size of its capital needs for railway development and other basic infrastructural investments, Hobson felt that the recent attempts to provide joint finance by three, and sometimes four, hitherto rival powers would be the prototype for the future. 'This large, joint interest will afford the surest basis of peace, at any rate for a generation, in the Far East,'[94] and led on to the development of international government. The old-fashioned imperialism of dominance and political control was giving way 'to an economic internationalism exercised with very little assumption of direct control, the minimum in fact that is found necessary to afford good security for the international assets'.[95] Hobson's *bouleversement* was complete. In *Imperialism: A Study* he had also anticipated that the financiers of the great powers might invade the Chinese market jointly. At that time, however, he expected that this would only provide the means whereby a vast, exploited, yellow workforce and army could be utilized to destroy European industry, to undercut the living standards of the Western working class, and to anaesthetize their growing political power.

The position adopted in the *Economic Interpretation of Investment* remained at the centre of Hobson's thought until the outbreak of war.[96] In 1914, for example, he contributed another article to the *Financial Review of Reviews* that reiterated many of the ideas of the 1911 book. Hobson was concerned here to point out that foreign investment had been more profitable than home during the previous twenty years and to persuade investors that a rational investment policy would lead to more funds going abroad. He also tried to reassure 'certain short-sighted patriots who see in this diversion of a growing proportion of national savings from home investment an injury to home industries'.[97] Foreign investment

---

[93] Ibid. 108–11.   [94] Ibid. 116.   [95] Ibid. 117.

[96] See also J. A. Hobson, 'Opening of New Markets and Countries', in G. Spiller (ed.), *Papers on Inter-racial Problems* (1911), 231–2.

[97] J. A. Hobson, 'Investment Safeguards under Changing Conditions', *Financial Review of Reviews* (June 1914), 643.

and increased international migration, he assured his readers, was 'rapidly imposing on the world a single standard of international civilisation through common acts of production and consumption and a general world-wide commerce'.[98] There was a benign invisible hand at work in international financial markets: 'Though each of these investors is not at all consciously concerned with making wealth for the rest of the world, but simply follows some line which he deems advantageous to himself, the operations of his intelligent and informed self-interest does lead him to co-operate in a policy of world-wide utility.'[99] The 'capitalist proletariat' was clearly no longer the mere 'catspaw' of cunning financiers.

Indeed, just before the war Hobson came fairly close to an outright acceptance of Norman Angell's philosophy. Angell was, perhaps, best described as an unreconstructed Cobdenite. He believed that the great industrial nations were now so economically interdependent, especially since the rise of international finance and banking, that a war between them would destroy the wealth of all of them. War was, therefore, totally irrational and could only be supported by relying on assumptions about economic structure which were hopelessly out of date. It followed from this that, once the politicians and the military men realized what economic interdependence entailed, war would disappear. There were, admittedly, one or two interests that benefited directly from war, such as the services and the armaments industry, but they could not prevail against a citizenry educated in the economic facts of life.[100] The need, which Hobson had so often stressed, for systematic changes in capitalism to eliminate war and imperialism, was also completely ignored by Angell and was replaced by an implicit faith in the growing rationality of an unreformed economic elite.

On occasion, Hobson himself talked as though a new sympathetic understanding between the great powers themselves was paralleling the coming harmony between developed and backward nations, and that the way to avoid war in future was simply to wait for the growth of international finance to bring Foreign Offices to their senses. In the *Economic Interpretation* he followed a lengthy quotation from

---

[98] Ibid. 647.   [99] Ibid. 653.
[100] N. Angell, *The Great Illusion* (1909). For a look at Angellism and its effects on educated thinking in Edwardian Britain, see H. Weinroth, 'Norman Angell and the Great Illusion: An Episode in Pre-war Pacifism', *Historical Journal*, 17 (1974).

The Great Illusion with the bold statement that 'modern finance is the great sympathetic system in an economic organism in which political divisions are of constantly diminishing importance'.[101] He went on to say:

That which Christianity, justice and humane sentiment have been impotent to accomplish through nineteen centuries of amiable effort, the growing consolidation of financial interests . . . seems likely within a generation to bring to consummation, namely, the provision of such a measure of international government as shall render wars between the great civilised powers in the future virtually impossible.[102]

Despite his new-found optimism about the economic future, he had occasional doubts, and not simply Angellite doubts, about the irrationality of nations. At a conference in 1911 he returned to the view that the need for markets in undeveloped territories was driven by lack of demand at home due to underconsumption. He also condemned much tropical trade as physically and morally degrading and as exploitation rather than development though he also felt that matters were improving.[103] A year later, in the context of a serious breakdown in industrial relations in Britain, he noted that the demand for overseas investments was so great that it was pushing up interest rates and prices and was putting capital in a stronger bargaining position than labour at home.[104] He was also still worried enough about the power of financiers, in the present state of capitalism, to offer occasional words of caution. The internationalism of capital would be a force for good in the long run but would have to be carefully watched in the short. In 1913, for example, while he strove to emphasize the irrationality of hostility to Germany, with whom Britain's trading and financial connections were growing closer year by year, he reminded his readers that there were 'certain nuclei' of thought, sentiment, and economic interest which had good reason to be in conflict with 'these harmonizing tendencies'. Some of these interests were 'the poisonous by-products of an imperfectly evolving modern industrialism, others are survivors of an obsolescent age of militarism and national

---

[101] *Economic Interpretation*, 121.
[102] Ibid. 122–3. Cf. also a speech on Angellism by Hobson in *Concord*, July 1913, pp. 71–2.
[103] 'Opening of Markets and Countries', 228–30.
[104] J. A. Hobson, 'The Causes of the Rise in Prices', *Contemporary Review*, 102 (1912), 489.

isolation'.[105] The danger presented by these traditional elements was evident enough to him during the crisis of 1914 when the Conservative party, facing Lloyd George's radical land proposals and another possible election defeat in 1915, came close to inciting the army in Ulster to mutiny to prevent Home Rule. Hobson interpreted this as a dangerous attempt by vested interests to try to win by force what they had failed to achieve by political persuasion and their growing desperation as the social reform movement got into its stride under the new democratic liberalism. Nonetheless, the fact that the propertied interests had been forced to such extremes was also, for him, a sign of how much had been achieved since the end of the Boer War, when the reaction against imperialism had set in.[106]

HOBSON'S DILEMMAS: A CRITIQUE

Hobson's vision of both the international economy and imperialism underwent substantial change between 1902 and 1911 and it is not easy to say exactly why. Occasionally, the change was apparent rather than real. Some of the differences between his position in *Imperialism* and in *International Trade*, for example, were partly the result of his temperamental inability to state his case in a balanced way and to demonstrate to his readers that the emerging global economy could be simultaneously both a spur to international harmony *and* a cause of imperialism. Trying to combine the life of a serious economic and sociological theorist with that of propagandist for liberalism did not help matters. He wrote too much and a lot of his work on sensitive political issues too often degenerated into a one-sided championing of the causes he supported and reinforced his natural tendency to go to extremes. Yet there was more to the problem than mere lack of balance. On issues such as the importance of international trade to capitalist development, the relation between that and imperialism, the role of financiers in economic development, and other big issues his views underwent fairly radical and fundamental change between *Imperialism* and *An Economic Interpretation of Investment.*

[105] J. A. Hobson, *The German Panic* (1913), 20. Cf. id., 'The Importance of Instruction in the Facts of Internationalism', *National Peace Council*, pamphlet no. 7 (1912), 4.
[106] J. A. Hobson, *Traffic in Treason* (1914).

It was once suggested that Hobson's radicalism was muted in general in the Edwardian period because he did not lay as much stress on the idea of underconsumption as he had before and that he had become more orthodox in his approach.[107] But this does not ring true: all that happened was that the theory of underconsumption was subsumed under the broader concept of surplus that reached its highest point of sophistication in these years. It has also been claimed that one reason why Hobson shifted his position so markedly is the resurgence of liberalism in Britain after the Boer War, his increasing confidence that the problems of surplus and underconsumption were being addressed, and his optimistic assessment of the coming of international harmony as a result.[108] There is some truth in this but it does not give enough emphasis to the fact that Hobson was constantly warning about the dangers of a revival of Conservatism and reminding fellow liberals of the power of the interests behind it: constant vigilance and a fear of reversal were his watchword in so many of his writings on domestic themes. His optimism was largely confined to his writings on foreign trade which often sat uncomfortably with his thoughts on the budgetary crisis of 1909, the House of Lords, and other national issues.

Hobson was neither the first nor the last person to hold two opposing views simultaneously but it is important to try to assess why he did so. At this point it is worth remembering that he was operating within a radical discourse that was itself implicitly contradictory. The James Mill tradition within radicalism saw foreign trade as a potential menace to progress because dependence upon it was an incitement to militarism and war. Hence the stress within that tradition on developing the domestic market as an antidote to aggression against foreigners. It is this version of radicalism, following Adam Smith's marginality thesis, which is predominant in *Imperialism* though Hobson never ceased to believe that a diminished but healthy foreign trade could encourage internationalism. On the other side, there was the Cobdenite version of history where the emphasis was upon extending foreign trade in order to break down the barriers between nations and increase interdependence. Hobson adopted a 'realist' version of this approach—one

[107] Nemmers thinks that Hobson entered a 'quasi-orthodox' phase after 1902. *Hobson and Underconsumption*, 69.

[108] My view in earlier years. See Cain, 'J. A, Hobson, Cobdenism and the Radical Theory of Economic Imperialism', 581–4.

that assumed imperialism had a role to play in the march of progress—in *International Trade* and in *An Economic Interpretation of Investment*. Any convincing explanation of the reasons for his move from the first to the second position, however, must be rooted in the events of the time and his reaction to them.

The chief spur to a shift from one pole of radical thinking to another was his hostility to the protectionist movement. It is not difficult to understand why Hobson should have become obsessed with the question of free trade in view of Chamberlain's massive assault upon it starting in 1903. Hobson was operating within a radical tradition where protection was historically associated with privilege, unearned increments, and autocracy and free trade with liberty, a fair distribution of income, and democracy. Moreover, Chamberlain the tariff reformer was also Chamberlain the imperialist; and, since imperialism was *the* enemy of progress as far as Hobson was concerned, it is hardly surprising that he should see protection and imperialism as inextricably intertwined, two aspects of the same deadly disease. In those circumstances it would have been extraordinarily hard for Hobson to admit that a protectionist policy could bring benefits in terms of employment and output. This is probably the chief reason why he insisted that free trade could do no economic harm and, as the corollary of this, that the only cause of unemployment was maldistribution of income and wealth. Moreover, as Chamberlain's tariff campaign got under way, Hobson's belief that, under free trade, foreign trade was of marginal or declining significance to the economy disappeared. The more he sang the praises of free trade and the more he claimed how beneficial it was, the more the marginality/relative decline thesis became an implausible one to defend. By 1910, as we have seen, he had completely abandoned his 1902 position, recognizing now that international trade was a vital part of the world economy and that its significance for Britain would most likely increase rather than decrease.

His commitment to the position that foreign trade was always a force for good also had revolutionary implications for his theory of imperialism. In 1902, he condemned imperialism as a diseased process, the outcome of an international flow of economic factors that were the by-product of an unhealthy domestic economy. But if foreign trade was a force for good in itself and vital to world prosperity—as he came to argue increasingly after 1903—then its effects in the underdeveloped world subject to imperialism had also to be accepted as positive. This is surely the principal reason why, by the time he wrote *An Economic Interpretation of Investment*, Hobson was talking of imperialism not as a curse hung around the necks of civilization throughout the globe but as a transitional phase in the relations between East and West. Whatever temporary hardships it brought, it was essentially an intermediate step on the way to a more dynamic world economy and one bringing with it a much more equitable distribution of resources between nations and amongst the different classes within nations.

Although brutally critical of privilege and monopoly, radicalism was fundamentally accepting of capitalism and saw it as a great engine of progress. It is the latter aspect of radicalism that came through most strongly in Hobson's writings in the ten years or so before the First World War. His defence of free trade, and the reasoning into which it led him, also point to the conclusion that Hobson was much less of an economic heretic than his adoption of that label implies. Someone who argued that the *only* cause of unemployment was maldistribution of resources and that if that maldistribution were corrected the economic system would work harmoniously, was offering a much less fundamental challenge to conventional economic thinking than was Keynes twenty years later, although, in political terms, Hobson would generally be regarded as the more unorthodox and dangerous of the two. Hobson was, or rather became, a classical economist in the Smith–Ricardo–Mill tradition who parted company with the main body on one—but only one—important issue, Say's Law. Langford Price, an economist with protectionist sympathies, noted this in responding to one of Hobson's free trade fusillades. Given his 'creed and antecedents' and his 'strong sympathies with socialistic aspirations' Price professed surprise at Hobson's Panglossian assumptions about the working of the economy under free trade and accused him of 'acquiescing thus complacently in the straitest and most characteristic dogma of old-fashioned individualist Economics'.[109]

Hobson's commitment to the classical approach had its great merits because it allowed him to continue to think in macroeco-

---

[109] L. L. Price, 'Protection, Free Trade and Unemployment', in P. J. Cain (ed.) *Free Trade and Protectionism*, vol. iv (Bristol, 1996), 158, 160. Price was responding to J. A. Hobson, 'Can Protection Cure Unemployment?', ibid. 53 (1909) but also commenting on the latter's *The Industrial System*.

nomic terms. In his mature years, he repudiated Marshallian neo-classical economics and the marginalist analysis at its base, even though he had done some pioneering work on the latter himself in the early 1890s. He objected to its individualist bias and its micro-perspectives that took attention away from the functioning of economic society as a whole and ignored the fact that output was socially, rather than individually, produced.[110] But his classicism, although compatible with his radical political philosophy, had its limitations. It was the classicist in him who took to writing for a financial journal which aimed at maximizing investors' incomes and proceeded on the blithe and convenient assumption that 'Capital, like manufactures, must be placed wherever it can secure the highest returns. In this way alone can the highest interests of the country be served.'[111] It may also explain why in contributing to it he, too, wrote as though the Smithian invisible hand had returned and that what was good for the foreign investor was always and everywhere good for the rest of humanity. It is probably also the reason why his opposition to the protectionist argument that the state should intervene in trade led him to claim that only individuals, not nations, traded with each other[112]—thus putting a large question mark against his own organicist approach to the economy. In these matters relating to foreign trade he was, in fact, much less unorthodox in his approach than some of the leading Chamber-lainite intellectuals such as Ashley, Amery, or Cunningham who developed their own organicist views in more intellectually chal-lenging and consistent ways. Free trade and the theory of surplus lay uneasily together. One product of the friction between them was a transformation in Hobson's theory of financial imperialism from one version that condemned the whole process as unnecessary, dangerous to liberalism, and exploitative of its victims to another that accepted it as inevitable, transitory, and a spur to world progress.

[110] See J. A. Hobson, 'Marginal Units in the Theory of Distribution', *Journal of Political Economy* 12 (1904); id., 'Marginal Productivity', *Economic Review*, 20 (1910). For Hobson in this context see J. Mahony, *Marshall, Orthodoxy and the Professionalisation of Economics* (1985).
[111] Investment Critic, 'Prejudices of Investors', 37.
[112] *International Trade*, 21.

CHAPTER SEVEN

Late Variations on a Famous Theme, 1914–1938[1]

HOBSON'S LATER YEARS

Hobson lived long beyond 1914, surviving not only total war but also the deepest economic depression in world history. He also lived to witness the beginning of the Second World War, dying in 1940 at the age of 81. He stayed active as a writer until the last few months of his life[2] and, although his fundamental approach to understanding the modern world did not change, Hobson did not become an intellectual dinosaur unable to respond to new stimuli. He read widely and was still, for example, capable of modifying and finessing his arguments on underconsumption in the mid-1930s. Indeed, it has been argued, his position on unemployment near the end of his life was much closer to that of Keynes than has usually been recognized.[3] Hobson was also capable of extending his range: he was a pioneer advocate of a League of Nations and most of his detailed writings on international government, which are still of interest today,[4] were produced after 1914 in response to the outbreak of world war, though the basic ideas with which he worked had all been announced earlier in his career. His renewed interest in furthering the cause of world government also inspired

---

[1] This chapter is a substantially revised and extended version of Cain, 'Variations on a Famous Theme'.

[2] His last publication was 'America in the War?', *South Place Monthly Record* (Dec. 1939). He died on 1 Apr. 1940.

[3] J. King, 'J. A. Hobson's Macroeconomics: The Last Ten Years', in Pheby (ed.), *J. A. Hobson after Fifty Years*.

[4] See Long, *Towards a New Liberal Internationalism*; see also id., 'Three Modes of Internationalism in the Work of J. A. Hobson', in Pheby (ed.), *J. A. Hobson after Fifty Years*; and B. Porter, 'Hobson and Internationalism', in Freeden (ed.), *Reappraising J. A. Hobson*.

his second attempt at biography. In 1919, he took advantage of the appearance of new material to add to Morley's classic account and 'to rescue the memory of Cobden from the narrow misinterpretations to which it has of late been subjected, by giving stronger emphasis to his international work'.[5] Besides remaining intellectually active he also became more politically influential after 1918. The Liberal party fragmented under the strain of running a war economy and Hobson took his New Liberalism[6] into the Labour party where he had some influence on aspects of policy in the 1920s, as we shall see. The Independent Labour party (ILP) adopted his views on surplus and underconsumption and he had an abiding influence on such key figures within the Labour movement as Tawney and Cole.[7] He was less acceptable to the younger Labour economists of the 1930s such as Durbin and Gaitskell:[8] but his stock was raised when Keynes paid him a handsome tribute and hailed the *Physiology of Industry* as a precursor of *The General Theory*.[9]

The cataclysmic events of 1914–40 also influenced his views on the links between capitalism and imperialism, sometimes profoundly. Although familiar arguments and familiar contradictions abound, Hobson kept thinking. He never gave the subject the degree of attention he had accorded it in *Imperialism* but his later writings occasionally showed a fertility of insight on a par with what he had achieved before 1914. To demonstrate this is the main task of this chapter, which also tries to answer a conundrum: why, if his views on the economic dynamics and significance of imperialism varied considerably over time, did Hobson choose to reprint *Imperialism* in 1938 without giving his readers any inkling that his views had often changed in the intervening years? This is followed

[5] Hobson, *Richard Cobden*, 11. See also Matthew, 'Hobson, Ruskin and Cobden', 22–30.

[6] The most detailed study of Hobson's thought after 1914 is Freeden, *Liberalism Divided*, though it does not cover his writings on imperialism. Freeden emphasizes the fact that liberal ideas still flourished, especially in the 1920s, even though the Liberal party was in deep decline and some of its major intellectual figures had to find other party affiliations.

[7] For Tawney see Freeden, *Liberalism Divided*, 313. For Hobson's influence on G. D. H. Cole, see A. W. Wright, *G. D. H. Cole and Socialist Democracy* (Oxford, 1979), 181 ff.

[8] E. Durbin, *New Jerusalems: The Labour Party and the Economics of Democratic Socialism* (1985), esp. 43–4, 137–8.

[9] On the Keynes–Hobson coming together see Clarke, *Liberals and Social Democrats*, 226–34, 273–4, and id., 'Hobson and Keynes as Economic Heretics', in Freeden (ed.), *Reappraising J. A. Hobson*.

by a brief summary of Hobson's changing views on the phenomenon of imperialism over forty years of writing about it. The chapter then ends with an attempt to explain how, by the time the Second World War broke out, *Imperialism* was on the way to becoming the classic text we know today.

HOBSON AND THE FIRST WORLD WAR

The outbreak of war in 1914 came as a complete surprise to Hobson—as well it might given the optimistic tone of many of his writings in the Edwardian period—and its length and savagery shook his faith in the future of humanity.[10] Looking back, he wrote nostalgically about the pre-1914 radical vision which rested on the belief in 'the existence of some immanent reason in history working towards harmony and justifying optimism' and which totally underestimated the power of the irrational in human life and the ability of vested interests to turn that irrationality to account.[11] Nonetheless his optimism did not disappear upon the declaration of war: his attitudes only changed significantly as hostilities became more all-encompassing in their effects and as the idea of 'business as usual' gave way to the intensities of total war. As late as March 1915 he was writing about overseas investment very much as he had prior to the war, lauding foreign investment and complaining that Treasury restrictions on capital flows were discouraging saving, harming the City and exporters, and thus threatening the overseas assets that were the greatest source of Britain's strength in its fight against Germany.[12]

In the same year, however, and in one of his most influential books, Hobson linked the war with imperialism, claiming that, fundamentally, conflict had broken out because of economic antag-

[10] Hobson was one of the organizers of the British Neutrality Committee formed in July 1914 with the aim of keeping Britain out of the war. See M. Swartz, 'A Study in Futility: The British Radicals at the Outbreak of the First World War', in Morris (ed.), *Edwardian Radicalism*. For Hobson's activities during the war see *Confessions*, ch. 8.

[11] J. A. Hobson, 'Why the War Came as a Surprise', *Political Science Quarterly*, 35 (1920), 344–5. This was reprinted as ch. 1 of *Problems of a New World* (1921). See also *Confessions*, 94.

[12] J. A. Hobson, 'Investment under War Conditions', *Financial Review of Reviews* (Mar. 1915), 12.

onisms centred on claims about imperial possession. He reckoned, for example, that German militarism had been boosted by the fears of German businessmen about the closing of foreign markets, especially the fear that British empire markets would be limited if tariff reform succeeded in Britain.[13] Not surprisingly, Hobson now put more stress than he had done just before 1914 on the argument that underconsumption in industrial countries was the prime cause of imperial expansion. He also reminded his readers of the dangers involved in conflicts between financial groups using national power to gain exclusive control of trade and investment openings in 'backward' countries. At this early stage in the war, however, Hobson still saw it as a temporary hazard on the road to progress. While vehemently condemning 'national groups of capitalists' who 'employ political weapons to gain their private ends',[14] he still made the Cobdenite claim that 'the free movement of capital and goods and men from one country to another is in its normal operation a pacific force, binding the different creditors and debtor nations together by mutual advantages'. In 1915 he was confident that 'the firmly woven bonds of commerce and investment and the tidal flow of labour, which in spite of some obstructions, pulse continuously with more power throughout the world, are constantly engaged in bringing into closer union the arts of industry, the standards of living, the habits, desires and thoughts of men'.[15] Wartime moves in favour of tariffs were dismissed as 'the last death struggles of obscurantist economics enlisted in the ranks of militarism'. Though the internationalism sponsored by commerce and finance had not prevented war from breaking out, Hobson insisted that this was 'no sufficient reason for disparaging it as a material and spiritual support of the new pacific order'.[16] The horrors of war were, he thought, more likely to quicken the pace towards internationalism than arrest it.[17]

Without specifying exactly how the reactionary forces making for imperialism might be rooted out, Hobson in 1915 focused his attention on the future of the 'backward' nations dominated by Europe. Just before the war, Hobson had considered that they would be natural beneficiaries of the increasing economic co-operation between the imperialist powers. Now he reverted to a position

---

[13] J. A. Hobson, *Towards International Government* (1915), 133.
[14] Ibid. 139 n. 1.   [15] Ibid. 195.   [16] Ibid. 195–6.   [17] Ibid. 149–53.

closer to that he had held in *Imperialism*, namely that the penetration and development of the poorest parts of the world could only take place without exploitation and conflict if some international supervisory body, like a League of Nations, were created.[18] He was worried, even then, that the possible exclusion of Germany from such a League might provoke 'a wide "conscious" imperialism of the victors which would in the long run prove no less dangerous to the peace of the world than the national imperialism of the past'.[19] Clearly Hobson feared, even at this early stage of the war, that an 'inter-imperialism' of the kind he had warned about in *Imperialism* might be its result. On the whole, however, he felt that, provided there was a movement towards 'economic democracy' in the industrial world, the League would be a force for progress and would insist upon the Open Door for trade in the underdeveloped world, ensuring that the latter received the full economic and social benefit of their contact with advanced capitalism. Overall, the tone of *International Government* was closer to the optimistic speculations of *An Economic Interpretation of Investment* than it was to the more pessimistic message of *Imperialism*, though it contained no explicit analysis of the international economy.[20]

As the war dragged on and as its impact upon everyday life became more pervasive, Hobson was increasingly alarmed at the possibilities of a serious erosion of liberal economics and liberal values. The reconstruction of Asquith's Liberal government in 1915, which brought in Conservative cabinet ministers, and its replacement late in 1916 by a coalition between Lloyd George's supporters and Conservative 'social imperialists' including the infamous Alfred Milner of Boer War notoriety, helped to convince Hobson that the dangers were real. Many of his fellow radicals acquiesced in the drift of policy because they could see no alternative to the crushing defeat of 'Prussianism',[21] but Hobson always hankered after an

---

[18] Ibid. 127–48.

[19] Ibid. 144–6. See also J. A. Hobson, *A League of Nations* (1915), 20.

[20] For critical discussion of Hobson's ideas as set out in *International Government* see K. E. Miller, *Socialism and Foreign Policy* (The Hague, 1967), 64–8; K. E. Waltz, *Man, the State and War* (1959), 145–56; Long, *Towards a New Liberal Internationalism, passim*.

[21] Clarke, *Liberals and Social Democrats*, ch. 6.

honourable peace based on the assumption that both sides shared the blame for the war equally. By 1916–17 he was thoroughly convinced that the coalition was determined to use the war not only to crush Germany but to organize the whole British Empire on a permanent war footing and that the imperialist forces were now in the ascendant as they had been during the Boer War.

What particularly concerned him at the time was the apparent drift towards an autarkic state as the war progressed.[22] The so-called McKenna duties were imposed in 1915 to restrict luxury imports. Much more significant, from Hobson's perspective, were the Paris Agreements of 1916 which envisaged a self-contained economic bloc, including all the Allies and their imperial posses-sions, which would be organized to discriminate against the Central Powers not only during the war but after it. The Agreements arose from the pessimistic assumption that Germany could not be defeated and that the war might end with an unsatisfactory truce, leaving the two armed camps facing each other. Once the truce had been declared, the Allies expected an assault on world markets by German industry that would throw their economies into disarray.[23] But Hobson interpreted the Agreements as a blatant attempt by vested economic interests to prolong the conflict and thus retard the advance of economic internationalism and economic democracy. He felt that they posed a fundamental threat to international economic relations that was 'nothing short of treason against the cause of civilisation'. If international commerce was curtailed, it would 'destroy every mode of higher intercourse . . . reverse the course of civilisation and drive back to barbarism'.[24] To counter the threat, Hobson, as a member of the executive council of the Union of Democratic Control set up in 1914 to fight 'secret diplomacy' and to encourage a swift peace honourable to both sides, persuaded the UDC to add the following to its list of demands:

That the European conflict shall not be continued by economic war after the military operations have ceased and that British policy shall be directed

[22] On free trade in Britain in the age of war and depression, see Howe, *Free Trade and Liberal England*, 295–308.

[23] On the Paris Agreements see P. Cline, 'Winding down the War Economy: British Plans for Peacetime Recovery, 1916–19', in K. Burk (ed.), *War and the State* (1982); Cain and Hopkins, *British Imperialism*, 443–5 and references therein.

[24] J. A. Hobson, *The New Protectionism* (1916), 115–16. Cf. 58–9.

towards promoting the fullest commercial intercourse between nations and the preservation and extension of the open door.[25]

Hobson also set himself to oppose the claim, popular in wartime, that before 1914 the German state had been in some way plotting the downfall and economic enslavement of the Allies and that the only effective counter to this was protection and exclusion. He emphasized how Britain's own power had developed under free trade; how Germany's fears that Britain would soon follow Chamberlain's ideas and impose tariffs had worsened relations between the powers before 1914; and how Germany's increasing competitiveness had to be met by better scientific and technical education rather than by a self-defeating protectionism which would simply perpetuate the worst kind of militarism and imperialism.[26] More specifically, he claimed that one major source of conflict was Germany's frustrated desire for colonial possessions in Africa.[27]

'DEMOCRACY AFTER THE WAR'

One fruit of the war was that it spurred Hobson to a closer examination of the origins of pre-1914 imperial expansion. Between 1898 and 1902, when he first analysed the phenomenon, his argument had been comprehensive in scope but, except in the case of South Africa, rather vague in the details. Now he took the analysis of specific episodes in imperial history much further than before.

In his early writings on imperialism, Hobson had been aware of the distinction between what is now called 'formal' and 'informal' empire.[28] In his wartime writings the distinction is more obvious. The inclusion of the Balkans in the list of areas subject to imperialist pressures made it plain that Hobson saw imperialism in an even

---

[25] M. Swartz, *The Union of Democratic Control in British Politics in the First World War* (Oxford, 1971), 78. The UDC was at one with Hobson in his stress on the economic origin of modern wars. See the Executive Committee of the Union of Democratic Control, *Memorandum on the Proposed Economic War* (1916), 5.

[26] *The New Protectionism*, chs. 5 and 8.

[27] J. A. Hobson, 'Africa and the War', *Labour Leader*, 7 June 1917, 6.

[28] As his long discussion of the Western penetration of China in *Imperialism: A Study* indicates.

wider perspective than before 1914,[29] though he still thought of it as the exploitation of the backward nations of the world rather than the global struggle for the 're-division of the world' envisaged by his Marxist contemporaries.[30] In 1917 he was more than ever convinced that financial forces were fundamental to imperialism and that the problem had become more acute in recent times because of the spread of industry and industrial competition: the intensity of the drive for cheap sources of raw material supply and the rapid increase in productivity in industrial countries had exacerbated the underconsumption problem by increasing savings as a proportion of income. Hence the growing pressure before 1914 for overseas outlets for surplus capital and the manipulation of governments by investors determined to defend their growing 'fixed stake' in weak, defenceless countries.[31] International trade was still largely a force for good: but when countries were weak and defenceless they became a prey to financial exploitation and international rivalry that could end in war. In 1902 Hobson had been prepared to outlaw imperialist adventures by the simple device of persuading governments to 'an absolute repudiation of the right of [their] subjects to call upon their Government to protect their persons and their property for injuries or dangers incurred on their private initiative'[32]—although this could only have worked if social reform had already changed the nature of capitalism. Now, in 1915–16 he urged the need for international government to encourage the peaceful joint development of these territories on the lines he had envisaged in *An Economic Interpretation of Investment* in 1911.[33]

In 1916, when specifying recent instances of imperialism, Hobson cast his net rather wider than he had in the past, mentioning not only British acquisitions but a range of European ones. The French–German conflict in Morocco was a conflict between rival firms over mineral deposits; the Italian adventure in Libya was 'in essence a gigantic coup of the Banco di Roma'; Persia 'came into modern politics as an arena of struggle between Russian and British

---

[29] Hobson, *Democracy after the War*, 89; *The New Protectionism*, 120.

[30] The best introduction to this aspect of Marxist imperialism is still E. Stokes, 'Late Nineteenth Century Colonial Expansion and the Attacks on the Theory of Economic Imperialism: A Case of Mistaken Identity?', *Historical Journal*, 12 (1969).

[31] *Democracy after the War*, 83.

[32] *Imperialism*, 359.

[33] *The New Protectionism*, 121, 128–34.

bankers'; and Turkey and the Balkans were drawn into the imperialist struggle 'because they lay along the route of German economic penetration of Asia'.[34] At this juncture, Hobson looked on imperialism after 1880 as something to be expected at that stage of human history. Governments could hardly stand aside, not simply because of the intense competition for place, but because their citizens assumed that it was the duty of the state to secure the right conditions abroad for the enterprise of their nationals. Although undertaken initially in support of private businesses, the signing of commercial treaties, consular arrangements, and other activities of the state benefited the public at large by widening the area of trade.[35] Even the promotion of chartered companies and the vigorous support of particular investment groups could not have been prevented. 'Upon the whole, it would be urged that this policy of pushful business, aided by political support, has made for enlarged and freer commercial intercourse and has been essential to the work of developing distant markets and more remote resources.'[36] Such thinking was in line with what he had written in 1911 but it was accompanied by the claim that what was needed now was some international body which would supervise the development of backward countries and offer open access to them.[37] In *The New Protectionism* he did not say whether this could only be achieved after the reform of capitalism and the achievement of economic democracy, or whether it was possible even in the present state of capitalism; though in his pamphlet on the League of Nations, written in 1915, he had assumed the former.[38]

In 1917, Hobson published *Democracy after the War*, the most comprehensive indictment of British imperialism he had written since *Imperialism: A Study*. The fundamental cause of the war was, he declared, 'colonial and imperial antagonisms'[39] which were economic at base and stimulated hostile and competing protectionist and expansionist systems and activated militarism among the great powers. Militarism was an essential part of unreformed capitalism.[40] It acted simultaneously as a means for disposing of surplus wealth, for grabbing territory for investment abroad, and for quelling the discontented masses. Hobson laid special stress on

---

[34] Ibid. 119–20.   [35] Ibid. 122–5.   [36] Ibid. 126.   [37] Ibid. 126–34.
[38] *A League of Nations*, 15–17.
[39] *Democracy after the War*, 38.
[40] Ibid. 27.

the last of these. The problem for elites living on 'improperty' was that the masses had begun to understand the injustice inherent in the existing structures of society, to question imperialism, and to demand reform. Militarism was improperty's chief defence, diverting attention away from domestic struggles to the enemy without and giving elites an excuse to suppress liberty and to squash the enemy within. Hobson pointed to the deliberate cultivation of anti-German feeling, naval rearmament, and the Ulster crisis of 1914 as early manifestations of the militarist reaction to the threat of real democracy in Britain. It was now reaching its apotheosis in the mass slaughter of the war, conscription, and the regimentation of social and economic life that accompanied war. Moreover, those who benefited most from militarism were intent on retaining the authoritarian structures erected during the war even when the fighting was over.[41] Hobson clearly felt that the war offered another opportunity to bring into existence the kind of imperialist state that he had warned against in *Imperialism*,[42] though now he had a stronger sense of the importance of industry within economic elite structures than he had in 1902.

In *Democracy after the War*, Hobson also turned his attention to Britain's recent imperial record. He offered an analysis of some major cases of imperial expansion at a level of detail unrivalled since *The War in South Africa* and never subsequently improved upon. The emphasis on finance as *causa causans* was marked. He prefaced the case studies with the observation that, although foreign investment could only be transferred through the export of goods or services, the objectives of exporters and investors were different. Most exporters had their major assets at home and if they lost a market there was a good chance they could find another. Investors, however, had a 'fixed and lasting stake' in foreign countries. They might even have more of their wealth placed abroad than at home, so they had an interest in war and imperialism if it improved the value and security of their assets.[43] He still felt that the relationship between financial power and imperial policy during the Boer War was crystal clear. The motives of politicians, the public, even Rhodes

---

[41] Ibid. esp. chs. 2 and 3.

[42] The fact that Milner, one of Hobson's Boer War villains, was a member of Lloyd George's war cabinet after 1916 can only have reinforced Hobson's sense of déjà vu.

[43] Ibid. 83. The emphasis here may reflect the influence of his friend H. N. Brailsford, *The War of Steel and Gold* (1914).

himself were basically non-commercial but they were used by the financiers who suborned the public through the press and controlled government and elite opinion through economic influence. 'When the war was trembling in the balance, the widespread ownership of mining shares in hundreds of influential local circles all over the country secretly assisted to mobilise public opinion in favour of determined action.'[44] Other cases, though, were 'more baffling to analyse'.[45] Turning to the British occupation of Egypt (an event only referred to in passing in *Imperialism*),[46] Hobson conceded that 'the position of Egypt on the route to India made it appear important to our statesmen that our Government should have a hold upon the country'. He could not believe, however, that in the purchase of the Suez Canal shares and in their reactions to the claims of English bondholders, 'English diplomacy was using finance, instead of being used by it'. To assert that, he thought, meant ignoring the 'plain fact that the political motive in each instance lay idle until it was stimulated into activity by the more energetic and constructive policy of the financier'.[47]

His analysis of great power policy in China before 1914 came to the same conclusions but again showed a feeling for the complexity of the issues which had sometimes been missing in earlier writings. He decided, for example, that Russia and Japan did not have specifically economic motives for their penetration of China but were 'activated primarily by considerations of territorial and political aggrandizement'.[48] (In an article written around this time Hobson also argued that French motives in the scramble for Africa were non-economic.[49]) Admitting, also, that in the case of Britain's entanglements in political and economic agreements with other powers in China, 'it is not possible to prove how far the initiative was taken by the financial groups, how far by the Foreign Offices', he went on to consider whether or not the British saw China's growing indebtedness as a way of making the latter politically dependent. He then explained that the British government's role in the various consortia which had provided China with finance over the previous generation was mainly to protect the interests of powerful financial groups in Britain against the 'healthy competition' offered by

---

[44] *Democracy after the War*, 84–7.   [45] Ibid. 87.
[46] *Imperialism*, 54, 108, 199.   [47] *Democracy after the War*, 90.
[48] Ibid. 95.   [49] 'Africa and the War'.

financiers, from other nations and from Britain, excluded from the consortia. It seemed evident to him that, rather than governments having political objectives in China which required carefully controlled financial backing, the financial groups within the consortia were actually using government to further their own ends: 'for the businessmen of the Great Powers, China is a huge field of commercial and financial exploitation and their respective Governments with their shifty policies are tools for its profitable working.'[50]

In 1917, his general conclusion about pre-1914 imperialism was the same as his judgement on the specific case of South Africa. 'Justice, humanity, prestige, expansion, political ambition, all conspired to dwarf the significance of the business motive. But persistence, point, direction and intelligible aim belonged to the latter.' Investor power was more potent than other kinds because it 'is more concentrated, wielded more skilfully, and is more direct in its action'.[51] Contrary to the argument he had advanced just before war broke out, Hobson was now convinced that, unless there had been a fundamental change in social structures and the growth of international government as a result, the great powers were bound to have come to blows over the spoils of imperialism. In the present state of relations, no agreements on division of territory could last long because the powers always fomented conflict by excluding some of their number and because the parties to the agreements were often impelled by ambitious greed to break them at a later date.[52] Neither 'inter-imperialism' nor international government seemed likely in the grim year of 1917 when peace seemed impossibly far away. Though he could not know it, Hobson's views had fallen closer into line with those of Bukharin and Lenin, though he never analysed imperial conflict in terms of 'uneven development' and he did not believe that the war was the beginning of the end of capitalism.

America's entry into the war initially raised Hobson's hopes that the conflict might lead to fundamental changes in capitalism and to a secure peace under a League of Nations. But the actual peace settlement was bound to be a severe disappointment. As constituted, the League seemed to him merely a tool of the victorious Allies, as the exclusion of Germany and Russia showed. Also, although

---

[50] *Democracy after the War*, 95–100.
[51] Ibid. 84–5.   [52] Ibid. 93.

Hobson felt that the policy of holding colonies as League man-
dates—which set limits on the exclusive use of a territory's resources
by the occupying power and suggested certain safeguards for the
local population—was good in itself, it was immeasurably weakened by the fact that it was only applied to the colonies forcibly
taken from Germany after 1918, while the Allies' own imperial
possessions remained under exclusive control.[53]

The latter years of the war brought forth Hobson's most emphatic
and detailed account of financial imperialism and an argument that,
to some extent, this imperialism had been inevitable given the structure of society in the advanced industrial countries. The thesis of
The New Protectionism and of *Democracy after the War* was in
many ways the same as in *Imperialism*, and the gains from imperialism were attributed to the rentiers and their allies. There was,
however, one key difference. In *Imperialism* a large part of foreign
trade and investment was seen as unnatural, the part associated
directly with imperialism was expected to grow and salvation
required its curtailment: in the wartime works it was still seen, as
in 1903–14, as mainly benign in effect, vital to the civilizing of man
and to the creation of a peaceful world community. The lesson he
drew from the war was not that economic internationalism had
failed but that it had not yet gone far enough to overcome 'the
barbarous traditions of a dateless past'. In the aftermath of war,
Hobson recognized that the United States was now the most
powerful nation on the planet. He was hopeful that it would extend
its influence across the globe after the war, combating the tendency
to protectionism in Europe by a wholehearted commitment to international free trade and by giving positive support to a genuinely
reformist League of Nations.[54]

THE 1920S: IMPERIALISM AND WORLD DEVELOPMENT

Hobson resigned from the Liberal party in 1916 in disgust at the
McKenna duties and the abandonment of the historic commitment

---

[53] J. A. Hobson, *The New Holy Alliance* (1919).
[54] J. A. Hobson, *The Morals of Economic Internationalism* (New York, 1920).
The quotation is from p. 16. See also J. A. Hobson. 'America's Place in the World',
Contemporary Review, 118 (1920).

to free trade they implied.[55] Two years later, after standing as an independent candidate in the 1918 election, he joined the Labour party in company with other pre-war Liberals shocked by Lloyd George's political delinquency and his association with social imperialists such as Milner in the war cabinet.[56] Labour had acceptably radical views on 'the Great War and the Bad Peace' and a good track record on the issues of free trade and opposition to imperial expansion. Joining Labour brought Hobson closer to the centre of political life: as early as 1918 he was chairman of a party committee on trade policy and wrote a paper for the Labour Economic Advisory Committee attacking arguments for imperial preference.[57] Hobson was also closely associated with the radical intellectuals, such as Leonard Woolf and Sydney Olivier, who formed the Labour Party Advisory Committee on Imperial Questions and who stressed the importance of native rights, economic development, and preparation for self-government within the dependent empire.[58] Within the party there was also a good deal of sympathy towards Hobsonian underconsumptionist explanations of depression and unemployment, two phenomena that loomed large in political and economic thinking in Britain in the 1920s.[59] Hobson's own writings in the 1920s mirror this political concern and most of his comments on empire and imperialism at this time were related to it.

It was the consequences of the Russian Revolution, however, which first drew from Hobson an interesting new extension of his ideas on the economics of imperialism. In 1902 he had insisted that the common man in industrial societies was a loser as a result of imperialism. In *An Economic Interpretation of Investment* he had claimed gains for everyone involved in the process. Now he began to think more in terms of gains made by Western working men, as well as capitalists, at the expense of the peoples in the dominated lands. In *Democracy after the War* Hobson had tacitly admitted

---

[55] *Confessions*, 126.
[56] See C. A. Cline, *Recruits to Labour: The British Labour Party, 1914–31* (New York, 1963).
[57] P. S. Gupta, *Imperialism and the British Labour Movement, 1914–64* (1975), 26–35.
[58] S. Howe, *Anticolonialism in British Politics: The Left and the End of Empire, 1918–1964* (Oxford, 1993), 47–8.
[59] The Independent Labour party adopted Hobsonian explanations for depression after 1923. See R. E. Dowse, *Left in the Centre: The Independent Labour Party, 1893–1940* (1966), 97–9.

that social imperialism was compatible with some improvement in living standards but he had not linked this with foreign trade or payments.[60] In 1920–1, he was claiming that the Bolshevik Revolution had made it obvious to existing elites that they could only survive by offering the masses a higher standard of comfort. This, he thought, could most easily be achieved by some redistribution of the gains extracted from labour in the underdeveloped world:

A portion of the surplus gains can be utilized to support a relatively high level of comfort for the Western working classes who will insist upon higher real wages, shorter hours, adequate provision against unemployment, ill health, old age and other emergencies. The workers would take their share partly in higher money wages, partly in lower prices for imported products, partly in social services rendered by a State which drew a large tax revenue from leasing 'Crown lands' in the colonies and protectorates to licensed business syndicates and from taxation of the high incomes derived from this exploitation.[61]

Hobson thought in 1920 that the League of Nations might be an instrument for such a new policy of 'inter-imperialism' by the victors, who would attempt 'to establish an economic peace by substituting a race cleavage for a class cleavage'.[62]

In the 1920s, Hobson took it for granted that imperial territory in 'backward' areas would become more important to the world economy in future. Partly because of wartime destruction of primary producing capacity in Europe during the war, the prices of many tropical products was set to rise and the desire to control the areas that produced them had intensified.[63] After taking many of Germany's colonies, Britain had a practical monopoly on supplies of some tropical goods thus making it easier to use empire as a means of placating the working classes. But Britain's position was dangerous: it was bound to be challenged by the 'have not' powers in the near future.[64] Hobson's insight into this aspect of social imperialism[65] brought him closer to the Marxist inter-

---

[60] *Democracy after the War*, 192–3.

[61] *Problems of a New World*, 185–6   [62] Ibid. 183, 227–34.

[63] In this context his prediction that Japan would make a concerted effort to conquer China was prescient. Ibid. 223.

[64] Ibid. 219–20, 224–6.

[65] The continuity with pre-war analysis is confirmed, however, by Hobson's description of the process as parasitic. Ibid. 29, 185.

pretation of imperialism. Lenin had consistently explained the adherence of part of the working class to imperialism before 1914 to the creation of an 'aristocracy of labour' fed on the profits of imperialist exploitation.[66] Hobson arrived at this conclusion independently: there is no evidence that he had read Lenin's famous pamphlet.

The political interests he had developed and his preoccupation with the labour question in the 1920s found its most famous outlet in his co-authorship of the Independent Labour party document *The Living Wage* (1926). This pamphlet, largely based upon Hobson's economic ideas, was centrally concerned with raising living standards in Britain by lifting the level of mass consumption, partly through family allowances and partly through policies designed to raise wages generally.[67] At the end of the document the authors briefly considered the effect of raising wages on the export sector in Britain. They recognized that raising wages could have adverse consequences for employment in industries which, in the 1920s, were struggling with ever-intensifying foreign competition. Faced with this difficulty, they pinned their hopes upon the prospects for increased productivity as wages rose and upon other methods of reducing costs, including state purchase of essential imports of food and raw materials. On the whole, though, they were pessimistic about the future of exports, relying on the hope that increased domestic demand would compensate for the loss of foreign markets. But the problem was not resolved in the document: the authors admitted that more exports might be needed because imports could well increase as incomes rose, and working-class interests in cheap food precluded any discussion of protection.[68]

[66] Hobson's writings at this time contradict McIntyre's view that neither he nor Brailsford subscribed to the theory of labour aristocracy as proposed by Lenin and always thought that the Western working class were the losers from imperialism. S. Mcintyre, *A Proletarian Science: Marxism in Britain, 1917–1933* (Cambridge, 1980), 211.

[67] Hobson's approach was rejected by the Labour party at its 1928 Labour conference in favour of Fabian ideas, though it can be argued that the former would have served the party better during the crisis of 1929–31 when it was in government. See N. Thompson, 'Hobson and the Fabians: Two Roads to Socialism in the 1920s', *History of Political Economy*, 26 (1994).

[68] H. N. Brailsford, J. A. Hobson, A. Creech Jones, and E. F. Wise, *The Living Wage* (1926), esp. 42–5. There are extracts in *J. A. Hobson: a Reader*, ed. Freeden, 197–9. See also Dowse, *Left in the Centre*, 130–1.

One of Hobson's chief concerns at this time was to try to resolve the dilemma posed by the desire to redistribute income in Britain and the possibility that this might price exports out of foreign markets, increase unemployment, and reduce demand.[69] In the ILP document there was a cursory mention of the fact that one way of boosting export sales was to increase the income of undeveloped parts of the world, especially those within the empire.[70] Hobson brought this idea to the centre of attention in the 1920s. In doing so, he ignored the emphasis in *The Living Wage* on the need for state purchase of imports and he also emphatically denied the assumption that increasing home demand could compensate for the loss of foreign: Britain's living standards depended on a high level of international trade and the international economy was in urgent need of expansion. 'An industrial country cannot in the long run live on the home market. It must continually seek more foreign areas in which to buy and sell and invest and develop.'[71] At the same time, Hobson rejected protection for British industry. He was now willing to admit that protection could increase output and employment within a nation, albeit at the expense of the rest of the world, something he had consistently denied before 1914.[72] Nonetheless he still felt that, in the long run, protection would reduce competitiveness, exacerbate the maldistribution of income, and add to the pressures making for imperialist aggression.[73]

Any lasting solution to the problem of unemployment and low living standards depended, therefore, on the growth of international economic co-operation under free trade. Hobson was encouraged by the idea that the rise of international cartels was slowly bringing the lessons of interdependence home. At the same time, he still feared that what could emerge from the war was 'a vast international "sweating system"' exploiting blacks to raise wages for white workers and serving 'to produce quiescence and connivance with the new phase of inter-imperialist capitalism'.[74] He found

---

[69] J. A. Hobson, *The Economics of Unemployment* (1922), esp. 97–8; id., *The Conditions of Industrial Peace* (1927), 106–8; id., *Rationalisation and Unemployment* (1930), 120–3; id., *Poverty in Plenty: The Ethics of Income* (1931), 69–74.

[70] *The Living Wage*, 51.

[71] *Rationalisation and Unemployment*, 117–18. See also *The Economics of Unemployment*, 102, 140; and *The Conditions of Industrial Peace*, 108–9.

[72] *The Economics of Unemployment*, 100–1, 155–6.

[73] *The Conditions of Industrial Peace*, 108–9; *Poverty in Plenty*, 73–4.

[74] J. A. Hobson, 'Half the World in Political Subjection: The New Imperialism', *New Leader*, 11 March 1927, p. 6. Also, *The Conditions of Industrial Peace*, 110–11.

this as morally repugnant as he had in 1921: but now he also argued that this kind of exploitation was self-defeating in the longer term because it would reduce the demand for industrial goods abroad, slow down the rate of world growth, and leave the underconsumption problem untouched.[75] Britain's problems could only be solved by a co-ordinated policy of raising living standards among Britain's European industrial competitors and in the underdeveloped world. In the first place:

If we are to retain within our national area the volume of trade and employment needed to maintain our growing population upon a rising standard of life, we must come to some definite arrangement with other countries supplying the world market to march along the same road of economic progress at something like the same pace. Unless we do this, an ever stronger tendency will operate to draw industries from this country and place them in countries where the net costs of production are lower.[76]

Secondly, the rapid development of the non-industrial world was an imperative necessity:

the pressure of expansion in our foreign markets more and more takes the shape of seeking trade in backward countries, and as a struggle for this trade with exporters from countries who were once our customers. That enormous potential markets exist in Africa, China and elsewhere there can be no doubt, but the expansion of these markets requires a complete reversal of the economic exploitation that has hitherto prevailed in the relations between advanced and backward countries. So long as a large part of the food and raw materials raised in tropical and other backward, non-industrial countries is the product of ill-paid and servile labour, the low consumption of imported manufacturers in these countries will serve as a real restraint on the productivity and full employment of manufacturing trades in the exporting nations. A policy of better distribution of income in this country requires, therefore, to be supported by a corresponding movement in other countries both in direct competition with us as exporters of manufactured goods and those which produce the food and raw materials we require and receive in payment for our manufacturers.[77]

Britain's particular problem of underconsumption could only be solved as part of a worldwide plan to raise living standards all

---

[75] *The Conditions of Industrial Peace*, 112; *Rationalisation and Unemployment*, 117; *Poverty in Plenty*, 77.
[76] *The Economics of Unemployment*, 104.
[77] *Rationalisation and Unemployment*, 123–4.

round.[78] In taking this line, Hobson was anticipating the post-1945 drive to develop the 'Third World' that accompanied decolonization. How this was to be achieved, however, he did not say except to express the hope that the League of Nations would evolve into a body capable of world economic leadership. Like the Labour party itself, Hobson in the 1920s shifted from the negative position that the League was merely a tool of the capitalist interests who had been victorious during the war, towards the view that, however imperfect it might be, it did represent the beginnings of political internationalism.[79] Similarly, the designation of certain colonies by the League of Nations as mandated territories subject to League supervision was now seen in a better light. It was 'a first dim formal expression'[80] of the need for international co-operation to develop the poorer nations of the world and Hobson now wanted to see the mandate system extended to include all European colonies and protectorates in Africa and Asia. If this were done, 'a large step would be taken towards regulating that competition for tropical and other resources that has hitherto been the chief obstacle to peace between nations and to the development of the wealth of the world for the good of mankind'.[81] The Labour party's own commitment to empire development in the 1920s and 1930s was very poor and was not pursued with any vigour until the early 1940s.[82] Before then, the party and the trade unions merited the Orwellian gibe that they were uncritical of empire because they knew how much British living standards depended on the exploitation of Britain's subjects

[78] Hobson saw development as a global issue rather than simply one confined to colonial territories arguing that 'for the expansion of our export trades in the near future, Russia, China and South America offer far greater possibilities than any portion of our empire'. *The Conditions of Industrial Peace*, 110.

[79] H. R. Winkler, 'The Emergence of Labour Foreign Policy in Britain, 1918–29', *Journal of Modern History*, 28 (1956). In 1930, Hobson was arguing the need for a new international economic order 'the forms of which it is perhaps premature to discuss'. *Rationalisation and Unemployment*, 125.

[80] J. A. Hobson, *Wealth and Life* (1929), 393.

[81] J. A. Hobson, *The Evolution of Modern Capitalism* (1926 edn.), 493.

[82] On Labour party indifference to empire in the 1920s see Gupta, *Imperialism and the British Labour Movement*, 71–80. In the Colonial Development Act, 1929, the Labour government did offer aid to poorer colonies in the form of British exports, though the amounts involved were very small and the main concern was to relieve British unemployment. Ibid. 135–40. For the change of policy in the 1940s see Howe, *Anticolonialism in British Politics*, 135–8.

abroad.[83] But, as his 1920s writings show, Hobson was not open to this kind of criticism.

Hobson's writings on imperial matters in the 1920s and early 1930s were closer in spirit to the *Economic Interpretation of Investment* than they were to *Imperialism* or to *Democracy after the War*, although the heady optimism of the 1911 book was missing. Economic interdependence was assumed in all his work at this time; and the growth of free trade internationalism was presented as crucial both to the progress of the working man in Europe and to rescue colonial peoples from servitude and exploitation. He still thought imperialism was a transitory phase in mankind's development, that the nation state that fostered imperialism had fulfilled its historic function, and that organizations like the League of Nations were the halting beginnings of 'federal world-government'.[84] At the back of Hobson's mind there was occasionally the thought that, in a truly reformed industrial democracy, international trade flows might be much reduced, but he evidently believed that, in practice, the most likely avenue to peace and internationalism lay through the growth of international economic co-operation. Faced with the impending creation of a protected British Empire in 1930, which he deplored,[85] he wrote

In a 'new moral world' organized on the basis of equitable exchange this economy will be superseded. In such a world a better apportionment of the product to the workers in every country would furnish a much larger volume of demand in the national market that the surplus available for export would be restricted, and its price would be higher than it is at present. But until such organization of world resources is available, each nation will find it advantageous to buy what it needs in the wide market, without loading the producers with costs of production heightened by a tariff and its consumers with the heaped up burdens of those higher costs as they emerge in high retail prices.[86]

[83] See the views of Orwell as reported in Howe, *Anticolonialism in British Politics*, 47–8.

[84] J. A. Hobson, 'The Saving Faith of Internationalism', *Contemporary Review*, 135 (1929), 691, 692–3.

[85] He said that Empire preference would 'prove to be a conspicuous landmark in the annals of human folly'. J. A. Hobson, 'The British Empire in Conference', *Nation* (New York), 17 Dec. 1930.

[86] J. A. Hobson, 'The New Protectionists', *Nineteenth Century and After*, 108 (1930), 319. Nonetheless, he had private doubts about the efficacy of free trade policies at this time. See Freeden, *Liberalism Divided*, 123.

THE 1930S: BACK TO 'IMPERIALISM: A STUDY'

As economic depression settled on the world in the 1930s the capitalist order came under increasing strain and warfare between the major industrial nations became more of a possibility. In response to such dispiriting events, Hobson was forced to move from the position that capitalism could progress by peacefully developing backward nations, hopefully under the benevolent eye of the League of Nations. By the late 1930s, the world crisis was leading him back towards views on the relations between domestic economic change, foreign trade and payments, and imperialism which were close to those he had held during the Boer War: a coincidence which made it seem reasonable to him to republish *Imperialism* in 1938.

This intellectual shift was, however, only clear at the very end of his life: even in the mid-1930s, he still believed in the practical possibilities of Cobdenism. Looking back in 1934, Hobson felt that, before 1920, capitalism had kept emergent democracy at bay by a series of concessions on welfare and wages that had ensured that the popular will had little influence over the workings of the economic system or the imperialism it spawned. Economic collapse—which he assumed to be the result of a massive underconsumption crisis—had drastically altered the political map. Capitalism's survival now depended upon 'rationalization' and planning, producing fascism on the Continent and a less formalized shift to the political right in Britain. On the other hand, the depression had heightened mass consciousness about the injustice of the system and the threat it posed to democracy and freedom. 'Improperty' and democracy were beginning to confront one another more openly: the crisis had brought with it possibilities for good.[87] Fascism, he thought, could not solve the economic crisis since the fundamental problem of maldistribution of property and income would remain.[88] A thoroughgoing 'inter-imperialist' exploitation of the underdeveloped world could alleviate the problem temporarily, though it would also lead to the spread of industrialization and add to the overproduction problem eventually.[89] But inter-imperialism now looked unlikely. With Japanese aggression in Manchuria and growing British imperial protection in

---

[87] J. A. Hobson, *Democracy and A Changing Civilisation* (1934), 31–42.
[88] Ibid. 43–4, 47–50, 132.   [89] Ibid. 50–2.

mind, Hobson pointed out that most industrial nations were resorting to more autarkic forms of imperialism and the number of open markets was shrinking. By now Hobson was beginning to think that another world war might be inevitable since it was a crude but effective method of reducing oversaving by 'destructive waste'.[90]

Nonetheless, in *Democracy*, Hobson claimed again that imperial self-sufficiency was 'quite impracticable' and that an extensive foreign trade was vital if populations were to be 'employed and contented'.[91] 'Closed States' tended to be autocratic and militaristic and were incompatible with the 'full productivity' of the industrial system.[92] His remedy for the troubles of the time included not only economic democracy but also the freest and widest range of international trade. In 1934 he was still optimistic enough to believe that, as awareness of the deficiencies of the capitalist system became more widespread, economic democracy would triumph and that free trade internationalism would eventually reassert itself.[93]

The marked faith in the importance of an extensive international division of labour both to the economic well-being of nations and as the economic bedrock of a future peaceful world order, was much less evident in Hobson's last works. His book *Property and Improperty*, written as the Civil War in Spain began, showed evidence of views on international trade much nearer to those of *Imperialism*. He agreed with the pacifist Norman Angell that conquest of another nation at a similar level of development to ourselves could bring no advantage to a conqueror and that, in this sense, European war was an absurdity: but he insisted that gains could be made through conquest and domination of countries at a lower level of civilization. However, he was now certain that if 'businessmen and settlers' or even 'export traders' and members of elite groups in government could be beneficiaries, the nation as a whole could not. Protectionist imperialism might bring gains to one country but if everyone practised it the gains were cancelled out and consumers were generally worse off as a result. He was also emphatic that imperialism could not make Germany or Japan or Italy more prosperous in general.[94] Moreover, he claimed that a reformed, democratic Britain should put foreign trade in the hands

---

[90] Ibid. 52–6.   [91] Ibid. 52, 54–5.   [92] Ibid. 162.   [93] Ibid. 163.
[94] J. A. Hobson, *Property and Improperty* (1937), 106–10, 124–30.

of the state. 'Socialized' trades would thereafter have little surplus left over for foreign investment, though Hobson did add that the private business which remained should be allowed the freedom to put its funds abroad: 'hugging all our savings for purely national development is inimical to the growth of economic internationalism which in the long run makes for peace and world security.'[95] The implication, however, was that there would be less involvement with the international economy in the new order. In an article published in 1938 Hobson wrote:

the equitable distribution of opportunities, income and property, within our nation will not only ensure peace and progress, but by a diminished pressure on the need for external markets for our goods and capital, by reason of the increased volume of home consumption, will abate the perils of aggressive imperialism and of international conflict.[96]

As in the early 1900s, Hobson was now thinking in terms of an internationalism based on a greater degree of self-sufficiency than was envisaged in the Cobdenite scheme of things.

The year 1938 saw a third edition of *Imperialism*—the first new edition for thirty-three years. Hobson justified reprinting it, with only a few minor statistical additions to the main text, by claiming that 'the chief perils and disturbances associated with the aggressive nationalism of today, though visibly influenced and accelerated by the Great War and the Bad Peace, were all latent and discernible in the world a generation ago'.[97] In the introduction he wrote for the new edition there was nothing to contradict the assumption in the text that both an extended international division of labour and imperialism held few benefits for the mass of mankind. As in *Property and Improperty*, Hobson argued that imperial aggression was costly to nations but beneficial to organized business interests. He also gave more prominence than before to the idea that the purpose of imperial aggression was to divert the attention of peoples otherwise growing steadily more conscious of the injustice of the existing economic order. This policy could end in war but war did have the merit of getting rid of oversaving. The loss of capital

[95] Ibid. 203.
[96] J. A. Hobson, 'Thoughts on our Present Discontents', *Political Quarterly*, 9 (1938), 55.
[97] *Imperialism* (1938 edn.), p. v; (1988 edn.), p. [44].

in the war of 1914–18 had been made up in the 1920s, which were times of rapid world growth and prosperity. Oversaving had only become chronic again in the depression of the 1930s—hence the imperial aggression of Japan, Germany, and Italy and their hostility to the huge, now protected, British Empire.[98] The policy might also end in revolution as the masses finally grew impatient with the system, but, as Hobson said,

> if as many close investigators of the business world appear to hold, the capitalism which has prevailed for the past few centuries is in any case destined to disappear it may seem better for its defenders to endeavour to prolong its life by political pressure for external markets than to succumb without a struggle to popular demands for a state socialism or a policy of social services, the expenses of which shall consume the whole of the surplus profit.[99]

Hobson left his readers to infer that he had always stood by the analysis of the international economy that underlay *Imperialism* when first written. He referred again to the theoretically possible, but practically unlikely, idea of an inter-imperialism: 'a project which might have given the whole of Western capitalism another generation of active profitable survival'.[100] But, of course, in the reprinted text, the argument that 'inter-imperialism' would most likely lead to the de-industrialization of the West, and the spoliation of industrial democracy, remained unmodified. In explaining this, it cannot be argued that Hobson was merely justifying himself for reprinting an ancient text since, as we have seen, views similar to those expressed in the 1938 introduction to *Imperialism*, and in the body of that work, had already appeared in *Property and Improperty* and elsewhere. By the time he came to reprint *Imperialism*, his faith in the practical possibilities of a Cobdenite solution to the world's ills had again receded. As he put it in 1937, it was important to 'perceive the necessity of establishing economic peace at home as the prior conditions of the attainment of a peaceful

---

[98] Ibid. (1938 edn.), pp. xiv–xvi; (1988 edn.), pp. [53–5]. Hobson felt the problem had been aggravated by the British abandonment of free trade in 1932.

[99] Ibid. (1938 edn.), p. xx; (1988 edn.), p. [59].

[100] Ibid. (1938 edn.), p. xxi; (1988 edn.), pp. [59–61]. It should be noted that at this point in the 1988 edition some pages are unfortunately transposed. The order of reading is pp. 59, 61, 60, 62.

internationalism',[101] a sentiment in perfect accord with those he had expressed in 1902 and which must have made reprinting *Imperialism* seem appropriate.

The Problem of Power

In 1938, Hobson also published his autobiography. In this he confessed that, although he felt that his economic interpretation of the origins of the Boer War was still valid, his interest in South Africa had led him 'for a time into an excessive and too simple advocacy of the economic determination of history' and that, at that time, he had 'not yet gathered into a clear perspective the nature of the interaction between economics, politics and ethics needed for anyone who might wish to claim the title of Sociologist'.[102] This seems a rather strange statement to make given his agreement to publish *Imperialism* again. It also underestimates what he had achieved in that book. As we have seen, Hobson's analysis of the springs of imperialism even in 1902 was rather more subtle in places than the famous 'Finance manipulates . . .' argument alone suggested.[103] However, it was true that financial conspiracy was the strongest theme in *Imperialism* and it had surfaced again in later works such as *Democracy after the War* though, in the latter book, he was willing to admit that some imperialist activity in Africa and the Far East was inspired by non-economic motives. What this passage in the *Confessions* reflects is that, in the mid-1920s, he did begin to advance a somewhat more elaborate thesis about the relations between the economic and political forces involved in imperialism than any he had considered since Part II of *Imperial-ism*. Power, he then argued, was derived ultimately from control 'over persons not things',[104] and failure to understand this was a weakness of all purely economic interpretations of history. Property was valued because of the control it gave over people and insofar as the motives for imperialism were 'self-assertion' and 'acquisitiveness'.

To the former, the primacy may be accorded, in the sense that individual or collective self-assertion, or lust for power, which impress men to take or

---

[101] *Property and Impropery*, 106.
[102] *Confessions*, 63–4.   [103] See *supra*, Ch. 4.
[104] J. A. Hobson, *Free Thought in the Social Sciences* (1926), 181.

enforce rule over others, uses the arts of acquisition both as a means to the furtherance of this end, and as instruments for the direct satisfaction of positive self-feeling.[105]

To imperial statesmen 'the gain-seeking of traders and investors' was something that could be 'pressed into the imperial service'; the 'desire for power then becomes the nucleus of a "complex" round which gather various other instructive drives with their emotional and ideological contributions'.[106] Even so, he felt that the 1882 occupation of Egypt and the Boer War remained 'instructive instances of the utilization of national force by private business', and he concluded that the evidence available 'seems to support the view that power politics furnish the largest volume of imperialist energy though narrow economic considerations mainly determine its concrete application'[107]—a position not too far from his original famous statements.

In the late 1930s, he took this line of thinking further by claiming that property was desired 'for power over other human beings and for the prestige which attaches to ownership and power' especially when it had been acquired without labour.[108] Imperial possession and expansion fed a sense of national power and importance just as property acquired by individuals satisfied individual self-esteem.

It is not necessary to prove that such acquisitions are profitable in the narrower economic sense for the possessing nation: the looser, loftier sense of predatory ownership suffices to give them value . . . Unless and until this individual group greed and pride can be dispelled by a keener sense of justice and good of others the exposure of illusions about the purely economic gains of aggressive foreign policies and imperialism will not suffice for peace and security.[109]

This was what made it possible for elites to mobilize popular sentiments in favour of imperialism and to use imperialism as a means of diverting attention from the class struggle at home.[110] The shift in analysis at this point probably owed something to Hobson's recent close study of Veblen who had written powerfully about the ability of the 'dynastic interests' in Germany to turn the vast

---

[105] Ibid. 192–3.   [106] Ibid. 181.   [107] Ibid. 192 n.1, 193.
[108] *Property and Improperty*, 13–14, 24.
[109] Ibid. 121–2.   [110] Ibid. 112–17.

capitalist energies of their country to their own ends.[111] Moreover, the shape that Hobson's reasoning took on this issue in 1937 was consistent with the argument in *Imperialism* that national economic gain from colonialism and imperialism was impossible. Nonetheless, in reprinting *Imperialism* in 1938 without referring to any of his other writings on the subject, Hobson was unwittingly suppressing this line of reasoning along with most of the other new ideas he had had on the subject since the Boer War.

CONSTRUCTING 'HOBSON': THE EMERGENCE OF A CLASSIC TEXT, 1914–1938

Hobson republished *Imperialism: A Study* in 1938 not only because the views expressed in it seemed appropriate to the times but also because the interest shown in it had increased dramatically. *Imperialism* is now a classic work, standing alongside Hilferding's *Finance Capitalism,* Lenin's *Imperialism, the Highest Stage of Capitalism,* and Schumpeter's *Imperialism* as one of the canonical texts with which any informed student of late nineteenth- and early twentieth-century European imperialism has some familiarity. This status was only achieved slowly: if Hobson's interpretation of imperialism still has some currency it must not be forgotten that it was rejected by many within the Liberal party and the wider progressive movement at the time of its first publication. His work was never entirely neglected though it had more purchase in the United States than it had in Britain. It was only in the 1930s that Hobson began to be generally recognized, by leading intellectuals and propagandists of the time as well as by historians, as an outstanding theorist of imperialism. However, the process by which *Imperialism* became accepted as a classic text also helped to obscure the fact that he had written on the subject on many other occasions for half a century. It also encouraged an excessive interest in Hobson as a purely economic theorist of imperialism and led readers to neglect Part II of the book. In the late 1930s, Hobson himself contributed to the emergence of this very limited version of his life's

---

[111] See J. A. Hobson, *Veblen* (1936). Veblen's key work in this regard was *Imperial Germany and the Industrial Revolution* (1915). Veblen's influence on Hobson is traced in S. Edgell and R. Tilman, 'John Hobson: Admirer and Critic of Thorstein Veblen', in Pheby (ed.), *J. A. Hobson after Fifty Years.*

work. He did nothing to counter the hardening conviction that he had written only one book of significance on the theme of imperialism though he had the opportunity to do so on more than one occasion.

As we have seen, *Imperialism* was not very well received even in New Liberal circles when first published, and the impact of Hobson's ideas before 1914 was very limited. Sydney Olivier was sympathetic to a Hobsonian approach and Brailsford gave the thinking embodied in *Imperialism* emphatic intellectual endorsement,[112] but it did not become a standard part of the repertoire of anti-imperialism. There was, for example, no hint of Hobson's leading ideas in Ramsay MacDonald's widely read *Labour and the Empire* (1907) despite the latter's association with the Rainbow Circle.[113] L. T. Hobhouse, Hobson's close intellectual ally on matters of domestic reform, endorsed the concept of surplus and did accept that the Boer War was inspired by financial imperialism: but otherwise he contented himself with the vaguer notion of a 'plutocratic imperialism'.[114] And, of course, Hobson distanced himself from many of the conclusions of *Imperialism* in the run-up to the First World War as the publication of *An Economic Interpretation of Investment* testified. All in all, it is not surprising that no attempt was made to reissue *Imperialism* again after 1905.[115]

The arguments of *Imperialism* began to attract attention after 1914, but it was not until the late 1930s that the interest in the book was sufficient to justify a third edition. The outbreak of war certainly gave a fillip to Hobson's arguments. Bernard Shaw, who had written the equivocal *Fabianism and the Empire* in 1900, offered a much more clear-cut analysis of the outbreak of war in August 1914. 'Capital badly wanted at home, is sent abroad after cheap labour into undeveloped countries; and the financiers use the control of our army and fleet, which they obtain through the control of Parliament solely to guard their unpatriotic investments. That is

---

[112] Brailsford, *The War of Steel and Gold*.

[113] Ramsay MacDonald fairly represented the views of Labour supporters in distinguishing between a good imperialism (which brought civilization) and a bad one, as in the Boer War. P. Ward, *Red Flag and Union Jack: Englishness, Patriotism and the British Left* (1998), 67–8.

[114] L. T. Hobhouse, *Democracy and Reaction* (2nd edn. 1909), 43. Cf. p. 171.

[115] It is worth recording that the second edition of *Imperialism* was published with financial support from Hobson's friends, suggesting that, without subsidy, it would not have been published at all. See the frontispiece to the 1905 edition.

the root of the present mischief.'[116] Shaw continued to take this line in the 1920s and 1930s[117] and, although he did not mention Hobson, he certainly helped to create an atmosphere sympathetic to the argument of *Imperialism*.[118] Olivier, now a prominent colonial administrator, and E. D. Morel and Leonard Woolf, both associates of Hobson in formulating a colonial policy for the Labour party[119] argued strongly for an economic theory of imperialism in the 1920s and took it for granted that the war was an imperialist one.[120] Although he thought of expansion as part of a 'general instinctive desire' driven on by the 'governing class', Morel was particularly worried about the influence of 'powerful financial interests' in exploiting Africa and destroying its development.[121] He also wanted to restrict European intervention in Africa in the manner suggested by Hobson and to ensure free trade. Woolf's analysis and prescriptions were essentially similar though neither he nor Morel actually cited Hobson's book and neither mentioned underconsumption. Like Hobson, Woolf denied that African imperialism benefited anyone in Europe except a small elite group and claimed that the politicians who took the decisions 'are themselves set in motion by another small group of persons, the financiers, traders, and capitalists, who are seeking particular economic ends in Africa'. Woolf also believed that the imperial project could end in catastrophe with a 'revolt of the "beneficiaries" against their guardians and benefactors'.[122] A few years later, he wrote that the chief spur to European imperialism in the Middle East and Asia was finance in the form of railways and mining companies.[123]

Imperialism also began to attain a certain academic respectability after 1919 especially in the United States. As Clarke noted,

[116] Shaw to the *Daily News*, 11 Aug. 1914; repr. in A. Chappelow, *Shaw—'The Chucker-Out': A Biographical Exposition* (1969), 411.

[117] See G. B. Shaw, *The Intelligent Woman's Guide to Socialism and Capitalism* (1928), esp. 140–5, 152–3.

[118] In his 'Common Sense about the War' (1914), Shaw argued for its capitalist imperialist origins but mentions Hobson only once, in the context of a discussion of diplomacy towards Belgium and its consequences. See G. B. Shaw, *What I Really Said about the War* (1931), 55, 84–5, 160.

[119] Gupta, *Imperialism and the British Labour Movement*, 53–7. McIntyre, *A Proletarian Science*, says that Hobsonian explanations of imperialism were common amongst Labour supporters (211).

[120] Lee, *Fabianism and Colonialism*, 170–83.

[121] E. D. Morel, *Africa and the Peace of Europe* (1917), pp. xxiv, 38.

[122] L. Woolf, *Empire and Commerce in Africa* (1920), 317, 319, 367.

[123] L. Woolf, *Imperialism and Civilisation* (1928), 60–5.

Hobson's unorthodox economic ideas 'found a kinder reception' in America than they did in Britain'.[124] After the war, it was cited in the bibliography of Achille Viallete's *Economic Imperialism and International Relations during the Last Fifty Years* (1923) though, ironically, Viallete's analysis was closer to *An Economic Interpretation of Investment* than it was to that in *Imperialism*. The latter was then noted approvingly in Parker Moon's well-known historical survey of the 1920s with its sympathy for economic interpretations of events.[125] L. H. Jenks also recognized Hobson as an important theorist of economic imperialism in his own pioneering work on the history of British overseas investment, though he appeared to know Hobson through *The Evolution of Modern Capitalism* rather than *Imperialism* and he associated Hobson with Marxist analyses of finance capitalism.[126] Jenks argued strongly for a financial theory of imperialism in the case of Egypt and the Ottoman Empire and asserted that Disraeli's purchase of the Suez Canal shares 'symbolized the advent of foreign investment as one of the abiding interests of British foreign policy'.[127] In his reconstruction of Europe's vast pre-war overseas investments and their consequences, Herbert Feis also recognized *Imperialism* as 'the most capable critical analysis of the political and economic results of British foreign lending', though his own analysis had little in common with Hobson's.[128] In the 1930s, scholarly interest in America in the relations between private foreign investment and international conflict grew. In his state-of-the-art book of the mid-1930s, the product of a larger collaborative academic effort investigating the causes of war, Eugene Staley quoted the *Psychology of Jingoism* with approval but eschewed the word 'imperialism' as too imprecise to be useful to the social scientist and did not mention *Imperialism*.[129] He also denied that expansion in Africa and Asia

[124] See Clarke, *Liberals and Social Democrats*, 48; Veblen's review is in *Journal of Political Economy*, 12 (1903). Hobson's reception in America is a theme well worth exploring further.

[125] P. T. Moon, *Imperialism and World Politics* (1926), esp. 538–40. Hobson wrote an enthusiastic review, 'Half the World in Political Subjection', 6.

[126] L. H. Jenks, *The Migration of British Capital to 1875* (1927; repr. 1963), 339.

[127] Ibid. 293, 325. Jenks also noticed Hobson's underconsumptionist doctrine (p. 81).

[128] H. Feis, *Europe, the World's Banker, 1870–1914* (Clifton, NJ, 1930; repr. 1974), 84.

[129] E. Staley, *War and the Private Investor: A Study in the Relations of International Politics and International Private Investment* (1935), 232–4, 416 n. 1.

had been a cause of war between the great powers though he did recognize that private foreign investment was sometimes a critical factor in subordinating smaller, weaker nations to more powerful ones.[130] Staley may not have recommended Hobson's major text but he may have increased interest in it by asking just those questions which had inspired the latter to write *Imperialism* over thirty years before.

Hobson's academic acclaim thus came at first mainly from across the Atlantic. In Britain itself, the Hobsonian flag was kept flying in the 1930s by G. D. H Cole, socialist intellectual and enthusiast for the theory of underconsumption,[131] who called Hobson 'one of the greatest living economists'.[132] Cole and Postgate's hugely influential textbook *The Common People* offered an economic approach to expansion in Africa and Asia close to Hobson's own in *Imperialism*. Foreign investment in tropical products was highlighted as a key element in imperialism since investments were placed in areas that 'needed the safeguard of the strong hand of imperialist intervention'.[133] Even greater help was at hand. Lenin had praised Hobson's analysis of imperialism in his now-famous pamphlet of 1916. Lenin had used Hobson's work as a stick to beat his Marxist opponents, especially Karl Kautsky, delighting in pointing out how the English liberal had a more acute understanding of the true nature of imperialism than the so-called 'Pope of Marxism'. He naturally disdained Hobson's 'bourgeois' belief that imperialism could be eliminated in a reformed capitalism. Similarly, he poured scorn on the notion that the imperialist powers could come together to divide up the world peacefully: the uneven development of capitalism would ensure that conflict was endemic and the pressure to 'redivide the world' chronic. Yet Lenin was also seriously interested in Hobson's analysis of contemporary capitalism as parasitic. He used it as part of his own argument that capitalism

[130] Ibid. ch. 13.

[131] Wright, *G. D. H. Cole and Socialist Democracy*, 182–3, 195. See also Cole's obituary tribute to Hobson in *Economic Journal*, 50 (1940).

[132] See Cole's review of Hobson's autobiography in *Political Quarterly*, 9 (1938), 440.

[133] G. D. H. Cole and R. Postgate, *The Common People, 1746–1938* (1938). The 1938 edition had only a very small bibliography with no mention of sources on imperialism. In the second edition, which repeats the text of 1938 on imperial expansion, *Imperialism* is cited along with such scholarly works as Viallete, Feis, and Jenks. See Cole and Postgate, *The Common People, 1746–1946* (1946), 705.

was 'overripe' and that the world war was part of its death struggles. His endorsement, of no account when he was merely the leader
of a small extremist Communist group, became an important means
of ensuring the fame of *Imperialism* once he had become established
as an iconic figure on the left after the Russian Revolution.[134]

In the late 1930s, when Japan and Italy had invaded China and
Abyssinia respectively, and Germany was claiming restitution of
her pre-war colonies, a new Leninist 'redivision of the world'
seemed imminent.[135] The ILP in the 1930s had accepted an anti-
colonial stance at odds with Hobson's continued interest in active
colonial development under European supervision: but their argument of 1938 that the coming war was due to a clash between
'Have' and 'Have Not' powers for imperial territory derived as
much from a Hobsonian as a Marxist lineage[136] and implicitly
demonstrated how the two approaches could be conflated. Amongst
left intellectuals the process began in earnest in the late 1930s. In
1936, John Strachey used Lenin extensively to show that the war
of 1914–18 had been an imperialist war and that another was on
the way.[137] But reading Lenin led him back to *Imperialism*: and two
years later he hailed Hobson's 'once famous now neglected' text as
a significant precursor of Lenin's work and as 'the highest point of
development ever reached by liberal thought in Britain'.[138] Similarly,
Leonard Barnes, who had also previously ignored Hobson, gave
him equal billing with Lenin in his new book published just before
war broke out and used them both to construct his own analysis
of the crisis of the times.[139] Hobson's approach to imperialism
was, according to Barnes, 'well in line with Marxist doctrine'. He
thought of Lenin's work as a 'careful supplement' to *Imperialism*,[140]

---

[134] See ch. 8 of V. I. Lenin, 'Imperialism, the Highest Stage of Capitalism' (1916),
in *Collected Works*, xxii (Moscow, 1964). Bill Warren, *Imperialism: Pioneer of
Capitalism* (1980), establishes Hobson's influence on Lenin, and on those influenced
by Lenin, but, since he wished to decry Lenin's interpretation of imperialism, he
was inevitably disparaging about Hobson's own work.

[135] For Labour's response to German claims see Gupta, *Imperialism and the
British Labour Movement*, 237–42.

[136] Howe, *Anticolonialism in British Politics*, 1–2, 67–71, 109.

[137] John Strachey, *The Theory and Practice of Socialism* (1936), 232–41.

[138] J. Strachey, *What Are We To Do?* (1936), 85–9.

[139] Cf. *The Duty of Empire* (1935), 265–72, with *Empire or Democracy?* (1939),
79, 101, 194–6, 249. For a brief description of Barnes's importance see Howe,
Anticolonialism in British Politics, 132–4.

[140] Barnes, *Empire or Democracy?*, 195.

and his reformist attitude to capitalism meant that he was closer in spirit to Hobson than he was to the former.[141]

Unselfconsciously no doubt, Strachey and Barnes were helping into the world that double-headed monster, the 'Hobson–Lenin' theory of imperialism, which had such wide publicity after 1945 and which is still a matter of active controversy today. The association of Hobson's theory with Marxism was also made in academic circles. In a closely reasoned attack on *Imperialism* in 1935, the American diplomatic historian William Langer gave Hobson the credit for having inspired the Marxist critique of empire.[142] Also lending a hand were some front-rank British academics whose attention was attracted by the increasing sympathy shown towards economic explanations of Britain's recent imperial history.[143] In the most authoritative of pre-war surveys of the imperial past, Hobson's 'able and interesting book' was noted as one important link in a theoretical chain running from Malthus through to Lenin; and, though an overall economic interpretation of empire building was seriously questioned, the South African war was cited as the 'most distinct, not to say glaring, example of the impact of finance upon politics'.[144] The intensely partisan production of 1902 was developing into the 'must-read' text of modern times and the edition of 1938 was a stage in that progress.[145] Yet the elevation of the book to canonical status had its costs. The reading of Hobson as a precursor of Lenin meant that attention was fixed mainly on the economic arguments of Part I of *Imperialism* and the rich historical, political, and sociological discussions of Part II were neglected, almost forgotten. The cords connecting Hobson to the radical tradition from which his book had sprung were cut as he emerged under the false appellation of proto-Marxist. Moreover, apart from scattered references to *The Evolution of Modern Capitalism* and to *The*

[141] Hobson gave no indication of ever having read Lenin's *Imperialism*.

[142] W. L. Langer, 'A Critique of Imperialism', *Foreign Affairs*, 14 (1935–6).

[143] W. K. Hancock, *Survey of British Commonwealth Affairs*, vol. ii, Pt. I (1940), 2, noted the connection between Lenin and Hobson. He also remarked that 'to Marxian theorists and an increasing proportion of the ordinary public the "imperialist" is a robber and a bully' (p. 1), thus suggesting that the audience for a Hobsonian approach to imperialism was growing.

[144] W. H. B. Court, 'The Communist Doctrines of Empire', in Hancock, *Survey of British Commonwealth Affairs*, 297–9.

[145] Hobson's autobiography also received a welcoming review from the American Marxist P. M. Sweezy, 'J. A. Hobson's Economic Heresies', *Nation* (New York) (Aug. 1938), 209–10.

Psychology of Jingoism, critics of the 1920s and 1930s knew Hobson only through *Imperialism*. The latter's decision to reprint *Imperialism* without serious amendment also left the impression that he had only ever held one set of opinions. In his 1938 preface, he gave little indication of the development of his own thinking on the subject and did not take the opportunity to comment on the views of others except in the case of Norman Angell. Apart from noting that *Imperialism* relied too much on economics in explaining expansion there was nothing in his autobiography to challenge the idea of undeviating commitment to one viewpoint. A rich and tangled history of changing opinions and fresh insights stretching over forty years was thus eclipsed and forgotten.[146]

HOBSON ON IMPERIALISM: A SUMMARY

Imperialism was undoubtedly Hobson's greatest contribution to the debate on the causes of imperial expansion after 1870. However, he wrote on imperial themes for fifty years and it is perhaps time to rescue some of that other material from obscurity. As we have seen, his approach sometimes changed markedly and he never ceased to produce new ideas on the subject until he was 80 years old. Summarizing such a long history is not easy but it is important at this stage to try to produce an overall picture of Hobson's leading ideas and their evolution, if only to emphasize that the 'Hobson' who has filled these pages is a much more complex entity than the one discussed in the preceding section.

In the early 1890s, Hobson considered the extension of foreign trade to be vital to the growth of the British economy and to the nation's welfare and stability and he had little hesitation in supporting imperial expansion for the sake of new markets. His views could often be characterized as 'free trade imperialist': but he also showed some sympathy for the idea of empire unity and

[146] Some reviewers of the *Confessions* and *Imperialism* complained that Hobson failed to show how his theory fitted the facts of the 1930s and that he had missed an opportunity to compare his ideas with those of his successors. The prominent economist A. G. B. Fisher welcomed the reprint of the latter but commented that 'it is a little disappointing to find that even in the Introduction to the new edition, little effort is made to fit the events of recent years into the doctrinal foundations'. He went on to say that 'a good deal has been written on imperialism since 1902, and it would be stimulating to have Mr. Hobson's critical judgement applied to the writers who followed him'. *Economic Journal*, 48 (1938), 534.

protection and thus anticipated some aspects of Chamberlain's programme of constructive imperialism. By 1898 he had wholly abandoned this position. Capitalism in Britain, he now decided, was based on a maldistribution of property, and its product, oversaving, sometimes found an outlet in foreign investment and trade and could result in imperialism. This remained his fixed conviction throughout the rest of his life. Nonetheless, his thoughts on the exact nature of the connection between what he later called 'impropery' and imperialism, and on the ways in which the one might be reformed and the other eliminated, were not always the same. He held different views at different times on the interrelations between, on the one hand, the broad flows of international trade and finance and, on the other, economic imperialism as a specific problem arising from it.

In *Imperialism: A Study*, his most important single statement of the problem, Hobson asserted, on the basis of shaky statistical evidence, that trade with the imperial territories acquired after 1870 was small. Given the assumption that overseas investments could only be transferred through exports, it followed that the capital invested in new territories was also small, but Hobson sometimes left his readers with the impression that the amounts involved were more substantial. He also asserted, again using questionable figures, that the benefits from imperial expansion went to financiers and their immediate allies only and that the costs were paid by the nation as a whole both directly and in terms of lost opportunities for domestic growth. He also believed that, if capitalist development were to continue unhindered and on the same lines, the future exploitation of Africa and, in particular, Asia would dramatically increase the amount of trade and capital involved in imperialism. In this sense, what had happened in South Africa mattered to Hobson not just in its own right but also because of the much greater upheaval in international economic and political relations it foreshadowed. Should imperialism triumph completely, the under-developed world would be forcibly industrialized and its indigenous economy and culture destroyed. Simultaneously, industry, the great carrier of progress and liberty in Europe and America, would also be eliminated and replaced by a service economy dominated autocratically by financial capitalists. In 1902, Hobson believed that this dreadful outcome could be prevented through social reform which, by redistributing income to the poor, would eliminate oversaving, increase domestic trade and investment dramatically, and reduce foreign trade and investment to low levels. European industrial society would then survive and develop on much more democratic lines; and the underdeveloped world, free of the pressures of heavy foreign investment and the competition between the European powers for markets, would also be allowed to grow in ways suited to local genius and traditions. The implication of the analysis was that imperialism was the outcome of a diseased capitalism, a parasitic growth upon it, and could only be rooted out by a transformation in the nature of that capitalism. From this perspective, imperialism existed because capitalist development had been perverse and need never have existed at all.

In *Imperialism*, Hobson also claimed that imperialism was a conspiracy hatched by a few financiers who, because they had a much clearer perception of what they wanted than other interested parties, were able to use the press to fill the masses with enthusiasm for empire and to persuade the governments of industrial societies to use public funds to back private economic interests. He repeated these claims on many occasions subsequently. However, in the course of developing his argument in *Imperialism*, he sometimes subverted this position. He suggested, at different times, that imperialism benefited principally industrial interests, at least in the United States; that it was the outcome of a coalition of business interests wherein finance was important but not pre-eminent; and that these interests were often as irrational in their beliefs and actions as any jingoistic supporters of expansion. Throughout the discussion there was a tension in Hobson's thought between an inherited British radicalism, which emphasized the conspiratorial nature of finance, and a more systematic argument based on his developing ideas about the connection between oversaving and the changing nature of advanced capitalism evident in the emergence of the large corporation and the trust. Later, in the 1906 edition of *The Evolution of Modern Capitalism*, Hobson emphasized the structural argument more strongly, showing that the financier emerged out of the formation of large corporate business in the United States and Germany and that the latter was also becoming a more potent force in Britain. This suggested the growth of a union or interplay between finance and industry that was far more complex than was implied by the one-sided 'finance manipulates' thesis that Hobson is best known for.

Hobson continued to produce ever more sophisticated ideas about the links between finance and imperialism in the Edwardian period and to warn the public of the dangers of a recrudescence of the latter. Yet, simultaneously, he introduced a markedly different set of arguments. Spurred on by the urgent need to defend free trade from Chamberlain's attacks, he now began to picture the international economy as a fundamentally benign force transforming the economic and political prospects of the whole world. In this case, the extension of the international division of labour, of which imperialism was a part, itself created the means through which capitalism would evolve to a 'higher' stage and 'economic democracy' would eventually be achieved. Imperialism could then appear as a more or less necessary stage in the march towards a prosperous and peaceful world economic society. This line of thinking was most evident in *An Economic Interpretation of Investment*, published in 1911. In this work, Hobson argued strongly for a clear connection between economic growth and the growth of foreign trade and investment and claimed that the international division of labour mitigated the effects of oversaving and underconsumption though it could not eliminate them. The economic penetration of the under-developed world was now described as a process bringing benefits to both industrial and 'backward' nations, one which did not threaten the survival of industrialism in the Western hemisphere or necessarily imply the destruction of the distinctive economic cultures of the dominated. Capitalist inequalities still existed and led to imperialism; but they were now presented as phenomena in the process of transformation by the same international economic process Hobson had condemned so bitterly in *Imperialism*. In 1902, Hobson had expected the development of an 'inter-imperialism' amongst advanced nations intent on exploiting the masses throughout the world. In 1911, he repeated the prediction but now thought that this same inter-imperialism would provide the foundations for global growth, international government, and world peace. In 1902, his solution to imperialism depended upon internal transformation amongst the dominant countries and the emergence of a world of largely self-subsistent, albeit free-trading, nations. In 1911, he was looking towards a much more Cobdenite future of mutually interdependent nations, one where the path to world economic justice and international peace would be made more sure the greater the extent and complexity of their economic interaction.

Imperialism and *An Economic Interpretation of Investment* represent the two extreme positions Hobson took up on the subject of imperialism in his mature writings as a New Liberal thinker. His other major statements fall somewhere in between. *Democracy after the War* was closer to *Imperialism* in its analysis of the dominant role played by finance in imperial expansion but retained some of the attitudes to the international economy developed in *Economic Interpretation*. Most of his writings on the subject in the 1920s were watered-down and amended versions of the latter. Although he never offered any new revolutionary interpretation of imperialism, Hobson was never content merely to repeat old ideas. Many of his later writings were valuable in developing particular arguments or expressing new insights. *Democracy after the War* contained an extended discussion of the 'finance manipulates' theme of *Imperialism* with much more attention paid to specific cases. In the inter-war period he introduced new material about the effects of the exploitation of empire on living standards in Britain and he became an early advocate of what was later called development economics. After the First World War, Hobson also began to consider seriously the possibility that the pursuit of power might be as crucial as the desire for economic gain in stimulating expansion. Despite these additions, it remained the case that, broadly speaking, his writings converged around the two different poles of thought represented by his books of 1902 and 1911.

As indicated earlier, these rather contradictory positions were a reflection of a basic tension in radical thinking whose origin was in the eighteenth century and in Adam Smith's ambivalent attitudes to the value of international economic intercourse.[147] Hobson veered from one stance to the other depending on the signs of the times. When there was peace, social reform in the leading industrial nations was in prospect, and militarism appeared to be in abeyance, he thought of international trade and international interdependence as benign forces contributing to economic democracy and transforming imperialism into internationalism. Hobson's most confident espousal of this approach was just before the First World War, but he offered a more cautious version of such Cobdenism in the 1920s. When the international economy collapsed or imperialist war broke out or was threatened, Hobson lost faith in pure

---

[147] See *supra*, Ch. 3.

Cobdenism and fell back on the hope that social and economic revolution from within the industrial nations would kill off 'improperty'. Economic democracy would then develop on a domestic basis and, because the pressures for aggressive economic expansion were eliminated, genuine internationalism would flourish. During the Boer War, for example, he clearly thought that the existing international economy was too diseased to be a transmitter of progress. The reissue of *Imperialism* in 1938 implied that he had returned to that view once the spread of fascism had begun to make a second world war appear inevitable.

Nonetheless, it could be argued that, once clearly established as a theme in his writings after 1903, the Cobdenite optimism that infused *An Economic Interpretation of Investment* became the strongest and most persistent component of his thought. He certainly clung on to key elements of it during the First World War and even during the early part of the 1930s, when the world economy appeared to be in ruins. No other book of Hobson's was so full of insight into the causes and meaning of imperialism or so detailed in its discussion of the impact of imperial expansion in Britain and overseas as was *Imperialism: A Study*. Yet it also presented him in his blackest mood: his more optimistic writings are probably more representative of his thought in general. In bad times, Hobson may have resorted to a kind of 'Liberalism in one Country' approach to progress but his deepest instincts were that Cobden was right and that economic globalization would eventually bring about world government and world peace. What remained consistent throughout his life was the belief that, sooner or later, economic democracy and internationalism would triumph over elitism and imperialism: what frequently changed was his understanding of how, and how soon, the transformation would occur.

Hobson was not a consistent thinker. His views on imperialism not only changed sharply over his lifetime: he was also quite capable of offering widely divergent arguments to different audiences simultaneously as he did, for example, between 1903 and 1914.[148] Given

---

[148] His changeful opinions, especially on the links between international trade and imperialism, suggest a certain lack of intellectual rigour. However, it is worth remembering that even so great a thinker as Keynes could shift position dramatically at times. A convinced free trader for most of his life, he argued strongly for protection and greater self-sufficiency in the depression of the 1930s and he supported his case

his frequent and sometimes dramatic shifts of emphasis it comes as no surprise that he remained a 'puzzle' even to his fellow radical H. N. Brailsford. Looking back admiringly at his mentor and friend, Brailsford detected a yawning inconsistency in Hobson's work on imperialism. Hobson had continually claimed that imperialism would never be got rid of until economic democracy came into existence 'and yet he went on hopefully laying the foundations of international Government, while over a great part of the world that operation had at best only just begun'.[149] Brailsford here conflated two different streams of thought, the first best represented by *Imperialism*, the other by *Economic Interpretation* but his bewilderment is understandable since Hobson often changed from one stance to another without any acknowledgement of the fact and without explaining clearly what he was about. Only very rarely did he explicitly offer these two distinct developmental trajectories as alternative possibilities, as in his article of 1930[150] when the world was finely balanced between the modest economic progress of the 1920s and the depression and chaos of the next decade.

Essentially, Hobson was pursuing a utopian dream of world prosperity and peace, and his intellectual arguments were often readjusted to fit in with whatever political and economic means, domestic or international, seemed likely to offer the best prospect for its fulfilment at any time.[151] 'Utopian' may seem the wrong appellation for Hobson since it refers specifically to those who looked backward for their ideal society to a world of 'agrarian calm felicity'[152] once thought to exist. Hobson himself was rather a 'euchronian', one of those who projected 'the good place, good state of consciousness and good constitution' into a 'good future time' that men would fashion for themselves with the aid of reason, science, and technology.[153] Some euchronians saw capitalism as a mere stage on the way to this felicitous future; others felt that a

---

with the claim that foreign trade was diminishing as a proportion of national income over time. J. M. Keynes, 'National Self-Sufficiency', *Yale Review* (1933); repr. in *The Collected Writings of John Maynard Keynes*, ed. D. Moggridge, xxi (Cambridge, 1982), 233–46.

[149] H. N. Brailsford, *The Life and Work of J. A. Hobson* (Oxford, 1948), 26.
[150] 'The New Protectionists'.
[151] For a discussion of utopian thinking within which Hobson can be comfortably accommodated, see Kumar, *Utopianism*.
[152] F. E. and F. P. Manuel, *Utopian Thought in the Western World* (1979), 20.
[153] Ibid. 4.

market society, purged of its imperfections, would form the ideal economic base for its realization. Owen, Fourier, Marx, and Morris are representative of the former, the socialist, tradition. Paine, Spencer, Cobden, and Hobson are major figures in the latter liberal-radical landscape, all more or less involved in the field of 'applied utopistics'.[154]

In the liberal-radical tradition, the 'new moral world' was a capitalist one of individualism which offered, not a communistic equality but rather equality of opportunity. In Cobden's and Spencer's time it was still possible to believe that the major barrier to the achievement of the ideal was the survival of the remnants of feudalism. The New Liberalism's, and Hobson's, great achievement was to identify capitalist monopoly and inequalities as the major hindrance to the growth of a pure capitalism and to campaign for its reform. But, in so doing, Hobson came up against the dilemma that earlier radicals had faced: that the same extension of international trade which offered the possibilities of spreading the new moral world of industry could also, while the 'classes' remained powerful, be a carrier of war and imperialism. One answer was patiently to assume that the growth of international interdependence would itself lead eventually to the demise of international conflict and imperialism; another was to concentrate on domestic reform and thus create a smaller but purer international economy that would encourage internationalism. Hobson offered either a domestic or an international remedy for imperialism depending on the political and economic circumstances of the time. But those who read only *Imperialism* or the *Confessions* would never know either that he had been an uncritical supporter of imperial expansion in his youth or that, once the scales had fallen from his eyes, he advocated not one method of interpreting capitalist imperialism but two.

[154] Ibid. 20.

CHAPTER EIGHT

Hobson Lives? Finance, Finance Capitalism, and British Imperialism, 1870–1914

Hobson's writings on imperialism, especially *Imperialism: A Study*, will always be significant to historians of late nineteenth- and early twentieth-century Britain. This is partly because his views have had such a strong influence on attitudes to imperialism and imperial expansion and have so powerfully influenced the historiography. His work is also important because of its role in the development of a distinctively British radical discourse which had its origins in the eighteenth century and because it illuminates the thinking of a small, but highly vocal, section of the British public on matters of central significance to the nation at a particular moment in its historical evolution. But can Hobson's work give any aid to the present-day historian trying to understand the dynamics of imperial expansion in the late nineteenth and early twentieth century? Is *Imperialism* a living text or is it simply a document whose influence lies in the past rather than the present?[1] In giving tentative answers to these questions, the limitations of the exercise should be carefully noted. The chapter is concerned with the usefulness or otherwise of Hobson's economic diagnosis of the causes of imperialism as expressed in *Imperialism*, more particularly Part I of that book and those sections of Part II considered in detail in Chapter 4 above, in the 1906 edition of *The Evolution of Modern Capitalism*, and in *Democracy after the War*. No attempt is made

---

[1] For an earlier attempt to assess Hobson's current usefulness see Cain, 'Hobson Lives? Finance and British Imperialism, 1870–1914'.

to try to assess the value of most of the rest of Part II of *Imperialism* or of *An Economic Interpretation of Investment* or many of his other writings. Hobson's lifelong interest in the relation between imperialism and economic development is also left out of consideration here. To do justice to all facets of Hobson's thinking recorded in these pages would require another book.[2] Another limitation placed on the discussion is that, for the sake of brevity, the empirical data used here covers the period 1870–1914 only.

FOREIGN INVESTMENT AND THE BRITISH ECONOMY

Since Hobson was so concerned to forge links between foreign investment and imperial expansion it is necessary to begin by assessing the former's significance to the British economy in his time. Hobson's approach has been attacked in recent years by those who claim that foreign investment was neither a new nor a particularly important feature of British economic life at the time he was writing. So, in order to test the relevance of any Hobsonian theory of imperialism it is first necessary to review the importance of foreign investment to the economy of Britain in the later nineteenth century.[3] Conventional assessments of British overseas investments all show that sustained flows of funds abroad were very much a phenomenon of the later nineteenth century and the Edwardian period. Total overseas assets owned by British subjects rose from around £200–30 million in 1850 to £700 million by 1870 and £2 billion in 1900 before reaching £4 billion just before the First World War.[4] At the latter date, the assets brought in a return of about £200 million per annum, equivalent to about 8 per cent of the national income. These magnitudes, which are broadly consistent with the statistics Hobson used, have recently been questioned and it has been argued that the figure for total assets owned abroad in 1913 should be

---

[2] Another Hobson is the subject of Long's *Towards a New Liberal Internationalism*.

[3] For a brief survey of the evidence see Cain and Hopkins, *British Imperialism*, 161–5.

[4] P. L. Cottrell, *British Overseas Investment in the Nineteenth Century* (1975), 11–14, 23, 31. See also Davis and Huttenback, *Mammon and the Pursuit of Empire*, table 2.1, pp. 40–1.

written down by about one-third with adjustments made for earlier dates accordingly.[5] Even if the downward revision were universally accepted as reasonable, the rise in foreign investment after 1850 would still be one of the most marked features of later nineteenth-century economic development. In fact, the experts have received the assault on orthodoxy somewhat sceptically even though it is admitted that the conventional totals are based upon inadequate data.[6] Besides this, the discussion on the extent of British investments overseas has largely been concerned with portfolio investment, that is with capital placed in foreign-owned firms. It is now becoming accepted that the amount of direct investment—involving the establishing of British firms abroad—has been neglected and previously under-recorded. Any downward revision of the figures for portfolio investment must, therefore, be compensated for by a more generous assessment of direct forms of capital export.[7] Given the present state of research, it is reasonable to accept the well-established figures for British foreign investment as roughly accurate. Foreign investment became a key feature of the British economy in the late nineteenth and early twentieth century and, with outflows averaging around 5 per cent of the national income between 1850 and 1913, was not a 'comparatively insignificant' item as one famous historian of British imperialism recently claimed.[8]

Who were the foreign investors? It is necessary to remember again that Hobson's analysis of imperialism is an extension and a repositioning of a long-running radical discourse on imperialism, one that always emphasized the connection between imperial expansion on the one hand and privilege, monopoly, and 'unearned increments'

[5] D. C. M. Platt, *Britain's Overseas Investments on the Eve of the First World War* (1986), esp. table 2.3, 60. For similar arguments see id., 'British Portfolio Investment Overseas before 1870: Some Doubts', *Economic History Review*, 2nd ser. 33 (1980).
[6] C. H. Feinstein, 'Britain's Overseas Investments in 1913', *Economic History Review*, 2nd ser. 43 (1990).
[7] P. Svedberg, 'The Portfolio-Direct Composition of Private Foreign Investment Revisited', *Economic Journal*, 88 (1978): M. Wilkins, 'The Free-Standing Company, 1870–1914: An Important Form of British Direct Foreign Investment', *Economic History Review*, 2nd ser. 41 (1988); M. Wilkins and H. Schroter (eds.), *The Free-Standing Company in the World Economy, 1830–1996* (Oxford, 1998); T. A. B. Corley, 'Britain's Overseas Investments in 1914 Revisited', *Business History* 36 (1994).
[8] R. E. Robinson. 'The Excentric Idea of Imperialism, with or without Empire', in W. J. Mommsen and J. Osterhammel (eds.), *Imperialism and After: Continuities and Discontinuities* (1986), 270.

on the other. Imperial expansion was paid for by the Many: it benefited the Few, a complex of interests that had historically centred
on the dominant territorial aristocracy and on the state it was
alleged to control. In the radical understanding of the mechanics of
imperialism the financiers and financial institutions of the City of
London had always played their part. The importance of bodies
such as the Bank of England and the East India Company in the
complex workings of the aristocratic state at home and abroad
were well recognized. Hobson's innovation was to seize on the
growing evidence that 'financial imperialism' was becoming a
more important part of the whole and, via his arguments about the
relation between underconsumption, oversaving, and foreign
investment, to give it a centrality in radical explanation it had never
had previously. In investigating the main sources of foreign investment, Hobson was true to his radical inheritance in arguing that it
originated largely in the south of England. He developed this line
of thinking fully in 1909–10 but the outlines of it are clearly
discernible in *Imperialism*.[9] For Hobson, the south was the home
of a 'moneyed class', a large non-industrial middle and upper class,
where incomes often came from rentier sources including foreign
investments. Imperialism was largely an endeavour to find openings
for the surplus savings of this class, whose power was enhanced
because they were culturally and socially integrated into the traditional circles that held the major share of power in Britain. They
were closely tied to the financiers, politicians, soldiers, professional
men, and administrators who had a direct interest in expanding
employment on the frontiers of empire.

Hobson woefully underestimated the dynamic qualities of the
City and of the service-driven economy of the south-east of England
as a whole that was the leading sector of the British economy after
1880. But recent work on the geographical distribution of stockholders in imperial and foreign enterprises does show a high
concentration of overseas investors with London addresses, though
there was a strong interest in foreign or imperial enterprise in
Lancashire and parts of Scotland. Moreover, although merchants
showed a preference for foreign investment, studies of the occupational structure of overseas investors have shown that manufacturers as a whole were far more interested in domestic than in

---

[9] *Imperialism*, 151, 314–15, 384–5; and 'The General Election: A Sociological
Interpretation', 113 ff.

overseas stocks. Also, insofar as manufacturers showed an interest in overseas endeavours, those who did so were predominantly from the London area. By contrast, the group with the most decided preference for investment overseas has been recently described as 'peers and gents'.[10] These findings are controversial, especially since having a London address did not necessarily mean that a business or an investor had his main business there. However, they do fit with evidence from other sources showing traditional money beginning to flow into overseas enterprise, a trend that partly reflected the steady decline in the profitability of agriculture after 1870. A great deal of saving in Britain was also made by those who, like the landed aristocracy, were cut off socially and institutionally from industrial employment and contacts and looking for safe outlets. Domestic opportunities for investment of the latter kind were limited after 1870 and rates of interest on government bonds, railway paper, and other suitable stocks were low. Returns on equivalent overseas investments were only marginally higher than on domestic stocks but it must be remembered that the returns on the latter must have fallen to much lower levels without the steady opening up of overseas opportunities.[11] Thus funds naturally flowed abroad into government stock, public utilities, and similar investments that were expected to bring a secure and steady return from an area much wider than the formal bounds of the British Empire. The flow, it appears, was determined as least as much by sociological divisions within Britain as it was by the search for greater profit.[12] Hobson would have found no difficulty in accepting that conclusion since he always believed that the savings of the rich were not much influenced by changes in interest rates. Nor would he have been surprised by the evidence of an increasing social intimacy and intermarriage between millionaire bankers and the non-industrial elites who ran government in Britain, or by the appearance of a new stage in the evolution of what has been termed 'gentlemanly capitalism' wherein City finance had greater scope than hitherto.[13]

[10] Davis and Huttenback, *Mammon and the Pursuit of Empire*, ch. 7.

[11] W. P. Kennedy, *Industrial Structure, Capital Markets and the Origins of British Economic Decline* (Cambridge, 1987), 145.

[12] Davis and Huttenback, *Mammon and the Pursuit of Empire*, 211.

[13] Y. Cassis, *City Bankers* (Cambridge, 1994), chs. 6 and 7. Cain and Hopkins, *British Imperialism*, esp. 182–3. For an earlier attempt to use Hobson's regional analysis to understand British imperialism see P. J. Cain, 'J. A. Hobson, Financial Capitalism and Imperialism in Late Victorian and Edwardian Britain', *Journal of Imperial and Commonwealth History*, 13 (1985).

There is some evidence to suggest that heavy flows of British capital overseas were inimical to industrial development in Britain as Hobson claimed in *Imperialism*.[14] The great surges of foreign investment in the 1880s and during the Edwardian period were accompanied by low rates of growth of output and investment in manufacturing in Britain even though the traditional export areas benefited from overseas flows of funds. By contrast, low levels of foreign investment in the 1890s were paralleled by a revival in manufacturing growth despite a severe slowdown in industrial exports.[15] Evidence of this kind has recently been used to provide a more directly Hobsonian view of the British economy in the late nineteenth and early twentieth centuries. Kennedy, for example, has claimed that, whatever benefits heavy foreign investment may have conferred on the major export industries and their regions, its effects on domestic investment as a whole were adverse. He believes that home investment was lowered partly because free trade encouraged Britain's debtors to pay their dues by exporting manufactured goods to her, thus lowering profits and discouraging investment. This is not an argument Hobson could have accepted since he was always an ardent free trader who saw protectionism merely as a device used by vested interests to improve their own position at the expense of the mass of consumers. But Kennedy also argues that home investment was low in part because high levels of foreign investment led to a maldistribution of income in favour of rentiers and lowered effective demand for industrial commodities.[16] It is also worth noting here that Hobsonian explanations for the ebbs and flows of overseas investment have also recently been brought back into the front-line of discussion. Edelstein's analysis of overseas investment flows is principally drawn up on neo-classical assumptions about the downward tendency of the rate of investment in response to limited home opportunities. However, he does pinpoint two periods, in the late 1870s and in 1901–3, when 'desired' savings overshot 'desired' domestic investment opportunities considerably. In his considered opinion, these bouts of Hobsonian oversaving may have triggered off the great foreign investment booms of the 1880s and 1905–13. Without foreign outlets, these savings would have

---

[14] *Imperialism*, 132–3.
[15] Cain and Hopkins, *British Imperialism*, ch. 6.
[16] Kennedy, *Industrial Structure*, 153–63. For another argument for underconsumption drawn directly from Hobson see P. K. O'Brien, 'The Costs and Benefits of British Imperialism, 1846–1914', *Past and Present*, 120 (1988).

been kept in idle balances and severe depression could have resulted.[17] These are highly controversial claims and the relationship between home and overseas investment is a particularly hotly disputed area of recent research.[18] But Kennedy's and Edelstein's work along with that on the geographical and occupational origins of investors does mean, at the very least, that a Hobsonian analysis of the British economy and its overseas ramifications can lay some claim to attention.

THE COSTS AND BENEFITS OF IMPERIALISM

A discussion of the importance of foreign investment to the British economy leads on naturally to a consideration of the costs and benefits of the British imperial project. True to his radical inheritance, Hobson believed that imperial expansion into heavily populated territories where extensive white settlement was impossible brought more costs than benefits to the nation and that the only true beneficiaries were the small group of financiers who controlled policy. Kennedy's conclusion is broadly in line with Hobson's on the economic side: Britons would have been better off keeping their savings at home and finding new ways of boosting domestic productivity. However, Edelstein's analysis of oversaving, despite its Hobsonian overtones, implies that foreign investment mitigated or overcame depression in Britain and that to some extent empire, as an outlet for investment, brought gains to the economy. However, it was Davis and Huttenback who were most influential in reviving interest in a Hobsonian approach when they provided a new armoury of statistics to try to prove that, while the overall gains from foreign investment were insufficient to cover the costs, elites gained most from foreign and colonial investments while paying a very small part of the taxes necessary to defend them.[19]

Davis and Huttenback's findings have encouraged a wider debate on the worth of empire.[20] Starting from the counterfactual

[17] M. Edelstein, *Overseas Investment in the Age of High Imperialism: The United Kingdom, 1860–1914* (1982), 254–6.
[18] For a thorough overview of the main arguments, see S. Pollard, *Britain's Prime and Britain's Decline, 1870–1914* (1989), ch. 2.
[19] Davis and Huttenback, *Mammon and the Pursuit of Empire*, 244–52.
[20] The main contributions are: O'Brien, 'Costs and Benefits'; A. Offer, 'The British Empire, 1870–1913: A Waste of Money?', *Economic History Review*, 2nd ser. 46

proposition that Britain had no empire after 1870, and using a variety of assumptions about the level of world development that would have been attained in the circumstances, Edelstein recently concluded that Britain's empire was beneficial to her in material terms. Depending on assumptions made, he computes the gains from trade at between 1.6 and 4 per cent of GNP in 1870 and 3.8–6.5 per cent in 1913. However, owing to subsidies on investments in the biggest borrowers, the settlement colonies,[21] gains on investment in empire only compute to 0.3 per cent of GNP in 1870 and 0.5 per cent in 1913 at best.[22] Imperial defence costs are estimated at one-half of the total British military spending, thereby accounting for about 1.1 per cent of GNP in 1870 and 1.5 per cent in 1913. On this basis, empire was worth having and its value increased over time. Edelstein's figures are interesting in this context because they indicate that the returns from empire were rising between 1870 and 1914[23]—a fact that Hobson might not have found too surprising—and that the main beneficiaries of imperialism were those involved in trade, rather than investors and financiers, a finding which contradicts Davis and Huttenback as well as Hobson. Of course, Edelstein's conclusions relate to the whole of empire: his work needs considerable refinement to determine whether the acquisition of colonies in the 1880s and 1890s was cost effective on his criteria and to make a direct comparison between his arguments and those of Hobson possible.

Starting with Hobson, his own calculations of costs and benefits were somewhat haphazard and unsatisfactory. At his most extreme, from the second edition of *Imperialism* onwards, he claimed that the territories occupied after 1870 provided Britain with a total trade of only £17 million (£9 m. exports, £8 m. imports) at the turn of the century. Moreover, according to Hobson, the only gain from

(1993); id., 'Costs and Benefits, Prosperity and Security', in A. Porter (ed.), *Oxford History of the British Empire*, iii (Oxford, 1999); M. Edelstein, 'Imperialism: Costs and Benefits', in R. Floud and D. N. McCloskey (eds.), *The Economic History of Modern Britain*, ii: 1860–1939 (Cambridge, 1994); P. J. Cain, 'Was it Worth Having? The British Empire, 1850–1950', *Revista de historia economia*, 16 (1998).

[21] Investments in the colonies were granted trustee status that had the effect of lowering the cost of borrowing.

[22] On some assumptions gains from investments proved negative. Edelstein, 'Imperialism: Costs and Benefits', 207–10.

[23] 1914 was probably the point of highest profitability. Using Edelstein's assumptions, it has been argued that profitability had clearly declined by 1937. See Cain, 'Was it Worth Having?', 372–4.

this trade was the profit upon it which, using his own figure of 5 per cent, would equal £850,000 per annum. It is worth remembering, however, that in the first edition Hobson had actually produced evidence which suggested that trade with new territories, including Egypt and the Transvaal, was worth about £52 million (£23 m. exports, £29 m. imports) in 1900 and a 5 per cent return on that would have been £2.6 million. Without offering any precise information, Hobson assumed that the return on British investment in these territories was considerably greater than on trade and that these gains had been made mainly by the 'little group of financial kings' who floated overseas loans.[24] Manufacturers and traders in general paid more in taxes to support this increased war expenditure than they gained in benefits: the reverse was true of financiers.[25]

All Hobson's claims were contentious and some were simply wrong. His figures for total trade ignored services such as shipping and insurance that could have been worth £2–5 million per annum depending upon whether the statistics from the first or second editions were used. Using his own profitability criterion, this would have brought in gains of £100,000–250,000 annually. Hobson assumed that gains from trade came only from profits because most exports could be sold at home for a smaller return but fell into the error of comparing *net* returns on trade with *gross* returns on investment. To be consistent, Hobson would have had to apply the same criterion to overseas investment as to trade because he always argued that what was saved was invested and that savings not sent abroad would find a niche domestically, though at a lower rate of return. Let us assume that investments in Egypt and South Africa were worth about £200 million in 1900 and that Britain had invested £40 million in the other sixteen colonies and protectorates listed by Hobson in later editions of *Imperialism*.[26] If there had been an average 1.1 per cent difference in returns on home and imperial investment[27] then the net income on investment in new possessions

---

[24] *Imperialism*, 57.

[25] For an extended discussion see *supra*, Ch. 4.

[26] New British financial issues for the whole of the dependent empire other than India between 1870 and 1900 totalled £48 m. Davis and Huttenback, *Mammon and the Pursuit of Empire*, table 2.1, pp. 40–1.

[27] M. Edelstein, 'Realised Rates of Return on British Domestic and Foreign Investments in the Age of High Imperialism' *Explorations in Economic History*, 13 (1976), table 7, p. 314, computes the difference over the period 1870–1914 at 1.1% per annum though the gap was more favourable to foreign investment only in

would have been about £2.5 million, or about the same as the returns on trade implied by Hobson's statistical evidence in the first edition of *Imperialism*. In other words, using his original assumptions and figures, it cannot be proved that investors as a whole got greater benefits than manufacturers and traders from extending the empire after 1870.

Hobson's own statistics and methods imply that, taken together, the overseas trade and investment associated with new empire were of little significance to British growth since, at best, they produced gains of roughly £5.5 million or 0.4 per cent of GNP in 1900. Yet Hobson's profitability measure for overseas trade, based on the 'marginalist' approach he inherited from Adam Smith, is itself very questionable and measuring Hobson by Edelstein's standards rather than his own produces interesting results. Edelstein's 'strong' assumption is that, if dependent empire territories had been independent, Britain would have sent only one-quarter of its actual exports to them and one-fifth of its capital investment, though returns on the latter would have been twice as high. If, in 1900 Britain had sent £23 million of exports to new possessions and had invested £250 million in them at 6 per cent per annum then, assessed by Edelstein's methods, the gains from trade would have been £18 million, or just over 1 per cent of GNP, and from investment £9 million or 0.5 per cent. On these criteria, new acquisitions were worth rather more to the nation than Hobson believed and manufacturers and traders gained more than did investors. One conclusion that can be drawn from this investigation is that, whatever method of calculation is used, it does not appear that investors made disproportionately large gains from empire. Of course, this leaves open the possibility that individual financiers, the people Hobson was most interested in, could have made substantial personal gains and that these people had a special influence with government and could influence policy on the frontiers.

As for costs, Hobson's attribution of the whole of the increase in defence expenditure to imperial expansion is clearly wrong. Edelstein's own figures are based on allocating half of all expenditure to imperial defence and expansion in the period 1870–1914

1870–6, 1887–96, and 1910–13. Davis and Huttenback, on the other hand, believe that domestic investment was more profitable than foreign on average after 1880. *Mammon and the Pursuit of Empire*, 107 and App. 3.2, p. 117.

though some other historians think that all spending on the navy and a considerable part of army costs would have been payable even if Britain had not possessed a formal empire.[28] Exactly how much the expansion into Africa and Asia after 1870 actually cost could only be determined by detailed research: it is possible that it was accomplished by using already existent resources with all the pressure for increases in expenditure coming from other quarters. It seems likely the cost in the 1880s and 1890s was only a very small fraction of the total defence bill and it is more than possible that the gains were larger than the cost, especially when it is considered that Hobson's method of computing the value of trade was very conservative. Even what Robinson and Gallagher called 'scraping the bottom of the barrel' in tropical Africa[29] may have paid its expenses with the benefits, such as they were, being widely diffused. Nonetheless, it must not be forgotten that assessments of costs are very time dependent. Edelstein's approach compares 1870 and 1913, two years of 'normal' defence expenditure. His assessment would have looked very different if he had taken the Boer War period when army costs alone rose to about 5 per cent of GNP, and it was precisely that period that most concerned Hobson and provoked him to write *Imperialism*.

It should also be remembered that, even if the empire was of overall material benefit to Britain and the benefits were diffused across the nation, it was still open to Hobson to argue that the resources could have been used to better effect at home in raising productivity. As O'Brien has noted, if Hobson was right and there was chronic underconsumption in Britain then the resources devoted to defending empire might well have been better employed in raising demand, investment, growth, and productivity domestically.[30] Finally, it must never be forgotten that Hobson was as much concerned with the moral outcome of imperialism as he was with its material costs. Even if it could be proved that imperial expansion brought direct material benefits to all in Britain in the short run, Hobson could still have objected to it if, in his view, it threatened liberty and democracy in a longer perspective.

[28] Edelstein, 'Imperialism: Costs and Benefits', 212; Offer, 'The British Empire', 232–4.

[29] R. E. Robinson and J. Gallagher, 'The Partition of Africa', in F. H. Hinsley (ed.), *New Cambridge Modern History*, xi (Cambridge, 1967), 593.

[30] O'Brien, 'Costs and Benefits', 170.

HOBSON AND THE SCRAMBLE FOR TROPICAL AFRICA

It is now well recognized that the swathe of tropical territories in West and East Africa and in parts of Asia occupied by Britain in the late nineteenth century attracted only very limited amounts of British capital. Davis and Huttenback concluded that the whole of the dependent empire other than India accounted for only about 5 per cent of all British overseas investments in 1914 and their findings only confirmed what had long been understood.[31] The fact that many of the African and Asian areas absorbed into the empire saw very little of the huge surge in foreign investment after 1870 has led some historians to dismiss Hobson's approach to imperialism as misguided and founded on crude statistical errors.[32]

For Norman Etherington the lack of correspondence between foreign investment and extension of territorial possession in the tropical regions of Africa and Asia in the late nineteenth century presents no real problem for a Hobsonian approach. He has argued that Hobson was not interested in the scramble for Africa, which he explained in the traditional radical manner. Etherington believes that Hobson's theory was intended to apply only to the period from 1895 onwards, when the South African crisis ushered in a new phase of capitalist imperialism and when the latter anticipated Lenin's argument about imperialism resulting from the beginning of the finance capitalist phase of development.[33] The emphasis Etherington places on Hobson's concerns about the future course of imperialism is salutary: but his thesis about the latter's views on the African partition cannot be sustained. In *Imperialism*, Hobson clearly indicated that his new theory was meant to encompass the assimilation of 'backward' areas into the empire after 1870 and was therefore directly applicable to the scramble.[34]

[31] Davis and Huttenback, *Mammon and the Pursuit of Empire*, 40–1.

[32] D. K. Fieldhouse, 'Imperialism: An Historiographical Revision', *Economic History Review*, 2nd ser. 14 (1961–2). For a wider attack on economic theories of imperialism in general see id., *Economics and Empire* (1974), ch. 3. For a dismissal of all theories of economic imperialism see R. Hyam and G. Martin, *Reappraisals in British Imperial History* (1975), 1.

[33] Etherington, *Theories of Imperialism*, ch. 4.

[34] *Imperialism*, 15–27. For a convincing modern demonstration, at least in relation to Hobson, see A. M. Eckstein, 'Is There a "Hobson–Lenin Thesis" on Late Nineteenth Century Colonial Expansion?', *Economic History Review*, 2nd ser. 44 (1991).

The fact that only small amounts of capital flowed to many of the territories acquired in the late nineteenth century has encouraged the idea that Hobson's theory is invalid generally and that it fails not just because it gives too much weight to economic forces but also because it puts too much emphasis on events in the metropolis in explaining expansion. The late Ronald Robinson, the most brilliant critic of classical economic theories of imperialism, rejected all 'Eurocentric' explanations because, he claimed, they defined imperialism almost 'wholly in terms of metropolitan drives projecting on passive peripheries'.[35] In his view, imperialism could only be understood as an 'interactive process' in which a wide variety of European 'inputs', economic and non-economic, came together with an equally varied range of collaborative forces outside Europe to produce a spectrum of imperial relations from a vague paramountcy on one side to formal rule on the other. Imperialism was not a simple function of European economic development, a stage in its progress. European inputs into the periphery were not significant enough in themselves to produce imperialism. Robinson argued instead that, in the white colonies where British economic inputs were of relatively greater significance, the imperial element in the relationship melted away rapidly; in Africa and Asia, where the economic link with the metropole was much weaker, the extension of imperial authority was most marked.[36] Purely Eurocentric theories are inadequate and there is force in the claim that 'when imperialism is looked at as an interactive process, its true metropolis appears neither at the centre nor on the periphery, but in their changing relativities'.[37] Nonetheless, despite the attempt to achieve a balance between metropole and periphery, Robinson and other critics of Hobson sometimes underrate the power of the former. As will be argued below, even when foreign investment was limited in size it could exercise a disproportionately large influence on the frontiers of empire. Moreover, the importance of foreign investment on some of the frontiers of empire was considerable, as was the case with both South Africa and Egypt, two areas of great interest to Hobson. The result is that the metropolitan economic contribution to imperialism can be underrated: if Hobson ignored the reactions on the periphery, Robinson sometimes falls into the opposite trap

---

[35] Robinson, 'The Excentric Theory of Imperialism', 268.
[36] Ibid. 268–9.   [37] Ibid. 271.

of leaving the metropolitan economy and polity too much out of account.

At the time of writing *Imperialism*, Hobson made little effort to describe the geographical distribution of foreign investment or to link changes in that distribution with movements of the imperial frontier. He was clearly aware that a great deal of British capital went to white-settled areas, including the United States,[38] yet his writing was often loose enough to leave the impression that substantial amounts were invested in the tropical African and Asian territories acquired after 1870. Nonetheless, the consensus among Hobson scholars is that he was aware that only marginal amounts of capital went to tropical acquisitions[39] and that these areas attracted 'less substantial speculative and manufacturing interests'.[40] However, for Hobson's theory to be applicable to the tropics, it is not necessary for capital investment by the imperial power to be large. If financiers were able to use political clout in placing their surpluses abroad, or could use the state to defend their stakes, it would be reasonable to call this 'financial imperialism' even if the amounts of money involved were small. Moreover, as Trevor Lloyd has shown, even when British investments were modest, they could have a disproportionate influence in establishing the British presence and in transforming Africa, particularly through the creation of the chartered companies in West, East, and South Africa. Such companies were financed through the City and were vital to the extension and preservation of British authority in their regions.[41]

If Hobson's theory still has some applicability to the case of tropical Africa and Asia where British capital was never in abundant supply, it is also the case that some of the imperialist episodes that interested him most involved much more substantial sums of British and other European savings. The 'dependent empire' may only have received small draughts of British capital: but Egypt and South Africa—designated somewhat misleadingly as a 'foreign country' and a 'white-settled colony' respectively in the trade statistics of the

---

[38] *Imperialism*, 62–3.

[39] See Porter, *Critics of Empire*, 218; Clarke, 'Hobson, Free Trade and Imperialism', 311.

[40] Cain and Hopkins, *British Imperialism*, 311. For manufacturing interests in tropical Africa see Hynes, *The Economics of Empire*.

[41] T. Lloyd, 'Africa and Hobson's Imperialism', *Past and Present*, 55 (1972). For a similar argument see Allett, *New Liberalism*, 151–3. It should be noted that Lloyd argued generally that capital flows had little to do with imperial expansion in Africa.

time—were very important outlets for British savings at different periods. At the time of the occupation, Egyptian long-term government debts were valued at about £70 million, there was short-term paper on the market worth about half of that amount, and Britons had the biggest stake in both. Investments in South African gold mines alone were valued at £75 million at the outbreak of the Boer War and again British investors were the key players.[42] Is a Hobsonian explanation of imperial expansion applicable to them and to the case of China, another area that loomed large in Hobson's thinking?

THE EGYPTIAN CRISIS AND THE OCCUPATION OF 1882

The occupation of Egypt in 1882 presents an interesting test of a theory of financial imperialism and in recent years historians have come to favour explanations of the occupation that Hobson would have found congenial.[43] Forty years ago, in *Africa and the Victorians*, Robinson and Gallagher put far more emphasis upon strategic considerations than economic ones. In their study of the 'official mind', it was assumed that British interest in the Egyptian economy was slackening as the latter slid into crisis in the mid-1870s and struggled to pay back the debts it had accumulated with France and Britain over the previous thirty years. Robinson and Gallagher also noted the determination of British officialdom not to be manoeuvred into action by outraged holders of Egyptian stock. Instead, they saw French initiatives—stemming mainly from bondholder pressure—as crucial in pushing Britain into a reluctant confrontation with the Egyptian problem for fear of a loss of influence over the Suez Canal, Britain's chief concern and a vital link on the road to India. They insisted that there was no real intention to intervene directly in Egypt until the middle of 1882 when nationalist riots in Alexandria finally convinced the authorities that law

---

[42] R. Owen, *The Middle East in the World Economy, 1800–1914* (1981), 127; Cain and Hopkins, *British Imperialism*, 321.

[43] There are brief introductory accounts in Cain and Hopkins, *British Imperialism*, 312–17; C. Newbury, 'Great Britain and the Partition of Africa, 1870–1914', in Porter (ed.), *Oxford History*, 632–4; A. L. al-Sayyid-Marsot. 'The British Occupation of Egypt from 1882', ibid., 651–4.

and order had broken down. Only then did it become essential to fill the void left by the collapse of the Khedival government on which the British had relied and to curb the militaristic nationalism of Urabi Pasha and his supporters who were now threatening Egypt with anarchy.[44]

Hobson was well aware of the claims that British policy was determined by the Suez Canal and the India route, claims that were widely popular in his own day. Nonetheless, he believed that the political excuses were only used as a cover to hide the real financial motives.[45] A closer inspection of the workings of the official mind in recent years has undermined many of Robinson and Gallagher's assumptions and given more credence to Hobson's point of view. From the British perspective, Suez never approached the Simonstown base at the Cape in strategic importance, nor was its security raised as an issue until the crisis in Egypt was on the brink of resolution by force. The attempt to portray the French as the forward party, with the British reacting to them, also fails to convince. The pressure of French investors for greater control over their stake in Egypt was a strong influence on their government's actions there in the early stages of the crisis, but their anxieties had eased by 1880 precisely because of greater British involvement and the security for investments it appeared to offer. By the early 1880s, French political interest had also switched to Tunis leaving the British with a fairly free hand in Cairo. Nor can it be claimed that Egyptian anarchy forced British intervention. The rise of the nationalist forces, which threatened the European-supported power structure in Cairo, was accompanied by remarkably little social upheaval. The new political forces, once they began to gain power, had no intention of repudiating Egypt's external economic obligations, still less of driving the considerable European population out of the country. So, since neither the French nor the Egyptians themselves can be said to have forced the British into action, the causes of British intervention need to be explained with reference to the perceptions and the actions of the British themselves.[46]

---

[44] Robinson and Gallagher, *Africa and the Victorians*, ch. 4.

[45] Hobson, *Democracy after the War*, 89–90.

[46] A. G. Hopkins, 'The Victorians and Africa: A Reconsideration of the Occupation of Egypt', *Journal of African History*, 27 (1986).

British interests in the Egyptian economy were extensive. Besides the interest in finance, Egypt provided British cotton exporters with their largest market in Africa.[47] The Conservative government which had to address the Egyptian problem before 1880 was unflinchingly determined that all debts should be paid and played a vigorous part in reorganizing the latter's finances. Under the cover of the government's unofficial but determined involvement, British holdings of Egyptian stock increased significantly at the turn of the decade while French interest dwindled. There is little doubt that the Suez Canal purchase and government involvement in setting Egyptian finances to rights encouraged British investors to take up the stock and led them to believe that the state had a duty to intervene on their behalf if the worst should occur.[48] Unfortunately the impositions of British officials, practising a brutal Gladstonianism in cutting public expenditure, overseeing debt repayment, and making Egypt creditworthy again in the eyes of London and Paris, led to a sustained nationalist reaction. By 1879, the British government seems to have assumed that Egypt would have to be taken under direct control since 'orientals' clearly could not be trusted to run a country on sound economic principles.[49]

Gladstone's incoming administration of 1880 made no such initial assumptions and was inclined at first to look with favour on Urabi's movement as representing a liberal nationalism with which Britons could sympathize. In Egypt, by contrast, British officials under pressure to relax their rigid policies of financial orthodoxy came increasingly to see Egyptian assertiveness as 'anarchy' and 'disorder'.[50] They eventually convinced the government in Britain, preoccupied with Irish affairs, of the justice of their case and of a threat to capitalist order of Egypt. Similar anxieties amongst British investors and traders involved in Egypt pushed the government in

[47] D. A. Farnie, *The English Cotton Industry and the World Market, 1815–1896* (Oxford, 1979), 91, 182–3. I am grateful to Roger Lloyd-Jones for reminding me of this source.

[48] Hopkins, 'The Victorians and Africa', 379, 381. See also B. R. Johns, 'Business, Investment and Imperialism: The Relationship between Economic Interest and Growth of British Intervention in Egypt, 1838–82' (unpub. Ph.D. thesis, University of Exeter, 1981), esp. 75–92, 107, 215, 253–4, 281–2.

[49] R. A. Atkins, 'The Conservatives and Egypt, 1875–1880', *Journal of Imperial and Commonwealth History*, 2 (1974), 200.

[50] A. Scholch, 'The "Man on the Spot" and English Occupation of Egypt', *Historical Journal*, 19 (1976).

the same direction, until the riots in Alexandria—which the British mistakenly assumed were inspired by Urabi Pasha's supporters—then provided an excuse for intervention.[51]

Once the collaborators who supported the Khedival regime had lost their authority, neither the official mind in Egypt nor their counterparts in Britain could bring themselves to believe that Urabi's supporters were capable of sustaining the law and order which would ensure financial stability. The sticking point for the British was undoubtedly the claim of the Chamber of Notables, the nationalists' 'parliament', to be consulted on budgetary questions. Wilfred Blunt the British aristocratic apologist for Urabi, recorded the following conversation with Lord Granville, the Foreign Secretary, in March 1882. Granville asked:

'Will they give up the claim of the Chamber to vote the Budget?' I told him I feared it was hopeless to expect this, as the deputies were all of one mind. 'Then', he said, 'I look upon their case as hopeless. It must end by their being put down by force.' I told him I could not believe the English Government could really intervene on such a plea, to put down liberty. But he maintained his ground and I left him much dissatisfied.[52]

Many Liberals felt a strong urge to avoid the embarrassing question of a connection between the campaign to suppress Urabi and Britain's economic interests. It was for fear of such embarrassment that Granville was persuaded to strike out of the document explaining Britain's conduct to other interested powers a passage admitting that Egyptian attempts at financial control had been the prime reason for Britain's hostility to the new men in Cairo.[53] It was for the same reason that the defence of Suez and the strategic importance of Egypt was emphasized in British explanations of their action, even though the Canal did not play a prominent part in the discussions preceding the intervention.[54] Political discomfort

---

[51] Id., *Egypt for the Egyptians! The Socio-political Crisis in Egypt, 1878–82* (1981), esp. ch. 3; M. E. Chamberlain, 'The Alexandria Massacres of 11 June 1882 and the British Occupation of Egypt', *Middle Eastern Studies*, 13 (1977).

[52] W. S. Blunt, *Secret History of the Occupation of Egypt* (1907; repr. 1969), 221–2.

[53] M. E. Chamberlain, 'Sir Charles Dilke and the British Intervention in Egypt, 1882: Decision Making in a Nineteenth Century Cabinet', *British Journal of International Studies*, 2 (1976), 238–9.

[54] See Dilke's memo for the cabinet of 4 July 1882 in S. Gwynn and G. M. Tuckwell, *The Life of Sir Charles W. Dilke*, i (1917), 465.

also had a role to play in shaping the radicals' own response. The Egyptian crisis was the first occasion on which the radicals marked down City usurers as the chief architects of imperialism.[55] Perhaps their zeal in identifying finance and its allies in the press, bureaucracy, and military also owed something to the natural desire to hide the uncomfortable fact that support for the adventure had come from the radicals' traditional strongholds in the industrial provinces where fears for the future of the Egyptian market were strong.[56] It took Hobson twenty years to come to terms, as a radical himself, with the evidence that financial imperialism in London was sometimes aided by industrial imperialism in the provinces.[57]

Hobson had good reason to believe that the Egyptian occupation was an example of financial imperialism but he misunderstood the way in which finance influenced policy. He thought that the controllers of finance were unique in knowing exactly what they wanted and could thus manipulate politicians and others into following their own prescriptions. In truth, during the Egyptian crisis financiers were no better placed than were politicians to understand clearly what was happening in Egypt nor were they ever sure what policies to adopt at each stage in the crisis. It was often the ill-founded anxieties of financial interests, whether in Egypt or the City, rather than 'clear sighted calculation', which increased the desire to intervene. Financiers did not have the power, the resolution, or the foresight to manipulate Salisbury or Gladstone in the manner Hobson assumed.[58] On the other hand, an intricate chain of connections had been built up between City financiers, politicians, administrators, and other interested parties in Britain that had an enormous influence in deciding the form British interest in Egypt would take. These commitments and obligations were the touchstone of Anglo-Egyptian relations, the crucial point about which the whole crisis revolved.[59] In that sense, it is surely correct

---

[55] Blunt, *Secret History*, 211, 214, 241, 294–5.

[56] Chamberlain's reactions are interesting in this context. See R. Jay, *Joseph Chamberlain: A Political Study* (Oxford, 1981), 67–9; and J. Chamberlain, *A Political Memoir, 1880–92*, ed. C. D. Howard (1953), 70–81.

[57] See *supra*, Ch. 4.

[58] Though, of course, Hobson had recognized at one point in *Imperialism* that financiers might be as much prisoners of imperialist ideologies as any other interests involved. See *supra*, Ch. 4.

[59] Even Gladstone had holdings of Egyptian stock. See *The Gladstone Diaries*, ed. H. C. G. Matthew, x (Oxford, 1990), p. lxxii.

to say that British financial capitalism, rather than the financiers themselves, was the 'governor of the imperial engine'.

THE ORIGINS OF THE BOER WAR: IMPERIALISM IN SOUTH AFRICA IN THE 1890S

Hobson did not regard South Africa as the most important arena of British imperial activity, as we have seen. However, the accident of circumstances meant that he paid that country more attention than any other. He also came to believe that the Boer War crisis revealed more plainly than ever before the forces lying behind British expansion overseas, so his arguments about causality in this case require detailed scrutiny. During his visit in 1899 he became convinced that the financiers who controlled the mining industry that had sprung up in the Boer republic of the Transvaal after the discovery of gold in 1886 were the vital force behind imperialism in South Africa and he stuck to this belief for the rest of his life. The mining capitalists' determination to rid themselves of President Kruger's restrictive monopolies, and their frustration at the Transvaal's inability or unwillingness to organize a cheap black labour supply had, he believed, inspired the Jameson Raid of 1895; and in his view, the Boer War was undertaken with the same objectives in mind and with the intention of remedying the failure of Jameson. Before his visit to South Africa and on occasions thereafter, Hobson claimed that economic progress was unifying South Africa naturally. He believed that a federal union of states would eventually emerge and that it would probably maintain a loose association with Britain as did the other major settler colonies. Rhodes's folly destroyed this possibility and opened the way to war by igniting the fires of Afrikaner nationalism and immeasurably strengthening the Transvaal's desire for independence. Hobson recognized Rhodes's political dreams but, both before and during the war, he argued that these ambitions were of less importance than the latter's search for profit. In later years he was more willing to accept the importance of Rhodes's ideological devotion to empire as a motivating factor though he coupled that admission with a claim that Rhodes was of less importance that the most powerful financiers such as Eckstein and Beit, whom he thought of as the central figures in the small cabal who controlled South Africa's capital resources. This knot of cosmopolitan capitalists harnessed the ambitions of leading politicians to their own ends: from Hobson's perspective, Chamberlain as Colonial Secretary after 1895 and Alfred Milner, appointed High Commissioner in South Africa in 1897, were instruments of capitalist ambition. The wider public was also entrapped by the mining capitalists' control of the press that helped convince them that the republic was denying basic political rights to immigrant Britons and that it was a hindrance to civilization and to progress.

Hobson was also acutely aware of the connection between policy in South Africa and the wider issue of empire unity as championed by Chamberlain. In *Imperialism* his worst fear was that, under Chamberlain's leadership, the forced unity imposed on South Africa by war would be the prelude to the emergence of a tariff-protected 'Greater Britain', a merging of Britain with its white-settled offshoots that would consolidate the power of finance within the empire. Hobson understood the character and intensity of the financial links between Britain and the settlement colonies in everything from agricultural mortgages to state and municipal debts. He believed such indebtedness had given British finance a strong interest in promoting colonial sub-imperialism, as was the case in South Africa itself, and a policy of imperial unity based on protection could, he thought, only heighten this interest. It would encourage big business and monopoly throughout the empire, stimulate further oversaving and foreign investment, and increase the pressure for expansion both in Britain and on the white periphery, thus entangling the metropolis in the colonists' own imperialist schemes and precipitating more conflicts with other powers. Hobson suggested this as a possibility: he was hopeful that it would not come to pass. He thought it more likely that the democratic tradition in the colonies would engender resistance to the militarism and taxation involved in imperialism and that the fear of being dominated by Britain in any close federation would make them averse to Chamberlain's vision of the future and keep them free of the policy of 'delegated imperialism'[60] that imperial federation might allow. Indeed, Hobson felt that, despite their own contribution to victory, once the struggle was over the militarism and

---

[60] *Imperialism*, 349.

expense of the Boer War would be sufficient to condemn Chamberlain's strategy in colonial circles.[61]

Most of Hobson's arguments about mining finance as a causal
agent in the Boer War have been emphatically rejected over the years
by a succession of historians who have emphasized the political
motives behind British aggression.[62] As they point out, Britain
had long hoped for federation in South Africa on the lines of the
Canadian confederation: Lord Carnarvon, who had supervised
the Canadian legislation in 1867, failed in the late 1870s to incorporate the small, landlocked, and impoverished Afrikaner republics,
the Transvaal and the Orange Free State over whom Britain had
always claimed paramountcy, in a federal scheme. The federation
was desired not, as was once thought, to ensure control of the Cape
naval base since that control was not in doubt either then or during
the crisis of the 1890s. Rather, the objective was to strengthen both
the local economy and ties with the mother country so that the
South African connection would minister to the strength of the
empire rather than act as a drain on its resources and be able to act
as a positive force in a crisis.[63] By the 1890s, when gold had raised
the Transvaal from its role as marginal state to the fastest growing
sector of the subcontinent, federation came to be seen as a way of
preventing the republic from becoming the focus of an economic
and political movement which would produce what the Selborne
memorandum famously called a 'United States of South Africa'
rather than another Canada.[64] Rhodes was enlisted in this struggle
to contain the Transvaal. His British South Africa Company got
its charter in 1889 because Salisbury's government saw it as a cheap

[61] 'The new Imperialism kills a federation of free self-governing states: the colonies
may look at it but they will go their way as before.' Ibid. 353.

[62] The classic text is Robinson and Gallagher, *Africa and the Victorians*, 410–61.
For the most comprehensive recent expression of this point of view see I. R. Smith,
The Origins of the South African War, 1899–1902 (1996), the main conclusions of
which are summarized in id., 'The Origins of the South African War (1899–1902):
A Reappraisal', *South African Historical Journal*, 22 (1990). For a brief survey of
the background events see C. Saunders and I. R. Smith, 'Southern Africa, 1795–
1910', in Porter (ed.), *Oxford History*; and Cain and Hopkins, *British Imperialism*,
318–27.

[63] R. L. Cope, 'Strategic and Socio-economic Explanations for Carnarvon's South
African Confederation Policy: The Historiography and the Evidence', *History in
Africa*, 20 (1987).

[64] Robinson and Gallagher, *Africa and the Victorians*, 434–7. On the importance
of federation in the 1890s see J. S. Marais, *The Fall of Kruger's Republic* (Oxford,
1961).

means of reasserting British authority in the region. The policy succeeded insofar as the BSAC's annexations of Mashonaland and Matebeleland cut off the Transvaal's expansion north. But since Rhodes found no gold his northern conquests failed to offset the republic's steady rise to centrality in the South African economy and polity.[65]

Rhodes's plot to overthrow Kruger's government—hastened by his failure to find gold elsewhere—received tacit support from government in Britain but Jameson's invasion was disastrously premature and succeeded only in ruining Rhodes's political reputation, inflaming Afrikaner nationalist sentiment, and strengthening Kruger's hand against the growing liberal elements in the Transvaal.[66] Several attempts have been made to provide a Hobsonian explanation for the Jameson Raid but none has proved satisfactory. Blainey argued that the conspirators amongst the mining capitalists were those involved in deep mining, where returns were poor, while those who stood aloof were outcrop miners with an assured profitability.[67] After serious criticism, revealing that many mining capitalists were both outcrop and deep miners,[68] the argument was reformulated and it was claimed instead that the enthusiasts for revolution were those who, even if their profits were healthy in the short term, needed heavy capital investment to maintain long-term viability and felt threatened by the ramshackle Afrikaner state's restrictions and monopolies.[69] Now even that argument appears discredited. Deep miners and outcrop miners, enthusiasts for Rhodes's schemes, and those who were sceptical or uninterested, all had similar capital needs and possibilities for profit in 1894–5. It seems impossible to read off the mining magnates'

[65] On the BSAC see J. S. Galbraith, *Crown and Charter: The Early Years of the British South Africa Company* (Berkeley, 1974) and id., 'The Origins of the British South Africa Company', in J. E. Flint and G. Williams (eds.), *Perspectives of Empire* (1973), 148–71. See also I. R. Phimister, 'Rhodes, Rhodesia and the Rand', *Journal of Southern African History*, 1 (1974). The most comprehensive recent biography of Rhodes is R. I. Rotberg, *The Founder: Cecil Rhodes and the Pursuit of Power* (Oxford, 1988), but the most accessible remains J. Flint, *Cecil Rhodes* (1974).

[66] Smith, *Origins of the South African War*, ch. 3.

[67] G. Blainey, 'Lost Causes of the Jameson Raid', *Economic History Review*, 2nd ser. 18 (1965).

[68] See in particular R. V. Kubiceck, 'The Randlords: A Reassessment', *Journal of British Studies*, 11 (1972); and id., *Economic Imperialism in Theory and Practice: The Case of South African Mining Finance, 1886–1914* (Durham, NC, 1979).

[69] R. Mendelsohn, 'Blainey and the Jameson Raid: The Debate Renewed', *Journal of Southern African Studies*, 6 (1980).

political views from their economic circumstances:[70] Robinson and Gallagher's view that the Raid was more a search for imperial *gloire* than a pecuniary expedition appears to have been vindicated.

Opponents of Hobsonian explanations are right to point out that, after 1895, the mining capitalists in South Africa had lost much credibility and were subject to suspicious scrutiny by politicians who feared, with some justice, that the former would make their own peace with the Transvaal's President, Paul Kruger. He proved willing to make important concessions that reduced mining costs considerably and weakened the mine owners' desire to be rid of his regime.[71] Given their suspicion of the intentions of the mining magnates, Chamberlain and Milner put their faith in the non-Boer immigrants, or Uitlanders, to solve the imperial problem. Selborne's memorandum was concerned with the emergence not of a Boer-dominated South Africa but of one led by the immigrant settlers who, it was assumed, would eventually become predominant in the Transvaal. Chamberlain and Milner were both worried that a settler-dominated Transvaal might either resist inclusion in the empire or, if it joined, do so in a manner that added little or nothing to the empire's overall strength. To counter such a possibility they championed the immigrants' claims for voting rights in the Transvaal, both as a means of overthrowing Boer power there and in the hope that the immigrants would associate their liberties with British imperialism and thus bind themselves to British aims in South Africa.[72] They also gave voting rights priority because it was an issue that could rouse the British public to indignation and one that eventually provided a justification for military action.[73] The mine

[70] E. N. Katz, 'Outcrop and Deep Level Mining in South Africa before the Anglo-Boer War: Re-examining the Blainey Thesis', *Economic History Review*, 2nd ser. 48 (1995). There is a brief summary of the debate in I. R. Phimister, 'Unscrambling the Scramble for Southern Africa: The Jameson Raid and the South African War Revisited', *South African Historical Journal*, 28 (1993), 208–10.

[71] P. Harries, 'Capital, State and Labour on the 19th Century Witwatersrand: A Reassessment', *South African Journal of History*, 18 (1986).

[72] For Chamberlain's attitudes see Smith, *Origins of the South African War*, 224–5. The fact that many of the immigrants were foreigners, including Germans, and that the Boers were seen as 'outriders of German expansionism', added to the unease about the future. See B. Nasson, *The South African War, 1899–1902* (Oxford, 1999), 39. Chamberlain and Milner wanted to be in a position to encourage a specifically British immigrant flow.

[73] On the importance of public opinion see A. N. Porter, *The Origins of the South African War: Joseph Chamberlain and the Diplomacy of Imperialism, 1895–1899* (Manchester, 1980) , esp. 246–7.

owners were expected to support the campaign for political rights on the grounds that their needs would be best met in a modern liberal state. The press they controlled was certainly an effective weapon in convincing the public of the justice of the cause: but Milner used it more effectively than the capitalists themselves.[74]

Hobson misunderstood the relationship between finance and politics in South Africa. He pictured the major political figures like Chamberlain and Milner as servants of mining capitalists but in doing so he failed to appreciate their aims properly and underrated their power. This is best illustrated by a closer examination of British government policy after the failure of the Jameson Raid.[75] Like Hobson himself, many Liberals and some Conservatives expected that a federated South Africa loosely tied to the British Empire would emerge naturally and were happy to settle for that.[76] On their side, however, Chamberlain and Milner were not interested in such links between mother country and colony because they thought it far too fragile and unpredictable and would do nothing to enhance the collective strength of the British Empire in the face of the mounting challenge of its enemies. What they strove for was a much stronger connection with a united South Africa within a cohesive imperial union, one that could only be ensured by vigorous political action. Imperial unity was a very live political issue in Britain in the 1890s and Chamberlain was a central figure promoting it. As Colonial Secretary, he was also very active in assisting at the birth of the Australian federation, an event he saw as a big step in the right direction and one that pointed the way South Africa would hopefully soon follow.

Chamberlain's determination to force the issue in 1898–9 and to persuade the Unionist government in Britain to support him over voting rights for immigrants was strongly influenced by the escalating alarm over the Transvaal's continued growth in status and power and his perception that, if the republic remained independent, it would very soon destroy all his hopes for South Africa

---

[74] Smith, *Origins of the South African War*, 212–14.

[75] For a study of British diplomacy in this period see Porter, *The Origins of the South African War*; and for a shorter version, see id., 'British Imperial Policy and South Africa, 1895–9', in P. Warwick and J.-J. van Helten (eds.), *The South African War: The Anglo-Boer War, 1899–1902* (1980).

[76] Some members of the British cabinet took this line in the run-up to war. Smith, *Origins of the South African War*, 268–9.

and undermine fatally his wider ambitions for the empire. One key source of this mounting disquiet was the ramifying consequences of Kruger's lease in 1894 of Portuguese railway lines that gave him an outlet to the sea independent of the Cape Province and Natal, the centres of British power in South Africa.[77] Kruger's arrival in Delagoa Bay enhanced the Transvaal's economic independence and also made it more likely that the republic would link up with foreign powers, especially Germany, in ways that would embarrass and weaken Britain in South Africa and elsewhere. The 1898 Anglo-German treaty, which agreed on shares in Mozambique should the Portuguese empire collapse and reserved Delagoa Bay for Britain, was supposed to lessen the threat of German influence: but in Colonial Office eyes it made matters rather worse by allowing for foreign development of the facilities at Lourenço Marques in order to encourage trade. The CO forecast a sharp increase in German trade and shipping which would strengthen the Transvaal but undermine Britain. They also forecast that German capital would develop the port sufficiently to allow it to be used as a coaling station or even as a naval base, giving Germany a hitherto un-attained position in Southern Africa, making her a stronger ally of the Transvaal, and giving her extra bargaining counters in disputes elsewhere in the world. It was also suggested that a vitalized Delagoa Bay could be used to undermine Britain's financial position in South Africa. Germany might use shipping subsidies to attract the flow of South African gold and thus promote Berlin as a gold market at the expense of London, undercutting the Bank of England's ability to command gold and thus weakening its con-trol of the world's central monetary mechanism. Moreover, rapid growth of the port and its railways would allow the Transvaal to cut down its traffic with the Cape and Natal. This would reduce railway income, make payments on the provinces' heavy debts in London more difficult causing problems in the City, and, by increasing their desire to come to terms with the Transvaal, weaken the provinces' links with Britain even further.

Some of the CO's dire warnings can be dismissed as fantasies, hatched in the overheated atmosphere of the Queen's Jubilee celebrations and the Fashoda incident. There is no evidence, for

[77] The rest of this paragraph depends on P. Henshaw, 'The "Key to South Africa" in the 1890s: Delagoa Bay and the Origins of the South African War', *Journal of Southern African Studies*, 24 (1998).

example, that their fears about gold supplies had any impact where it mattered—in cabinet, in the Treasury, or at the Bank of England.[78] Despite Hobson's attempt to associate him with finance, it is clear that Chamberlain was not worried about Britain's future financial dominance of South Africa or the City of London's ability to compete in the wider world, both of which he took for granted. The CO's concerns about German penetration and loss of trade did, however, tell with him: as that very unusual entity, a leading politician with a background in manufacturing, what concerned him and his supporters was Britain's emerging industrial weakness in competition with America and Europe and the fact, as they saw it, that the free trade cosmopolitanism in which City finance flourished was exacerbating it.[79] Chamberlain feared that, if Britain's industrial strength was undermined, its internal stability would be damaged, its military and naval strength would ebb away, the empire would disintegrate, and its place as a great world power would be lost to Germany or the United States even if it remained a global leader in finance and international services.[80] As an antidote he proposed an imperial union, with protection if necessary, which he hoped would grow strong enough to match the United States in wealth and power. A federation of the South African states was a crucial stepping stone on this journey: if it failed to materialize, or if Britain had to rest content with an 'informal' free trade empire there based on finance while its industrial export base was competed away,[81] then the outcome would be a state with only a tenuous connection with Britain and the wider imperial unity project would be undermined.

[78] Those who argue that gold supplies were a key issue in British policy include S. Marks and S. Trapido, 'Lord Milner and the South African State Reconsidered', in M. Twaddle (ed.), *Imperialism, the State and the Third World* (1992). But see J.-J. van Helten, 'Empire and High Finance: South Africa and the International Gold Standard, 1890–1914', *Journal of African History*, 23 (1983), and R. Ally, *Gold and Empire: The Bank of England and South Africa's Gold Producers 1886–1926* (Johannesburg, 1994), ch. 1. There is a useful summary of approaches in Phimister, 'Unscrambling the Scramble for Southern Africa', 208–16, 219–20.

[79] J. L. Garvin, *The Life of Joseph Chamberlain, iii: 1895–1900* (1934), 23.

[80] Though he did warn later in his career that the City of London's prosperity would eventually be undermined if British industry should decline. Cain and Hopkins, *British Imperialism*, 195–6.

[81] The Transvaal's tariff independence was a bar to federation and a threat to British trade interests. Phimister, 'Unscrambling the Scramble for Southern Africa', 218–19.

Despite their reservations about the great mining magnates, Chamberlain and Milner needed the mining capitalists' support because the prosperity of mining was vital to South African growth and therefore to the flows of British capital and emigrants who were the key to establishing 'Britishness' as central to South Africa's future. Milner's single-minded determination to get the mines quickly back to work after 1902, even if it involved the politically sensitive policy of importing Chinese labour, is testimony to that. Yet prioritizing mining in this way did not mean policy dominance by mining capitalists in the manner described by Hobson: although the renewed profitability of the mines was at the top of Milner's agenda the policy only made complete sense in terms of the wider programme that he and Chamberlain were pursuing. Apart from their suspicions about the ultimate intentions of Rhodes and the other mining capitalists, it is not difficult to see why, given their ideological stance, Chamberlain and Milner should have distrusted the idea that financial dominance alone would produce the outcomes they desired in South Africa. Mining capitalism might well benefit from the opening of Delagoa Bay but Britain's position in South Africa could easily have been weakened as a result. There was also evidence to hand, for example, that some of the links between the City and the Transvaal could undermine Britain's geopolitical strategy in South Africa. It is true that Kruger found it very difficult to borrow money except in Britain and that Nathan Rothschild (who was very closely associated with Rhodes and had extensive South African mining interests)[82] was able to monitor the ways in which Kruger disposed of the loan he arranged for the latter in 1892. Yet it is also the case that, although intended to control him, the loan gave Kruger the opportunity to use other funds he commanded to forge the vital railway link to the Portuguese-held coastline that emphasized the economic dominance of the Transvaal over the Cape by making it independent of the latter's rail and road system.[83] In other words, British financial dominance, which many

[82] On the Rothschild–Rhodes connection and Rothschild's extensive South African interests see N. Ferguson, *The World's Banker: The History of the House of Rothschild* (1998), 876–89; R. V. Turrell and J.-J. van Helten, 'The Rothschilds, the Exploration Company and Mining Finance', *Business History*, 28 (1986).
[83] K. E. Wilburn, 'Engines of Empire and Independence: Railways in Southern Africa', in C. B. Davis and K. E. Wilburn (eds.), *Railway Imperialism* (1991), 32–5.

in Britain took to be sufficient to ensure control in South Africa by informal means,[84] could actually enhance the Transvaal's independence and power and undermine the 'Greater Britain' that was the ultimate objective of both Chamberlain and Milner.[85]

Looking back at the war, Jan Smuts the Boer/Afrikaner liberal who later became a collaborator with British imperial aims in South Africa, thought that 1895–1905 was an aberrant (and misguided) period in British imperial policy-making.[86] The 'empire and industry' strategy was certainly an unusual one. Most leading politicians in Britain assumed that financial strength was the key to economic success on the global stage and that the country's industrial fortunes were dependent on that rather than the reverse; and they would have been satisfied with a less formal link between Britain and her white settlements. Chamberlain's and Milner's concern for the fate of industry, and their sense that the time in which to remedy the problem was short, gave an edge to South African policy missing before and contributed to a resolution of the crisis by war. This stark and rigid geopolitical outlook lay behind Milner's policy of pushing the Uitlander issue hard in 1898–9 and forced uncomfortable choices on numerous political and economic entities hitherto undecided between the two opposed power structures in South Africa. In face of gathering political crisis, foreign capital decided to back a British solution to the problem if only to end uncertainty.[87] Milner's strategy also forced other elements in South Africa to choose sides. In Natal, the result of his call to patriotism was that the province came out wholeheartedly for war for fear that anything less that complete defeat for the Transvaal would open them later to devastating economic reprisals.[88] However, what is also of great interest from a Hobsonian perspective is that there was a significant

---

[84] Ferguson, *The World's Banker*, 889–90.

[85] Kruger's railway independence, and the so-called 'Drifts Crisis' it provoked, so alarmed the British government that they considered military action against the Transvaal. The crisis may also have persuaded the government to give their unofficial backing to Rhodes's plans that ended in the Jameson fiasco. See K. E. Wilburn, 'The Drifts Crisis, the "Missing Telegrams" and the Jameson Raid: A Centennial Review', *Journal of Imperial and Commonwealth History*, 25 (1997).

[86] Smith, *Origins of the South African War*, 157–60.

[87] J.-J. van Helten, 'German Capital, the Netherlands Railway Company and the Political Economy of the Transvaal', *Journal of African History*, 19 (1978), 386–8.

[88] R. Ovendale, 'Profit or Patriotism: Natal, the Transvaal, and the Coming of the Second Anglo-Boer War', *Journal of Imperial and Commonwealth History*, 8 (1980).

shift in opinion in mining circles in 1898–9. By then the capital costs of the deep mines had begun to rise sharply[89] while relations with Kruger's regime deteriorated and new taxes on mining were raised. With future profitability again under threat, the mining magnates were also subject to a ferocious campaign in the Transvaal press intended to undermine the Uitlander reform movement by dividing the white mineworkers from the owners and portraying the latter as exploiters and parasites.[90] Although the Chamber of Mines was never united on the issue, it is evident that at least some of the most prominent mining capitalists had sound economic reasons for supporting a military solution to the crisis in 1899.

Finance did not manipulate the patriotic forces that led to an imperial war in South Africa in the manner indicated by Hobson in Part I of *Imperialism*. Policy in 1899 was determined by wider geopolitical and economic strategies and the development of financial capitalism sometimes undermined that policy and had to be brought into line with it. Nor was finance monolithic and certain of itself in the way Hobson suggested. Mining capitalists were sometimes divided on what policy it was best to pursue and some City activities undermined and contradicted others: a Transvaal/German development of Delagoa Bay might have boosted mining profits and cheered one end of the City but it would also have badly affected the returns on Cape and Natal railways and depressed another part of it. Nonetheless, mining capitalists were a critical part of the coalition of forces that Chamberlain and Milner brought together in the crisis of 1898–9 and financial concerns were important in more subtle ways in creating a new South Africa. The resort to war did not produce the kind of British South African state that Chamberlain and Milner desired partly because, as Hobson noted, the South African economy simply was not attractive enough to British immigrants. The Liberal government that followed after 1906 had to accept a Boer/Afrikaner-dominated union rather than a Canadian type of federation. Within that union, mining capitalism might not have been hegemonic but it was free to develop and prosper. Moreover, one key element in encouraging a union on these

---

[89] Phimister, 'Unscrambling the Scramble for Southern Africa', 215.
[90] A. H. Jeeves, 'The Rand Capitalists and the Coming of the South African War, 1896–1899', *South African Journal of Economic History*, 11 (1996), 70–5.

terms was the perception that it was vital to ensure that South Africa had a government with tax-raising powers sufficient to give it credit in London and in the City. That credibility was vital to allow South Africa to borrow funds to build the infrastructure that would provide the economic cement needed to bind the British, Afrikaner, and foreign communities together within the union and give it long-term stability.[91] Thereafter, Britain's economic authority in South Africa rested mainly on monetary and financial props and continued to operate effectively until after 1945. In that sense, South Africa remained a part of Britain's 'invisible empire' of finance (as did other emerging Dominions such as Australia and New Zealand) though in ways which Ritortus understood rather better than Hobson.[92] The collaborative links between Britain and South Africa were also strong enough to ensure that the latter gave active support to the metropolis in both world wars, something Hobson did not expect. There was financial imperialism in South Africa though it did not operate in the way Hobson claimed.

BRITAIN AND CHINA, 1895–1914

Although his name is linked most frequently with the African partition, Hobson regarded the scramble for control of China in the twenty years before the First World War as the single most important event in the contemporary history of imperialism. The political battle between the great powers to divide China into 'spheres of interest' was thought by Hobson to be the preliminary to an invasion of European and American surplus savings. In his view the governments of Britain and other powers were working directly on behalf of financial interests who needed the authority of their states to help them subdue the Chinese and to clear the way for capitalist exploitation. If necessary, the great powers would come together in an 'inter-imperialism' designed to provide the vast

---

[91] These were important considerations in the mind of Lord Selborne, who was High Commissioner in South Africa at the time of the Union and who had a big influence on the final settlement. See D. E. Torrance, *The Strange Death of Liberal Empire: Lord Selborne in South Africa* (Liverpool, 1996).

[92] On British financial imperialism in the Dominions see Cain and Hopkins, *British Imperialism*, chs. 8 and 21. For Ritortus see *supra*, Ch. 4

infrastructural investments needed for rapid development in China, while sheltering under the capitalist 'law and order' provided by the intrusion of Western power. Hence, although he had little time for any argument suggesting that tropical African colonies might prove useful economic assets in the future, China's potential interested him greatly and he believed that visions of Chinese plenty were driving forward the sinister forces that were bringing China under European and Japanese control.

In the heyday of early Victorian optimism, the British assumed that free trade was sufficient in itself to galvanize backward peoples into capitalist development; and this benign medicine was forced on the Chinese in the wars between 1840 and 1860. The result of free trade was deeply disappointing partly because the complexities of 'underdeveloped' economies could not be unravelled by free trade treaties; partly because, especially in China, the authorities remained stubbornly unyielding in their hostility to European culture.[93] Successive British governments, carefully monitored by a Parliament deeply suspicious of state expenditures, were reluctant to commit themselves to stronger action to increase penetration.[94] In China, for example, they were only roused into action to support British business in the 1880s when other European powers began to try to undermine British predominance at Peking.[95] But the great turning point came in 1895 when China, defeated by Japan in war, was forced by the latter to pay an indemnity and as a result had to raise foreign loans for the first time. As Chinese military and financial independence began to weaken so European penetration increased. British policy was to try to interest the other great powers in maintaining the political and territorial integrity of China. At the same time, the British wanted to ensure that the Yangtze Valley, where British trade was mainly concentrated, was demarcated a 'sphere of interest' and that all major capital projects there—which

[93] For introductions to these themes see J. Osterhammel, 'Britain and China, 1842–1914', in Porter (ed.) *Oxford History*; P. Lowe, *Britain and the Far East: A Survey from 1819 to the Present* (Manchester, 1981); Cain and Hopkins, *British Imperialism*, ch. 13.

[94] D. C. M. Platt, *Finance, Trade and Politics in British Foreign Policy, 1815–1914* (Oxford, 1968), Pt. II, chs. 2 and 4; D. McLean, 'Finance and "Informal Empire" before the First World War', *Economic History Review*, 2nd ser. 29 (1976).

[95] D. McLean, 'Commerce, Finance and British Diplomatic Support in China, 1885–6', *Economic History Review*, 2nd ser. 26 (1973).

were the key to political as well as economic control—should be under British authority.[96]

These initiatives were supposed to create the conditions under which British capital would flow into China confirming British predominance there. The Foreign Office was vigorous in claiming concessions for railways and mines, but the amount of capital forthcoming from the City was often disappointingly small. Capital would not flow unless investors felt their money was safe: but China was an insecure place and the foreign incursions often made this worse by undermining the authority of China's governing elites.[97] Since the City was a free market, open to persuasion in some ways but impossible for politicians to command, it was difficult to overcome its reluctance and many of the concessions extracted from a reluctant Chinese government remained on paper only. A good example of the problems faced was provided by the Shanghai–Nanking railway concession which the Foreign Office had extracted from the Chinese government and which was intended to open up further the Yangtze Valley, the most important area for British trade. The Foreign Office enlisted the support of the Hongkong and Shanghai Bank (HKSB) and other powerful local institutions. Yet the attempt to raise a loan for the railway in London in 1905 was a flop because the City, with the Boxer rebellions of 1900 still fresh in the memory, was unconvinced about the security of the investment.[98] Fiascos of this kind sometimes drove the British authorities to enlist the support of rather dubious characters in order to raise funds and interest.[99] Clearly, Hobson's vision of eager financiers prodding politicians into action was far from the mark.

However, British governments were more successful in solving problems when they made terms with foreign capitalists and their governments and arranged common development schemes. This

[96] L. K. Young, *British Policy in China, 1895–1902* (Oxford, 1970), ch. 4. The most detailed account of the scramble period is E. W. Edwards, *British Diplomacy and Finance in China* (Oxford, 1987).

[97] C. B. Davis, 'Financing Imperialism: British and American Bankers as Vectors of Imperial Expansion in China, 1908–20', *Business History Review*, 56 (1982).

[98] For the frustration felt in the Foreign Office see Edwards, *British Diplomacy and Finance*, 70.

[99] Including the speculator Edmund Davis, described as one who would 'cheat his blind grandmother at cards'. I. R. Phimister, 'The Chrome Trust: The Making of an International Cartel', *Business History*, 38 (1996), 79.

policy was first adopted in 1895 when Britain organized a joint loan by all interested parties to cover the costs of the indemnity demanded by Japan after the war.[100] Co-operation took a new direction from 1904 when, after the Anglo-French Entente of that year, some railway concessions were taken up in partnership with France.[101] The obvious attraction here was that the French money market was more amenable to political pressure than was the British and that schemes involving more than one great power gave a stronger sense of security and encouraged investors. Moreover, European bankers and concessionaires felt a similar pressure to co-operate as they became increasingly aware of their dependence on the stability of the Chinese government and its revenues. The British government, and its chief ally the HKSB, tried hard to turn this in their favour. Encouraged by the Foreign Office and benefiting from the patient diplomacy of Charles Addis, the rising star at the London office, the HKSB worked to bring American and German capital as well as French into consortia to build railways: in the process, the bank even acquired four German directors.[102] The Foreign Office and the HKSB also had a less exacting but still difficult task to perform in the matter of public loans. They wanted the Chinese government to be able to borrow and they wanted to ensure that all foreign players involved in China had a piece of the action. By 1909–10, the success of the international railway consortia was such that the same national groups of finance capitalists were beginning to form the basis for international public loans to China. Given that China was an insecure place (the collapse of the dynasty in 1911 was proof enough of that) allowing China to borrow involved British governments in giving quasi-official backing to loans floated in London.[103] The 'inter-imperialism' of the great powers Hobson described in *Imperialism* and, more approvingly, in *An Economic Interpretation of Investment* was fore-shadowed in these policies though they proved less resilient in the long term than he expected.

---

[100] D. McLean, 'The Foreign Office and the First Chinese Indemnity Loan, 1895', *Historical Journal*, 16 (1973).

[101] E. W. Edwards, 'The Origins of British Financial Cooperation with France in China, 1903–6', *English Historical Review*, 86 (1971).

[102] R. A. Dayer, *Finance and Empire: Sir Charles Addis, 1861–1943* (1988), 55–64.

[103] Addis believed that the Bank of England had offered unofficial but powerful guarantees for holdings in the 1895 Indemnity loan. Ibid. 38.

The Foreign Office also sought to control China's finances by preventing its government from dealing with whom it pleased when raising foreign loans. Indeed, Hobson accused them of acting on behalf of a tight-knit bunch of influential financiers who had conspired to monopolize the Chinese loan market. As proof he cited in evidence the Foreign Office's determination to obstruct the attempt by the Crisp Syndicate in London to lend money to the Chinese government in 1912.[104] As Yuan shi-k'ai tried to establish himself as leader in the wake of the 1911 rebellion, Charles Addis of the HKSB convinced the Foreign Office that, to prevent any foreign powers from using the crisis as an excuse to dismember China, the Four Power Consortium which had arisen out of the international railway groupings should be widened to include Russia and Japan. The six powers should then jointly issue a loan to stabilize the regime, but only if Yuan agreed to the imposition of further financial checks which would finally put Chinese budgets firmly under foreign control: the fate of China's new rulers was to be that which had already befallen the Khedive in Egypt and the Sultan at Constantinople. Addis also persuaded the Foreign Office that the HKSB should once again control the British end of the loan and act as the prime negotiator with foreign banking groups. However, Birch Crisp, a merchant banker with interests in Brazil and Russia, stepped in to offer to raise a loan of £10 million for China in London. Yuan, determined if possible to avoid further foreign interference in Chinese affairs that was raising nationalist antagonism and threatening the stability of his already shaky regime, was, of course, keen to accept.[105]

The Foreign Office disassociated itself from the Crisp Syndicate and did its best to dissuade investors in London from taking up the Syndicate's Chinese issues. In this it was ultimately successful but only after a considerable struggle. Taking advantage of a surge of optimism in the City about the prospects for growth in China under the emerging regime, Crisp skilfully played upon the resentments which had built up over the years, in the City and elsewhere, about the relationship which had developed between the Foreign Office and the HKSB bank and the privileged position the latter and its associates had acquired in Chinese finance. He had strong support

---

[104] *Democracy after the War*, 96–8.
[105] For Addis's part in the drama see Dayer, *Finance and Empire*, 64–70.

on the Stock Exchange and in other parts of the City for daring to challenge the 'establishment'. Crisp also attacked the cosmopolitanism of the Foreign Office and the HKSB and their associates, using the rising hostility to Germany in Britain (the naval race had begun in earnest in 1909) to complain about the German directors on the HKSB board and to decry some of the consortia agreements. He also capitalized on the frustrations of British manufacturers with interests in China who had similar objections to the government's cosmopolitanism. To ensure security for loans, for example, Britain had allowed the Chinese to raise tariffs that hit Lancashire cotton-exporting interests. In an effort to persuade foreign capital into his railway schemes Addis, with government backing, had also agreed to forbid any preferential access for British firms in railway building and supplying materials. That, too, had raised an outcry since foreign governments had often no scruples about reserving orders for their own nationals. The Foreign Office only managed to resolve the crisis in the end by persuading the HKSB to broaden the base of its support in the City but Crisp and his friends were still excluded.[106] It also had to agree that industrial and railway loans should be excluded from consortia provisions and left to the free market in future.

In *Democracy after the War*, Hobson admitted that the 'European powers may have been actuated in part by the principle that it was best to act in concert so as to prevent loans from individual groups which would be used to obtain political advantages for particular countries as against the general advantage of China itself'. But he also believed that the financiers involved 'ran this policy for all it was worth' because it meant that interlopers like Crisp could be prevented from lending money to China and ensured that the existing lenders could maintain a monopoly and thus obtain better terms from the Chinese government.[107] The present historical consensus is that British governments came to prefer the creation of international consortia for fear that a 'free for all' lending policy would encourage the other great powers to pursue policies that threatened Chinese unity and make development impossible. They were also concerned to restrict the number of British banks and other financial institutions who could take part in loans because

---

[106] On events in the City see Kynaston, *The City of London*, 564–71.
[107] Hobson, *Democracy after the War*, 99.

they believed that free competition would allow the Chinese government to borrow without accepting the financial discipline necessary
to solvency and long-term growth. Hobson was, therefore, probably wrong to infer that the consortia were determined to exploit
China in a naked manner but, nonetheless, the relationship between
the British government, the HKSB bank, and a few other business
groups interested in China had become a very intimate and exclusive one by 1912 and marked a new stage in the evolution of British
financial capitalism.

CONCLUSION: FINANCE, FINANCE CAPITALISM, AND IMPERIALISM

The verdict on Hobson at this point must be that the questions he
asked were of real interest to students of British imperialism but
that the answers he offered sometimes did not fit the known facts
very well. His approach has some relevance to current controver-
sies about British economic development and its regional peculiarities in a period of heavy foreign investment and it is still possible
to argue, on Hobsonian underconsumptionist lines, that imperialism was a net loss to the British nation. On the other hand, the
evidence available does not indicate that financiers made spectacular gains from imperial expansion at everyone else's expense:
insofar as gains were made they accrued to sellers of British exports
just as much as, or even more than, they did to City investors and
those gains may have been widely diffused. Nonetheless, despite the
fact that the gains made by investors were less than he believed, the
case studies do show, as he insisted, that finance was a prime mover
on the imperial frontier in Africa and China.[108]

Where Hobson went wrong was in his forthright view of the
relationship between finance and politics: finance was often crucial

---

[108] Recent work on South-East Asia, for example, also supports the belief that a
Hobsonian approach to expansion still has some purchase. In the case of Burma, for
example, it appears from recent scholarship that the timing of the occupation in 1885
was strongly influenced by the intelligence passed on to British governments by City
firms with connections in Burma. See A. Webster, 'Business and Empire: A
Reassessment of the British Conquest of Burma in 1885', *Historical Journal*, 43
(2000). For other evidence of links between City finance and expansion in the region
see id., *Gentlemen Capitalists: British Imperialism in South East Asia, 1770–1890*
(1998).

to expansion, financial conspiracy was not. Even in Egypt, where the financial motives for occupation were obvious, there is no evidence to support Hobson's continuously reiterated assertion that ruthless financiers manipulated much less visionary and hesitant politicians to serve their clearly understood ends. Hobson adopted the conspiratorial solution to the problem of finding the link between economic power and political action partly because of his radical heritage and partly because it seemed to fit the facts of the South African case, the one with which he was most heavily involved personally. Yet, in practice, the relations between finance and politics were much more complex and flexible and every case had its unique configuration of forces. In Egypt, City bankers and statesmen stumbled through to a resolution of a crisis whose causes and ramifications neither quite understood and occupation was a rather desperate attempt to rescue a financial policy no longer amenable to mere informal influence. In South Africa after 1895, though the support of mining finance was crucial to the success of policy, the leading financiers were to some extent harnessed to a policy driven by Chamberlain and his supporters that had implications far beyond South Africa itself. Politicians also orchestrated the process in China. Their aims were fairly clear but both British and foreign financiers were reluctant to get involved and had to be persuaded by government before they would offer the support that made these aims realizable. Modern research has also revealed that financiers and politicians sometimes had competing objectives and moved in different directions: the financial and political arms of expansion had to be constantly readjusted to each other. The advance of the financial frontier in Egypt and in South Africa undermined traditional policy there and provoked political action intended to bring them back into alignment. In China, the problem was the opposite: policy ambition ran ahead of the financial wherewithal needed to make it viable and the latter had to be coaxed into catching up with the former.

In assessing Hobson's usefulness to scholars today it is important to remember that, although financial conspiracy was a central thread in his writings, there were times when he offered more subtle approaches to understanding the drive for expansion overseas. First, on a number of occasions in *Imperialism*, he spoke of financiers not as leaders but as vital elements in a coalition of forces with an interest in overseas expansion and exploitation. At these moments, he thought of imperialism as the outcome of what Gramsci was later to call an 'historical bloc', based on cultural as well as material foundations, that exercised 'hegemony' in Britain. Those who have argued that 'gentlemanly capitalism' was the main force behind British policy at this time take a similar view. They see expansion as driven by a coalition of City-centred finance and traditional aristocracy with industry, despite its economic importance, on the margins in policy terms. On this reading, British imperialism involved a dynamic intercourse between a restless financial capitalism, constantly opening new avenues for growth abroad, and an elite with a long pedigree for whom an expanding imperial frontier offered great opportunities for reproduction both of their wealth and their status as authority figures.[109] Events in Egypt in the 1880s and in China after 1895 are explicable in these terms. Reading Hobson can still illuminate this process although far more attention should now be given to discussing the strains and conflicts between the various parts of the power elites he described, especially since such tensions often produced novel policies and movements.

Secondly, Hobson forecast the emergence of a new kind of financial capitalism in Britain and one that promised greater prominence for industry. In a penetrating discussion of *Imperialism* and its relationship with later Marxist thought, Giovanni Arrighi has argued that scholars are faced with 'two diverse and incommensurable conceptions of "finance capital"' and that 'for Hobson, the expression "finance capital" (or analogous terms he employed) designated a *supranational* entity which had almost no links with any productive apparatus: whereas for Hilferding, it referred to an entity of a *national* character whose ties with the productive apparatus tended to be extremely close'.[110] There is much truth in this analysis and it was when Hobson was thinking on the lines described by Arrighi that he was inclined to see finance as not only a separate but as an overwhelmingly dominant force. Nonetheless, only fragmentarily in *Imperialism* but with greater emphasis in *The Evolution of Modern*

---

[109] Cain and Hopkins. *British Imperialism, passim.* For the view from an aristocratic perspective see D. Cannadine, *Ornamentalism: How the British Saw their Empire* (2001).

[110] G. Arrighi, *The Geometry of Imperialism: The Limits of Hobson's Paradigm* (1978), 25. The italics are Arrighi's.

Capitalism, Hobson did sometimes suggest that the capitalist world was becoming more like that described by Hilferding and by Lenin. The financial capitalism described in Part I of *Imperialism* controlled the state apparatus and commanded the other forces with an interest in imperial expansion, but it had little structural connection with industry. In Part II, however, and in other writings Hobson did link large-scale industrial businesses with finance and not simply because foreign investment was associated with the export of British manufactured goods. The growth of monopoly in British industry was not as marked as in America but even at the turn of the century he believed that it was sufficient to enhance profits for the large, well-organized businesses at the expense of their lesser brethren and thus reduce the profits and growth potential of the latter. Judging from the second edition of *The Evolution of Modern Capitalism*, Hobson expected the growth of monopoly in British industry to lead to the emergence of a finance capital on German or American lines. A new breed of financier, leading corporate industrial enterprises, would arise alongside the older-style City moguls whose interest in manufacturing was perfunctory. He also forecast that, if protection were introduced to pay for the South African war or to further imperial federation schemes, the pace of growth of big business in Britain would accelerate. There was then the possibility of a further stimulus to oversaving and foreign investment leading to the expansion of the imperial frontier especially in Asia, outbreaks of war between the powers, and a vicious spiral of militarism in Europe and America that would threaten the survival of industry, liberty, and democracy.[111] Hobson thought that capitalism was adopting new and more complex shapes in Britain and that the political and military forces—the institutions of the state—connected with it would themselves change in composition over time producing novel alliances with capitalism.[112] He also believed that, unless social reform changed the distribution of income and wealth, those persons and

---

[111] I have benefited greatly here from reading the following: Etherington, *Theories of Imperialism*, ch. 4; Nowell, *Hobson's Imperialism*; Magnusson, 'Hobson and Imperialism'; A. Brewer, *Marxist Theories of Imperialism: A Critical Survey* (2nd edn., 1990), 78–81.
[112] Allett sees Hobson as thinking in terms of what was later called a 'military-industrial complex'. *New Liberalism*, 149–51.

institutions with a direct or indirect interest in supporting imperialism would grow.

Etherington is quite right to say that Hobson believed that this phase of capitalist development was beginning to develop in the late 1890s and that it was spawning a new kind of imperialism wherein the state had a much more active part. There were signs of a marked shift in policy towards the less developed parts of the empire at that time which were consistent with such a belief on Hobson's part. As Colonial Secretary after 1895, Chamberlain led a drive to use state funds to create the infrastructural investments in the underdeveloped empire that he hoped would initiate rapid growth and make the empire stronger and more self-sufficient. The resources involved were very limited but the consequences on the periphery were sometimes critical to local development and could also trigger movements in the imperial frontier. Chamberlain's initiatives were reflective of profound changes taking place in the structure of the economy and new perspectives on Britain's position in the world as its industrial pre-eminence and export markets came into question. They were accompanied by the rise of big business in new parts of the empire such as the South African diamond and gold mining giants and the Ashanti Goldfields Corporation in West Africa.[113] They also brought into being a new set of relationships between the Treasury, the Colonial Office, the Crown Agents, and a host of financial, commercial, and industrial concessionaires which represented just that kind of configuration of interests which Hobson argued, in Part II of *Imperialism*, was the greatest beneficiary of expansion.[114] Seen in this light, the Boer War was only a more spectacular example of the same policy.[115]

[113] On the latter see R. E. Dumett, *El Dorado in West Africa: The Gold Mining Frontier, African Labour and Colonial Capitalism in the Gold Coast* (Athens, Oh., 1998), 280–92.

[114] For Chamberlain's new imperial policy see R. M. Kesner, *Economic Control and Colonial Development: Crown Colony Financial Management in the Age of Joseph Chamberlain* (Oxford, 1981); for shorter accounts see also M. Havinden and D. Meredith, *Colonialism and Development: Britain and its Tropical Colonies, 1850–1960* (1993), 86–91, and E. E. H. Green, 'The Political Economy of Empire, 1880–1914', in Porter (ed.), *Oxford History*, 351–3. On the Crown Agents and their connections with the Colonial Office and with business, see D. Sunderland, 'Principals and Agents: The Activities of the Crown Agents for the Colonies, 1880–1914', *Economic History Review*, 2nd ser. 52 (1999).

[115] On this theme see the important statement by N. Etherington, 'Theories of Imperialism in Southern Africa Revisited', *African Affairs* 81 (1982), esp. 396–401.

In this case, the state helped organize, and relied for its efficacy upon, a coalition of forces in South Africa in which an emergent mining/finance capitalism had become a vital part. Shula Marks has emphasized that in South Africa there was a 'subtle interweaving of a common world-view, a common acceptance of the centrality of the mining industry and its profitable development' which, despite their many disagreements, brought politicians and capitalists together. She also stressed 'the essential seamlessness of the economic, political, ideological and military drives for imperialism'[116] which, in this context, indicate that Hobson's rather more open-ended discussion of the sources of imperial expansion in Part II of *Imperialism* are more relevant to understanding the crisis than the more simplistic judgements of *The War in South Africa* and Part I of *Imperialism*.

The first and second editions of *Imperialism* appeared at a time when there was a real possibility that the electorate would embrace Chamberlain's vision of a protectionist empire, and the book was a warning of the dire consequences that would follow such a political upheaval. Hobson was acutely aware that, if implemented with zeal, 'Constructive Imperialism' could transform the economic structure of the nation, encourage the growth of big industrial business in Britain, and forge new links between the state, industry, finance, politics, and empire. Chamberlain's attempts to encourage economic development in the dependent territories after 1895 and his launch of the Tariff Reform campaign from 1903 showed that he was definitely set upon such a transformation in the hope of encouraging those forces that he believed would unite the empire more closely. He wanted to create a new economic and political coalition, a fresh 'historical bloc' with industry at its centre, because he was convinced that the existing coalitions supported a free trade cosmopolitanism that threatened the survival of Britain as a global power in the twentieth century. Had he succeeded he might have introduced a new kind of 'industrial imperialism', with finance as its handmaiden. Hobson's perception of the future was somewhat different. He thought that, if the Constructive Imperialists succeeded, they would accelerate the emergence of finance

---

[116] S. Marks, 'Scrambling for South Africa', *Journal of African History*, 23 (1982), 113.

capitalism, on the lines laid out in the 1906 edition of *Evolution*, where large-scale industry would be brought under the control of a new kind of cosmopolitan finance. Moreover, he believed that the long-term consequences of the rise of finance capitalism could include the destruction of industry in Britain and other parts of Europe.

In retrospect, Hobson's biggest mistake—though a perfectly understandable one at the time—was to take Chamberlain and the political forces he represented too seriously. Constructive Imperialism never managed to capture the imagination of the majority of the voting public. Chamberlain's plans for empire development did not get far[117] and in 1906 the tariff reform campaign was decisively rejected by the electors. Industry was itself split over free trade, kept its distance from City finance, and lacked the coherence to assert itself politically. The combination of social reforming liberalism and Milnerite social imperialism which Lloyd George toyed with in 1909–10 achieved a brief reality in the latter's war cabinet in 1916–19—and formed the backdrop to *Democracy after the War*—but fell apart rapidly when peace came.[118] And, although it alarmed Hobson and may have been a factor in persuading him to reprint *Imperialism* in 1938, the imperial preference policy adopted by the National government in 1932 was merely a very pale reflection of the original vision of a united, protected empire. Big business certainly grew rapidly in importance and it began to make an impact on British policy in areas such as China in the 1930s.[119] Yet its links with the City and with government never developed as Hobson predicted and it did not emerge as the champion of an aggressive, militaristic imperialism in quite the way he thought it might at the beginning of the century. One of the ironies of Hobson's life is that he spent so much of his time warning the British public about a danger that, if far from imaginary, never actually took shape in the way he expected. His consolation might be that his own work

---

[117] The struggle between the Treasury and Chamberlain over state support for development is well illustrated in R. E. Dumett, 'Joseph Chamberlain, Imperial Finance and Railway Policy in British West Africa in the Late Nineteenth Century', *English Historical Review*, 90 (1975).

[118] Searle, *The Quest for National Efficiency*, ch. 6; Cain and Hopkins, *British Imperialism*, 442–9.

[119] Cain and Hopkins, *British Imperialism*, 606–13.

as a crusading liberal reformer and critic of imperialism played some small part in preventing its emergence.[120]

[120] Looking at Hobson's approach to capitalist imperialism from a current perspective, it seems clear that many of the issues discussed in *Imperialism* are still relevant to modern debates about the development of the world economy. As a new phase of what Hobson called 'internationalism' and what we call 'globalization' takes place, there are increasing concerns being expressed about the effects of international capital in de-industrializing the West, skewing income and wealth distribution in favour of those already rich, and exploiting the labour of Asia and Africa. (For an introduction to these themes see A. G. Hopkins (ed.), *Globalization in World History* (2002).) Moreover, there are remarkable parallels between the way in which recent critics such as S. Haseler in *The Super-Rich: The Unjust World of Global Capitalism* (2001) and N. Klein in *No Logo* (2000) have diagnosed these problems and the way Hobson worked in *Imperialism*. In Klein's case, for example, this includes a concern with the way the media create new languages to gloss over the disturbing or horrifying aspects of international business and also with the increasing influence of big business on government. In this sense, Hobson's writings may still be relevant in a more immediate sense than has been discussed in this chapter. It is no surprise that the recent work with which Hobson's has most affinity is American. The radical tradition, running through such figures as Veblen, C. Wright Mills, and J. K. Galbraith, is much stronger in the United States than it is in Britain where it has been overlaid by various strands of Marxism, not all of them refined enough to reveal what E. P. Thompson once called 'the peculiarities of the English'.

Bibliography of
Works Cited

(Place of publication is London unless otherwise stated)

1. WORKS BY HOBSON

(a) Individual works

'A London Letter', *Derbyshire Advertiser and Journal* (1887–97).

The Physiology of Industry: Being an Exposure of Fallacies in Existing Theories of Economics (1889; repr. Bristol 1992) [with A. F. Mummery].

'The Cost of a Shorter Working Day', *National Review*, 15 (1890).

Problems of Poverty: An Inquiry into the Industrial Condition of the Poor (1st edn. 1891; 2nd edn. 1895; 3rd edn. 1899).

'The Law of the Three Rents', *Quarterly Journal of Economics*, 5 (1891); repr. in *Hobson: Writings on Welfare and Distribution*, ed. Backhouse

'Can England Keep her Trade?', *National Review*, 17 (1891); repr. in *Hobson: Writings on Imperialism and Internationalism*, ed. Cain.

'The Element of Monopoly in Prices', *Quarterly Journal of Economics*, 6 (1892); repr. in *Hobson: Writings on Welfare and Distribution*, ed. Backhouse.

Review of S. N. Patten, *The Theory of Dynamic Economics*, *Economic Journal*, 2 (1892).

'The Academic Spirit in Education', *Contemporary Review*, 63 (1893).

'Rights of Property', *Free Review*, 1 (1893).

'The Influence of Machinery upon Employment', *Political Science Quarterly*, 8 (1893).

'The Subjective and Objective View of Distribution', *Annals of the American Academy of Political and Social Science* 4 (1894). repr. in *Hobson: Writings on Welfare and Distribution*, ed. Backhouse.

The Evolution of Modern Capitalism: A Study in Machine Production (1st edn. 1894; 3rd edn. 1906; 5th edn. 1926).

Co-operative Labour on the Land (1894) [ed. with introd. by JAH].

'Monopoly Rents of Capital', *National Liberal Club: Political Economy Circle Transactions*, 2 (1895).

'The Meaning and Measure of Unemployment', *Contemporary Review*, 67 (1895).

'The Economic Cause of Unemployment', *Contemporary Review*, 67 (1895).

'Mr. Kidd's "Social Evolution"', *American Journal of Sociology*, 2 (1895).

The Problem of the Unemployed: An Enquiry and an Economic Policy (1896; repr. 1993).

'The Decay of English Agriculture', *Commonwealth*, 1 (1896).

'Human Cost and Utility', *Economic Review*, 6 (1896); repr. in *Hobson: Writings on Welfare and Distribution,* ed. Backhouse.

'Ethics of Empire', *Progressive Review* (Aug. 1897) [pub. under pseudonym 'Nemo'].

'The Influence of Henry George in England', *Fortnightly Review*, NS 62 (1897).

John Ruskin: Social Reformer (1st edn. 1898; 3rd edn. 1904).

'Is England a Free Trade Country?', *Reformer*, 15 Sept. 1898.

'The Ethics of Industrialism', *New Age* (1898), 468–9, 487, 503, 519, 554, 585.

'Edward Bellamy and the Utopian Romance', *The Humanitarian* (New York), 13 (1898).

'Free Trade and Foreign Policy', *Contemporary Review*, 74 (1898); repr. in *Hobson: Writings on Imperialism and Internationalism*, ed. Cain.

'What Peace?', *Ethical World*, 28 Jan. 1899.

'The Economics of Bargaining', *Economic Review*, 9 (1899); repr. in *Hobson: Writings on Welfare and Distribution*, ed. Backhouse.

'Foreign Competition and its Influence on Home Industries', *Co-operative Wholesale Societies Annual* (1899).

'"The White Man's Burden"', *Ethical World*, 18 Feb. 1899.

Leading article, *Ethical World*, 27 May 1899, p. 323.

Review of E. S. Talbot, *Degeneracy: Its Causes, Signs and Results* (1898), *Ethical World*, 27 May 1899.

Note on 'Jewish Financiers', *Ethical World*, 3 June 1899, p. 350.

Note on 'The Ethical Societies and Imperialism', *Ethical World*, 10 June 1899, p. 366.

Note on 'Financial Jews', *Ethical World*, 10 June 1899, p. 366.

'Issues of Empire', *Ethical World* (July 1899), 404–5, 419–20, 437–8, 450–1.

'The Psychology of the War Spirit', *Ethical World*, 9 Dec. 1899, p. 723.

The Economics of Distribution (1900; repr. New York, 1972).

The War in South Africa: Its Causes and Effects (1900; repr. New York. 1972).

'The Ethics of Industrialism', in S. Coit (ed.), *Ethical Democracy: Essays in Social Dynamics* (1900).

'Capitalism and Imperialism in South Africa', *Contemporary Review*, 77 (1900); repr. in *Hobson: Writings on Imperialism and Internationalism*, ed. Cain.

'The Proconsulate of Milner', *Contemporary Review*, 78 (1900).

'The Inevitable in Politics', *Ethical World* (Sept. 1900), 563, 579–80, 594.

Letter on 'John Brown's Body', *Ethical World*, 6 Oct. 1900, p. 639.

The Social Problem: Life and Work (1901; repr. Bristol, 1996).

The Psychology of Jingoism (1901).

'The Commercial Value of Imperialism', *Speaker*, 2 Nov. 1901.

'Imperialism as an Outlet for Population', *Speaker*, 9 Nov. 1901.

'Economic Parasites of Imperialism', *Speaker*, 16 Nov. 1901.

'Imperialism the Policy of Investors', *Speaker*, 23 Nov. 1901.

'The Financial Direction of Imperialism', *Speaker*, 30 Nov. 1901.

'Imperialism based on Protection', *Speaker*, 7 Dec. 1901.

'Socialistic Imperialism', *International Journal of Ethics*, 12 (1901).

'The Industrial Future of South Africa', *Co-operative Wholesale Societies Annual* (1901).

'The Economic Taproot of Imperialism', *Contemporary Review*, 81 (1902).

'The Scientific Basis of Imperialism', *Political Science Quarterly*, 17 (1902).

'Imperialism and the Lower Races', *British Friend* (1902), 53–5, 81–3, 129–32.

'The Approaching Abandonment of Free Trade', *Fortnightly Review*, NS 71 (1902).

Imperialism: A Study (1st edn. 1902; 2nd edn. 1905; 3rd edn. 1938; repr. 3rd edn. 1988).

'The Inner Meaning of Protectionism', *Contemporary Review*, 84 (1903); repr. in *Hobson: Writings on Imperialism and Internationalism*, ed. Cain.

International Trade: An Application of Economic Theory (1904).

'Herbert Spencer', *South Place Magazine*, 9 (1904); repr. in *Hobson: A Reader*, ed. Freeden.

'Marginal Units in the Theory of Distribution', *Journal of Political Economy*, 12 (1904); repr. in *Hobson: Writings on Welfare and Distribution*, ed. Backhouse,

'The Occupations of the People', *Contemporary Review*, 88 (1905).

'The American Trust', *Economic Review*, 14 (1905).

Canada Today (1906).

'The Ethics of Internationalism', *International Journal of Ethics*, 17 (1906); repr. in *Hobson: Writings on Imperialism and Internationalism*, ed. Cain.

'The Insurrection in Natal', *Tribune*, 23 Mar. 1906.

'The Condition of Foreign Labour', *Tribune*, 28 Aug. 1906.

'The New Aristocracy of Mr. Wells', *Contemporary Review*, 89 (1906).

The Fruits of American Protection: The Effects of the Dingley Tariff upon the Industries of the Country and Especially the Well-Being of the People (1907).

'England's Duty to the Russian People', *South Place Magazine*, 12 (1907).

'The Art of Panic Making', *South Place Magazine*, 14 (1908).

The Crisis of Liberalism: New Issues of Democracy (1909; repr. Brighton, 1974).

The Industrial System: An Inquiry into Earned and Unearned Income (1st edn. 1909: 2nd edn. 1910; repr. 1993).

'South Africa as an Imperial Asset', *English Review*, 3 (1909); repr. in *The Crisis of Liberalism* and in *Hobson: Writings on Imperialism and Internationalism*, ed. Cain.

'Can Protection Cure Unemployment?', *National Review*, 53 (1909).

'The Investment of British Capital Abroad', *Labour Leader*, 12 Feb. 1909.

A Modern Outlook (1910).

'The General Election: A Sociological Interpretation', *Sociological Review*, 3 (1910); repr. in *Hobson: Writings on Imperialism and Internationalism*, ed. Cain.

'Social Parasitism', *English Review*, 4 (1910).

'Marginal Productivity', *Economic Review*, 20 (1910); repr. in *Hobson: Writings on Welfare and Distribution*, ed. Backhouse.

'The Two Englands', *Nation*, 5 (1910); repr. in *A Modern Outlook*.

The Science of Wealth (1st edn. 1911; 4th edn. 1950).

An Economic Interpretation of Investment (1911).

'Opening of Markets and Countries', in G. Spiller (ed.), *Papers on Interracial Problems* (1911).

'The Importance of Instruction in the Facts of Internationalism', *National Peace Council*, pamphlet no. 7 (1912).

'The Causes of the Rise in Prices', *Contemporary Review*, 102 (1912).

The German Panic (1913).

Speech on Angell's *The Grand Illusion*, Concord (July 1913), 71–2.

Traffic in Treason: A Study of Political Parties (1914).

'Investment Safeguards under Changing Conditions', *Financial Review of Reviews* (June 1914).

Work and Wealth: A Human Valuation (1st edn. 1914; repr. 1993).

'Investment under War Conditions', *Financial Review of Reviews* (Mar. 1915).

Towards International Government (1915).

A League Of Nations (1915).

The New Protectionism (1916).

Democracy after the War (1st edn. 1917; 3rd edn. 1919; repr. 1998).

'Africa and the War', *Labour Leader*, 7 June 1917, p. 6.

Richard Cobden: The International Man (1918; repr. Brighton, 1968).

The New Holy Alliance (1919).

The Morals of Economic Internationalism (New York, 1920).

'America's Place in the World', *Contemporary Review*, 118 (1920).

'Why the War Came as a Surprise', *Political Science Quarterly*, 35 (1920); repr. in *Problems of a New World* and in *Hobson: Writings on Imperialism and Internationalism*, ed. Cain.

Problems of a New World (1921).

The Economics of Unemployment (1922).

Free Thought in the Social Sciences (1926).

The Living Wage (1926) [with H. N. Brailsford, A. Creech Jones, and E. F. Wise].

The Conditions of Industrial Peace (1927).

'Half the World in Political Subjection: The New Imperialism', *New Leader*, 11 Mar. 1927, p. 6.

Wealth and Life: A Study in Values (1929).

'The Saving Faith of Internationalism', *Contemporary Review*, 135 (1929).

Rationalisation and Unemployment: An Economic Dilemma (1930).

'The New Protectionists', *Nineteenth Century and After*, 108 (1930).

'The British Empire in Conference', *Nation* (New York), 17 Dec. 1930.

Poverty in Plenty: The Ethics of Income (1931).

Democracy and a Changing Civilisation (1934).

Veblen (1936).

Property and Improperty (1937).

Confessions of an Economic Heretic (1938).

'Thoughts on our Present Discontents', *Political Quarterly*, 9 (1938).

'America in the War?', *South Place Monthly Record* (Dec. 1939).

(b) Collections of Hobson's writings

J. A. Hobson: Writings on Welfare and Distribution, ed. R. E. Backhouse, (Bristol 1992).

J. A. Hobson: Writings on Imperialism and Internationalism, ed. P. J. Cain (Bristol, 1992).

J. A. Hobson: a Reader, ed. M. Freeden (1988).

2. OTHER PRIMARY SOURCES

(a) Official documents

Minority Report of the Royal Commission on Depression in Trade and Industry, Cd. 4893 (1886).

Annual Statement of Trade of the United Kingdom with Foreign Countries and British Possessions, Cd. 549 (1901).

Parliamentary Debates (Lords), iv (1909).

(b) Books and articles

ADAMS, BROOKS. 'The Commercial Future, I—The New Struggle for Life among Nations (From an American Standpoint)', *Fortnightly Review*, NS 65 (1899).

ANGELL, N. *Patriotism and Three Flags* (1903).
—— *The Great Illusion* (1909).
Anon. 'The Paradox of Imperialism', *Monthly Review* (Oct. 1900).
—— 'The Empire and Militarism', *Monthly Review* (Nov. 1900).
—— 'Expansion and Expenditure', *Edinburgh Review*, 197 (1903).
—— 'Foreign Politics and Common Sense', *Edinburgh Review*, 197 (1903).
—— *Fabian News* (Feb. 1903) [review of *Imperialism*].
ASHLEY, W. G. *The Tariff Problem* (1903).
BALL, SIDNEY. 'The Social Ideal', *Economic Record*, 9 (1899).
BARNES, L. *The Duty of Empire* (1935).
—— *Empire or Democracy?* (1939).
BELLAMY, E. *Looking Backwards* (1888).
BIRCHENOUGH, H. 'Do Foreign Annexations Injure British Trade?', *Nineteenth Century*, 41 (1897).
—— 'Lord Rosebery on the Dangers to British Trade', *Nineteenth Century*, 48 (1900).
BIRDWOOD, Sir J. *The Industrial Arts of India*, 2 vols. (1880).
BLUNT, W. S. *Secret History of the Occupation of Egypt* (1907; repr. 1969).
BOSANQUET, B. *The Philosophical Theory of the State* (1899).
BRADLAUGH, C. *Labour and Law* (1891).
BRAILSFORD, H. N. *The War of Steel and Gold* (1914).
BRIGHT, J. (ed.), *Speeches on Questions of Public Policy by John Bright, M.P.*, ed. J. E. Thorold Rogers, 2 vols. (1868).
CAIN, P. J. (ed.), *Empire and Imperialism: The Debate of the 1870s* (South Bend, Ind., 1999).
CALCHAS, 'Will England Last the Century?', *Fortnightly Review* NS 69 (1901).
CARNEGIE, A. 'British Pessimism', *The Nineteenth Century* 49 (1901).
CHAMBERLAIN, J. *A Political Memoir, 1880–92*, ed. C. D. Howard (1953).
—— et al. *The Radical Programme* (1885), ed. D. Hamer (Brighton, 1971).
CHURCHILL, W. S. *The People's Rights* (1909; repr. 1970).
CLARK, J. B. 'Distribution as Determined by a Law of Rent', *Quarterly Journal of Economics* 5 (1891).
CLARKE, W. 'The Future of the Canadian Dominion', *Contemporary Review*, 38 (1880).
—— 'The Industrial Basis of Socialism,' in Shaw and Bland (eds.), *Fabian Essays*. repr. in *William Clarke*, ed. Burrows and Hobson.
—— 'The Genesis of Jingoism', *Progressive Review*, 1 (1897). repr. in *William Clarke*, ed. Burrows and Hobson.
—— 'Is Democracy a Reality?', *Progressive Review*, 2 (1897).
—— 'Political Defects of the Old Radicalism', *Political Science Quarterly*, 14 (1899). repr. in *William Clarke*, ed. Burrows and Hobson.

—— 'The Social Future of England', *Contemporary Review*, 78 (1899), repr. in *William Clarke*, ed. Burrows and Hobson.

—— *William Clarke: A Collection of his Writings*, ed. H. Burrows and J. A. Hobson, (1908).

COBBETT, WILLIAM *The Opinions of William Cobbett*, ed. G. D. H. Cole and M. Cole (1944).

COBDEN, R. *Speeches on Questions of Public Policy by Richard Cobden*, *M.P.*, ed. J. Bright and J. E. Thorold Rogers, 2 vols. (1870).

COLE, G. D. H. Review of Hobson's *Confessions*, *Political Quarterly*, 9 (1938).

—— and POSTGATE, R. *The Common People, 1746–1938* (1st edn. 1938; 2nd edn. 1946).

COLQUHOUN, A. R. *China in Transformation* (1898).

CONANT, C. A. 'The Economic Basis of "Imperialism"', *North American Review*, 167 (1898).

COURT, W. H. B. 'The Communist Doctrines of Empire', in Hancock, *Survey of British Commonwealth Affairs*.

COURTNEY, L. 'What is the Advantage of Foreign Trade?', *Nineteenth Century*, 53 (1903).

CROSS, J. W. 'British Trade in 1898: A Warning Note', *Nineteenth Century*, 45 (1899).

CROZIER, J. B. 'How to Ruin a Free Trade Nation', *Fortnightly Review*, NS 71 (1902).

DESMOLINS, M. *Boers or English: Who Are in the Right?* (1900).

DILKE, C. W. *Greater Britain: A Record of Travel in English-Speaking Countries during 1866 and 1867* (1868).

'Drifting', the Author of [Ellis Barker]. 'The Defence of the Empire: An Open Letter to Lord Salisbury', *Contemporary Review*, 79 (1901).

—— 'The Economic Decay of Great Britain', *Contemporary Review*, 79 (1901).

ELLIOT, R. 'The English Radicals', *Edinburgh Review*, 191 (1900).

FARADAY, E. R. 'Some Economic Aspects of the Imperial Idea', *Fortnightly Review*, NS 64 (1898).

FARRER, LORD, 'Does Trade Follow the Flag?', *Contemporary Review*, 74 (1898).

FEIS, H. *Europe, the World's Banker, 1870–1914* (Clifton, NJ, 1930; repr. 1974).

FISHER, A. G. B. Review of third edition of *Imperialism*, *Economic Journal*, 48 (1938).

FLUX, A. W. 'The Flag and Trade', *Journal of the Royal Statistical Society*, 62 (1899).

FROUDE, J. A. 'England and her Colonies', *Fraser's Magazine*, 81 (1870); repr. in Cain (ed.), *Empire and Imperialism*.

FROUDE, J.A. 'The Colonies Once More', *Fraser's Magazine*, 82 (1870); repr. in Cain (ed.), *Empire and Imperialism*.

—— 'England's War', in *Short Studies on Great Subjects*, iii (1907).

—— *Oceana: or England and her Colonies* (1886).

GIFFEN, Sir G. The Excess of Imports', *Journal of the Royal Statistical Society*, 62 (1899).

—— 'Are We Living off Capital?' (1901), in *Economic Inquiries and Studies* (1904).

—— 'Our Trade Prosperity and the Outlook', *Economic Journal*, 10 (1900).

GLADSTONE, W. E. 'Aggression on Egypt and Freedom in the East', *Nineteenth Century*, 2 (1877); repr. in Cain (ed.), *Empire and Imperialism*.

—— 'England's Mission', *Nineteenth Century*, 4 (1878); repr. in Cain, *Empire and Imperialism*.

—— *The Gladstone Diaries*, ed. H. C. G. Matthew, 10 (Oxford, 1990).

GREEN, T. H. *Prolegomena to Ethics* (4th edn. 1899).

GORST, J. L. 'The Oriental Character', *Anglo-Saxon Review*, 2 (Sept. 1899).

GREG, W. R. 'Foreign Policy of Great Britain: Imperial or Economic?', *Nineteenth Century*, 4 (1878).

GREY, EARL. *Memoir of Hubert Hervey* (1899).

GWYNN, S., and TUCKWELL, G. M. *The Life of Sir Charles W. Dilke*, 2 vols. (1917).

HALLETT, H. S. 'British Trade and the Integrity of China', *Fortnightly Review*, NS 63 (1898).

HAMMOND, J. L. 'Colonial and Foreign Policy', in *Liberalism and the Empire* (1900).

HANCOCK, W. K. *Survey of British Commonwealth Affairs*, vol. ii, Pt. I (Oxford 1940).

HARRIS, C. A. 'Foreign Investments', in R. Inglis Palgrave (ed.), *The Dictionary of Political Economy*, ii (1900).

HART, R. 'The Peking Legation: A National Uprising and International Episode', *Fortnightly Review*, NS 68 (1900).

HERTZFELD, A. G. 'Our Falling Trade', *Westminster Review*, 150 (1898).

HILFERDING, R. *Finance Capital: The Latest Stage of Capitalist Development* (1910; repr. 1981).

HIRST, F. W. 'Imperialism and Finance', in *Liberalism and the Empire* (1900).

—— *British Capital at Home and Abroad* (1911).

HOBHOUSE, L. T. 'The Foreign Policy of Collectivism', *Economic Review*, 9 (1899).

—— *Democracy and Reaction* (1st edn. 1904; 2nd edn. 1909).

—— *Liberalism* (1911; repr. Oxford, 1964).

HUBBARD, E. 'American "Trusts" and English Combinations', *Economic Journal*, 12 (1902).

Investment Critic, 'Prejudices of Investors', *Financial Review of Reviews* (Dec. 1912).

JENKS, L. H. *The Migration of British Capital to 1875* (1927; repr. 1963).

KERSHAW, J. B. C. 'The Future of British Trade', *Fortnightly Review*, NS 62 (1897).

KEYNES, J. M. 'Great Britain's Foreign Investments', *New Quarterly* (1910); repr. in *The Collected Works of John Maynard Keynes*, ed. D. Moggridge, xv (Cambridge, 1971).

—— 'National Self-Sufficiency', *Yale Review* (1933); repr. in *The Collected Writings of John Maynard Keynes*, ed. D. Moggridge, xxi (Cambridge, 1982).

KIDD, B. *Social Evolution* (1894).

—— *The Control of the Tropics* (1898).

—— *The Principles of Western Civilisation* (1902).

—— 'Imperial Policy and Free Trade', *Nineteenth Century*, 54 (1903).

KINGSLEY, M. *West African Studies* (3rd edn. 1964).

LANGER, W. L. 'A Critique of Imperialism', *Foreign Affairs*, 14 (1935–6).

LENIN, V. I. 'Imperialism, the Highest Stage of Capitalism' (1916); repr. in *Collected Works*, xxii (Moscow, 1964).

LILLY, W. S. Review of Pearson, *National Life and Character*, *Quarterly Review*, 177 (1893).

—— ' "Collapse of England" ', *Fortnightly Review*, NS 72 (1902).

LORIA, A. *Economic Foundations of Society* (1902).

MACDONALD, J. A. MURRAY. 'The Liberal Party', *Contemporary Review*, 79 (1900).

—— 'The Imperial Problem', *Contemporary Review*, 80 (1901).

MACDONALD, J. R. 'The Propaganda of Civilisation', *International Journal of Ethics*, 11 (1900–1).

MACROSTY, H. W. 'The Growth of Monopoly in British Industry', *Contemporary Review*, 75 (1899).

—— 'Organisation or Protection?' *Fortnightly Review*, NS 71 (1902).

—— 'Business Aspects of British Trusts', *Economic Journal*, 12 (1902).

MALLOCK, W. H. 'The Alleged Economic Decay of Great Britain', *Monthly Review* (Sept. 1901).

MALTHUS, T. R. *Principles of Political Economy* (1820).

MARSHALL, A. *Principles of Economics* (variorum edn. Cambridge, 1961).

MASTERMAN, C. F. G. (ed.). *The Heart of the Empire* (1901).

MILL, J. *Commerce Defended* (1805); repr. in *James Mill: Selected Economic Writings*, ed. D. Winch (Edinburgh, 1966).

MILL, J. S. *Essays on Some Unsettled Questions in Political Economy* (1844); repr. in id., *Collected Works*, iv (Toronto, 1967).

—— *Principles of Political Economy* (1st edn. 1848); repr. in id., *Collected Works*, iii (Toronto, 1965).

MILNER, Sir A. *England in Egypt* (1892).

MOON, P. T. *Imperialism and World Politics* (1926).

MORE, Sir T. *Utopia* (Cambridge, 1989).

MOREL, E. D. *Africa and the Peace of Europe* (1917).

MORGAN-BROWNE, H. 'But Are We Decaying?', *Contemporary Review*, 79 (1901).

—— 'Is Great Britain Falling into Economic Decay?', *Contemporary Review*, 80 (1901).

MORLEY, J. *The Life of Richard Cobden*, ii (1881).

MORRIS, W. 'How We Live and How We Might Live' (1884); repr. in *Political Writings of William Morris*, ed. A. L. Morton (1973).

—— *News from Nowhere* (1890).

MUIRHEAD, J. H. 'What Imperialism Means', *Fortnightly Review*, NS 68 (1900).

MURRAY, G. 'The Exploitation of Inferior Races in Ancient and Modern Times: An Imperial Labour Question with a Historical Parallel', in *Liberalism and the Empire* (1900).

OGDEN, H. J. *The War against the Dutch Republics in South Africa: Its Origins, Progress and Results* (Manchester, 1901).

OGNIBEN. 'The United States of Imperial Britain', *Contemporary Review*, 81 (1902).

OLIVIER, S. 'The Moral Basis of Socialism', in Shaw and Bland (eds.), *Fabian Essays*.

PAINE, T. *The Rights of Man* (Everyman edn. 1966).

PAISH, Sir G. 'Great Britain's Investments in Other Lands', *Journal of the Royal Statistical Society*, 72 (1909).

—— 'Great Britain's Capital Investments in Individual Colonies and Foreign Countries' *Journal of the Royal Statistical Society*, 74 (1911).

PEARSON, C. H. *National Life and Character* (1893).

—— 'The Causes of Pessimism', *Fortnightly Review*, NS 54 (1894).

PEARSON, K. *National Life from the Standpoint of Science* (1901).

PERRIS, G. H. 'The New Internationalism', in S. Coit (ed.), *Ethical Democracy* (1900).

PRICE, L. L. 'The Economic Possibilities of an Imperial Fiscal Policy', *Economic Journal*, 13 (1903).

—— 'Protection, Free Trade and Unemployment', in P. J. Cain (ed.), *Free Trade and Protectionism*, vol. iv (Bristol, 1996; first pub. 1909).

REINACH, P. S. Review of *Imperialism: A Study*, *Political Science Quarterly*, 18 (1903).

RICHARD, H. *Mr. Chamberlain's Defence of the War* (1882?).

RICHIE, D. G. *Darwinism and Politics* (1889).

—— 'War and Peace', *International Journal of Ethics*, 11 (1901); repr. in id., *Studies in Political and Social Ethics* (1902).

RITORTUS. 'The Imperialism of British Trade—I & II', *Contemporary Review*, 76 (1899).

ROBERTSON, J. M. *The Fallacy of Saving* (1892).
—— *Patriotism and Empire* (1898).
—— *The Eight Hour Day* (1899).
ROBINSON, E. VAN D. 'War and Economics', *Political Science Quarterly*, 15 (1900).
RUSKIN, J. *Unto This Last, The Crown of Wild Olive, and Sesame and Lilies*, in *The Works of John Ruskin*, ed. E. T. Cook and A. Wedderburn, xviii (1905).
—— *Fors Clavigera*, in *Works of John Ruskin*, ed. E. T. Cook and A. Wedderburn, xxviii (1907).
SAMUEL, H. *Liberalism: An Attempt to State the Principles and Proposals of Contemporary Liberalism in England* (1902).
—— 'The Cobden Centenary', *The Nineteenth Century*, 55 (1904).
SANDERS, L. ' "The Yellow Peril" ', *Anglo-Saxon Review* (Dec. 1900).
SCHUMPETER, J. A. *Imperialism* (1919); repr. in R. Swedberg (ed.), *Joseph A. Schumpeter: The Economics and Sociology of Capitalism* (Princeton, 1991).
SEEBOHM, F. 'Imperialism and Socialism', *Nineteenth Century*, 7 (1880); repr. in Cain (ed.), *Empire and Imperialism*.
SEELEY, J. R. *The Expansion of England* (1883).
SHAW, G. B. 'The Economic Basis of Socialism', in Shaw and Bland (eds.) *Fabian Essays*.
—— 'The Transition to Social Democracy', in Shaw and Bland (eds.) *Fabian Essays*.
—— 'Socialism for Millionaires', *Contemporary Review*, 69 (1896); repr. in id., *Essays in Fabian Socialism* (1932).
—— *Fabianism and the Empire* (1900).
—— *The Intelligent Woman's Guide to Socialism and Capitalism* (1928).
—— *What I Really Said about the War* (1931).
—— and Bland, H. (eds.), *Fabian Essays in Socialism* (1889).
SMILES, S. *Self Help*, ed. A. Briggs (1958).
SMITH, A. *An Inquiry into the Nature and Causes of the Wealth of Nations* (Oxford, 1976).
SMITH, GOLDWIN. 'The Greatness of England', *Contemporary Review*, 34 (1878).
—— *In the Court of History: An Apology for Canadians who are Opposed to the Boer War* (1902).
SPENCER, H. *Principles of Sociology*, i (1876).
—— *The Man versus the State* (1884).
—— *Facts and Comments* (1902).
STALEY, E. *War and the Private Investor: A Study in the Relations of International Politics and International Private Investment* (1935).
STEAD, W. T. *The Americanisation of the World* (1902).
STRACHEY, J. *The Theory and Practice of Socialism* (1936).

STRACHEY, J. *What Are We To Do?* (1938).

SWEEZY, P. M. 'J. A. Hobson's Economic Heresies', *Nation* (New York) (Aug. 1938).

TALBOT, E. S. *Degeneracy: Its Causes, Signs and Results* (1898).

TOWNSEND, M. *Europe in Asia*(1901).

Union of Democratic Control, *Memorandum on the Proposed Economic War* (1916).

VEBLEN, T. Review of *Imperialism, Journal of Political Economy,* 12 (1903).

—— *The Theory of Business Enterprise* (1904).

—— *Imperial Germany and the Industrial Revolution* (1915).

VIALLETE, A. *Economic Imperialism and International Relations during the Last Fifty Years* (1923).

VOGEL, J. 'Greater or Lesser Britain', *Nineteenth Century,* 1 (1877); repr. in Cain (ed.), *Empire and Imperialism.*

WADE, J. *The Extraordinary Black Book* (1831).

WALLACE, A. R. 'The Seamy Side of Imperialism', *Nineteenth Century,* 75 (1899).

WALLAS, G. 'Property under Socialism', in Shaw and Bland (eds.), *Fabian Essays.*

WALPOLE, S. Review of Pearson, *National Life and Character, Edinburgh Review,* 178 (1893).

WEBB, S. 'The Rate of Interest and the Laws of Distribution', *Quarterly Journal of Economics,* 2 (1888).

WILLIAMS, J. H. 'The Theory of International Trade Reconsidered', *Economic Journal,* 39 (1929).

WILSHIRE, H. G. 'The Significance of the Trust', *Wilshire's Magazine* (Nov. 1901).

WILSON, A. J. 'The Immorality and Cowardice of Modern Loan-Mongering', *Contemporary Review,* 73 (1898).

—— 'The Art of Living on Capital', *Contemporary Review,* 75 (1899).

—— 'Trade Prosperity and Government Waste', *Contemporary Review,* 75 (1899).

WOOLF, L. *Empire and Commerce in Africa* (1920).

—— *Imperialism and Civilisation* (1928).

3. SECONDARY WORKS ON HOBSON

(a) Books and articles

ALLETT. J. *New Liberalism: The Political Economy of J. A. Hobson* (Toronto, 1981).

—— 'New Liberalism, Old Prejudices: J. A. Hobson and the "Jewish Question"', *Jewish Social Studies,* 49 (1987).

—— 'The Conservative Aspect of Hobson's New Liberalism', in Freeden (ed.), *Reappraising J. A. Hobson.*

—— 'The Moral Philosophy of J. A. Hobson', in Pheby (ed.), *J. A. Hobson after Fifty Years.*

ARRIGHI, G. *The Geometry of Imperialism: The Limits of Hobson's Paradigm* (1978).

BACKHOUSE, R. E. 'J. A. Hobson as a Macroeconomic Theorist', in Freeden (ed.), *Reappraising J. A. Hobson.*

—— 'Mummery and Hobson's *The Physiology of Industry*', in Pheby (ed.), *J. A. Hobson after Fifty Years.*

BRAILSFORD, H. N. *The Life and Work of J. A. Hobson* (Oxford, 1948).

CAIN, P. J. 'J. A. Hobson, Cobdenism and the Radical Theory of Economic Imperialism, 1898–1914', *Economic History Review*, 2nd ser. 31 (1978).

—— 'International Trade and Economic Development in the Thought of J. A. Hobson before 1914', *History of Political Economy*, 11 (1979).

—— 'Hobson's Developing Theory of Imperialism', *Economic History Review*, 2nd ser. 34 (1981).

—— 'Hobson, Wilshire and the Capitalist Theory of Capitalist Imperialism', *History of Political Economy*, 17 (1985).

—— 'J. A. Hobson, Financial Capitalism and Imperialism in Late Victorian and Edwardian Britain', *Journal of Imperial and Commonwealth History*, 13 (1985).

—— 'Variations on a Famous Theme: Hobson, International Trade and Imperialism, 1902–38', in Freeden (ed.), *Reappraising J. A. Hobson.*

—— 'Hobson Lives? Finance and British Imperialism, 1870–1914', in S. Groenweld and D. Wintle (eds.), *State and Trade: Government and the Economy in Britain and the Netherlands since the Middle Ages* (Zutphen, 1992).

—— 'Free Trade, Social Reform and Imperialism: J. A. Hobson and the Dilemmas of Liberalism, 1890–1914', in A. Marrison (ed.), *Free Trade and its Reception, 1815–1960: Freedom and Trade*, i (Manchester, 1998).

—— 'British Radicalism, the South African Crisis and the Origins of the Theory of Financial Imperialism', in Omissi and Thompson (eds.), *The Impact of the South African War* (2002).

CLARKE, P. F. 'Hobson and Keynes as Economic Heretics', in Freeden (ed.), *Reappraising J. A. Hobson.*

—— *Liberals and Social Democrats* (Cambridge, 1978).

—— 'Hobson, Free Trade and Imperialism', *Economic History Review*, 2nd ser. 34 (1981).

COLE, G. D. H. 'John A. Hobson, 1858–1940', *Economic Journal*, 50 (1940).

COPPOCK, D. J. 'A Reconsideration of Hobson's Theory of Unemployment', *Manchester School*, 21 (1953).

DAVIS, H. B. 'Hobson and Human Welfare', *Science and Society*, 21 (1957).

ECKSTEIN, A. M. 'Is There a "Hobson–Lenin Thesis" on Late Nineteenth Century Colonial Expansion?', *Economic History Review*, 2nd ser. 44 (1991).

EDGELL, S. and TILMAN, R. 'John Hobson: Admirer and Critic of Thorstein Veblen', in Pheby (ed.), *J. A. Hobson after Fifty Years*.

—— and TOWNSHEND, J. 'John Hobson, Thorstein Veblen and the Phenomenon of Imperialism: Finance Capitalism, Patriotism and War', *American Journal of Economics and Sociology*, 51 (1992).

EMY, H. V. *Liberals, Radicals and Social Politics, 1892–1914* (Cambridge, 1973).

ETHERINGTON, N. 'The Capitalist Theory of Capitalist Imperialism', *History of Political Economy*, 15 (1983).

—— *Theories of Imperialism: War, Conquest and Capital* (1984).

FREEDEN, M. 'J. A. Hobson as a New Liberal Theorist', *Journal of the History of Ideas*, 34 (1973).

—— 'Biological and Evolutionary Roots of the New Liberalism in England', *Political Theory*, 4 (1976).

—— *The New Liberalism: An Ideology of Social Reform* (Oxford, 1978).

—— *Liberalism Divided: A Study in British Political Thought, 1914–1939* (Oxford, 1986).

—— (ed.). *Minutes of the Rainbow Circle, 1894–1924* (1989).

—— (ed.). *Reappraising J. A. Hobson: Humanism and Welfare* (1990).

—— 'Hobson's Evolving Conceptions of Human Nature', in Freeden (ed.), *Reappraising J. A. Hobson*.

—— 'J. A. Hobson as a Political Theorist', in Pheby (ed.), *J. A. Hobson after Fifty Years*.

KADISH, A. 'Rewriting the Confessions: Hobson and the Extension Movement', in Freeden (ed.), *Reappraising J. A. Hobson*.

—— 'The Non-canonical Context of The Physiology of Industry', in Pheby (ed.), *J. A. Hobson after Fifty Years*.

KEARNS, J. '*Fin-de-Siecle* Geopolitics: Mackinder, Hobson and Theories of Global Closure', in P. J. Taylor (ed.), *Political Geography in the Twentieth Century: A Global Analysis* (1993).

KING, J. E. *Economic Exiles* (1988).

—— 'J. A. Hobson's Macroeconomics: The Last Ten Years', in Pheby (ed.), *J. A. Hobson after Fifty Years*.

LEE, A. J. 'John Atkinson Hobson, 1858–1940', in J. M. Bellamy and J. Saville (eds.), *Dictionary of Labour Biography*, i (1972).

LLOYD, T. L. 'Africa and Hobson's Imperialism', *Past and Present*, 55 (1972).

LONG, D. 'Three Modes of Internationalism in the Work of J. A. Hobson', in Pheby (ed.), *J. A. Hobson after Fifty Years*.

—— Towards a New Liberal Internationalism: The International Theory of J. A. Hobson (Cambridge, 1996).

MAGNUSSON, L. 'Hobson and Imperialism: An Appraisal', in Pheby (ed.), J. A. Hobson after Fifty Years.

MATTHEW, H. C. G. 'Hobson, Ruskin and Cobden', in Freeden (ed.), Reappraising J. A. Hobson.

MEADOWCROFT, J. Conceptualising the State: Innovation and Dispute in British Political Thought, 1880–1914 (Oxford, 1995).

MITCHELL, H. 'Hobson Revisited', Journal of the History of Ideas, 26 (1965).

NEMMERS, E. E. Hobson and Underconsumption (Amsterdam, 1956).

NOWELL, G. 'Hobson's Imperialism: A Defence', in R. M. Chilcote (ed.), The Political Economy of Imperialism: Critical Appraisals (Boston, 1999).

PHEBY, J. (ed.). J. A. Hobson after Fifty Years (Basingstoke, 1994).

PORTER, B. 'Hobson and Internationalism', in Freeden (ed.) Reappraising J. A. Hobson.

PORTER, B. C. Critics of Empire: British Radical Attitudes to Colonialism in Africa, 1895–1914 (Cambridge, 1968).

RICHMOND, W. H. 'John A. Hobson: Economic Heretic', American Journal of Economics and Sociology, 37 (1978).

SCHNEIDER, M. 'Modelling Hobson's Underconsumption Theory', in Pheby (ed.), J. A. Hobson after Fifty Years.

—— J. A. Hobson (1996).

SEMMEL, B. The Liberal Ideal and the Demons of Empire: Theories of Imperialism from Adam Smith to Lenin (Baltimore, 1993).

THOMPSON, N. 'Hobson and the Fabians: Two Roads to Socialism in the 1920s', History of Political Economy, 26 (1994).

TOWNSHEND, J. J. A. Hobson (Manchester, 1990).

—— 'Hobson and the Socialist Tradition', in Pheby (ed.), J. A. Hobson after Fifty Years.

WOOD, J. C. 'J. A. Hobson and British Imperialism', American Journal of Economics and Sociology, 42 (1983).

—— British Economists and the Empire (1983).

(b) Unpublished doctoral theses

JOHNS, B. R. 'Business, Investment and Imperialism. The Relationship between Economic Interest and Growth of British Intervention in Egypt, 1838–82' (unpub. Ph.D. thesis, University of Exeter, 1981).

LEE, A. J. 'The Social and Economic Thought of J. A. Hobson' (University of London, 1970).

TOWNSHEND, J. 'J. A. Hobson and the Crisis of Liberalism' (Southampton University, 1973).

4. OTHER SECONDARY WORKS

ALLY, R. *Gold and Empire: The Bank of England and South Africa's Gold Producers 1886–1926* (Johannesburg, 1994).

AL-SAYYID-MARSOT, A. L. 'The British Occupation of Egypt from 1882', in Porter (ed.), *Oxford History*.

ANTONY, P. D. *John Ruskin's Labour: A Study of Ruskin's Social Theory* (Cambridge, 1983).

ARMITAGE, W. H. G. *Heavens Below: Utopian Experiments in England, 1560–1960* (1961).

ATKINS, R. A. 'The Conservatives and Egypt, 1875–1880', *Journal of Imperial and Commonwealth History*, 2 (1974).

BANERJI, A. K. *Aspects of Indo-British Economic Relations, 1858–1898* (Bombay, 1982).

BARKER, T. C. 'London: A Unique Megalopolis?', in T. C. Barker and A. Sutcliffe (eds.), *Megalopolis: The Giant City in History* (1993).

BAXENDALE, J. '"I Had Seen a Lot of Englands": J. B. Priestley, Englishness and the People', *History Workshop Journal*, 51 (2001).

BELLAMY, R. *Liberalism and Modern Society: An Historical Argument* (1992).

BENNETT, G. (ed.). *The Concept of Empire: Burke to Attlee, 1774–1947* (1953).

BERNSTEIN, G. L. *Liberalism and Liberal Politics in Edwardian Britain* (Winchester, Mass., 1986).

BETTS, R. A. 'The Allusion to Rome in British Imperial Thought in the Late 19th an early 20th Centuries', *Victorian Studies*, 15 (1971).

BIAGINI, E. F. *Liberty, Retrenchment and Reform: Popular Liberalism in the Age of Gladstone, 1860–1880* (Cambridge, 1992).

BICKERS, R. *Britain in China: Community, Culture and Colonialism* (Manchester, 1999).

BLAINEY, G. 'Lost Causes of the Jameson Raid', *Economic History Review*, 2nd ser. 18 (1965).

BLEWETT, G. *The Peers, the Parties and the People: The General Elections of 1910* (1972).

BOSS, H. *Theories of Surplus and Transfer: Parasites and Producers in Economic Thought* (Cambridge, 1990).

BREWER, A. *Marxist Theories of Imperialism: A Critical Survey* (2nd edn. 1990).

BURROW, J. *A Liberal Descent: Victorian Historians and the English Past* (Cambridge, 1981).

—— *Whigs and Liberals: Continuities and Change in English Political Thought* (Oxford, 1988).

BUTLER, J. *The Liberal Party and the Jameson Raid* (Oxford, 1968).

CAIN, P. J. 'Capitalism, War and Internationalism in the Thought of Richard Cobden', *British Journal of International Studies*, 5 (1979).

—— 'Political Economy in Edwardian Britain: The Tariff Reform Controversy', in A. O'Day (ed.), *The Edwardian Age: Continuity and Change* (1979).

—— 'The Economic Philosophy of Constructive Imperialism', in C. Navari (ed.), *Politics and the Spirit of the Age* (Keele, 1996).

—— 'Was it Worth Having? The British Empire, 1850–1950', *Revista de historia economia*, 16 (1998).

—— 'Tradition and Innovation: The City of London, 1870–1914', in J.-P. Dormois and M. Dintenfass (eds.), *The British Industrial Decline* (1999).

—— 'British Free Trade, 1850–1914: Economics and Policy', *ReFRESH*, 29 (1999).

—— and HOPKINS, A. G. *British Imperialism, 1688–2000* (2001).

CANNADINE, D. *Ornamentalism: How the British Saw their Empire* (2001).

CASSIS, Y. *City Bankers* (Cambridge, 1994).

CHAMBERLAIN, M. E. 'The Alexandria Massacres of 11 June 1882 and the British Occupation of Egypt', *Middle Eastern Studies*, 13 (1977).

—— 'Sir Charles Dilke and the British Intervention in Egypt, 1882: Decision Making in a Nineteenth Century Cabinet', *British Journal of International Studies*, 2 (1976).

CHAPMAN, S. 'Rhodes and the City of London: Another View of Imperialism', *Historical Journal*, 23 (1985).

CHAPPELOW, A. *Shaw—'The Chucker-Out': A Biographical Exposition* (1969).

CLAEYS, G. 'Justice, Independence, Industrial Democracy: The Development of John Stuart Mill's Views on Socialism', *Journal of Politics*, 49 (1987).

CLINE, C. A. *Recruits to Labour: The British Labour Party, 1914–31* (New York, 1963).

CLINE, P. 'Winding down the War Economy: British Plans for Peacetime Recovery, 1916–19', in K. Burk (ed.), *War and the State* (1982).

COLLINI, S. 'Liberalism and the Legacy of Mill', *Historical Journal*, 20 (1977).

—— *Liberalism and Sociology: L. T. Hobhouse and Political Argument in England, 1880–1914* (Cambridge, 1979).

—— *Public Moralists: Political Thought and Intellectual Life in Britain, 1850–1950* (Oxford, 1991).

—— WINCH, D., and BURROW, J. *That Noble Science of Politics: A Study in Nineteenth Century Intellectual History* (Cambridge, 1983).

COPE, R. L. 'Strategic and Socio-economic Explanations for Carnarvon's South African Confederation Policy: The Historiography and the Evidence', *History in Africa*, 20 (1987).

CORLEY, T. A. B. 'Britain's Overseas Investments in 1914 Revisited', *Business History*, 36 (1994).

COTTRELL, P. L. *British Overseas Investment in the Nineteenth Century* (1975).

COURT, W. H. B. *British Economic History, 1870–1914: Commentary and Documents* (Cambridge, 1965).

CROOK, P. *Benjamin Kidd: Portrait of a Social Darwinist* (Cambridge, 1984).

—— *Darwinism, War and History* (Cambridge, 1994).

CROUZET, F. *The Victorian Economy* (1982).

CURTIN, F. D. 'Aesthetics in English Social Reform: Ruskin and his Followers' in H. Davis, W. C. DeVane, and R. C. Bald (eds.), *Nineteenth Century Studies* (Ithaca, NY, 1940).

CUTHBERTSON, G. 'Preaching Imperialism: Wesleyan Methodism and the War', in Omissi and Thompson (ed.), *Impact of the South African War*.

DAVIS, C. B. 'Financing Imperialism: British and American Bankers as Vectors of Imperial Expansion in China, 1908–20', *Business History Review*, 56 (1982).

DAVIS, L. E., and HUTTENBACK, R. A. *Mammon and the Pursuit of Empire: The Political Economy of British Imperialism, 1860–1912* (Cambridge, 1986).

DAWSON, M. 'Liberalism in Devon and Cornwall, 1910–1931: "The Old Time Religion"', *Historical Journal*, 38 (1995).

DAYER, R. A. *Finance and Empire: Sir Charles Addis, 1861–1943* (1988).

DEN OTTER, S. *British Idealism and Social Explanation: A Study in Late Victorian Thought* (Oxford, 1996).

DOWSE, R. E. *Left in the Centre: The Independent Labour Party, 1893–1940* (1966).

DUMETT, R. E. 'Joseph Chamberlain, Imperial Finance and Railway Policy in British West Africa in the Late Nineteenth Century', *English Historical Review*, 90 (1975).

—— *El Dorado in West Africa: The Gold Mining Frontier, African Labour and Colonial Capitalism in the Gold Coast* (Athens, Oh., 1998).

DURBIN, E. *New Jerusalems: The Labour Party and the Economics of Democratic Socialism* (1985).

EDELSTEIN, M. 'Realised Rates of Return on British Domestic and Foreign Investments in the Age of High Imperialism', *Explorations in Economic History*, 13 (1976).

—— *Overseas Investment in the Age of High Imperialism: The United Kingdom, 1860–1914* (1982).

—— 'Imperialism: Costs and Benefits', in R. Floud, and D. N. McCloskey (eds.), *The Economic History of Modern Britain*, ii: *1860–1939* (Cambridge, 1994).

EDWARDS, E. W. 'The Origins of British Financial Cooperation with France in China, 1903–6', *English Historical Review*, 86 (1971).

—— *British Diplomacy and Finance in China, 1895–1914* (Oxford, 1987).

ELDRIDGE, C. C. *Disraeli and the Rise of a New Imperialism* (Cardiff, 1996).

EMY H. V. 'The Impact of Financial Policy on English Party Politics', *Historical Journal*, 15 (1972).

ETHERINGTON, N. 'Theories of Imperialism in Southern Africa Revisited', *African Affairs*, 81 (1982).

FARNIE, D. A. *The English Cotton Industry and the World Market, 1815–1896* (Oxford, 1979).

FEINSTEIN, C. H. 'Britain's Overseas Investments in 1913', *Economic History Review*, 2nd ser. 43 (1990).

FERGUSON, N. *The World's Banker: The History of the House of Rothschild* (1998).

FETTER, F. A. *Capital, Interest and Rent: Essays in the Theory of Distribution* (Kansas City, 1977).

FIELD, H. J. *Towards a Programme of Imperial Life: The British Empire at the Turn of the Century* (Oxford, 1982).

FIELDHOUSE, D. K. 'Imperialism: An Historiographical Revision', *Economic History Review*, 2nd ser. 14 (1961–2).

—— *Economics and Empire* (1974).

FLINT, J. E. *Cecil Rhodes* (1974).

GALBRAITH, J. S. 'The Pamphlet Campaign on the Boer War', *Journal of Modern History*, 24 (1952).

—— 'The Origins of the British South Africa Company' in J. E. Flint and G. Williams (eds.), *Perspectives of Empire* (1973).

—— *Crown and Charter: The Early Years of the British South Africa Company* (Berkeley, 1974).

GALLAGHER, J., and ROBINSON, R. E. 'The Imperialism of Free Trade, 1815–1914', *Economic History Review*, 5 (1953–4).

GARSIDE, R. W. *The Measurement of Unemployment: Methods and Sources in Great Britain, 1850–1970* (1980).

GARVIN, J. L. *The Life of Joseph Chamberlain*, iii: *1895–1900* (1934).

GRAMSCI, A. *Selections from the Prison Notebooks*, ed. Q. Hoare and G. Nowell Smith (1971).

GREEN, E. E. H. *The Crisis of Conservatism: The Politics, Economics and Ideology of the Conservative Party, 1880–1914* (1995).

—— 'The Political Economy of Empire, 1880–1914', in Porter (ed.), *Oxford History*.

GREENSLADE, W. *Degeneration, Culture and the Novel* (Cambridge, 1994).

GUPTA, P. S. *Imperialism and the British Labour Movement, 1914–64* (1975).

HAMER, D. A. *John Morley: Liberal Intellectual in Politics* (Oxford, 1968).

304   Bibliography

HANNAH, L. *The Rise of the Corporate Economy* (2nd edn. 1983).

HARLING, P. *The Waning of 'Old Corruption': The Politics of Economical Reform in Britain, 1779–1846* (Oxford, 1996).

—— and MANDLER, P. 'From "Fiscal-Military" State to Laissez-Faire State, 1760–1850', *Journal of British Studies*, 32 (1993).

HARRIES, P. 'Capital, State and Labour on the 19th Century Witwatersrand: A Reassessment', *South African Journal of History*, 18 (1986).

HARRIS, J. *Unemployment and Politics. A Study in English Social Policy, 1880–1914* (Oxford, 1972).

HARVIE, C. *The Lights of Liberalism: University Liberals and the Challenge of Democracy* (1976).

HASELER, S. *The Super-Rich: The Unjust World of Global Capitalism* (2001).

HAVINDEN, M., and MEREDITH, D. *Colonialism and Development: Britain and its Tropical Colonies, 1850–1960* (1993).

HENSHAW, P. 'The "Key to South Africa" in the 1890s: Delagoa Bay and the Origins of the South African War', *Journal of Southern African Studies*, 24 (1998).

HEYCK, T. W. *The Transformation of Intellectual Life in Victorian England* (1982).

HIRSCHMAN, A. *The Passions and the Interests: Political Arguments for Capitalism before its Triumph* (Princeton, 1977).

HOLMES, C. *John Bull's Island: Immigration and British Society, 1871–1971* (1988).

HOPKINS, A. G. 'The Victorians and Africa: A Reconsideration of the Occupation of Egypt', *Journal of African History*, 27 (1986).

—— (ed.). *Globalization in World History* (2002).

HOUGHTON, W. E. (ed.). *The Wellesley Index of Victorian Periodicals*, vols. i, ii (Toronto, 1966, 1972).

HOWE, A. C. *Free Trade and Liberal England* (1997).

—— 'Free Trade and the Victorians', in A. Marrison (ed.), *Free Trade and its Reception, 1815–1960* (1998).

HOWE, S. *Anticolonialism in British Politics: The Left and the End of Empire, 1918–1964* (Oxford, 1993).

HUGHES, J. BEAUMONT. 'The Press and the Public during the Boer War 1899–1902', *Historian*, 61 (1999).

HUTCHISON, T. W. *A Review of Economic Doctrines, 1870–1929* (Oxford, 1953).

HYAM, R., and MARTIN, G. *Reappraisals in British Imperial History* (1975).

HYNES, W. G. *The Economics of Empire: Britain, Africa and the New Imperialism, 1870–1895* (1979).

INGLIS, F. *Radical Earnestness: English Social Theory, 1880–1980* (1982).

JAY, R. *Joseph Chamberlain: A Political Study* (Oxford, 1981).

JEEVES, A. H. 'The Rand Capitalists and the Coming of the South African War, 1896–1899', *South African Journal of Economic History*, 11 (1996).

JONES, P. D. *The Christian Socialist Revival, 1877–1914: Religion, Class and Social Conscience in Late Victorian England* (Princeton, 1980).

JOYCE, P. *Visions of the People* (1991).

KATZ, E. N. 'Outcrop and Deep Level Mining in South Africa before the Anglo-Boer War: Re-examining the Blainey Thesis', *Economic History Review*, 2nd ser. 48 (1995).

KENNEDY, W. P. *Industrial Structure, Capital Markets and the Origins of British Economic Decline* (Cambridge, 1987).

KESNER, R. M. *Economic Control and Colonial Development: Crown Colony Financial Management in the Age of Joseph Chamberlain* (Oxford, 1981).

KLEIN, N. *No Logo* (2000).

KOEBNER, R., and SCHMIDT, H. D. *Imperialism: The History and Significance of a Political Word, 1840–1960* (Cambridge, 1964).

KOSS, S. *The Pro-Boers* (Chicago, 1973).

KREBS, P. M. *Gender, Race and the Writing of Empire: Public Discourse and the Boer War* (Cambridge, 1999).

KUBICECK, R. V. 'The Randlords: A Reassessment', *Journal of British Studies*, 11 (1972).

—— *Economic Imperialism in Theory and Practice: The Case of South African Mining Finance, 1886–1914* (Durham, NC, 1979).

KUMAR, K. *Utopianism* (1991).

KURER, O. 'J. S. Mill and Utopian Socialism', *Economic Record*, 68 (1992).

KYNASTON, D. *The City of London: Golden Years, 1890–1914* (1995).

LAITY, P. 'The British Peace Movement and the War', in Omissi and Thompson (eds.), *Impact of the South African War*.

LAWRENCE, J. 'Popular Radicalism and the Socialist Revival in Britain', *Journal of British Studies*, 31 (1992).

LEE A. J. 'The Radical Press', in A. J. A. Morris (ed.), *Edwardian Radicalism, 1900–1914: Some Aspects of British Radicalism* (1974).

LEE, C. H. 'Regional Growth and Structural Change in Victorian Britain', *Economic History Review*, 2nd ser. 34 (1981).

—— *The British Economy since 1700: A Macroeconomic Survey* (Cambridge, 1986).

—— 'The Service Sector, Regional Specialisation and Economic Growth in the Victorian Economy', *Journal of Historical Geography*, 10 (1984).

LEE, F. *Fabianism and Colonialism: The Life and Thought of Sydney Olivier* (1988).

LOWE, P. *Britain and the Far East: A Survey from 1819 to the Present* (Manchester, 1981).

McBriar, A. M. *Fabian Socialism and English Politics, 1884–1918* (Cambridge, 1966).

—— *An Edwardian Mixed Doubles: the Bosanquets versus the Webbs. A Study in British Social Policy, 1890–1929* (Oxford, 1987).

McCarthy, J. P. *Hilaire Belloc: Edwardian Radical* (1978).

Maccoby, S. (ed.). *The Radical Tradition, 1763–1914* (1952).

McIntyre, S. *A Proletarian Science: Marxism in Britain, 1917–1933* (Cambridge, 1980).

McKenzie, J. M. *Orientalism: History, Theory and the Arts* (1995).

McLean, D. 'Commerce, Finance and British Diplomatic Support in China, 1885–6', *Economic History Review*, 2nd ser. 26 (1973).

—— 'The Foreign Office and the First Chinese Indemnity Loan, 1895', *Historical Journal*, 16 (1973).

—— 'Finance and "Informal Empire" before the First World War', *Economic History Review* 2nd ser. 29 (1976).

Mahony, J. *Marshall, Orthodoxy and the Professionalisation of Economics* (1985).

Manuel, F. E., and Manuel, F. P. *Utopian Thought in the Western World* (1979).

Marais, J. S. *The Fall of Kruger's Republic* (Oxford, 1961).

Marks, S. 'Scrambling for South Africa', *Journal of African History*, 23 (1982).

—— and Trapido, S. 'Lord Milner and the South African State Reconsidered', in M. Twaddle (ed.), *Imperialism, the State and the Third World* (1992).

Marrison, A. *British Business and Protection, 1903–1932* (Oxford, 1996).

Marsh, J. *Back to the Land: The Pastoral Impulse in England from 1880 to 1914* (1982).

Matthew, H. C. G. *The Liberal Imperialists* (Oxford, 1973).

—— *Gladstone, 1809–1898* (Oxford, 1996).

Mendelsohn, R. 'Blainey and the Jameson Raid: the Debate Renewed', *Journal of South African Studies*, 6 (1980).

Michie, R. C. *The City of London* (1991).

Miller, D. 'Peter Kropotkin (1842–1921): Mutual Aid and Anarcho-communism', in J. A. Hall (ed.), *Rediscoveries* (Oxford, 1986).

Miller, K. E. *Socialism and Foreign Policy* (The Hague, 1967).

Mitter, P. *Much Maligned Monsters: A History of European Reactions to Indian Art* (Oxford, 1977).

Morris, A. J. A. (ed.). *Edwardian Radicalism, 1900–1914: Some Aspects of British Radicalism* (1974).

—— *C. P. Trevelyan, 1870–1956: Portrait of a Radical* (1976).

Murray, A. K. *The People's Budget, 1909–10: Lloyd George and Liberal Politics* (Oxford, 1980).

Nasson, B. *The South African War, 1899–1902* (Oxford, 1999).

Newbury, C. 'Great Britain and the Partition of Africa, 1870–1914', in Porter (ed.), *Oxford History*.

Nicholls, D. 'The English Middle Class and the Ideological Significance of Radicalism, 1760–1886', *Journal of British Studies*, 24 (1985).

O'Brien, D. P. *The Classical Economists* (Oxford, 1975).

O'Brien, P. K. 'The Costs and Benefits of British Imperialism, 1846–1914', *Past and Present*, 120 (1988).

Offer, A. 'Ricardo's Paradox and the Movement of Rent in England, c1870–1914', *Economic History Review*, 2nd ser. 33 (1980).

—— *Property and Politics: Landownership, Law, Ideology and Urban Development in England* (Cambridge, 1981).

—— 'Empire and Social Reform: British Overseas Investment and Domestic Politics, 1908–14', *Historical Journal*, 26 (1983).

—— 'The British Empire, 1870–1913: A Waste of Money?', *Economic History Review* 2nd ser. 46 (1993).

—— 'Costs and Benefits, Prosperity and Security', in Porter (ed.), *Oxford History*.

Omissi, D., and Thompson, A. S. (eds.). *The Impact of the South African War* (2002).

Osterhammel, J. 'Britain and China, 1842–1914', in Porter (ed.), *Oxford History*.

Ovendale, R. 'Profit or Patriotism: Natal, the Transvaal, and the Coming of the Second Anglo-Boer War', *Journal of Imperial and Commonwealth History*, 8 (1980).

Owen, R. *The Middle East in the World Economy, 1800–1914* (1981).

Peel, J. Y. D. *Herbert Spencer on Social Evolution* (Chicago, 1972).

Phimister, I. R. 'Rhodes, Rhodesia and the Rand', *Journal of Southern African History*, 1 (1974).

—— 'Unscrambling the Scramble for Southern Africa: The Jameson Raid and the South African War Revisited', *South African Historical Journal*, 28 (1993).

—— 'The Chrome Trust: The Making of an International Cartel', *Business History*, 38 (1996).

—— 'Empire, Imperialism and the Partition of Africa', in S. Akita (ed.), *Gentlemanly Capitalism, Imperialism and East Asia* (2002).

Pick, D. *Faces of Degeneration: A European Disorder, c1848–1918* (Cambridge, 1989).

Pierson, S. *Marxism and the Origins of British Socialism: The Struggle for a New Consciousness* (Ithaca, NY, 1973).

Platt, D. C. M. *Finance, Trade and Politics in British Foreign Policy, 1815–1914* (Oxford, 1968).

Platt, D. C. M. 'British Portfolio Investment Overseas before 1870: Some Doubts', *Economic History Review* 2nd ser. 33 (1980).

—— *Britain's Overseas Investments on the Eve of the First World War* (1986).

POCOCK, J. G. A. *The Machiavellian Moment: Florentine Political Thought and the Atlantic Republican Tradition* (Princeton, 1975).

POLLARD, S. *Britain's Prime and Britain's Decline, 1870–1914* (1989).

PORTER, A. N. *The Origins of the South African War: Joseph Chamberlain and the Diplomacy of Imperialism, 1895–1899* (Manchester, 1980).

—— 'British Imperial Policy and South Africa, 1895–9', in P. Warwick, and J.-J. van Helten, (eds.), *The South African War: The Anglo-Boer War, 1899–1902* (1980).

—— (ed.). *Oxford History of the British Empire*, iii (Oxford, 1999).

PORTER, B. C. *The Lion's Share: A Short History of British Imperialism* (3rd edn. 1996).

READMAN, P. 'The Conservative Party, Patriotism and British Politics: The Case of the General Election of 1900', *Journal of British Studies*, 40 (2001).

RICCI, D. M. 'Fabian Socialism: A Theory of Rent as Exploitation', *Journal of British Studies*, 11 (1969).

RICHTER, M. *The Politics of Conscience: T. H. Green and his Age* (1964).

ROBINSON, R. E. 'The Excentric Idea of Imperialism, with or without Empire', in W. J. Mommsen, and J. Osterhammel, (eds.), *Imperialism and After: Continuities and Discontinuities* (1986).

—— and GALLAGHER, J. 'The Partition of Africa', in F. H. Hinsley (ed.), *New Cambridge Modern History*, xi (Cambridge, 1967).

ROTBERG, R. I. *The Founder: Cecil Rhodes and the Pursuit of Power* (Oxford, 1988).

SAID, E. W. *Culture and Imperialism* (1993).

SAUL, S. B. *The Great Depression, 1873–1896: Myth or Reality?* (1969).

SAUNDERS, C., and SMITH, I. R. 'Southern Africa, 1795–1910', in Porter (ed.), *Oxford History*.

SCHNEER, J. *London 1900: The Imperial Metropolis* (New Haven, 1999).

SCHOLCH, A. 'The "Man on the Spot" and English Occupation of Egypt', *Historical Journal*, 19 (1976).

—— *Egypt for the Egyptians! The Socio-political Crisis in Egypt, 1878–82* (1981).

SCHUMACHER, E. F. *Small is Beautiful: A Study of Economics as if People Mattered* (1973).

SCHWARTZ, L. D. *London in the Age of Industrialisation: Entrepreneurs, Labour Force and Living Conditions, 1750–1850* (Cambridge, 1992).

SEARLE, G. R. *The Quest for National Efficiency: A Study in British Politics and Political Thought* (Oxford, 1971).

—— *Eugenics and Politics in Britain, 1900–1914* (Leiden, 1976).

—— *Corruption in British Politics* (Oxford, 1987).

SEMMEL, B. *The Rise of Free Trade Imperialism: Classical Political Economy, the Empire of Free Trade and Imperialism, 1750–1850* (Cambridge, 1970).

—— *John Stuart Mill and the Pursuit of Virtue* (New Haven, 1984).

SKINNER, Q. 'Meaning and Understanding in the History of Ideas', *History and Theory*, 8 (1969); repr. in J. Tully (ed.), *Meaning and Context: Quentin Skinner and his Critics*, (Princeton, 1988).

SMITH, I. R. 'The Origins of the South African War (1899–1902): A Reappraisal', *South African Historical Journal*, 22 (1990).

—— *The Origins of the South African War, 1899–1902* (1996).

SPEAR, J. F. *Dreams of an English Eden: Ruskin and his Tradition in English Social Criticism* (1984).

STALEY, C. E. 'A Note on Adam Smith's Version of the "Vent for Surplus" Model', *History of Political Economy*, 5 (1973).

STEDMAN JONES, G. *Outcast London: A Study in the Relationship between Classes in Victorian Society* (Oxford, 1971).

STOKES, E. 'Late Nineteenth Century Colonial Expansion and the Attacks on the Theory of Economic Imperialism: A Case of Mistaken Identity?', *Historical Journal*, 12 (1969).

SUNDERLAND, D. 'Principals and Agents: The Activities of the Crown Agents for the Colonies, 1880–1914', *Economic History Review*, 2nd ser. 52 (1999).

SVEDBERG, P. 'The Portfolio-Direct Composition of Private Foreign Investment Revisited', *Economic Journal*, 88 (1978).

SWARTZ, M. *The Union of Democratic Control in British Politics in the First World War* (Oxford, 1971).

—— 'A Study in Futility: The British Radicals at the Outbreak of the First World War', in Morris (ed.), *Edwardian Radicalism*.

TAYLOR, M. 'Imperium et Libertas? Rethinking the Radical Critique of Imperialism during the Nineteenth Century', *Journal of Imperial and Commonwealth History*, 19 (1991).

TAYLOR, M. W. *Men versus the State: Herbert Spencer and Late Victorian Individualism* (Oxford, 1992).

THOMPSON, A. S. 'The Language of Imperialism and the Meanings of Empire: Imperial Discourse in British Politics, 1895–1914', *Journal of British Studies*, 36 (1997).

—— *Imperial Britain: The Empire in British Politics c1880–1930* (1999).

THOMPSON, E. P. *William Morris: Romantic to Revolutionary* (1977).

TORRANCE, D. E. *The Strange Death of Liberal Empire: Lord Selborne in South Africa* (Liverpool, 1996).

TREGENZA, J. *Professor of Democracy: The Life of Charles Henry Pearson, 1830–94* (Cambridge, 1968).

TURRELL, R. V. and VAN HELTEN, J.-J. 'The Rothschilds, the Exploration Company and Mining Finance', *Business History*, 28 (1986).

VAN DER VEN, H. 'The Onrush of Modern Globalization in China', in Hopkins (ed.), *Globalization in World History*.

VAN HELTEN, J.-J. 'Empire and High Finance: South Africa and the International Gold Standard, 1890–1914', *Journal of African History*, 23 (1983).

—— 'German Capital, the Netherlands Railway Company and the Political Economy of the Transvaal', *Journal of African History*, 19 (1978).

VINCENT, A., and PLANT, R. *Philosophy, Politics and Citizenship: The Life and Thought of British Idealists* (1984).

VINCENT, J. *The Formation of the Liberal Party, 1857–1868* (1966).

WALTZ, K. E. *Man, the State and War* (1959).

WARD, M. *Gilbert Keith Chesterton* (1944).

WARD, P. *Red Flag and Union Jack: Englishness, Patriotism and the British Left* (1998).

WARREN, BILL, *Imperialism: Pioneer of Capitalism* (1980).

WASSERSTEIN, B. *Herbert Samuel: A Political Life* (Oxford, 1992).

WEBSTER, A. *Gentlemen Capitalists: British Imperialism in South East Asia, 1770–1890* (1998).

—— 'Business and Empire: A Reassessment of the British Conquest of Burma in 1885', *Historical Journal*, 43 (2000).

WEINROTH, H. 'Norman Angell and the Great Illusion: An Episode in Prewar Pacifism', *Historical Journal*, 17 (1974).

WELLS, G. A. (ed.). *J. M. Robertson (1856–1933): Liberal, Rationalist and Scholar* (1987).

WILBURN, K. E. 'Engines of Empire and Independence: Railways in Southern Africa', in C. B. Davis and K. E. Wilburn, (eds.), *Railway Imperialism* (1991).

—— 'The Drifts Crisis, the "Missing Telegrams" and the Jameson Raid: A Centennial Review', *Journal of Imperial and Commonwealth History*, 25 (1997).

WILKINS, M. 'The Free-Standing Company, 1870–1914: An Important Form of British Direct Foreign Investment', *Economic History Review*, 2nd ser. 41 (1988).

—— and SCHROTER, H. (eds.). *The Free-Standing Company in the World Economy, 1830–1996* (Oxford, 1998).

WILLIAMS, R. *Keywords: A Vocabulary of Culture and Society* (1976).

WINCH, D. *Classical Political Economy and the Colonies* (1965).

WINKLER, H. R. 'The Emergence of Labour Foreign Policy in Britain, 1918–29', *Journal of Modern History*, 28 (1956).

WOOLF, W. *From Radicalism to Socialism: Men and Ideas in the Formation of Fabian Socialist Doctrines, 1881–1889* (New Haven, 1975).

WORBOYS, M. 'The Emergence and Early History of Parasitology', in K. S. Warren and Z. Bowers (eds.), *Parasitology: A Global Perspective* (New York, 1983).

WRIGHT, A. W. *G. D. H. Cole and Socialist Democracy* (Oxford, 1979).

YOUNG, L. K. *British Policy in China, 1895–1902* (Oxford, 1970).

Index